THROUGH THE AGES

A HISTORY OF THE CHRISTIAN CHURCH

Ernest Trice Thompson

JOHN KNOX PRESS
ATLANTA

© Marshall C. Dendy 1965
Printed in the United States of America
Second Printing 1976

CONTENTS

The Church Universal: "One Body and One Spirit"

1
THE CHURCH:
ITS NATURE AND MISSION

IN THE MONTHS that follow we shall be finding out more about the church, the church which has brought the "one story of the Bible" down through the ages to our present day, the church which is now scattered through the earth, the church of which we are a member, in which we worship, to which we contribute, through which we participate in the ongoing work of the Kingdom.

What is this "church" and what is its function or mission?

The word "church" itself is used rather loosely in modern speech. It refers often, most frequently, it may be, to a building, the structure which houses a worshiping congregation for two or more hours a week and stands stark and empty in the intervening hours. It refers at times to a congregation which gathers now and then for worship and instruction and then disintegrates, ceasing to be until its component parts are again reassembled. Again, the word describes a "denomination," the organization that coordinates the work of a number of such congregations—an organization which is distinguished from other similar organizations by some distinctive tradition or belief. The word may be used to describe a family of such denominations, divided by national barriers, or divided within a nation by some bitter memory or cherished belief, or only by historical accident. The word is also used at times to describe the church universal—the church as it has come down through the ages, as it has spread over all the earth; the universal church which includes all local congregations, all denominations and families of denominations; in other words, the entire vast company of believers. By some again the church is identified with the clergy, the ministers who stand in the pulpit and administer the sacraments, the professionals who are the organization's official representatives.

In the Bible, it should be noted, the church is never a building, but always a *people;* never a denomination, never a family of denominations, never the clergy as distinguished from the laity (in the New Testament there is no such distinction). The word, as used in the New Testament, describes either the total body of believers (Acts 9:31; 1 Cor. 12:28) or else a body of believers in a specified area, e.g., those worshiping in a particular house (Rom. 16:5) or those scattered through a city such as Corinth (1 Cor. 1:2). Yet the church remains one. As emphasized in Ephesians, "There is one body and one Spirit, just as you were called to the one hope that belongs to your call, one Lord, one faith, one baptism, one God and Father of us all, who is above all and through all and in all" (Eph. 4:4–6).

The English word "church" comes from a Latin word *kyriakon,* meaning "belonging to the Lord." The Latin word in turn was employed as roughly equivalent to the New Testament term, *ekklesia,* coming from two Greek words meaning "to call out from." Classical Greek authors used the word to describe any public gathering. The translators of the Hebrew Bible into Greek (the Septuagint) took *ekklesia* as one of two words to describe Israel as a people called out to the worship and service of God.

ORIGINS OF THE CHURCH

The Westminster Confession of Faith identifies the church simply with all God's people (the "elect" of all ages; this would go back even before Abraham). But Abraham and his family together mark the first "calling-out" of a special set-apart group. The call came originally to Abraham, to go out from his country, his kindred, and his father's house, to a land that God would show him. With the call came the promise, "I will make of you a great nation, and I will bless you, and make your name great, so that you will be a blessing" (Gen. 12:2). This promise was later confirmed by a covenant (Gen. 17), which was renewed with Isaac and Jacob, and ultimately at Mount Sinai was expanded into a covenant between God and his people Israel: "If you will obey my voice and keep my covenant," said the Lord, "you shall be my own possession among all peoples; . . . and you shall be to me a kingdom of priests and a holy nation" (Exod. 19:5–6).

Israel, however, failed to live up to her part of the promise. In Jesus' day the nation, or at least a portion of it, sought to observe with painstaking care the Law and Traditions in which God's will for the nation was expressed, but its mission to become a blessing, a kingdom of priests, mediating the blessings of God to all mankind, had been forgotten. Jesus first attempted to recall the nation to its true mission as church or People of God. Failing in this attempt, he turned to his disciples, choosing twelve as the nucleus of a new Israel. To Peter, who confessed him as the promised Messiah, came the fateful words, "You are Peter, and on this rock I will build my church, and the powers of death shall not prevail against it" (Matt. 16:18). In the Upper Room, Jesus broke bread and passed the cup in token and pledge of the New Covenant into which, in accordance with Jeremiah's prediction, God now entered with his people, those who accepted his redemptive love manifested in Christ.

When Jesus was crucified, it seemed for a moment—even to his chosen disciples—that his hopes for a new Israel had been disappointed. Then came the Resurrection, the Ascension, the outpouring of the Spirit at Pentecost, the beginnings of the Christian church, the church's gradual spread, beginning at Jerusalem, into the uttermost parts of the earth.

NATURE OF THE CHURCH

It will help us here to note some of the words used by members of the early church to describe this new beginning.

They were *believers*—believers in Jesus as the promised Messiah, as the unique Son of God, believers in the God whom they had come to know as the God and Father of their Lord and Savior, Jesus Christ. The term was suggested, it may be, by Jesus' words in the Upper Room, "Let not your hearts be troubled; believe in God, believe also in me" (John 14:1).

They were *brethren*—bound to one another by ties stronger than those of an earthly family. The term, it may be, was linked to Jesus' words, "Whoever does the will of God is my brother, and sister, and mother" (Mark 3:35).

They were *disciples*—learners, that is, in the school of Christ. As they used the term perhaps they recalled the words of Jesus, "You are not to be called rabbi, for you have one teacher, and you are all brethren" (Matt. 23:8).

They were *saints*—not in the modern sense of the term, but saints according to the meaning of both the Hebrew and Greek roots, in the sense that they had separated themselves from the unbelieving world and had dedicated or consecrated themselves to the service of God.

They were *those of the Way* (Acts 9:2)—the term found most frequently in the book of The Acts. It is indeed a suggestive term, for Christianity is a way of life, Jesus' way; it is a way of salvation, Jesus' way (see Acts 16:17); it is a way to God, Jesus' way, the only way. Perhaps usage of the term came from recollection of Jesus' words in the Upper Room: "I am the way, and the truth, and the life; no one comes to the Father, but by me" (John 14:6).

The name which gradually, in the course of time, was to supersede all others was given to the disciples first, Luke tells us, in Antioch (Acts 11:26). By whom the name was bestowed, or why, we are not told; but it is indicative. Here in Antioch Gentiles were first welcomed into the church in any numbers. What did these Gentiles and these Jews, formerly estranged, have in common? Most noticeably their faith in Jesus as the promised Messiah or Christ. Of him they spoke, of him they sang, him they worshiped as Son of God, and him they proclaimed as Savior and Lord. And so they came to be called— *Christ's men* or *Christians*.

Of all the various names given to the early Christian community this is the most significant, for it alone points directly to him from whom the church receives its life. Other names (like the names of our modern denominations) are on the margin: believers in what? brethren, why? disciples of whom? saints for what purpose? those of which way, of whose way? It is significant that the disciples were first called Christians in Antioch, where it first became apparent that in Christ barriers which divided men from their fellowmen must fall, and that believers in Christ were obligated—everyone "according to his ability"—to meet the material and spiritual needs of their fellowmen, not only at home but also abroad (Acts 11:19–30; 13:1–3).

Light is thrown on the nature of the church not only by the names applied to the early believers in Christ, but also by the metaphors or "images" employed by New Testament writers (particularly Paul) to picture the church to their readers. Paul S. Minear, in his suggestive book *Images of the Church in the New Testament,* recognizes eighty or more such images. The four master images mentioned most frequently, and about which other images may be gathered, he finds to be "the people of God," "the new creation," "the fellowship of faith," and "the body of Christ."

The first of these master images, that of *"the people of God,"* is found in fourteen New Testament writings (see particularly 1 Peter 2:9–10), and in seven others equivalent expressions are used, such as "Israel," or "the household of God." This image links Old and New Testaments, and indicates that the New Covenant, sealed by Jesus' death on the cross, replaces the Old Covenant made with Israel at Sinai, and that the people whom God has chosen to know him and in turn to make him known are now found in the church rather than in the synagogue.

The second master image (*"the new creation"*) stresses the church's mission in the world, or, rather, the end for which God has destined the church. As the first image looks to the past, linking Sinai and Calvary, the second looks to the future, the goal which God has in mind for mankind as a whole (see Eph. 1:9–10). It is in the church, Paul goes on to indicate, that this purpose is to be fulfilled, not by man's efforts, but primarily through God's action (Eph. 2—3). The church then individually and collectively is to be recognized as God's workmanship, a new creation, destined to include all mankind (see 2 Cor. 5:17; Eph. 2:10; Col. 1:15–20; Rev. 3:14; Rev. 21:1–5a). These passages indicate that God continues active in the world and that the church today is to be regarded as only the first fruits of a mighty harvest, which will include not only the multitude of the heavenly host, but also a new heaven and a new earth, in which there will be neither mourning nor crying nor pain any more, "for the former things have passed away."

The third master image (*saints*) stresses "the fellowship of faith." The emphasis here is on the human instruments as a community or fellowship, rather than as separate individuals, through whom God will accomplish his end—a community in which it is assumed that the Holy Spirit is actively at work. Paul has this image in mind when he addresses his letter "to the church of God which is at Corinth, to those sanctified in Christ Jesus, called to be saints together with those who in every place call on the name of our Lord Jesus Christ, both their Lord and ours" (1 Cor. 1:2). Members of the church are referred to as saints in no less than one hundred passages in eighteen different writings. As seen by the New Testament writers, the fellowship of the saints is entrusted with a task, in which each individual member has a part for which he has been equipped by the Holy Spirit.

The fourth image greatly stressed by some writers is that of the church as *"the body of Christ."* In the first two images the activity of God the Father is most in evidence; in the third image it is the activity of the Holy Spirit which is most in evidence; in the last image it is Christ who is to the fore. "He is the head of the body, the church; he is the beginning, the first-born from the dead, that in everything he might be preeminent" (Col. 1:18). God "has put all things under his feet and has made him the head over all things for the church, which is his body, the fulness of him who fills all in all" (Eph. 1: 22–23). It should be noted, however, that the activity of Father, Son, and Spirit is recognized in each of these images, and each image is used in association with, not in isolation from, the other images. The image of the body is particularly suggestive in that it stresses many-ness and one-ness, unity of many parts in a living whole, the relation of the members of the church to one another and to Christ. As a member of the Body of Christ each has his particular function, for which he has been equipped by the Holy Spirit (1 Cor. 12).

In his widely read book *The Nature and Mission of the Church,* Donald G. Miller summarizes some of the characteristics of the church as set forth in the New Testament:

(1) *"The church is divine, not human.* We do not make the

church by our efforts, we receive it as a gift from God. The church is not created by a group of religious men banding together to form it. It was created by God through the resurrection of Jesus Christ."

(2) *"The church is a fellowship of faith, not an institution.* The church does not consist of buildings or programs, but of people."

(3) *"The church is corporate, not individualistic.* . . . Just as a body is not made by collecting a hand here, and an arm there, and a foot somewhere else, and then putting them together, so the church is not made up of a group of isolated individuals who decide to unite for their common religious welfare. . . .

"Our faith is personal, but not individual. It is the personal in-grafting into a corporate reality."

(4) *"The church is universal, not local.* The church is not merely the particular congregation to which I belong, nor the denomination to which it adheres. When one unites with the church in any particular place, he unites with the church universal."

(5) *"The church is the body of the living Christ, not the perpetuator of His memory nor the guardian of a tradition.* . . . [It] has no existence unless the Spirit of the Living Christ lives in her *now.*"

(6) *" . . . the church exists not for her own sake, but solely for the glory of God."*[1]

We do not yet, however, have the complete picture of the church as it is set before us in the New Testament. To the present we have looked at it largely from its godly side—looking to the divine intention, to the church as it aspires to be, to the church as it exists in the mind of God. But the church also has its human side: The People of God have their limitations, the new creation retains many of the imperfections of the old, the fellowship of faith is frequently broken, the Body of Christ is not always responsive to its head. This picture too the Bible holds before us—in the Gospels, in the Acts, in the Epistles. The time came when the disciples forsook Jesus and fled; one betrayed him, and another denied him. Even after Pentecost Peter needs to be rebuked by Paul (Gal. 2:11). Writing "to the church of God which is at Corinth, to those sanctified in Christ" (1 Cor. 1:2), Paul recognizes that divisions have arisen within the body (1 Cor. 1:10–12), that "there is immorality among you, and of a kind that is not found even among pagans" (1 Cor. 5:1), that some are drunken even at the Communion service (1 Cor. 11:20–21), that there are those who deny the resurrection of the body (1 Cor. 15:12).

In the light of such facts we understand the biblical statements regarding the nature of the church. *It is a divine institution in that God is in it, and yet human, in that God does not abolish the weakness of the human flesh.* It is the People of God, but it includes those who are ignorant and those who are consciously or unconsciously disobedient to the divine will. It is the Body of Christ, in that it acknowledges Christ as its head, yet all too often in word rather than in deed. The church is one, and yet it has always been divided, never truly one, as our Lord prayed it might become.

So it was in the New Testament period; so it has been through history; so it is today. The local congregation of which each of us is a member, the denomination with which we are affiliated, the church in Russia as well as the church in the United States contain nuclei of devoted Christians: each, however, with its own imperfections, and also those less interested, and more than a few who live quite unworthily of the name they profess. Yet they too are members of the church, the Body of Christ. It is through the church so composed that Christ has carried its mission in the past and still continues to do so.

MISSION OF THE CHURCH

What is this mission? It is described in various figures, set forth in various forms in the New Testament.

"You are the salt of the earth," Jesus said to his disciples (Matt. 5:13). Salt in his day had a twofold function: to preserve food from decay, and to make it more tasty and palatable. So the People of God are to preserve society, to make life more zestful and tasty for all.

"You are the light of the world," Jesus continued. The world is walking in darkness; in our day it has come dangerously near to the abyss. Those who learn from Jesus have that truth about God (and man) which dispels the darkness. "Let your light so shine before men," said Jesus, "that they may see your good works and give glory to your father who is in heaven" (Matt. 5:14, 16).

"You are Peter [a rock]," said Jesus to the disciple who had just confessed that he was the Christ, the Son of God, "and on this rock I will build my church, and the powers of death shall not prevail against it. I will give you the keys of the kingdom of heaven, and whatever you bind on earth shall be bound in heaven, and whatever you loose on earth shall be loosed in heaven" (Matt. 16:18–19). The Kingdom of heaven is God's reign on earth and beyond the earth. To Peter first, and then to all disciples, Jesus has given the keys by means of which the doors of the Kingdom may be opened to men, its blessings made available to them, both here and hereafter. "To bind," "to loose," were technical terms. The rabbis bound when they forbade a course of conduct as contrary to the will of God; they loosed when they permitted a course of conduct as agreeable to the word of God. Peter and his fellow apostles would set forth ideals of conduct that would ever thereafter bind the conscience of believing men and women. It is the responsibility of the church to transmit these ideals.

After the Resurrection Jesus instructed his disciples, "Go . . . and make disciples of all nations, baptizing them in the name of the Father and of the Son and of the Holy Spirit, teaching them to observe all that I have commanded you," (Matt. 28:19–20). The purpose as indicated by Jesus is to make disciples of all nations; to accomplish this end, his disciples (the church) are first to baptize men in the name of the Father and of the Son and of the Holy Spirit. It is not the physical act that Jesus primarily had in mind, but the spiritual reality. The church is to bring men into living touch with God, who is Father, Son, and Holy Spirit. Second, it is to teach them, not merely to know, but also to observe all the things which he has commanded. The things which he has commanded are summarized in the two great commandments—love to God and love to man.

"God was in Christ reconciling the world to himself," writes Paul in 2 Corinthians 5:19–20. "So we are ambassadors for Christ, God making his appeal through us." It is his ultimate purpose, we are told in Ephesians 1:10, "to unite all things in [Christ], things in heaven and things on earth." And this purpose, we are further told, is to be realized first of all in the church, through the breaking down of the barriers that have hitherto divided man from his fellowmen, and then to be made known by the church to the principalities and powers in the heavenly places (Eph. 2—3).

According to these and other passages the task of the church is a total one: every nation, every area of truth it must seek to bring under subjection to Christ; all aspects of broken community are matters for its concern. The sinful barriers raised between men by nation, class, race, sex, occupation, education are to be destroyed at the foot of the cross.

In the light of this purpose we are to evaluate the work of the church in history, the program and work of our own denomination.

FOR CONSIDERATION

[A note on these questions: You will find at the end of each chapter a number of questions for readers to think about. These questions are not meant to review the chapter. Rather, they suggest the question: Since these things we have been discussing are so, then what? Few of the questions in this book have short, easy answers, few have guaranteed, foolproof, cast-iron answers. They are designed to make you think, not to see how well you can remember. Questions which are particularly difficult, or require some study, are marked with an asterisk (*). You may wish to use such questions as assignments to individuals or (better) groups, for study, discussion, and report to the class as a whole. It is not intended that all the questions in every chapter can be discussed and answered in one class meeting!]

*1. How would you explain what the church is to a nonchurchgoing friend? How would you express its full New Testament meaning? Do the New Testament names for the church help you to understand it?

2. Which of the images employed in the New Testament to picture the church is most meaningful to you? Why?

3. Dr. Donald G. Miller declares that, according to the New Testament teaching, the church is divine, not human, a fellowship of faith, not an institution. Do you accept these statements, or would you modify them?

4. How would you answer a man who excused his neglect of the church by emphasizing the frailties of its members?

5. Do you accept, or do you take exception to, the statement of the mission of the church as set forth in this chapter?

6. Is the New Testament mission of the church really understood and accepted by the membership of the church as a whole? of your congregation? Why do you think so? What more needs to be done in this regard?

York

Lincoln

London

Saxons

GERMANY

Vand

• Lyons

Milan

Rome

Hippo

Carthage

The Roman Empire About 300 A.D.

Part I
IN THE
ROMAN EMPIRE

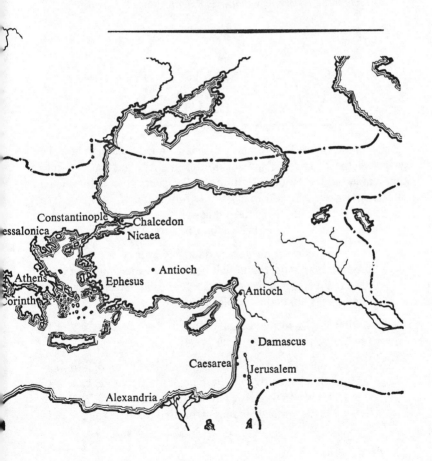

Constantinople Chalcedon
essalonica Nicaea

Athens Ephesus • Antioch
orinth Antioch

• Damascus

Caesarea Jerusalem

Alexandria

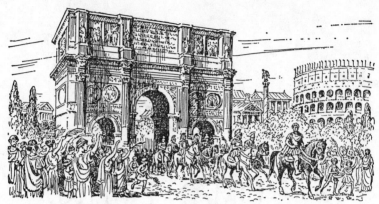

Constantine, First Christian Emperor, Entering Rome Triumphantly

2

THE CHURCH
WINS THE EMPIRE

IN THE BOOK OF THE ACTS a physician named Luke tells how the gospel of the risen Jesus spread—within a single generation—into the centers of the Roman Empire. In the years that followed the church grew even more rapidly. Pliny, governor of Bithynia (see Acts 16:7), disturbed over the rapid spread of Christianity in this province, wrote about A.D. 112 to the Emperor Trajan:

> ... many of every age, every rank, and even of both sexes, are brought into danger; and will be in the future. The contagion of that superstition has penetrated not only the cities but also the villages, and country places. ... [1]

In the middle of the second century, Justin, the first philosopher to be won to the new faith, wrote with pride:

> ... there is not a single race of men, whether among barbarians or Greeks, or by whatever name they may be called, of those who live in wagons or are called nomads or of herdsmen living in tents, among whom prayers and thanksgivings are not

20

offered through the name of the crucified Jesus to the Father and Maker of all things.[2]

Tertullian, at the century's end, boasted:

> We are but of yesterday, and we have filled every place among you—cities, islands, fortresses, towns, market-places, the very camps, tribes, companies, palace, Senate, and Forum. We have left you only the temples.[3]

By A.D. 323 perhaps one-tenth of the population of the Empire, ten million out of a hundred million, had been won to the new faith. The strength of the church was greater than these figures would indicate, for its adherents were more numerous in the cities, where the course of empire was determined, than in the countryside; and in the East, particularly North Syria and Asia Minor, where the earliest civilizations had arisen, than in the cruder and more imitative West. It drew especially from the influential middle class, but there were also many poor, and some of wealth, education, and social position. Only a change of attitude on the part of the government was necessary to bring the mass of the population flocking into the church.

The gospel had even spread beyond the empire—into the Tigris-Euphrates Valley, along the shores of the Black Sea, into Armenia, Arabia, and India; and some converts had been won among the Goths.

"Never in the history of the race has this record ever quite been equalled," declares Kenneth Scott Latourette:

> Never in so short a time has any other religious faith, or, for that matter, any other set of ideas, religious, political, or economic, without the aid of physical force, or of social or cultural prestige, achieved so commanding a position in such an important culture.[4]

This rapid growth is more impressive when we recall that it took place in spite of opposition by the state, rivalry on the part of other religions, and attacks by contemporary scholars seeking to exploit every weakness.

THE STRUGGLE WITH THE STATE

Early Christians had suffered at the hands of the Jewish authorities almost from the beginning (see Acts 3:1—4:31; 5:12–42;
7:38—8:3; 12:1–17) and later from mob action or at the hands of
local magistrates stirred up by Jewish or Gentile opponents (see Acts
13:50; 14:5–6, 19; 16:19–24; 17:5–9; 19:23–41; 21:27—28:30).
The Roman Government, however, remained a bulwark of protection (see Acts 18:12–17), and Paul made his final appeal to Caesar
with some hope of vindication (see Acts 25:1–12).

In A.D. 64, just three years after the final events described by
Luke in The Acts of the Apostles, a fire broke out in the city of
Rome, destroying a large part of the city. Many believed that the Emperor Nero had himself ordered the fire. Wrote Tacitus, the Roman
historian:

> ... to overcome this rumor, Nero put in his own palace as
> culprits, and punished with most ingenious cruelty, men whom
> the common people hated for their shameful crimes and called
> Christians. .... at the beginning, some were seized who made
> confessions [under torture, no doubt; or perhaps only that they
> were Christians]; then on their information, a vast multitude
> was convicted, not so much of arson as of hatred of the human
> race. And they were not only put to death, but subjected to in-
> sults, in that they were either dressed up in the skins of wild
> beasts and perished by the cruel mangling of dogs, or else put
> on crosses to be set on fire, and, as day declined, to be burned,
> being used as lights by night. Nero had thrown open his gar-
> dens for that spectacle, and gave a circus play, mingling with
> the people dressed in a charioteer's costume or driving in a
> chariot. From this arose, however, toward men who were, in-
> deed, criminals and deserving extreme penalties, sympathy,
> on the ground that they were destroyed not for the public good,
> but to satisfy the cruelty of an individual.[5]

This account is more interesting because it contains one of the
earliest references to Christ found in secular literature, because it reflects the contemptuous and uninformed attitude of cultured Romans
toward this new religious movement, and because it includes not only

a vivid account of the first persecution by the Roman Government, but also a statement of its effect on the minds of the people. In this persecution, according to the tradition of the church, Paul lost his life, being beheaded, as befitted a Roman citizen, and Peter was crucified with his head hanging downward, as he himself had requested. He was not worthy to die, he explained, as his Master had died.

At this time, or shortly thereafter, it came to be regarded as a capital crime merely to call oneself a Christian; and this continued to be the case until a Toleration Act was approved (though not uniformly observed) in the year A.D. 313.

Why was this the case, and why did persecutions continue to arise until finally a Christian emperor extended his sway over the entire empire and brought them to a sudden end?

Some persecutions, particularly in the earlier part of the period, were started by the people. Three charges in particular were leveled against Christians; all three aroused hatred and at times stirred up mobs. Christians were accused first of committing abominations— engaging in sexual immoralities in connection with their "love feasts," and drinking the blood of infants in their observance of the Lord's Supper. Wild rumors to this end were circulated and believed by the credulous as they have been through history regarding unpopular minorities. But such charges were soon discredited and ceased to be accepted. More serious was the charge of atheism—Christians did not worship the gods whose favor was essential for the prosperity and security of the state. Flood, earthquake, and pestilence were all attributed to the offended gods, who thus visited upon the people the results of the neglect and sacrilege of the Christians.

> If [wrote Tertullian] the Tiber floods the city, or the Nile refuses to rise, or the sky withholds its rain, if there is an earthquake, famine, or pestilence, at once the cry is raised: Christians to the lions.

In North Africa the practice passed into a proverb: "If there is no rain, lay the blame on the Christians."

The third charge brought against the early Christians was "hatred of the human race." We understand the basis for this curious charge when we recall that Christians were commanded to come out and be separate from their pagan neighbors (see 2 Cor. 6:14—7:1). Devout believers could not enjoy the popular amusements, because of their immoralities and their callous disregard of human life; they could not engage in civic affairs or attend the popular banquets because they involved sacrifices to idols. Their purer morals and their more spiritual and exclusive religion seemed to mark them as those who claimed to be superior persons, who disapproved of all who lived otherwise. Christians might be social among themselves, but for general purposes they were nonsocial to a degree that brought upon them the accusation of being haters of their fellowman.

Though in the beginning it was apt to be popular feeling that preceded and inspired state action, more and more as time went on the empire itself became concerned to stamp out the stubborn resistance of the Christians. This rigorous policy of the state, differing from its usual tolerant attitude toward various religious bodies, was justified by the charge of disloyalty leveled at the early Christians, based in large measure on their refusal to join in the worship of the emperor as divine. This national religion was regarded as essential if the many peoples included in the Roman Empire were to be held together in a common loyalty. Only the Jews (who offered no threat to the empire, and whose peculiarities in this regard were recognized and accepted) were spared such religious (and patriotic) acknowledgment. The mob that assaulted the house of Jason in Thessalonica accused Paul and Silas of "acting against the decrees of Caesar, saying that there is another king, Jesus" (Acts 17:6–7). This charge became more serious as the church continued to grow, and with it the power and authority of its chosen rulers, the bishops. As H. B. Workman writes:

> The student should beware, however, lest he overlook the momentous issues involved in the refusal of the State to allow any society or club to exist which had not first obtained official recognition, and the equally momentous refusal of the Church to obtain such recognition. The question is not one of legal technicalities or procedure, or the 'sheer obstinacy,' as Marcus Aurelius would have phrased it, of Christian fanatics, but points rather to one of those root antagonisms of principle the influence of which, in different forms, may be felt in the twen-

tieth as much as in the second century. By Roman theory the State was the one society which must engross every interest of its subjects, religious, social, political, humanitarian, with the one possible exception of the family. There was no room in Roman law for the existence, much less the development on its own line of organic growth, of any corporation or society which did not recognize itself from the first as a mere department or auxiliary of the State. The State was all and in all, the one organism with a life of its own. Such a theory the Church, as the living kingdom of Jesus, could not possibly accept either in the first century or the twentieth.[6]

The church underwent its second fiery trial during the reign of Domitian—in the decade of the nineties. It was particularly severe in Asia Minor, where Christians were most numerous. To encourage the Christians in this area to stand firm under this fierce assault and to assure them of the final victory, John the Aged wrote the book of Revelation. The Roman Empire, he predicted, would perish, but not the church of the Lord Jesus Christ. Those who died in Christ would receive their heavenly reward (Rev. 20:4). This persecution in time spent its force, and the church emerged as before, strengthened in the affections of the people.

In the year A.D. 112 Pliny, governor of Bithynia, wrote to the Emperor Trajan:

> It is my custom, lord emperor, to refer to you all questions whereof I am in doubt. ... In investigations of Christians I have never taken part; hence I do not know what is the crime usually punished or investigated, or what allowances are made. So I have had no little uncertainty whether there is any distinction of age, or whether the very weakest offenders are treated exactly like the stronger; whether pardon is given to those who repent, or whether a man who has once been a Christian gains nothing by having ceased to be such; whether punishment attaches to the mere name apart from secret crimes, or to the secret crimes connected with the name. Meantime this is the course I have taken with those who were accused before me as Christians. I asked them whether they were

Christians, and if they confessed, I asked them a second and third time with threats of punishment. If they kept to it, I ordered them for execution; for I held no question that whatever it was that they admitted, in any case obstinacy and unbending perversity deserve to be punished . . . [7]

To this letter Trajan replied:

You have adopted the proper course, my dear Secundus, in your examination of the cases of those who were accused to you as Christians, for indeed nothing can be laid down as a general ruling involving something like a set form of procedure. They are not to be sought out; but if they are accused and convicted, they must be punished—yet on this condition, that whoso denies himself to be a Christian, and makes the fact plain by his action, that is, by worshipping our gods, shall obtain pardon on his repentance, however suspicious his past conduct may be . . . [8]

see
P. 38

This was the general policy that continued to be followed by the government until A.D. 250. But though there was general toleration and only occasional persecution, the sword was always hanging heavily over the heads of Christians. If one incurred the ill will of a neighbor, if he was publicly charged, if mob action arose, or if a zealous official took it upon himself to enforce the law, then Christians suffered. One such persecution arose during the reign of Antoninus Pius (A.D. 155). It culminated in the burning of the aged Bishop Polycarp, one of the few surviving Christians whose memories ran back to the days of the apostles. The church never forgot the words of the venerable patriarch, when offered his life if only he would curse Christ: "Eighty and six years have I served Him," Polycarp replied, "and he did me no wrong. How can I blaspheme my king, that saved me?" A feeble slave woman, named Blandina, was the heroine of a persecution that broke out in the cities of Vienne and Lyons in southern France (A.D. 177). Her mistress, herself to be numbered among the martyrs, feared that Blandina because of bodily weakness might not bear as bold a witness as all hoped to bear under the tortures which were to come. Some indeed gave way, but Blandina stood firm, and it was she who more than any other upheld the spirits of the confessors. In their account of the persecution, distributed among the churches for their edification, the two churches in France recalled how

> The blessed Blandina last of all, having, like a high-born mother, exhorted her children and sent them forth victorious to the King, travelled herself along the same path of conflicts as they did, and hastened to them, rejoicing and exulting at her departure, like one *bidden to* a marriage *supper,* rather than cast to the wild beasts.[9]

The first systematic persecution of the church broke out in the year A.D. 250 and continued with interruptions for nine years. The Roman Empire at last gathered its energies to stamp out the growing faith which seemed to threaten its existence. Some Christians did not wait to be apprehended, but hastened to offer the prescribed sacrifices and so receive their certificates of exemption. In the judgment of the church, recalling Matthew 16:26, they had forfeited, not saved, their lives. Others went into hiding until the storm was over. Still others simply lay low and were overlooked. But there were men who endured the extreme of torture rather than deny Christ, the learned Origen, for example; still others went boldly to their death, like Cyprian, bishop of Carthage in northern Africa, who when the death sentence was pronounced cried, "Thanks be to God!" When the persecutions finally ceased, the church emerged purified and strengthened.

There followed a long period of peace, when it seemed that the offense of the Christian name might be forgotten. Then suddenly (in the year A.D. 303) under Diocletian, one of the ablest of the later emperors, there broke out a second systematic persecution, the most severe of them all, which continued in some parts of the empire for twenty years, and ended finally not in the destruction of the church, but in its victory. From this period comes the story of forty Christian soldiers, members of the "Thundering Legion," martyred at Sebaste in Lesser Armenia by being left naked on the ice of a frozen pond, with baths of hot water on the bank as a temptation to deny their Lord. Only one of the forty gave way, and his place was taken immediately by a member of the guard who had been converted by the constancy of the rest.

It was the Emperor Constantine who finally brought the persecutions to an end. He was the son of Constantius, one of the two senior emperors who with their corresponding juniors now governed the empire. By his wit and daring he eluded his scheming enemies who would detain him in the East, fled to Britain, and succeeded his father as one of the two emperors in the West. There followed shortly the decisive battle of Mulvian Bridge (north of Rome), in which Constantine won sole supremacy in the West. Constantine went into this battle with the monogram of Christ[10] emblazoned on his banners and from this time on acknowledged Christ as Lord, though he was not actually baptized until a week before his death. In the year A.D. 323 he defeated Licinius, ruler of the East, and became sole ruler of the empire. The church, for all practical purposes, had now become the church of the state.

What led Constantine to become a Christian? Historians can only surmise. The piety of his mother may have prepared the way—according to an uncertain tradition, she was the earlier Christian. Superstition probably played a part. Constantine dreamed, so he said, on the eve of the battle of the Mulvian Bridge (later the "dream" became a "vision") that he saw a sign in the sky, the cross of Christ, and under it these words, "In this sign, you shall conquer." Policy also may have helped to shape his decision. He was wise enough to see, perhaps, that the church had won the favor of the populace, and that with its aid he could best govern the empire. But religious faith was also involved. Constantine had his faults. But he was a strong and able ruler, and there is no reason to doubt his growing allegiance to Christ.

THE STRUGGLE WITH RIVAL RELIGIONS

The growth of the church in the early centuries is more striking when we recall that it faced the rivalry of other religions competing for the affections of the people.

The old pagan religions, the gods of Greece and Rome, had lost their hold on the minds of men, and offered no serious competition to the new religion. However, it has been said:

Religions do not die. They only pass, leaving immeasurable

traces of their doctrines and ceremonies in the religious systems that succeed them. The old religion of the Latins yielded
in large degree to Greek and Oriental beliefs, but none the
less it persisted in many ways and was a powerful element in
religious thought till the end of the Empire. And in its turn that
complex of Latin, Greek and Oriental concepts that we call
Roman religion did not entirely perish when Christianity won
its victory. In some of its phases it survived in the religious
practices, customs and beliefs of the early Christians, and
traces of it are extant to the present day.[11]

Such remnants of these older religions are embedded in our marriage customs, for example, the engagement ring, worn on the third
finger of the left hand, the bridal veil, the wedding feast (including
the wedding cake), and in some countries the wearing of garlands by
both bride and groom, the procession to the bridegroom's house and
the carrying of the bride over the threshold. Many of our Christmas
festivities stem from the same source, as do some of the present ac-
companiments of the Easter season—the bunny rabbit and the eggs.
The ancient religions gave an impetus also to the veneration of the
saints. The Latins attached some divine personality to every important process of nature. When Christianity finally vanquished the ancient gods, their functions were ascribed to the "saints." To this topic
we shall return.

The most serious religious competition offered to Christianity
came from the mystery religions (so called because of the secrecy
attached to their rites of initiation). These mystery religions came
from the East, and were spreading rapidly in the West along with
Christianity, with which they had some striking resemblances. They
believed, for example, in savior-gods, who died and rose again, and
in sacramental acts, which brought cleansing from sin, a new birth,
and the promise of immortality. The gods of the mystery religions,
however, were nebulous figures from an imaginary past, men, slain
against their will, who had become gods. They too succumbed finally
to the power of the crucified and risen Jesus, but not without leaving
their mark on the superior religion which supplanted them in the affections of the people.

Not only did they in part Orientalize the West and thereby
make it hospitable to a Palestinian Gospel, but they also awakened profound religious aspirations which only Christianity
could satisfy, and provided the new faith with a redemptive
terminology which enabled it readily to make contact with the
existing religious ideas of its converts.[12]

From the mystery religions, probably, came the growing belief that
the value of a sacramental act lies not so much in the religious experience symbolized as in the proper performance of the act itself, and
that the bestowal of divine grace is conditioned not by the spiritual
receptivity of the worshiper, but by the magical power of the ceremony itself.

THE STRUGGLE WITH CRITICAL INTELLECTUALS

Christianity won its victory in the Roman Empire in spite of opposition from the state, in spite of the rivalry of other religions, in
spite also of attacks launched in the second and third centuries by
contemporary intellectuals. The attacks then were much like attacks
on Christianity today by unsympathetic scholars: essentially, that its
beliefs are no more than superstitions, and that Jesus was no more
than a very imperfect man. The belittlement of Jesus Christ proved
ineffective and was soon dropped. But attacks against Christianity
itself—the absurdity of some of its doctrines and facts (such as the
resurrection of Christ)—were keenly pressed. None of its claims was
left unexamined (for which we can truly be grateful). The church in
turn possessed able defenders. They returned sensible answers to all
serious charges; they argued from the reasonableness of Christian
beliefs and from the practical effects Christian faith has in men. Every
martyr was one more bit of evidence for the power of Christ. They
advanced positive arguments for their claims, pointing not only to
fulfilled prophecy, and to the miracles performed by Christ, but also
to the moral effects of the gospel, to the rapid spread of Christianity,
to its reasonableness and its adaptation to the deepest needs of human
nature. As Origen declared in his reply to Celsus:

And so we shall go on believing in God according to the teaching of Jesus Christ, seeking to convert those blind on the sub-

ject of religion. Blind, they say, are we; but they themselves are blind. Seducers we, they say; but they lead men astray. Oh, what a noble seduction ours, that men should change from dissolute to sober living—or towards it; to justice from injustice —or tending that way; to wisdom from being foolish—or becoming such; and from cowardice, meanness and timidity, show courage and fortitude, not least in this struggle for the sake of our religion—for God the Creator of all things, and Jesus Christ even as all the prophets have spoken.[13]

EXPLANATION OF THE CHURCH'S GROWTH

How do we explain the growth of Christianity—in spite of persecution, in spite of the attraction of rival religions, in spite of attacks by leading literary figures?

In part, no doubt, by what Paul describes as "the fulness of the time" (Gal. 4:4, K.J.V.). As we look at the ancient world the stage seems to have been set for the birth of Christ—Christianity could not have grown so readily a few generations earlier, or a few generations later. The Roman Empire had gathered under its banner ancient lands, the founts of western civilization, around the Mediterranean; for a short period there was comparative peace, good roads bound the empire together; life was secure, men were free to travel. Greek language and culture had spread through the bounds of the Roman Empire; the missionaries could be understood wherever they went; a common culture had prepared the way for a common religion; philosophic thought tended toward belief in one God; the oriental mystery religions awakened in men's hearts a desire for redemption.

Basic of course was the revelation of God in Jesus Christ, the Christian message. Describing the church's victory over its rivals, Kenneth Scott Latourette concludes:

> Out of them all Christianity won partly because of its organization, with the fellowship and protection which the uprooted individuals of the Graeco-Roman world craved, partly because of its inclusiveness, partly because of its happy combination of adaptibility and intransigence, partly because it supplied better than any other what the ancient world was asking

of religion and philosophy, partly because of its Jewish heritage, its moral earnestness and power, and its miracles, but chiefly because of the quality of the life and the death of Jesus and the experiences which followed among his disciples. In the last analysis it was from Jesus that those qualities stemmed which gave to Christianity its victory over its rivals.[14]

But the success of the gospel cannot be accounted for by the fullness of the times, or even by the revelation of God in Jesus Christ—the Christian message—alone. We must also take into account the witness of believers, the Christian messengers.

One might gather from the book of The Acts that mass conversions accounted for the rapid growth of the church (Acts 2:41; 4:4). But there were no mass conversions, so far as we know, in the early church after the early sermons of Peter. One might then conclude that the growth of the church came from the missionary labors of men like Paul. But this does not seem to have been the case. There were no missionary societies, no missionary institutions, no organized efforts, so far as is known, in the period before Constantine, and yet in this period, less than three hundred years from the death of Christ, the mass of the Roman Empire, representing civilization in the West, was nominally Christianized.

Christianity grew naturally, it has been said, from within. Ordinary Christians witnessed to those with whom they came in contact. Celsus, one of Christianity's leading critics, scoffingly remarked that fullers and workers in wool and leather, rustic and ignorant persons were the most zealous propagators of Christianity and brought it first to women and children. Women and slaves introduced it into the home circle. Careful investigation reveals that Christianity in its growth followed the trade routes of the empire, and we recognize that merchants carried it with their goods. We find it in the army barracks and know that soldiers carried it from one post to another. Justin, the first philosopher to believe, had sought truth in many areas and in a number of philosophic schools. He was converted, he tells us, by a venerable old man whom he met walking on the shores of the sea. He taught now the new philosophy of Christ. Every Christian laborer, said Tertullian, boths finds out God and manifests him. As another has said, it was a case "of one loving heart setting another on fire."

It was not only the words that they spoke, but also the witness of *Love*
their lives. "Behold how these Christians love one another," the pagans are reported to have said. "The Jews do not allow any of their
own people to become beggars, and the Christians support not only
their own but also our poor . . . " Julian, the heathen emperor, wrote
after the death of Constantine, seeking in vain to turn the clock backward and breathe new vitality into a dying paganism. "It is matters
like this," he added, "which have contributed most to the spread of
Christianity: mercy to strangers, care for burying the dead, and the
obvious honourableness of their conduct."[15] It is "no wonder," says
Gwatkin, the Cambridge historian,

> if the Christians made an impression out of all proportion to   *START*
> their numbers. Conviction in the midst of waverers, fiery en-   *WITH*
> ergy in a world of disillusion, purity in an age of easy morals,   *THIS*
> firm brotherhood in a loose society, heroic courage in time of   *LIST*
> persecution, formed a problem that could not be set aside,
> however polite society might affect to ignore it: and the reli-
> gion of the future turned on the answer to it. Would the world
> be able to explain it better than the Christians, who said it was
> the living power of the risen Saviour?[16]

It was not only the *life* of the Christian community which invited
faith, but the *death* which so many of them were willing to die for the
sake of Christ. Not all Christians, as we have seen, were ready to give
their lives, but many were, and out of every persecution the church
came purified and strengthened. Their constancy and their courage
had won new converts for their cause. "The blood of the martyrs,"
Tertullian cried, "has become the seed of the church!"
In a word, Christians won the Roman Empire because, as T. R.
Glover once wrote, they "out-thought," "out-lived," and "out-died"
the pagan world.[17] And so it must be again.

FOR CONSIDERATION

1. Read Matthew 10:16–39; Romans 8:28–39; Revelation 5:6–
   14; 6:9–14. How does the story of the persecution of the
   church (pages 22–28) help us to understand how these words
   came to be written and preserved?

2. Absurd charges were circulated—and believed—regarding the early Christians. Why are people so ready in every age to accept unsubstantiated charges against unpopular minorities? How should such charges be met?

*3. A recent historian states:

In the long run no compromise was possible between those who recognized no power beyond the Roman state and those who held that the state, like any other human creation, was subject to a judgment whose ground lay hidden beyond history.[18]

Is this a valid judgment for the present day?

4. Was martyrdom in the early church necessary or desirable? Should Christians have conformed to the customs of the day and paid the expected honors to the emperor as divine?

*5. Christians in ancient times did not actually invite persecution. Should Christians today do so, behind the Iron Curtain, let us say, or behind the Bamboo Curtain? What should be our attitude toward our fellow Christians in these lands where the church exists only on sufferance, and at the cost of considerable subservience to the state? Where and when, in your estimation, should Christians prepare to take their stand against an anti-Christian state?

*6. If persecution arose against the church in our own land, would there be martyrs? When does one become a martyr? Can you give examples of faithfulness under difficulties in our own land, in our own time? Are there those subject to such pressure, such popular feeling, such threat of violence in our present time? Have you ever been persecuted for your faith? Why, or why not?

7. What are the chief rivals of the Christian faith today? How can we best deal with them, in the light of our study?

8. Early Christians maintained that "there is salvation in no one else, for there is no other name under heaven given among men by which we must be saved" (Acts 4:12). This position was steadfastly maintained in the first three centuries, when many other religions were vying for the allegiance of the empire. Today, influential figures, like the historian Toynbee, say that

Christianity must give up its claims to exclusiveness and make common cause with other high religions against the advancing paganism of our times. What would be your reply to this appeal?

*9. Many of the literary figures of the early Roman Empire were contemptuous of Christianity, which they did not really understand. What is the attitude of our literary intelligentsia today—our novelists, dramatists, scenario writers, and poets? How should the church meet attacks made today on its faith and morals?

10. The church in the first three centuries grew because the average Christian bore witness to his neighbor—because the Christian life, the Christian ethic, differing from that of the pagan world, commended itself to an increasing number of earnest men and women. Should the Christian church today be concerned primarily with adding new members to the roll, with statistical success, or with greater purity of life, with greater demonstration of Christian love?

Next Chapter: The shift from a persecuted church to a persecuting church. The shift from being the object of ridicule, to the position of authority.

Constantine Pacing Off the Boundary of His New Capital, Constantinople

3
CHURCH AND STATE ARE UNITED

THE CONVERSION OF CONSTANTINE and the establishment of his supremacy over the empire as a whole opened a new era in the history of the church, indeed, in the history of western civilization. It was the beginning of a long period, not yet entirely ended, in which church and state would be closely allied, a relationship which brought benefits, but also dangers, soon to be realized, for both church and state.

THE END OF PERSECUTION

The persecution of the church ceased, of course, during the reign of Constantine and also during the reign of his three sons, who succeeded him on the throne. They were followed in turn by Julian (known as Julian the Apostate), a nephew of Constantine, who threw off the mask of Christianity he had been forced to wear, sought in vain to breathe new life into the old paganism, and resumed the persecution of the church. This persecution grew increasingly severe, but ended shortly with the death of Julian. Expiring from wounds received in battle with the Persians, he is reported to have exclaimed, "O Galilean, thou hast conquered!" The story is no doubt legendary, but it expresses truth. Although paganism lingered on for many generations, it was dying, without hope of resurrection. Julian was the last pagan Roman emperor.

INCREASING FAVOR TO THE CATHOLIC CHURCH

Constantine, reigning as a Christian, retained the pagan title of Pontifex Maximus (Chief Priest). Wisely, he did not restrict the rights of other religious bodies. In various ways, however, he showed his favor to the Catholic faith. Sunday was made a day of rest (in the cities). Members of the clergy were exempted from some burdensome civic responsibilities. Money was given for aid in the construction of churches. Church courts, which had been erected in accordance with the Pauline injunction (1 Cor. 6:1–3), were recognized by the civil government and permitted to function alongside its own tribunals. Tremendously significant for the future relations of church and state was the erection of Constantine's new capital on the site of the ancient Byzantium. Old Rome with its ancient families, opposed to the new religion, retained much of its pagan atmosphere. The new Rome (Constantinople), chosen for its strategic location in the heart of the empire, was Christian from the outset.

Constantine's sons, all succeeding emperors after Julian, continued his policy of favor to the Catholic Church, as distinguished from the various dissenting or schismatical bodies that had arisen, and which continued to arise here and there through the church. It was now generally agreed that to maintain its strength in spite of all disintegrating forces the empire must possess a common religion, as found in a single church, which by this time could be none other than the Catholic (or "universal") Church.

INCREASING RESTRICTION OF PAGANISM AND DISSENT

Increasing favor to the Catholic Church, therefore, was accompanied by increasing restrictions on paganism and dissent. The beginning of the end for both came during the reign of Theodosius I (379–395), one of the more eminent emperors of the later Roman, or as now called, the Byzantine, Empire. The name comes from Byzantium, the earlier name for Constantinople, the more important capital of the empire from Constantine's time on.

Typical laws aimed at the repression of heathenism included in the Theodosian Code, drawn up under the orders of Theodosius II, are the following:

A.D. 399: Whatever privileges were conceded by the ancient laws to the priests, ministers, prefects, hierophants [priests] of sacred things ... are to be abolished henceforth, and let them not think that they are protected by a granted privilege when their religious confession is known to have been condemned by the law.

A.D. 399: If there are temples in the field, let them be destroyed without crowd or tumult. For when these have been thrown down and carried away, the support of superstition will be consumed.

A.D. 416: Those who are polluted by the error or crime of pagan rites are not to be admitted to the army nor to receive the distinction and honor of administrator or judge.

A.D. 423: Although the pagans that remain ought to be subjected to capital punishment if at any time they are detected in the abominable sacrifices of demons, let exile and confiscation of goods be their punishment.[1]

These and other laws were issued by the emperor for the protection of the empire. But church fathers approved, and cannot therefore be absolved from responsibility. It is indeed tragic that the church, which for so many generations had been a persecuted church, became so soon a persecuting church. Before Constantine, the church fathers whose writings have come down to us were generally opposed to Christian service in the army. Within less than a hundred years after Constantine, no non-Christian was permitted to serve in the army, or to hold any other position of trust in the empire. There were some cases of mob violence against non-Christians (most notably the murder of Hypatia, daughter of the philosopher, Theon, herself a talented exponent of Platonic thought). But it was small, insignificant in comparison with what the Christians themselves had suffered. Paganism was not the stuff from which martyrs were made.

Theodosius I moved not only against heathenism, but also against heresy and dissent from the orthodox belief. Significant here is his decree aimed at Arians, who denied the full deity of Christ:

> It is our will that all the peoples whom the government of our clemency rules shall follow that religion which . . . the pontiff Damasus [Bishop of Rome] and Peter, Bishop of Alexandria . . . follow; that is, that according to the apostolic discipline and evangelical doctrine we believe in the deity of the Father and the Son and the Holy Ghost of equal majesty, in a holy trinity. Those who follow this law we command shall be comprised under the name of Catholic Christians; but others, indeed, we require, as insane and raving, to bear the infamy of heretical teaching; their gatherings shall not receive the name of churches; they are to be smitten first with the divine punishment and after that by the vengeance of our indignation, which has the divine approval.[2]

Here again we observe that Theodosius was not moved solely by religious considerations. The Arian heresy (to be discussed more fully in a later chapter) threatened to divide and therefore to weaken the Roman Empire, beset by increasing dangers from within and without. But here also church leaders approved. Their philosophy of repression was best expressed by Augustine, the most influential theologian in the early church. In his day North Africa was rent by the Donatist schism (to be treated later). Augustine reasoned with the dissenters, but they would not heed. The civil authorities finally resorted to force, and many of the Donatists were reclaimed. As Augustine saw it, this meant that immortal souls had been saved from what otherwise would have proved to be eternal damnation. Merciful severity therefore was actually only an expression of Christian love. As Jesus taught in his parable of the Wedding Feast (Luke 14:16–24), so the parable was misinterpreted by Augustine, after persuasion had failed it was proper to use force, and so "compel people to come in."

Final suppression of paganism in the Byzantine Empire (i.e., the later empire when its main capital was Byzantium [Constantinople]) came during the reign of Justinian (A.D. 527–565), another of the stronger rulers, who shored up—temporarily—the now crumbling empire. According to his edict it was decreed that

> Those who have not yet been worthy of the venerable rite of baptism shall report themselves ... and go to the holy churches with their wives and children and all the household subject to them, and be taught the true faith of Christians, so that having been taught their former error henceforth to be rejected, they may receive saving baptism, or know, if they regard these things of small value, that they are to have no part in all those things which belong to our commonwealth, neither is it permitted them to become owners of anything movable or immovable, but, deprived of everything, they are to be left in poverty, and besides are subject to appropriate penalties.
>
> We also forbid that any branch of learning be taught by those who labor under the insanity of the impious pagans. ...
>
> If any one in our commonwealth, hiding himself, shall be discovered to have celebrated sacrifices or the worship of idols, let him suffer the same capital punishment as the Manichaeans ...
>
> Also we decree that their children of tender years shall at once and without delay receive saving baptism; but they who have passed beyond the earliest age shall attend the holy churches and be instructed in the Holy Scriptures, and so give themselves to sincere penitence that, having rejected their early error, they may receive the venerable rite of baptism ... [3]

By this time, however, both paganism and dissent from the Catholic faith had practically disappeared in the Byzantine Empire. There was little persecution and little suffering, because there was little opposition. Paganism had expired largely because of its own inherent weakness. Dissent was unable to maintain itself against the superior power and appeal of the one (Catholic) Church, which had behind it the full support of the state.

INCREASING PAGANIZATION

And yet paganism did not utterly vanish. Traces lived on now within the Christian church. As increasing favor was shown to the

Catholic Church by Constantine and his successors, as increasing restrictions were placed on heathenism outside the church, the population moved en masse into the church, bringing with them many of
their former beliefs, many of their former attitudes, many of their
former practices, baptized now in the name of Christ.

A single illustration will suffice. In the old Roman religion there
were deities for every important process of nature and of human life.
A Roman turned, for example, to his household gods to keep his
larder stocked, to Ceres to make his wheat field flourish, to Silvanus
to make his grain grow, and so to a host of other deities for other particular wants. After Constantine the functions of these gods were
taken over rapidly, and in some cases almost bodily, by the "saints."
Thus in Spain San Serapio came to be appealed to in case of stomach-
ache, Santa Polonia for toothache, San Jose for headache, San Ber-
nardo for indigestion, San George for an infected cut, Santa Quiteria
for dog's bite, Santa Dorothea for rheumatism, San Pedro for the
fever, and Santa Rita for the impossible. Santa Anna became the patron saint of women in childbirth in Naples and its neighborhood.
The prayers addressed to her were strikingly like those with which
pagan women had appealed to Juno Lucina. The earliest representations of the Madonna and Christ Child were similar to those of the
Egyptian Isis and Horus. It is difficult, if not impossible, to avoid the
conclusion that this massive development was accelerated by the
great influx into the church of half-converted heathens under the
stress of the repressive laws enacted by Christian emperors against
the old religions.

Increasing Secularization

Union of church and state under Constantine and his successors
led also to the increasing secularization or worldliness of the church.
As the church became more powerful men came to seek its high offices for other than purely spiritual ends. The rivalry between bishops
of important sees (a "see" was a bishop's district) became at times a
naked struggle for power and furnishes many an ugly chapter in the
subsequent history of the church. The emperors found it increasingly
necessary to control the church, to remove unruly bishops from their
posts, to elevate to this high office men on whom they could depend.

The church at the outset did not see the danger of this new situation. Constantine, for example, was asked by both parties to intervene in the conflict between Catholics and Donatists. As time went on emperors were able to exercise greater control over the church in the East than in the West. Constantinople was now their seat of power; Rome, dominated increasingly by its bishops and inheriting some of the old capital's ancient glories, in fact the entire western portion of the empire, was passing out of their political domain.

The difference finds some illustration in the diverse fortunes of John Chrysostom, bishop of Constantinople (*ca.* A.D. 345–407) and his contemporary, Ambrose, bishop of Milan (A.D. 337–397), at this time the emperor's administrative headquarters in the West.

John Chrysostom

Chrysostom ("the Golden-Mouthed") was perhaps the most eloquent preacher in the early church, and one of the most courageous. He was accustomed to preach through successive books of the Bible, expounding their meaning, and applying them practically to the life of his times. His expositions, more than most of those which have come down to us from ancient times, retain their value to the present day. The great preacher's happiest days were spent in Antioch, where, as a simple presbyter, he was free to proclaim the word to large congregations which gathered to hear him. His troubles began when he was carried forcibly to Constantinople and elected bishop against his will. Here the severe self-denial of his daily life rebuked the lax morals of both clergy and laity, his strict discipline aroused resentment, his rebuke of sin in high places as well as low made him enemies in every quarter. Particularly did he arouse the ire of the Empress Eudoxia. Once she had him banished, but a violent storm woke terror in her soul, and Chrysostom was recalled. He was no more cautious after this incident than before. In a famous sermon he compared the empress with Salome, who again dances, rages, and seeks the head of John. Furious, Eudoxia once again secured an order of banishment, and this time no storm came to his aid. Chrysostom's followers were banished, cruelly tortured, and killed. He himself was unmercifully harassed. To destroy his influence, he was moved farther and farther from the capital. Finally, after three years of suffering, he was exiled, being forced to travel by foot to Pityus, a small town on the shores of the Black Sea, the farthest, the most miserable place in the whole empire. His weakened constitution could no longer stand the brutalities to which he was subjected. Realizing that he was about to die he partook of the Communion, offered prayer, which closed with the words, "Glory be to God for all things," "and then having aroused himself at the last Amen, he stretched out his feet which had been so beautiful in their running as they brought salvation to the penitent and reproof to confirmed sinners." So Palladius, contemporary historian, described the end of John of Antioch, "known as St. John Chrysostom, who defied emperors and loved God."

Ambrose WEST

Ambrose, equally courageous, had a happier end. The son of a high government official, he became governor of a large portion of northern Italy, with his residence in Milan, then practically an imperial capital. As he entered the cathedral to preserve order in a disputed election, the chant was raised, "Ambrose for bishop!" Though as yet unbaptized, Ambrose finally accepted his election as the call of God. He proved to be an able administrator, as well as a strong preacher and a gifted theologian. A farseeing statesman, he developed positions which became basic for the church in the West regarding the relations of church and state. Ambrose held first that the Catholic Church had a right to protection by the state from heresy and dissent. Writes Palanque, an able Roman Catholic historian,

> His aim was to bring about a close union between the Church and the State so that, far from putting the various cults on an equal footing, the State should ever display, though without violence or the shedding of blood, its special and unique favour to Catholic worship and discourage all others.[4]

Under his prodding, pagan symbols were finally destroyed in Rome, and Arianism was suppressed by the Emperor Theodosius.

Ambrose held in the second place that the church, in its own realm, was completely independent. More clearly and more completely than any other ecclesiastic of the day he laid down the principle of ecclesiastical autonomy. "Divine things," he asserted, "are not subject to the imperial power. . . . The palaces concern the Emperor, the churches concern the bishop."[5] He informed the emperor bluntly that he was not the head of the church. In accordance with this position he resisted successfully all efforts of Justina, mother of the youthful Valentinian II, to secure a place for the worship of the Arians in Rome.

Ambrose held finally that the church was superior to the state in the moral and spiritual realm. "He desired to compel the civil power to respect the moral law, even in acts not possessing a specifically religious character, and he was prepared to secure this by inflicting the censures of the Church wherever necessary."[6] This claim was advanced most spectacularly in the case of the Emperor Theodosius himself. This autocratic emperor in a fit of anger had ordered a general massacre of the inhabitants of Thessalonica. Ambrose sent him a confidential letter exhorting him to do penance for his sin as King David had done. "I urge, I beg, I exhort, I warn," he wrote, and added, "I dare not offer the sacrifice [the Lord's Supper] if you intend to be present."[7] The emperor, after some deliberation, gave in, and did public penance for his sin. This penance is a very important event both for the church and the empire. It is the first time an emperor acknowledged a higher authority than himself, and the first time a bishop used his power to judge and to dictate to an emperor. The power of the monarch was no longer absolute; it was checked by the moral authority of leaders in the church. Both the public and the private acts of the high ruler are fair subjects for criticism and (if necessary) condemnation, by the church.[8]

In the following generation, the benefits and the dangers of the close relations between church and state inaugurated by Constantine would become more apparent.

FOR CONSIDERATION

1. Read Mark 12:17; Acts 5:29; Romans 13:1–7; 1 Peter 4:13–17; Revelation 18. What light do these various passages throw on the Christian's responsibilities to the state?
2. Wherein do you differ or agree with Ambrose in his views of the relations between church and state?

3. Should the church support legislation today for the protection of the Sabbath? Why do you think so?

*4. Exemptions of the clergy from responsibilities assumed by other citizens, begun by Constantine, still continue in our own land; exemptions from compulsory military service and from jury duty are examples. Is it proper that such exemptions should continue? What about exemptions of church property from taxation? Give reasons for your answer.

*5. On what rational grounds do we defend religious toleration? Are there limits to this toleration? Should children of Christian Scientist parents, for example, be required to accept inoculations which are against their religious principle, but which the community deems essential for its own physical protection? What about "conscientious objectors"?

6. Why is it dangerous for those in possession of truth—any truth —to attempt to suppress error by legislation or other force?

The next three questions are raised by Winthrop S. Hudson in his excellent little book, *The Story of the Christian Church*:[9]

7. Are churches always in danger when they become respectable, popular, and prosperous? [If so, why?] S A

8. Are there social pressures today which may result in increased church membership without any corresponding depth of Christian conviction? . . .

9. . . . What [if anything] is wrong with the contention that religion belongs in one sphere and political and economic issues in another?

CATholic = UNiversal

Emperor Valentinian III Ordering All Bishops to Obey Pope Leo I

CATHOLIC
UNIVERSAL
SEE P41

4
THE CHURCH
TIGHTENS ITS ORGANIZATION

THE FIRST FIVE HUNDRED YEARS were important years in the history of the church. During these years, when it endured persecution and emerged victorious as the church of the empire, it underwent changes which have determined its subsequent course in large measure down to the present day. In this period it tightened its organization, elaborated its worship, developed its discipline, clarified, and in a number of important areas, defined its beliefs. A large part of Christendom (Roman Catholics, Greek Catholics, Anglo-Catholics) believes that in each of these respects it was divinely led; Protestants agree only in part. In some particulars it appears to them that the church began to move in paths that would take them ever farther away from the scriptural norm.

We look first at ways in which the church began to tighten its organization.

THE FIRST CENTURY

In the New Testament period (the first century) we meet apostles, "gifted" men, and officers.

46

The Greek word "apostle," meaning originally a delegate, or messenger, or one sent with orders, came to be applied especially to the twelve disciples whom Jesus had selected out of the total number of his followers to be his constant companions and to become heralds of the Good News of the Kingdom. These apostles became men of particular prestige and authority, though that authority is nowhere specifically defined.[1] In the days immediately following the resurrection Matthias was chosen to take the place vacated by Judas (Acts 1:15–26). But nothing more is heard of Matthias, or in fact of most of the others who were included in the original group. Paul claimed to be an apostle, chosen by the Lord Christ himself, and therefore on an equal plane with those regarded as pillars of the church (see Gal. 1—2). Barnabas and others are termed apostles, not as successors of the original twelve but as messengers of the gospel to those who had never heard. The apostles as a distinct group finally ceased to exist; but their authority as Jesus' chosen spokesmen, as authorized expounders of the faith, became more firmly established with the passing years.

Paul in his Epistles refers to men who served the church in various capacities because of particular "gifts" which they had received from the Holy Spirit. All members of the church, Paul indicates, had some gift which they could use for the benefit of the whole (read 1 Cor. 12:1—14:5), but some had gifts which rendered them particularly useful to the community of believers, or in Paul's words, to "the body of Christ" (see 1 Cor. 12:27–31a; Eph. 4:11–12). Some of these men, apostles, prophets, and teachers, for example, served the church universal; others served the local church.

In addition to such gifted individuals (on whom the church in every age depends for a large part of its ministrations)—or better, we might say, included among these gifted individuals—were men who rendered services of such essential character that in time they came to hold a permanently recognized "office" in the church.

The two permanent officers that came to be accepted as such before the end of the first century were, first, elders (Greek, *presbyters*) or bishops (the terms being used interchangeably) and, second, deacons. In perhaps his earliest Letter (1 Thess. 5:12–13) Paul names no officers as such, but urges respect for "those who labor among you and are over you in the Lord . . . " In his First Letter to the Corinthians (12:28) he refers, among others, to helpers and administrators. His Letter to the Philippians, written from Rome as his ministry drew to a close, is addressed "to all the saints in Christ Jesus who are at Philippi, with the bishops and deacons," which suggests that by this time the administrators and helpers had become more important in the life of the church and were coming to be known as holders of a distinct office in the church. In his final Letters (if indeed they came in their present form from the hands of Paul), the qualifications and duties of these two officers are more specifically defined (see 1 Tim. 3:1–13; 5:17; and Titus 1:5–19, where "bishop" and "elder" seem to be synonymous terms for the same office).

The book of Acts, written later than the Pauline Epistles, assumes that the office of elder (or bishop) existed from the beginning. Luke speaks here of elders in the mother church at Jerusalem (Acts 11:30; 15:2; 21:18), which was indeed what one might expect, since the synagogues, with which the apostles were of course familiar, had themselves been governed by a board of elders. Luke tells us further that Paul appointed elders in the churches founded on his first missionary journeys (Acts 14:23) and that he addressed the elders of the church at Ephesus (Acts 20:17), referring to them as bishops in the course of his address (20:28 in the Greek). He does not mention deacons, but he does tell us how the early church at Jerusalem chose seven men "to serve tables" (the word "to serve" comes from the same Greek root from which comes the word "deacon"), particularly in the daily distribution of food. These seven men were regarded as deacons by later church fathers, and the church in Rome continued for many years, we are told, to have only seven deacons, because of the precedent set in Jerusalem.

It is possible that some men began to stand out as men of pre-eminent prestige or authority beyond that exercised or enjoyed by the elders or bishops as a whole, before the first century drew to a close. James, the brother of Jesus, seems to have enjoyed such prestige in Jerusalem (Acts 12:17; 15:13 f; 21:18). In the Jewish synagogues there was a permanent moderator, or presiding officer, as in the Sanhedrin itself, and James may have held such a position in the church at Jerusalem. In the Pastoral Epistles Paul is pictured as bestowing some authority on Timothy and Titus (see 1 Tim. 1:3; Titus 1:5), as his personal representatives. This in turn may have led to further developments in the following century.

THE SECOND CENTURY

In this century, the second century A.D., there were two important developments. First, the "gifted men" gradually disappeared, that is, as recognized servants of the church. The reason for this is apparent. The time came when men claiming to speak through the Spirit could no longer be trusted. Some were theologically unsound, going so far as to deny that Christ actually came in the flesh (1 John 4:1–5). They were in fact false prophets, as John declares, and as Jesus himself had earlier warned (Mark 13:5; cf. Acts 20:29–30). Others seemed to have had mercenary motives. In the Didache (rhymes with "did away"), one of the early Christian manuals, originating in the second century, the church is warned against men who come to a congregation asking for something more than simple lodging. So men claiming to speak in the Spirit came to be suspect unless the church had given them its imprimatur, unless, that is, they had been formally chosen, officially designated as officers in the church. And so, though this was not the intention, there ceased in time to be any place for "laymen" to serve the church in any official recognized capacity.

The second important development in this century was the emergence of what is termed the "monarchial" bishop. In the first century, "elder" and "bishop" appear to have been synonymous terms for the same office; in the second century, each congregation came to have a single bishop, vested with monarchial power over the congregation, and the elders (Greek word, *presbyters*) became his cabinet of advisers. Why this was the case, we cannot say, but the fact is evident. Ignatius, bishop of Antioch, for example, emphasizes the importance of the bishop in his letter to the Smyrnaeans (about A.D. 112):

> Avoid divisions, as the beginning of evil. Follow, all of you, the bishop, as Jesus Christ followed the Father; and follow the presbytery as the Apostles. Moreover, reverence the deacons as the commandment of God.[2]

Whatever the exact reason, it was not an unnatural development.

There were some obvious advantages in times of danger of having a single head who could make quick decisions; there would be a natural tendency to elevate the man who was accustomed to preside, to proclaim the word, to preside at the Lord's Supper. In addition, it was not a democratic age, rather an autocratic one which accepted the leadership principle, the principle of authority delegated from higher to lower; and, at first unconsciously perhaps, and later consciously, the organization of the church was molded on that of the Roman Empire, the most efficient political organization that the world had ever known.

THE THIRD CENTURY

In accordance with this same trend the authority of the bishops was enhanced in the centuries that followed. In the third century the bishop came to exercise authority not only over the church, probably knots of worshipers in his own city, but also over the congregations or churches in the surrounding area. He had in other words become what we now call a "diocesan" bishop. The presbyters (or elders), who in the second century had been his advisers, were now priests (a contraction of the Greek word *presbyter*), serving each his own church or congregation, under the general authority of his bishop. Deacons continued to busy themselves with the financial affairs of the parish, being particularly responsible for the care of the poor, all under the authority and control of the bishop.

By this time a clerical "order" or rank had developed, clearly distinguished from the laity, who were now dependent upon the clergy for the ministrations of grace. Members of the clergy gave their whole time to the service of the church, and secured their remuneration or support from the church. The "high brass" included bishops, presbyters (elders or priests), and deacons. The lower ranks included such subordinate posts as lectors or readers, subdeacons, acolytes (altar attendants), exorcists (specialists in expelling demons), "widows" (older women employed by the church to serve particularly among women; see 1 Tim. 5:9–10), and deaconesses. Bishops were elected ostensibly by the people; other members of the clerical order were nominated by the bishop, but also elected by the people. Admission to the clergy was through ordination, the laying on of hands, in accordance with New Testament (and Jewish) practice (see Acts 6:6; 13:3; 2 Tim. 1:6). Bishops were originally ordained, it would appear, by presbyters or elders, but by the end of the fourth century they were ordained only by bishops, and the laying on of hands by the bishops had become necessary for the ordination of presbyters or priests.

THE FOURTH CENTURY

In the fourth century the church began to model its organization more consciously on that of the empire, and this development was encouraged by the emperors, who preferred to have power concentrated in fewer hands and thus more easily controlled. In this century, "metropolitan" bishops appeared (later called "archbishops"). They were the bishops of the capital city of each Roman province. They presided over synodical councils, which were held now with some regularity, and which included all bishops within the province; they also exercised administrative authority over clergy and laity in their areas. In this century appear also "patriarchs," the bishops of the four most important sees (official seats or residences of the bishops) in the empire, those of Rome, Constantinople, Alexandria, and Antioch. Jerusalem also was regarded as a patriarchal see, because of its religious associations, but the bishop of this see never exercised the political and spiritual authority that was wielded by the other four. The bishop of Rome, to take an example, was in this century diocesan bishop of Rome and its environs, metropolitan bishop of southern Italy, and patriarchal bishop of the West, with undefined authority over all bishops in this area; and so with the other patriarchal bishops. The struggle for power that ensued between these rival claimants of spiritual (and political) power offers an ugly picture, and determined the course of many of the controversies that arose in this period.

THE FIFTH CENTURY

In the fifth century, one bishop, the bishop of Rome, began for the first time, to claim (not to exercise) universal supremacy in the church.

The church in Rome had been founded by unknown disciples in

New Testament times. When Paul wrote his Letter to the Romans in A.D. 55 the church had been in existence for several years (see Rom. 15:22–24). The Apostle later came to Rome, not free, as he had hoped, but a prisoner in bonds, and here, according to an early tradition of the church, he was finally martyred. Peter also probably visited Rome, and here he too, according to tradition, ultimately gave his life for Christ. A late tradition (about A.D. 185) holds that Peter was the first bishop of Rome, but according to all the evidence there was no single, monarchial bishop in this city until late in the second century. The church in Rome suffered severely, as we have seen, under Nero and again under Domitian, but it recovered quickly from both, and from A.D. 100 on was probably the largest single congregation in Christendom. One of its bishops (Victor, A.D. 189) threatened to excommunicate Eastern bishops who did not agree with him regarding the date of Easter, but this threatened action infuriated Polycrates, bishop of Ephesus and spokesman for the eastern bishops, as well as Irenaeus, influential ecclesiastic in what is now southern France.

In the fourth century, as we have seen, the bishop of Rome came to be recognized as patriarch of the West, claiming some authority over other bishops in this area. Such authority was not recognized, however, in the ancient sees of northern Africa, or by Ambrose and other strong ecclesiastics in northern Italy, or by the churches in the territories dominated by the new Germanic tribes breaking into the Roman Empire.

In the fifth century *a claim to universal supremacy was advanced for the first time* by a bishop in Rome—Innocent I. He based his claim on what he held to be a decision of the first ecumenical council to be held in the church, the Council of Nicaea (A.D. 325). Actually, however, the decision he quoted was one approved by the Council of Sardica, a council representing only a group of western bishops. In the Pelagian controversy, of which we shall speak later, Innocent ventured the bold assertion that in the whole Roman world nothing should be decided without the approval of the Roman bishop, and that especially in matters of faith all bishops must turn to Rome.

It was Leo I, however (A.D. 440–461), who is commonly spoken of as the first pope, and it was he who developed for the first time the claims still advanced by popes today, a claim based on the words of Jesus to Peter in Matthew 16:18–19. In addition Leo I exercised something like papal powers in the West (not, however, in the East).

To understand these claims and the degree to which they were actually realized we will have to wait until we have reviewed other developments in the church and in the empire, especially in western Europe. We may observe, however, that the claims of the Roman pontiffs were finally accepted by the newer churches arising from the ruins of the Roman Empire in the West; they were never accepted by the older churches in the East. The claim to universal supremacy advanced by bishops of Rome in the fifth century A.D. remains the great stumbling block between the Roman Catholic and the Eastern Orthodox Churches; it is rejected, of course, by all Protestants.

FOR CONSIDERATION

*1. Consider Acts 14:23; 15:6; 1 Timothy 3:1–10; 5:17; Titus 1:5–9. Is there scriptural basis for presbyterian church government here?

2. Is it desirable that the polity of the church be modeled on that of the New Testament?

3. Presbyterianism sought to organize itself in accordance with the New Testament pattern. To what extent did it succeed?

*4. What are the values of presbyterian government as contrasted with episcopal or congregational church government?

*5. What, if any, are the superior advantages of other types of church government to our own?

6. What do we mean by the doctrine of "the priesthood of all believers"?

7. Was the early church right or wrong in permitting distinctions between clergy and laity to arise? Why do you think so?

8. What are the mutual responsibilities of ministry and laity in the church today?

9. The New Testament church was served by "gifted" individuals, who were not elected to any office, but who had certain endowments which they employed in the service of the church. Are there such men today? What list of modern "gifts" would you draw up to put alongside Paul's list in 1 Corinthians 12:28?

10. Should we be willing to sacrifice some of the principles of our presbyterian church government if a wider church union on other grounds should appear to be advantageous?

11. What, if any, principles of our government would you not be willing to concede?

*12. What meaning does the organization of the church have for our present day? To what extent are we bound by the past in such measures? To what extent are we left free to order our organization as may seem best to us today?

13. If it is true that Christ left no detailed instructions for the outward organization of the church, does this mean that questions of church organization are to be regarded as of little consequence?

*14. If precedents can be found in the early church for the congregational, the presbyterian, and the episcopal types of church organization, on what ground must debates as to the proper form of church organization be settled?

*15. What does Matthew 16:18–19 really mean?

Christians Worshiping in San Mariae Maior, Founded in Rome, A.D. 432–40

5
THE CHURCH
ELABORATES ITS WORSHIP

IN THE FIRST FIVE HUNDRED YEARS of the church's history there were important developments in the field of worship, developments which have continued to influence all branches of the church, in one way or another, down to the present time.

OCCASIONS OF WORSHIP

Some Jewish Christians continued to observe the traditional Sabbath, in addition to the first day of the week when they gathered to celebrate their Lord's resurrection from the dead. Indications are that Gentile Christians, on the other hand, from earliest times observed only the Lord's Day as their accustomed day of worship. Paul declined to impose ceremonial elements of the Mosaic Law on his converts from the Gentile world (see Gal. 5:1–3, 13–14). In his letter to the Corinthian Christians it is plainly indicated that the congregation assembled on the first day of the week (1 Cor. 16:1–2; compare also Acts 20:7). In other letters Paul strenuously opposed efforts of the Judaizing Christians to fasten Jewish days of worship (including the

Sabbath) on the Gentile churches. To give in to such endeavors, he insisted, would be to return to a legal bondage from which the gospel had happily delivered them (see Gal. 4:8–10; Rom. 14:1–6; Col. 2:16–17). The earliest Christian writers after the New Testament times refer repeatedly to the fact that Christians worshiped on the first day of the week rather than on the Jewish Sabbath—because on this day Jesus rose from the dead. Thus Ignatius, bishop of Antioch, wrote in A.D. 112: "Those, then, who lived by ancient practices arrived at a new hope. They ceased to keep the Sabbath and lived by the Lord's Day, on which our life as well as theirs shone forth . . . "[1]

"We have nothing to do with Sabbaths, new moons or the Jewish festivals," Tertullian exclaimed at the end of the second century. "We have our own solemnities, the Lord's Day, for instance, and Pentecost."[2]

In addition to their worship on the Lord's Day, Christians were accustomed from earliest times to fast on certain days of the week, particularly on Friday, the day when Jesus died on the cross. On this day they refrained from eating any meat in which there was blood. Fish became the staple diet for this day (as it remains in Catholic homes to the present time).

There were also certain annual observances to which the church attached great importance from the earliest days, thus laying the foundation for what came to be known as the church year. Most important of these annual observances was that celebrating the resurrection of Jesus from the dead. Tertullian's words quoted above reveal that Pentecost was observed as the completion of the Easter season by the end of the second century. The day before Easter meanwhile (in some cases forty hours) was observed as a fast day. In the third century, Holy Week was drawn into the Easter cycle, and in the first quarter of the fourth century, during the period of the great persecution, the period of fasting was lengthened to forty days (the origin of our present Lenten observance). Epiphany (January 6), variously regarded as the day of Jesus' birth, his baptism, and the visit of the Wise Men, began to be observed in the East during the third century, and in the West in the century following. December 25 as the date of Jesus' birth was not celebrated in the West until the year A.D. 354, and in the East not until some time later. This particular date was almost certainly chosen to offset the pagan observance of this day as the birthday of the sun-god Mithras (Christianity's most dangerous rival in the fourth century). It has no real claim therefore to be regarded as the actual birth-date of our Lord. As "saint-worship" grew apace in the fourth and fifth centuries various days were set aside in which they were to be given particular honor. It was this multiplication of days, along with the superstitions which gathered about them, which later induced some of the Protestant Reformers to abandon the whole idea of a church year.

PLACES OF WORSHIP

Naturally church buildings were not erected in any large numbers during the years of persecution. The homes of wealthier Christians were made available for this purpose. In the oldest of these house-churches which has been recovered (dating from the period 232–256), there is a baptismal font; on the wall behind, a painting of the Shepherd and the Fall; and on the side walls, remains of paintings, including the healed paralytic, Peter and Christ upon the water, and the three women at the empty tomb. On occasion, when persecution became severe, in some cities, Christians went underground, and conducted their worship in the catacombs, the underground tombs which enclosed their dead. In the paintings on the catacomb walls and in the sculpture (bas-relief) of the sarcophagi we find the beginnings of Christian art. There were numerous symbols—the cross, Alpha and Omega, the anchor, the palm, the fish (the Greek word ICHTHUS gave the initials of "Jesus Christ, Son of God, Savior"), the dove, the hart (a kind of deer), the vine, and many others. There were also pictures, as indicated above, including some allegorical representations of Christ, the earliest being those of a Shepherd or Teacher.

When the persecutions ceased and Christianity became the accepted religion, church buildings began to be erected, some with state aid, and very costly. Naturally, they were modeled after familiar forms. In the East it was the Byzantine type, marked by rounded domes. In the West it was the basilican type, oblong, with portico, slanting roof, and at the end a rounded, tall, bay window or "apse." Men were seated on one side, and women on the other; pulpit and choir were in the center of the building. At the eastern end was the altar, adorned with costly cloths, a cross or crucifix, burning tapers, with a splendid copy of the Scriptures, and above all the tabernacle for the consecrated host (bread).

ELEMENTS OF WORSHIP

The church based its worship services on those of the synagogue, and there were from the beginning the basic elements which have continued to the present day. There was Scripture reading, first from the Old Testament and then from the New (the writings of the apostles; only gradually assembled and counted as Scripture); prayer, some spontaneous or free, other following set forms; Psalms, first, and later hymns (the oldest which has come down to us is "Shepherd of Eager Youth," written by Clement of Alexandria, about A.D. 200); a homily or sermon; and an offering.

Then, in addition, there were the sacraments. The word itself is not found in the New Testament and was first brought into the service of the church about A.D. 200 by the Latin Father, Tertullian. For many generations it was used rather loosely to describe a large number of rites which had some inner or spiritual significance. But the most important of these from the beginning were Baptism and the Lord's Supper.

BAPTISM

Baptism, employed by John the Baptist, then by Jesus' disciples, has been from New Testament times the rite of initiation into the church (see Matt. 28:19; Acts 2:38). But who were baptized? Believers only, or believers and their infant offspring? On this question there is a difference of opinion, so far as it relates to the New Testament period. Those who reject infant baptism point out that there are no instances of infant baptism recorded in the New Testament. Those who accept infant baptism point out that infants were circumcised under the Old Covenant and that baptism, which replaced circumcision as the rite of admission under the New Covenant, must likewise have included infants, unless there was some indication to the contrary, which clearly there is not; also that there are many instances of household baptisms referred to in the New Testament (Acts 10:48;

16:15, 33; 1 Cor. 1:16; 16:15), and that it is unreasonable to deny that infants were found in any of these homes. Irenaeus, about A.D. 185, is the first of the church fathers to refer clearly to the practice of infant baptism, but he does not mention it as though it were a novelty. Tertullian advised against the practice (about A.D. 200), not however on the ground that it was an innovation and so contrary to the teachings of the apostles, but on the ground of expediency. It was better, he urged, to postpone baptism until the adolescent years were past and one had sown his wild oats. Baptism thus postponed, he held, wipes out past sins, and enables one to start afresh. Origen, the greatest scholar in the early church, argued (about A.D. 225) for the practice, on the ground that it was apostolic. In the postbiblical church, infant baptism did not, however, become the general practice until the fifth century, and then chiefly on theological grounds. It was now believed that an infant was born in original sin and without baptism was eternally lost. With such beliefs it seemed dangerous to delay.

There is also uncertainty about the original mode of baptism. The New Testament records do not give us a clear picture. Good arguments can be presented for sprinkling, pouring, and immersion. Historians agree, however, that immersion was the most common form after New Testament times; also that pouring and sprinkling were accepted as alternative forms. The two latter forms became prevalent in the western churches in the fifth and sixth centuries, as the church spread into northern climes, and immersion became less desirable. Luther and Calvin both believed that immersion was the original form, but held that the form itself was immaterial.

In New Testament times, water baptism was a symbol of the remission of sins (Acts 2:38; 1 Cor. 6:11), of baptism with the Holy Spirit (Matt. 3:11; John 3:5), and of union with Christ (Rom. 6:4; Col. 2:12). In the second century it became rather a device which somehow conveys forgiveness and brings the new birth. This new and exaggerated importance that was henceforth attached to the rite was due perhaps to the influence of the popular mystery religions, which promised regeneration by such impersonal means.

THE LORD'S SUPPER

The Lord's Supper, observed from the earliest days in accordance with the Lord's commands (1 Cor. 11:25; Matt. 26:26; Mark 14:22; Luke 22:19), came originally at the end of a common meal, "the love feast," as was the case when Paul wrote his familiar words to the Corinthians (1 Cor. 11:17–26). By the middle of the second century, however, it had become a part of the regular worship service, and the most important part. Along with this change in observance came a change in theory, comparable to that which had taken place in connection with the sacrament of Baptism. In the first century the Lord's Supper had been a meal commemorating the death of Christ (see Luke 22:19; 1 Cor. 11:24, 26), and symbolizing the communion of believers with one another and with Christ (1 Cor. 10:16–17). In the second century it became a rite in which Christ was really present (though the mode of his presence was not defined) and through which participants became partakers of his eternal life. In the third century it came to be regarded as a sacrifice, in which Christ's body was re-offered by the priest and which inclined God to be gracious to the living and the dead. This was not the theory of "transubstantiation" (see p. 145) later developed and now held in the Roman Catholic Church, but it was a step in that direction. How can we explain such a departure from the New Testament ideal? It may be due, again, in part at least, to the influence of the popular mystery religions, along with Judaism and other ancient religions which gave a large place to sacrificial offerings.

Justin Martyr, writing about A.D. 150, describes Christian worship for the sake of a nonbeliever, as follows:

> On the day which is called the day of the sun there is an assembly of all who live in the towns or in the country; and the memoirs of the Apostles or the writings of the prophets are read, as long as time permits. Then the reader ceases, and the president speaks, admonishing us and exhorting us to imitate these excellent examples. Then we arise all together and offer prayers; and ... when we have concluded our prayers, bread is brought, and wine and water, and the president in like manner offers up prayers and thanksgivings with all his might; and the people assent with *Amen;* and there is the distribution and partaking by all of the Eucharistic elements; and to them that

are not present they are sent by the hand of the deacons. And they that are prosperous and wish to do so give what they will, each after his choice. What is collected is deposited with the president, who gives aid to the orphans and widows, and such as are in want by reason of sickness or other cause; and to those also that are in prison, and to strangers from abroad, in fact to all that are in need he is a protector.

We hold our common assembly on the day of the sun, because it is the first day, on which God put to flight darkness and chaos . . . and made the world, and on the same day Jesus Christ our Saviour rose from the dead . . . [3]

LITURGY

From this and other accounts it is clear that the earliest worship was simple. Liturgical forms—responses by the congregation, set prayers, as well as free or spontaneous prayer—were present, but they were brief. By the middle of the third century an important development occurred: the worship service came to be divided into two parts. The first part, consisting of Scripture reading, preaching, singing, and prayer, was open to everyone; upon completion of this public service all unbelievers and catechumens (candidates for admission) were escorted from the room by deacons, and the Lord's Supper, in which the service now found its climax, was observed in secret rites known only to the initiate. Why this development took place we cannot say. Perhaps it was due again to the influence of the mystery religions, all of whose initiatory rites were in secret, or it may have been to safeguard the Communion from profanation. These secret rites continued for a century, and when once again the full service became public, the service had been greatly expanded. Christianity was now the accepted religion. Church buildings had become more numerous and expensive. Furnishings and appointments had become lavish and ostentatious. "Incense, jeweled altars, and golden chalices were being increasingly utilized; and rituals were becoming longer and more complicated."[4]

In the judgment of some scholars, "the increasing emphasis on ceremonials, the increasing employment of the idea of objective sacrifice and of the term 'priest' and other Temple terminology, and the beginning of the distinctions between clergy and laity and between different orders of ministers ... all may be attributed in part to the influence of Judaism."[5] In addition, "it seems almost certain that Christians added colorful ceremonies, emphasized the 'mystery' of the Supper and guarded it carefully from all but the faithful, and utilized sacramental terminology in their worship practice for the express purpose of competing with the fascinating rites and rituals of the mystery religions."[6]

The more important question is: Was this development justified? Christianity has adopted and adapted much from the civilization around it in every age, and this has been one of the secrets of its enduring strength. After Constantine religious services, it is estimated, lasted for approximately three hours. By the end of the sixth century they had taken much the same form they have since retained in the Orthodox and Roman Catholic Churches. Had Christian worship been somewhat paganized in the process, or was it a natural movement preserving all essential elements in a more mature liturgy, and accommodating itself wisely to the desire in human nature for ritual and color and action? On this question there may be and is a wide difference of opinion.

LOWER CHRISTIANITY

Extremely important was the rapid development after Constantine of what is sometimes termed "Lower Christianity." By Lower Christianity is meant the worship (in some sense) of objects or beings less than God. Such "worship," as we have seen, became general after the great flood of half-converted heathen poured into the church, following the changed attitude of the state toward Christianity and all non-Christian religions.

Basically this expressed itself in the veneration of the saints. Increasingly, Christians prayed to the Christian martyrs, who, it was believed, had passed immediately into their heavenly reward. It was thought that they in turn would intercede with the Father or Son, who would listen more readily to their requests than to their own. As there had once been gods for every particular need, so, as we have seen, there soon came to be a saint for each such need.

Among the growing multitude of the saints, Mary, the mother of

Jesus, came to hold a pre-eminent position. The fact that she is not mentioned in the New Testament after the brief statement in Acts 1:14 that she was one of those gathered in the Upper Room after the death and resurrection of Christ would indicate that she held no particular place of honor in the earliest church. Church fathers in the first three hundred years have little to say regarding her. The so-called Apocryphal (nongenuine) gospels, however, reveal a developing popular interest in Mary, and it is to these Apocryphal gospels that most of the later legends regarding Mary can be traced.

In the third century, as asceticism (the life of monks, for example) came to be regarded as the Christian ideal of life, Mary came to be known as the "Virgin Mary." The doctrine that she was perpetually a virgin, that the brothers of Jesus were not the sons of Joseph and Mary, was not held universally in the church, however, until the latter part of the fourth century. It is true that the so-called brothers of Jesus may have been his cousins or sons of Joseph by an earlier marriage, but this is not a natural interpretation of the New Testament records; and the doctrine as it developed in the fourth century was due to theological, rather than biblical (or historical), considerations. By this time it was generally agreed that virginity was a holier estate than normal motherhood. The mother of Christ must therefore have been perpetually a virgin.

In the fifth century Mary came to be revered as the "Mother of God." This title, which can be traced back to Egypt in the early part of the third century, became a battle cry in one of the theological controversies which raged in the fifth century, and its use was sanctioned by the Council of Ephesus in the year A.D. 431. The "worship" of Mary may be said to have begun on that date.

Another title of honor ascribed to her in this period was "the Queen of Heaven." It was a title formerly applied to Isis, mother goddess of one of the most popular mystery religions.

It was in the fifth century too that Augustine, most influential theologian in the early church, taught what all Catholics were now prepared to believe, that Mary had lived without sin.

At the same time Mary had begun to be honored in a public cult, with festive days set aside in her honor, as an important part of the church year. Before Justinian (A.D. 527–565) these feasts in honor

of Mary commemorated gospel events—the Annunciation, the Na-
tivity, the presentation in the Temple—and found their justification
in Mary's relation to Christ. In the second half of the sixth century,
the Marian festivals were completed by those held in celebration of
her birth, her conception, and finally her death, or rather, her falling
asleep. These, as distinguished from the earlier feasts, were all concerned with Mary herself, not at all with Christ.

The cult of the martyrs, growing rapidly after the Constantinian
period, included also the veneration of their relics, portions of their
body, a bone, a bit of their hair, a portion of their clothes, some other
object with which they had come in contact. This usage was defended
by arguments based on the natural sentiments of the human heart.
When a father dies, his children cherish the clothes he has worn, the
ring which adorned his finger. The bodies of the saints, Augustine declared, were the organ and vessel of the Spirit and more intimately
linked with their personality than the objects just mentioned. A relic
thus by degrees came to be regarded as a protection for the person
who wore it. So we find a piece of a bone, or a tiny portion of the true
cross, worn around the neck or enclosed in a ring. And quite naturally it gave rise to numerous frauds, and to more than a little superstition. This cultus of relics aroused some resistance and criticism,
not only on the part of pagans, but also on the part of Christians, who
maintained that it was nothing more than a kind of transposed paganism. Jerome, one of the most influential of the church fathers, replied
thus:

> No, we do not adore the relics of martyrs, any more than
> we adore the sun, the moon, the angels, the archangels, or the
> seraphim. . . . We honour them in order to adore Him whose
> witnesses they were . . . ; we honor the servants in order that
> this honour given to them may be passed on to the Master who
> has said, "He who receiveth you, receiveth me."[7]

The veneration of pictures was justified in similar fashion. Honor
paid to the picture of the saint was in fact honor paid to him, and
through him to God the Father, and Jesus the Savior of all men. Similar veneration was paid to angels, though the cultus of the angels was
never so extensive as the cultus of the saints.

So by the end of the sixth century, the worship of the church had become greatly elaborated, and some tendencies had appeared which leaders of the Reformation would repudiate as contrary to the Scriptures.

FOR CONSIDERATION

1. What principles of worship are set forth in the following New Testament passages: John 4:23–24; 1 Corinthians 11:17–28; 14:26–35; 16:1–2; Colossians 3:16–17?

2. Look up the references to the Lord's Supper on page 60 and consider: Is this like the way the Lord's Supper is conducted in my church? It would interest you also to visit churches of different denominations and compare their liturgies with one another and with the New Testament picture.

3. To what extent should our worship be determined by the worship of the church in the first century? In the first five centuries? Is there value in following traditional forms of worship that link the church of today with the church of yesterday, the church of the twentieth century with the church of the early centuries?

4. What dangers are there in the growing use of liturgical forms?

5. How would you answer a Seventh-Day Adventist who insisted that the Fourth Commandment requires us to worship on the Jewish Sabbath (Saturday) rather than on the first day of the week?

6. Should the church today make more or less use of the church year (Christmas, Holy Week, Easter, Pentecost, for example)?

7. Should greater or less use be made of Christian art? Why? How?

8. If it could be proved (as it cannot) that immersion was the original form of baptism, would it follow that immersion is the only form of baptism?

9. What is the real significance of the Lord's Supper?

10. What attitude should Protestants take toward the Virgin Mary? What is the objection to the veneration of Mary as exhibited in the Roman Catholic Church?

11. Is the value attached to relics by devout Roman Catholics helpful, harmful, or harmless to the spiritual life of Roman Catholics?

Augustine Publicly Professing His Christian Faith

6
THE CHURCH
DEFINES ITS BELIEFS

IN THE FIRST FIVE HUNDRED YEARS of its existence, the church was compelled to define many of its beliefs: compelled by questions raised by believers, questions which demanded an answer; compelled particularly by the rise of heresies which threatened the church's very existence.

THE DOCTRINE OF THE CHURCH

One of the earliest of the doctrines that it was found necessary to consider was that of the church. How was the true church, the Catholic Church, to be distinguished from un-genuine churches, "heretical" (unorthodox) and "schismatical" (split-off)? That was a practical question on which the life of the church came to depend.

The word "catholic," we may observe, is not found in the Bible. It was used first, so far as we are aware, by Ignatius, bishop of Antioch, about A.D. 112, to distinguish the universal church, spreading now through the empire, from the various local congregations. By the latter part of this century it became necessary to distinguish this

church—the true church, Catholic (or "universal") not only in that
it was spread through the empire, but also in that it was the original
church, preserving continuity with the church of the previous generations—from the many new bodies, heretical or schismatical, springing up here and there.

Irenaeus, influential bishop of Lyons, in southern France, in the
year A.D. 185, wrote an important book, *Against the Heresies,* that
laid down a threefold standard which would henceforth determine the
church's thinking on this matter. The apostles, Irenaeus said in effect,
were the only authorized exponents of Christianity.

Only those churches, then, could be recognized as Catholic which
acknowledged (a) *the writings of the apostles,* (b) *the tradition of
the apostles,* and (c) *the bishops as successors of the apostles.* Each
of these three marks was essential. In the writings of the apostles was
to be found the gospel set forth by those whom Jesus appointed for
that purpose. Some of the heretics, however, claimed to have apostolic writings that the Catholic Church regarded as forgeries; and they
distorted words found in those writings which were regarded as genuine. It was necessary, therefore, to fall back on a second line of defense—the tradition of the apostles—which was preserved in the
baptismal creeds of the Catholic Churches. These baptismal creeds
differed in detail from region to region but agreed in essential content.
Some of the leading heretics, however, claimed that to them had been
given the secret teaching of the apostles—the more advanced teaching, which had not been entrusted to the church as a whole. Irenaeus
in reply asked, Where is the full teaching of the apostles most likely to
be found, with these false teachers who had no connection with the
apostles, or among the bishops who had come down in orderly succession from the apostles themselves—the bishops of Rome, for example, who could trace their lineage back to Peter, or bishops in the
East, whose line of descent could be traced back to John?

THE NEW TESTAMENT

The argument of Irenaeus was a good common-sense argument,
and from this time, we may say, these three marks became distin-
guishing characteristics of the early Catholic Church. The emphasis
which Irenaeus and other church fathers laid upon them was to have

further consequences, some good, some bad. It gave great stimulus, for example, to the formation of the New Testament canon. In the earliest days the only recognized Scripture was that which the church had inherited from Judaism, our Old Testament. From earliest days, however, the writings of the apostles were read alongside the Scripture in the worship service of the church and were regarded as fully authoritative, as inspired, indeed, by the Holy Spirit. About A.D. 140 Marcion, one of the most influential of the early heretics, repudiated the Old Testament Scriptures and offered in their stead an abbreviated Gospel According to Luke, and, with some editing, the various Letters of Paul (excluding the Pastoral Epistles). The church was compelled to draw up an accepted collection of the apostolic writings, a canon, to set over against this partial collection. In his famous work Irenaeus counted these writings as Scripture on a par with the older collection of writings. Tertullian, at the opening of the third century, began to speak of the two collections as the Old and New Testaments (or Covenants). Though the church was now agreed that inspiration in the stricter sense ended with the apostolic era and that the apostolic writings were Scripture alongside the "Old Testament," it was some time yet before scholars of the church were agreed as to the limits of the New Testament canon. There was agreement from the very beginning in regard to the four Gospels, the book of The Acts, and the thirteen Epistles of Paul. But the other books of our New Testament were not known equally through the church. Also, it was not clear just when the apostolic age had ended, or just which books had come from the hands of the apostles or those associated with them. The first New Testament canon (list of books) including all of the books found in our present New Testament, those and no others, was drawn up by Athanasius, bishop of Alexandria, in the year A.D. 367. This collection of writings was endorsed soon afterwards by various synods of the church, approved by the bishop of Rome, and accepted by Jerome for his new translation of the Bible into Latin. It remains the New Testament canon accepted by all branches of the Christian church. It is agreed that on these books and on these books alone we must depend for our knowledge of the revelation of God's love in Jesus Christ.

THE APOSTLES' CREED

The tradition of the church on which, as we have seen, Irenaeus laid so much emphasis, was preserved in the baptismal creeds of the early church. One of these early creeds, and one only, has been preserved particularly in the western church, and that is the baptismal creed of the church in Rome, the only church in the West which could trace its origins back to the apostles. This creed came to be known as *the Apostles' Creed,* not because it was written by the apostles (an old theory exploded five hundred years ago), but because it was thought to preserve the apostolic tradition. References to this creed can be traced back to the middle of the second century, though the earliest form in which it was known to us dates from the year A.D. 337. It continued to undergo slight changes—including the addition of "he descended into hell" (more properly, Hades)—until the eighth century, when it assumed the full form in which it is ordinarily repeated at the present time. It remains the oldest and best beloved creed in the Christian church, and is repeated in the morning service by churches of various communions throughout the world.

BISHOPS AS SUCCESSORS OF THE APOSTLES
Clement and Irenaeus

The idea that bishops were in some sense successors of the apostles is found first in a letter written by Clement, an elder or presbyter in the church at Rome, in the name of this large and influential church, to the church in Corinth. It was written about A.D. 96 and is the earliest writing in the church after those coming from the apostolic circle. The apostolic succession that Clement has in mind is, however, an orderly, historical, matter-of-fact succession of the presbyter-bishops who succeeded the apostles in the government of the church, and who should not, he argues, be put out of office without good reason. We hear nothing more of the idea for nearly a hundred years, until Irenaeus develops his matter-of-fact historical argument that bishops who can trace their succession back to the apostles are more likely to have the full truth of the gospel than the heretics who can claim no such relation. Irenaeus, however, does go just a bit further when he hints that the bishops in this line of apostolic succession have received a "gift" of the truth. This in time would come to mean that the bishops of the church assembled in an ecumenical council would be infallibly guided in their definition of the truth (the theory of the Greek Orthodox Church) and the theory that the bishop of Rome, as the successor of Peter, is infallible when he speaks officially as the head of the church regarding matters of faith and morals (the dogma of the Roman Catholic Church, as approved by the Vatican Council in the year A.D. 1870).

Cyprian and Leo

In the year A.D. 250 Cyprian, bishop of Carthage, wrote a very important work on the church, in which he gives the theory of apostolic succession a twist that puts it in an entirely new category from that suggested by Clement of Rome or by Irenaeus. According to Cyprian's theory, the bishops, as successors of the apostles, are representatives of Christ, possessing all the authority for their day that the original apostles had in theirs; as such, they are mediators between God and man, with full power to bind and loose—to forgive sins, that is, or to refuse to forgive; they become also the only channels of saving grace. Apart from such bishops the church indeed does not exist. This was to become *the Catholic theory of the church*. It differs from the present Roman Catholic theory only in that the full power of Christ, given first to the twelve apostles and then to their successors the bishops, was *vested in the bishops as a body,* not in one bishop, who as successor of Peter, the Prince of the Apostles, is himself the vicar of Christ.

This later claim was developed by Leo I, bishop of Rome, about A.D. 450. Bishops of Rome, as we have seen, had at times asserted themselves in ways that aroused indignation among their fellow bishops, and had at times claimed to hold their succession from Peter. Other bishops, accepting Cyprian's theory of apostolic succession, were prepared to award precedence in honor to the bishop of Rome, but nothing more. None of the early church fathers interpreted Jesus' words to Peter to mean that to Peter and to his successors, the bishops of Rome, full authority in the church had been granted; this, however, was the claim of Leo. It was a claim which bishops in the older parts of the empire would never accept; a claim, however, which would be acknowledged in time by the newer churches in the West.

Regarding the Trinity

A second belief which the church was compelled to define more exactly in the early centuries was that growing out of its faith in Jesus as the only begotten Son of God.

Divine attributes had been attributed to Jesus by the earliest generation of Christian writers, as in the New Testament itself, and from the beginning Jesus was worshiped as God. But if this were the case were there not two Gods—first, God the Father, and second, God the Son? This was the question which gave rise, in the third century, to what became known as the Monarchian heresy. Monarchianism comes from two Greek words meaning "a single ruler" (whence our word "monarch"). The Monarchians sought to preserve men's faith in one God along with their faith in Jesus as God's only Son. One wing of this movement, known in history as Dynamic Monarchians (the word "dynamic" coming from a Greek word meaning "power"), held that Jesus was a man given divine power first at the time of his baptism, when the Holy Spirit came upon him like a dove. He was later raised from the dead and rewarded for his faithfulness with a secondary divinity. This view held little attraction, however, for the church. A man who became a lesser God did not satisfy; nor could one preserve the unity of God by adding secondary deities.

More appealing was the view of Sabellius, whose heresy came to be known as "Sabellianism," or "Modalistic Monarchianism." He was understood by his opponents to teach that Son and Holy Spirit were only temporary manifestations or "modes" of God, the Father, like rays emitted and then withdrawn again into the sun. This was a simple explanation which men could easily grasp, but it was rejected by the church, on the ground that it preserved the unity of the Godhead at the expense of both Son and Holy Spirit. Each, according to this view, existed only as a *temporary* mode or manifestation of the one true God.

Tertullian

Many of the church fathers wrote in opposition to Monarchianism. Most important of these was Tertullian, who, in his response to Praxeas (a contemporary heretic), first brought the word "Trinity" into the church's vocabulary. "The Father is God," he wrote, "and

the Son is God, and the Holy Spirit is God, and each is God. . . .
These three are one thing, not one Person."

From his writings was drawn the formula which in time was to
become the mark of orthodoxy on the subject: in the Godhead there
is *one substance* and *three "persons."* By substance Tertullian, it is
generally agreed, meant essential being. But there is not the same
certainty regarding his use of the word "person." In the lawcourts
(and Tertullian had been a lawyer, before he came a Christian) the
word "person" was used to describe the role, perhaps the various
roles, in which an individual appeared before a court; in theatrical
terminology it applied likewise to the various roles or parts (dramatis
personae) played by a single actor in the course of the play. The
word was coming, however, to have the sense which it now holds in
ordinary speech—referring to an individual with his own distinct
personality. In which sense did Tertullian use the word? He did not
define his terms and we cannot therefore be sure. But it is now widely
agreed that for Tertullian the three "persons" were objective *modes
of being* rather than personalities in our modern sense. Tertullian's
definition did not in any case give an intellectual solution to the problem faced by the early church. It did guard against dangers on the
right and on the left—the danger on the one hand of believing in three
gods and the danger on the other hand of sacrificing the true and continuing personal nature of either Father, Son, or Holy Spirit. At the
same time it bears witness to what has always been the fundamental
faith of the church: that the Father is God, the Son is God, and the
Holy Spirit is God, and that there are not three Gods but one: one
God, Creator of the world and Father, who has made himself known
in a historic personage, Jesus of Nazareth, and who is active in our
life and the life of the church as the Spirit of holiness.

Tertullian's formula (in Latin) proved acceptable to the West,
where people took to simple formulas and were not overly fond of
speculation. In the more intellectual East, where Greek remained the
popular language, Tertullian did not have the same influence. Continued discussion here gave rise finally to the Arian controversy,
which racked the church, east and west, for the larger part of a century (A.D. 318–381).

Arius

Arius, who gave his name to this heresy, was a priest in charge of a suburban church in the city of Alexandria. He began the controversy by attacking publicly the views of his bishop, Alexander, who held that Jesus was of the same substance (Greek, *homo-ousios*, "same in essential being") with the Father, and that there never was a time in which he did not exist. Arius, on the other hand, seeking to preserve the unity of the Godhead, held that the Son had come into being through a creative act of God (the first of created beings), and that he was not of the same substance as the Father. He was therefore a secondary deity, thus pointing to the Holy Spirit as a god of still lower rank, subordinate to the Son as the Son was to the Father.

The controversy spread far beyond Alexandria and threatened to engulf the entire East. As one historian has written: "The debate was conducted with the violence of a political convention. Everybody entered into it. Men who met to transact business neglected their bargaining to talk theology. If one said to the baker, 'How much is the loaf?' he would answer, 'The Son is subordinate to the Father.' If one sent a servant on an errand, he would reply, 'The Son arose out of nothing.' Arius put his doctrine into verse, to popular tunes, and it was sung and whistled in the streets. The arguments were punctuated with fists and clubs."[1]

Constantine, who had only recently established his reign over the empire, recognized that there was a threat here, not only to the unity of the church but also to that of the state. He invited the bishops of the church to assemble, therefore, in Nicaea (outside of Constantinople) and reach agreement on this and other issues before the church. So assembled, in the year A.D. 325, the first "ecumenical" council of the church, i.e., a council composed of representatives from every part of the church. The council very quickly rejected the view of Arius, for which there was never any large popular support. After some prodding from the emperor, it adopted a creed which is the basis of our present *Nicene Creed*. This was the first creed adopted by an ecumenical council, speaking for the whole church. (It was also the first creed to become officially a standard of orthodoxy. Arius and his supporters, who refused to accept the decision of the council, were exiled from the empire.) In this creed the church confessed its faith "in one God the Father All-sovereign, maker of all things visible and invisible; And in one Lord Jesus Christ, the Son of God . . . *begotten not made, of one substance* [Greek, *homo-ousios*] *with the Father,* through whom all things were made . . ."[2]

The original question that had been raised involved only the deity of Christ. As the discussion continued, however, it became clear that this implied the deity of the Holy Spirit. So in the end the East accepted a trinitarian formula comparable to that which had already been accepted in the West. The final victory of this trinitarian faith was sealed by the second ecumenical council, which met in Constantinople in the year 381, and approved an enlarged form of the original creed of Nicaea, what is now known as the Nicene Creed (see *The Hymnbook,* page 12), and which is accepted by all branches of the Christian church as a statement of the orthodox faith.

Is Christ fully divine or is he not? Do we in Christ have to do with God himself, or with one who is somewhat less than God? Is God one who has made himself accessible to man (in Jesus), or does he himself remain forever inaccessible? The Arian view, which held that Jesus Christ is more than man but less than God, has appeared and reappeared at various times in the history of the church but has always been rejected as inadequate. The church has held and still does hold to the faith that *God was in Christ* reconciling the world to himself (2 Cor. 5:19) and that *the Holy Spirit is God in us, Christ in us.*

REGARDING THE PERSON OF CHRIST

While the church was still torn by the Arian controversy, another question was raised which would engage the attention of theologians for more than three centuries and in the end rend the church in the East, giving rise to dissenting groups which have continued to the present time. These were the so-called "Christological" controversies, concerning the relationship of the human and divine in Jesus Christ. If the Son—the second person of the Trinity—was fully divine, as proclaimed in the Council of Nicaea, and if the divine Son had become incarnate in human flesh, in what sense was he human?

In New Testament times there had been those who claimed that he was human only in appearance. The body in which he appeared was only an apparent body. John emphatically rejected this point of view in his first Letter (1 John 4:1–3). Doceticism, as it was called ("docetic" comes from a Greek root meaning "to seem"), never took firm root in the church.

Apollinarius

In the latter part of the fourth century, Apollinarius, bishop of Laodicea, advanced a new theory. He suggested that in the person of Jesus the divine Logos (meaning "Word" or "Reason"), referred to in John 1:1, took the place of the human spirit (i.e., his consciousness, reason, and will). Jesus possessed a human body and a human soul (life principle), but not the human spirit, not the human mind. The church rejected this theory (Apollinarianism, as it came to be called) in the second ecumenical council (Constantinople, A.D. 381), on the ground that it destroyed the full humanity of Christ.

The church, up to this time, had served notice that no view of the person of Jesus Christ was an adequate interpretation of Christ or in accord with all the facts in the case that did not recognize that Jesus of Nazareth was both fully human and at the same time fully divine. But how could this be?

Nestorius

An explanation offered by Nestorius, bishop of Constantinople, stirred up a new and even more bitter controversy. Nestorious held that the divine Word or Logos dwelt in the man Jesus somewhat as God dwells in a temple, or as he dwelt in the Old Testament prophets, or even as he dwells in all Christian believers, but it was emphasized that this occurred in another, uniquely complete and permanent way in the case of Jesus. The Logos dwelt in the man Jesus from his very first formation on throughout his whole life, conducting him to perfection. The man Jesus desired what God desired, willed what he willed. Through him, Deity spoke and acted for the salvation of mankind. This moral and spiritual unity between God and man in Jesus Christ, which might conceivably have been broken if Jesus, for example, had yielded to the temptations of Satan, finally became an indissoluble one. In Jesus Christ we have, then, a man so completely dominated and controlled by indwelling divinity (the second person of the Trinity) that we may think of him as one dual person—with two natures, one fully human, the other fully divine. Nestorius' able and determined opponent was Cyril, bishop of Alexandria. Modern historians are inclined to feel that Cyril's opposition was not only theologically, but also politically, motivated. He resented the growing prestige and ecclesiastical power of a rival ecclesiastical see. However this may be, Nestorius was condemned by the third ecumenical council which met in Ephesus in the year A.D. 431, on the ground that he proposed a Jesus who was two whole persons, not one, leaving God and man bound only loosely together in a union of wills; Jesus, then, had not only two natures (one human and one divine): he was actually two persons. After his condemnation, Nestorius retired into a monastery, and was later banished from the empire. Nestorianism, however, continued to spread. It was welcomed in Persia, then seeking to revive its ancient glories; in part, it may be, because it was not tolerated in the Roman Empire, with which Persia was at odds. It penetrated the Far East and reached the furthermost bounds of China. Centuries later, the Nestorian Church was perhaps the largest Christian body in the world, the Christian church of the Far East. In the thirteenth century Marco Polo tells us that the trade routes from Baghdad to Peking were lined with Nestorian chapels. Political changes, along with the rise of the Turks as a new and aggressive Mohammedan power, severed these Nestorian missions from their roots, and the Nestorians became a small band of Christians, found today mostly in Syria and in parts of India—a sturdy people who have maintained their faith in spite of tremendous odds.

The problem now was to find a formula that would recognize Jesus as being both fully human and fully divine and still one person. A venerable archimandrite (head of a monastery), named Eutyches, proposed a formula that brought on the third Christological controversy. Eutyches' solution, in brief, was that before the Incarnation we can distinguish two complete natures— a human nature and a divine nature; after the Incarnation, only one, the human nature having become completely absorbed in the divine nature. The church was not prepared, however, to accept a theory that acknowledged Jesus as human for only a limited time, and that before his birth. This theory, too much like Docetism, was rejected by the fourth ecumenical council meeting in Chalcedon in the year A.D. 451. This important gathering went further, approving a statement which is now known as the *Chalcedonian Creed,* one which is accepted by most of Christendom as setting forth the orthodox view of the person of Christ, as the Nicene Creed sets forth the orthodox view regarding the deity of Christ.

Key phrases of this creed are the following:

> We all with one accord teach men to acknowledge one and the same Son, our Lord Jesus Christ, at once complete in Godhead and complete in manhood, truly God and truly man ... one and the same Christ, Son, Lord, Only-begotten, recognized IN TWO NATURES, WITHOUT CONFUSION, WITHOUT CHANGE [these last two phrases were intended to rule out Eutychianism], WITHOUT DIVISION, WITHOUT SEPARATION [these two phrases were intended to rule out Nestorianism] ... the characteristics of each nature being preserved and coming together to form one person ...[3]

SUMMARY

As a consequence of the Christological controversies up to this point, the church had ruled out a number of inadequate explanations of the person of Christ, or to put it otherwise, inadequate views of the Incarnation, some of which are doubtless held by some Christians at the present time. They had repudiated, for example, the view that Jesus was not a man, but a God (Docetism). Again, they had repudiated the idea that Jesus was some kind of immediate being, neither God nor man in the full sense, but something between (Arianism). Also the view that Jesus began by being a man and ended by being a God (Dynamic Monarchianism). Also the view that Jesus was simply God or the eternal Son of God inhabiting a human body for thirty years on earth, so that while the living organism was human, the mind or spirit was divine (Apollinarianism). Also the view that Jesus was a man fully surrendered to the indwelling Deity (Nestorianism). Likewise the view that his manhood was swallowed up in his divinity (Eutychianism), as well as the idea that Christ was no more than a temporary mode of God's existence (Sabellianism). True, the "orthodox" view finally set forth in the Chalcedonian Creed does not give us an intellectual solution of the problem faced by the early church:

it does not explain how Jesus can be God and man in two natures and one person forever. But, like the doctrine of the Trinity, it warns against the dangers on both right and left: here the danger of so separating the divine and the human natures that Jesus becomes in fact two persons; and the danger of so uniting the two natures that one replaces the other, or that either is reduced, or minimized, or absorbed into the other. At the same time, it witnesses to the fundamental faith of the church in every age that we have to do with one who is fully God and who is at the same time fully man.

As a modern theologian has written:

> What the early Ecumenical Councils have done for us by their doctrinal decisions is the preliminary and negative task of repudiating the various errors, the heresies, which were always of the nature of over-simplifications. The definitions adopted were the right answers to the questions that were then being asked. But language is constantly changing and is always imperfect as a vehicle of meaning, and thus a theological question is never put in a really perfect form or in a form that will last for ever. . . . Athanasius spoke of the Nicene Creed as . . . 'a signpost against all heresies.' That is exactly what it was. By rejecting the various errors it protected the mystery. But it does not relieve successive ages of the task of thinking out the meaning of the mystery. That is the perennial task of theology: to think out the meaning of the Christian conviction that God was incarnate in Jesus, that Jesus is God and Man.[4]

Unfortunately there were some, particularly in Egypt and in Syria, who were not willing to accept the Chalcedonian Creed. This was due in part to theological questionings, a fear that the Chalcedonian formula left the way open to Nestorianism, that two natures— one fully human, the other fully divine—meant and could only mean two persons. It was due in large part also to the fact that Syria and Egypt, representing ancient peoples with their own proud history, were no longer happy in the Byzantine Empire, that they resented the control now exerted over them from Constantinople. The theological differences were the front behind which the opposing factions rallied. Monophysitism (coming from two Greek words meaning "one nature") was the new doctrine championed in the two lands of Syria and Egypt—a doctrine which held that after the Incarnation there remained only one nature—the divine nature, which possessed, however, certain human attributes. Still another heresy, offered as a possible compromise, came to be known as Monothelitism (coming from two Greek roots meaning "a single will"). According to this theory Christ had two natures (one human, the other divine) but only one will, which was divine rather than human. This compromise, however, proved unacceptable to both sides, and was repudiated at the sixth ecumenical council, which met in Constantinople in the year A.D. 681. "We preach," said this council,

> two natural wills, not contrary (God forbid), as the impious heretics assert, but his human will following his divine and omnipotent will, not resisting it nor striving against it, but rather subject to it.[5]

This, too, became a part of the orthodox doctrine. The theological division remained in the Byzantine Empire, however, until finally the Mohammedans swept over what we now call the Near East, which had been the home of so many ancient civilizations, along with the whole of northern Africa—after which it ceased to be a problem. Monophysites and Monothelites remained, but now outside the bounds of the empire.[6]

Four Monophysite churches (the Coptic Church in Egypt, the Ethiopian Church, the Jacobite Church in Syria, and the Armenian Church in Lebanon and Soviet Armenia) and one Monothelite Church (the Maronite Church in Syria) have survived to the present day—minority groups in a Mohammedan or Communist environment. Restricted in their activities, unable to maintain proper educational facilities, in the main desperately poor, they have become for the most part stagnant pools, contributing nothing to the ongoing stream of Christianity. Contributing nothing? Nothing but a faithful witness which centuries of oppression have not been able to overcome.

Today three approaches are being made to these ancient churches. The Roman Catholic Church seeks to attach them to their own body (giving rise to the so-called Uniat churches), the Anglican communion is seeking to raise the level of their leadership, other Protestant churches, including the Presbyterians, seek to win them to a purer evangelical faith.

Rejected Explanations of the Person of Christ (Heresies)

Docetism	Jesus wholly divine—his manhood an illusion	
Arianism	Jesus less than God—more than man	
Dynamic Monarchianism		
	Jesus a man	—who became a god
Modalistic Monarchianism (Sabellianism)		
	One God as (by turns) Father, Son, Spirit —Christ a temporary "mode" of God	
Apollinarianism	Jesus fully God	—only partially a man
Nestorianism	Jesus fully God	—fully man—two persons
Eutychianism	Jesus' manhood	—absorbed into his deity
Monophysitism	Jesus a God	—with human attributes
Monothelitism	Jesus God	—and man—without a human will

The orthodox doctrine as accepted at Chalcedon:
    Jesus—fully God—fully man—one person

THE DOCTRINES OF SIN AND GRACE

A fourth set of doctrines on which the church reached some measure of agreement in the early centuries (though here no official dogmas were adopted) were those dealing with man and his redemption.

Augustine

The most influential thinker in this area was Augustine (A.D. 354–430). In him, one modern historian had declared, "the ancient church reached its highest religious attainment since apostolic times." Though his influence in the East was to be relatively slight, owing to the nature of the questions with which he was primarily concerned, all Western Christianity was to become his debtor. Such superiority as Western religious life came to possess over that of the East was primarily his bequest to it. He was to be the father of much that was most characteristic in medieval Roman Catholicism. He was to be the spiritual ancestor, no less, of much in the Reformation.[7] Another competent historian speaks of him as "the most important figure in church history since Paul; a man who moulded the destiny of the Western Church for a thousand years."

Augustine was born in northern Africa (what is now Algeria) in the little town of Tagaste. His father, a man of some means, was able to give his son an excellent education, and he became in time a professor of rhetoric, a highly honored profession, in which he was able to earn a comfortable living. We are particularly concerned with Augustine's spiritual experience. His father was a pagan, an easygoing man of the world; his mother, on the other hand, was an earnest Christian, who desired above all else that her son should give his heart to Christ. It seemed for long as though she were doomed to disappointment. Augustine, high-minded and truth-seeking, struggling with the demons of sensuality, rejected Christianity as intellectually untenable. He chose instead Manichaeism, Christianity's most potent rival in the fourth century, which held that there were two ultimate principles in the universe, one of good, the other of evil, locked in mortal combat. As a Manichaean Augustine prayed, "Grant me chastity and continence, but not yet." Convinced at last of the intellectual and moral inadequacy of Manichaeism, he became a skeptic. He dismissed the faithful concubine who had borne him a son, became betrothed to a young girl whose station in life was comparable to that of his own, and entered into even less creditable relations with another. His moral life had reached its lowest level. Neoplatonism next attracted him. He learned here that evil had no positive existence, as the Manichaeans had taught. It was on the other hand negative, a lack of good, an alienation of the will from God. But power to overcome his sensuality was still lacking.

He had by now accepted a teaching appointment in Milan, then the western capital of the empire. He went to the cathedral to hear Ambrose because of his great skill as an orator, and found an answer to some of his intellectual difficulties. A letter came one day describing the life of Christian hermits in Egypt. Distressed that these ignorant monks had conquered temptations of the flesh, as he, with all his learning, had been unable to do, he rushed into the garden, where he heard a child in a neighboring house chanting, probably in play, "Tolle, lege [take up and read]." There was a copy of the Scriptures on a table in the gardenhouse. Augustine took it and opened to Romans 13:13–14: "Let us conduct ourselves becomingly as in the day, not in reveling and drunkenness, not in debauchery and licentiousness, not in quarreling and jealousy. But put on the Lord Jesus Christ, and make no provision for the flesh, to gratify its desires." Out of this experience came Augustine's conversion to the Christian faith. He quit his profession, gave himself to a careful study of the Scriptures, and returned to northern Africa, where he was elected, first presbyter, and then bishop at Hippo.

Augustine lived very simply, as a monk might. He lived with his clergy in one house; no women, not even his own sister, were admitted; there was no private ownership of property in the community. He conducted a kind of theological seminary there for years. He dressed in plain black, ate simple food seasoned only by reading or conversation. He made a strict rule against gossiping about the absent brothers. He was interested in the welfare of the poor; he also undertook the intellectual defense of Christianity against the major heresies of his own day; and his own teachings continued to guide the church both Roman Catholic and Protestant for generations to come, and remain as wells of inspiration even yet.[8]

Augustine's writings were voluminous, and he touched on and enriched almost every doctrine of the church. Two of these writings became classics, and have so remained to the present day.

The first of these is Augustine's famous *Confessions,* in which he describes in detail the spiritual experience which we have hastily sketched. The keynote is struck in the opening paragraph: "Thou hast made us for thyself [O Lord] and restless is our heart until it comes to rest in thee." In the pages that follow greater depths of devotion are sounded than in any writing since those of the Apostles. "Augustine's conception of religion as a vital relationship to the living God," it has been pointed out, "was of permanent influence." To a considerable degree it changed the popular conception of the Christian life.

A second influential work of Augustine was his *City of God.* It was written shortly after the Visigoths led by Alaric captured Rome, "the eternal city," and civilization, as men had known it for a thousand years, seemed on the verge of collapse. Pagans blamed the fall of Rome on its desertion of the ancient gods. Augustine demolished this contention and then developed a philosophy of history that was to have profound influence for many centuries to come. Throughout the ages, he said, there have been two cities (kingdoms or empires, we might say), and these two cities have been formed by two loves, one, the earthly city, "by the love of self even to the contempt of God," the other, the heavenly city, "by the love of God even to the contempt of self." The earthly city, whatever its form, is bound to disappear, for it bears within itself the seeds of its own destruction. The heavenly city alone will endure, for it alone enjoys the blessing of God. This abiding city exists in history as a real, though imperfect community, the members of which are involved in the earthly city. It is not identical with the visible catholic church and ought not to be confused with any of its cultural effects; and yet it is not a mere abstraction but a genuine fellowship—a fellowship of sinners who accept the forgiveness of God and in whom he has begun his new creation.

Augustine's fine distinction was not recognized by those who followed him. For many, ecclesiastical and civil rulers alike, the City of God came to be identified with the (Roman) Catholic Church. God's reign was to be established on earth under the control of the church.

Of tremendous influence also were Augustine's various writings on the doctrines of man and his salvation (sin and grace). His view of man can be summed up in three phrases—original righteousness, original sin, and original guilt. Augustine believed, with his immediate predecessors, that God had created man (Adam, the first ancestor of the human race) positively righteous, morally perfect, we might say, except that there was a possibility of sin. (Some of the earlier Greek fathers, it might be noted, held that man was created innocent, rather than righteous, with the possibility of turning either toward God or away from him.) Adam had fallen from this estate in which he was created by sinning against God, and all mankind, descending from Adam by ordinary generation, had fallen with him. Man's estate was now one of "total depravity"—a misleading theological term which suggests that man's nature was only evil, and as evil as it could possibly be. It means rather that man's whole nature was affected—that he was alienated from God in the totality of his being, that in him apart from God there was no possibility of redemption. It is from this basic sinfulness of man that all actual evil, individual and social, is derived. Augustine's view of man's predicament, we might note, was more serious than that of any of the church fathers who had preceded him. They held that all men because of Adam's sin had been morally sick; Augustine held that they were encompassed in moral and spiritual death: there must be a new creation if he was to live. In Augustine's view man was not only born totally depraved; he also bore the guilt of Adam's sin, and this was explained in Augustine's view by the fact that he was actually in Adam, and therefore had sinned in Adam. How, then, could man be saved? According to Augustine, only through God's action on his behalf. God chose (predestined) some to be saved, others to be lost; those elected were saved by divine grace (which was irresistible); they believed, were justified (forgiven, and declared righteous or just), and because God held them fast would certainly persevere to the end.

Variant Views

These doctrines of Augustine (shaped to some extent, no doubt, by his own religious experience) were challenged by a British monk, named Pelagius, who, it may be surmised, had had no such struggle with evil as had Augustine. Pelagius denied that doctrine of original sin—all men, like Adam, he insisted, had complete freedom to sin or not to sin; God did not elect, the choice was made by man. Pelagius gave no place to divine grace in the Augustinian sense (power within the self to do the right). God had sent Jesus to show the way. Man could follow through with the powers with which God had endowed him. The views of Pelagius were condemned by the third ecumenical council meeting in Ephesus (A.D. 431) and have been rejected ever since by the "orthodox" wing of the church. Augustine, though extreme in his views, saw more deeply than his defeated opponent into the nature of the human malady—man's deep estrangement from the origin and goal of his being.

Some, in essential agreement with Augustine, were compelled to demur. Leaders of this group, in southern France, came to be known as Semi-Pelagians. They held, in brief, that though man lacked moral ability to save himself, there was much that he could do, and that if he made the necessary effort God would come to his aid. God had elected those who he foresaw would make this requisite effort and who would accept his proffered aid.

This Semi-Pelagianism was rejected as inadequate by a western council, the Synod of Arles. A compromise solution was finally reached at the Synod of Orange (A.D. 529) which, when accepted by Pope Boniface II, brought the Semi-Pelagian controversy to an end, although Semi-Pelagian positions have never ceased to be held in the church.

The Synod of Orange affirmed that man, as a consequence of Adam's sin, had lost *all* power to turn unto God, and that *all good* in man was the *work of God*. It is "by the free gift of grace, that is, by the inspiration of the Holy Spirit," that we have even "the desire of believing." Predestination to evil was definitely rejected by the council. Grace was prevenient; that is, it preceded any act on the part of man. But the irresistibility of grace is nowhere affirmed, which would suggest that while divine grace is essential and precedes any movement toward God on the part of man, it may still be rejected. The reception of grace, however, was tied up with the sacrament of baptism, and infant baptism had become the general practice. As expressed by the Synod of Orange:

> We also believe this to be according to the Catholic faith, that grace having been received in baptism, all who have been baptized, can and ought, by the aid and support of Christ, to perform those things which belong to the salvation of the soul, if they labor faithfully.[9]

This opened the way to a doctrine of *salvation by works,* and it was in this direction that medieval Catholicism was to move.

For Gregory the Great (A.D. 540–604), who summed up the tendencies of the day and laid the basis for medieval thought, the Catholic Church was the ark of salvation, through which alone could man be saved. Baptism brought forgiveness for sins of the past, and grace by which man could win merit with God. For sins committed after baptism satisfaction must be given. In case of private sins, repentance and good works were sufficient. In case of public sins, there must be public confession; absolution (forgiveness) was then pronounced by the priest, to whom God had given power to bind and to loose, that is, to forgive or to refuse to forgive, and the performance of some good deeds was imposed by way of "satisfaction." After death the sinner could expect to go to purgatory, where he was finally purged of all sin and made ready for heaven. The Lord's Supper now found its chief value in cutting down the time spent in purgatory not only for the living but also for the dead. Men were helped along the way by the invocation of the saints.

"If we compare the Christianity of Gregory with that of Augustine," writes one of our eminent historians,

> we reach a remarkable result. Almost everything in Gregory has its roots in the teaching of Augustine, and yet scarcely anything is really Augustinian. That which was un-Augustinian in Augustine becomes the vital element of this Semi-augustinian. The fundamental spirit of Augustine has vanished, and superstition gained supremacy. Everything is coarser, more fixed, and ordinary. The controlling motive is not the peace of God which finds rest in God; but the fear of uncertainty, which seeks to attain security through the institutions of the church.[10]

Accepting such a theology the church moved into the Middle Ages, laying the foundations for a new civilization among the Ger-

---

DOCTRINES OF SIN AND GRACE

	Man	Election	Grace
Augustinianism	Total depravity (complete moral inability)	Unconditional (not based on God's foreknowledge)	Irresistible
Pelagianism	Complete moral ability	None	None, except as God has made his will known in Christ
Semi-Pelagianism	Partial moral ability (man can merit grace)	Conditional (based on God's foreknowledge)	Necessary (Man moves; God comes to his aid)
Moderate Augustinianism (Synod of Orange)	Moral inability (but man can accept or reject divine grace)	No reprobation (God does not elect any men to be eternally lost)	Prevenient (Man's faith is a response to God's prior approach to him)

manic tribes which had by now taken over what was left of the Roman
Empire in the West.

FOR CONSIDERATION

*1. Jesus and his apostles warned against the danger of false teach-
   ers. (See Matthew 7:15–20; 24: 24–25; Acts 20:29–30; 1 Timothy 4:1–5; 2 Peter 2:1–3; Jude, verses 3–4; 1 John 4:1–3.)
   What are the specific dangers against which we are warned?

2. What are the fundamentals of the gospel? (For New Testament
   statements, see John 3:16; Matthew 28:19–20; Acts 16:31; 1
   Corinthians 15:3–4; 1 Timothy 3:16; 1 John 4:1–3.)

3. Are the early creeds to be accepted as final or infallible statements of truth? What place, if any, should they have in the worship and educational program of the church?

4. What values do you find in the repetition of the Apostles' Creed
   Sunday after Sunday in the worship of the church? Are there any
   objections to such usage? In your judgment, should the phrase
   "holy Catholic Church," misinterpreted by some to refer to the
   Roman Catholic Church, be retained or modified? What about
   the phrase, "he descended into hell"? What does this phrase
   mean to the average worshiper?

5. Consider carefully the marks of the true church as set forth by
   Irenaeus. Were they the right answers for this particular time?
   To what extent are they valid today?

*6. Many of the differences which we find in the modern church can
   be traced back to the relative places of Scripture, tradition, and
   church. Protestants recognize the sole authority of Scripture, but
   church and tradition are by no means unimportant. Catholics
   tend to equate Scripture and tradition and to accept the church as
   the authoritative expounder of both. What in your opinion is the
   relative position of each?

7. Christian bodies are divided today over the question of apostolic
   succession. Churches which hold to this dogma and which think
   they can trace the ordination of their ministers back to the apostles themselves do not recognize other churches as being true
   churches, or the ministers of these churches as being true ministers qualified to administer saving grace through the sacraments.

This is one of the questions which come to the fore in any discussion of church union involving Presbyterians and Episcopalians. Episcopalians tend to reject any union unless Presbyterian ministers accept some form of reordination which insures that they too will be in the line of the apostolic succession. Should Presbyterian ministers submit to such reordination if other reasons for union are compelling?

8. Was the church contending for something more than mere trifles in the long, drawn-out Christological controversies? Why do you think so?

9. How can the Augustinian, the Pelagian, the Semi-Pelagian, and the moderate Augustinian view of man be most clearly stated in terms of today?

10. Why does the church today need to give more careful instruction in regard to the doctrines of the church?

Monks Copying the Scriptures and Other Christian Manuscripts

7
THE CHURCH SERVES
AND SURVIVES THE EMPIRE

IN ITS FIRST FIVE CENTURIES the church won the Roman Empire, church and state were united, the church underwent changes—it strengthened its organization, elaborated its worship, and clarified its beliefs. At the same time the church served and finally survived the empire.

THE CHURCH RAISED THE MORAL TONE OF SOCIETY

The influence that the church exerted upon society is difficult to measure. It may be assumed that the moral ideals of Christianity were higher than those of the pagan world. Stoicism taught a lofty ethical ideal, from which Christianity itself was able to learn, but it left little place for pity, or for sacrificial love, and it fell below Christianity in moral power. Some generally accepted evils the church opposed from the beginning—abortion, for example, and exposure of children (it was the custom for unwanted children to be left in open fields to die, or to be raised by those who took them up for a life of prostitution, it may be, or slavery); opposed also were games in the arena, where men were compelled to fight for their lives against men or beasts. These and other practices were outlawed only after Christianity came to power, and through its influence. The church did not wage war against slavery as an institution (such an effort could hardly have been contemplated at this particular stage in human history) but it was careful for slaves as individuals.

> Within the Church itself there was neither bond nor free. They were all brothers, or, as Paul wrote of Onesimus, "no longer a mere slave but something more than a slave, a brother beloved." Christianity created the spirit that ultimately undermined slavery. To the slave no less than to the free the church was open. It recognized the slave's personality as no longer 'res' [a thing, as defined by Roman law], but 'persona' [a person, of infinite worth in the sight of God].[1]

In one of the early works defending Christianity, *To Diognetus,* the author summed up:

> Christians cannot be distinguished from the rest of the human race by country or language or customs ... Yet, although they live in Greek and barbarian cities alike, as each man's lot has been cast, and follow the customs of the country in clothing and food and other matters of daily living, at the same time they give proof of the remarkable and admittedly extraordinary constitution of their own commonwealth. They live in their own countries, but only as aliens. They have a share in everything as citizens, and endure everything as foreigners. Every foreign land is their fatherland, and yet for them every fatherland is a foreign land. They marry, like everyone else, and they beget children, but they do not cast out their offspring. They share their board with each other, but not their marriage bed. ... They obey the established laws, but in their own lives they go far beyond what the laws require. They love all men, and by all men are persecuted ... They are reviled, and yet they bless; when they are affronted, they still pay due respect. ...

> To put it simply: What the soul is in the body, that Chris-

tians are in the world. The soul is dispersed through all the members of the body, and Christians are scattered through all the cities of the world. The soul dwells in the body, but does not belong to the body, and Christians dwell in the world, but do not belong to the world. ... The soul loves the flesh that hates it, and its members; in the same way, Christians love those who hate them. The soul is shut up in the body, and yet itself holds the body together; while Christians are restrained in the world as in a prison, and yet themselves hold the world together.[2]

"In the whole range of history," comments the historian Gwatkin, there is no more striking contrast than that of the Apostolic churches with the heathenism around them. They had short-comings enough, it is true, and divisions and scandals not a few, for even apostolic times were no golden age of purity and primitive simplicity. Yet we can see that their fulness of life, and hope, and promise for the future was a new sort of power in the world. Within their own limits they had solved almost by the way the social problem which baffled Rome, and baffles Europe still. They had lifted woman to her rightful place, re-stored the dignity of labour, abolished beggary, and drawn the sting of slavery. The secret of the revolution is that the selfish-ness of race and class were forgotten in the Supper of the Lord, and a new basis for society found in love of the visible image of God in men for whom Christ died.[3]

After Constantine the Christian ideals were more widely pro-claimed. As Will Durant has written in his *Age of Faith:*

For the first time in European history the teachers of mankind preached an ethic of kindliness, obedience, humility, patience, mercy, purity, chastity and tenderness, virtues ... admirably adapted to restore order to a de-moral-ized people, to tame the marauding barbarian, to moderate the violence of a failing world.[4]

Back of the Christian ethic was a new regard for the individual, for every individual, as an immortal soul for whom Christ had died.

THE CHURCH DEVELOPED PHILANTHROPY

Christianity not only raised the moral tone of society, it also developed philanthropy in a new and unheard of way. The early Christians "had all things in common" (Acts 2:44, 4:32), not in the sense that they ceased to hold private property, but in the sense that they had a strongly developed sense of "stewardship," which led them to give what was necessary for the common welfare; no one was permitted to suffer for lack of food or shelter. Later, as the church grew and this simple method of caring for the material needs of the congregation no longer sufficed, seven men were chosen to see that no one was overlooked in the distribution of food (Acts 6:1–6). As the church began to expand in the Roman Empire one congregation contributed of its abundance to those who lacked (Acts 11:27–30; Gal. 2:10; 1 Cor. 16:1–4; 2 Cor. 8—9). This concern for the material wants of fellow Christians continued to grow in the centuries following. Local congregations cared for the poor (not only their own, but according to Julian the Apostate, "ours" as well), they looked after the fatherless and the widows, they gave attention to prisoners and captives, they made provision for the unemployed, they arranged for the burial of the dead. They were so generous to the needy that Lucian, a cultivated non-Christian, scoffed,

> their law-giver persuaded them that they were all brethren, and that when once they come out and reject the Greek gods, they should then worship that crucified sophist and live according to his laws. Therefore they despise all things and hold everything in common.[5]

This cultivated man of the world could not understand how anyone could give so lavishly to perfect strangers. But the common people, as we have seen, were impressed. "Behold how these Christians love one another," they said. It was this exhibition of Christian love, according to the pagan emperor Julian, that more than anything else explained the success of the early church.

The philanthropy of the church was so highly developed by Constantine's time that it gradually took over the care of the poor and needy throughout the empire; in its care, and under its auspices, there was now developed for the first time in human history a definite and systematic scheme for the relief of human need. In addition to poor relief there were organized monasteries, deaconries, hospitals, hostelries, orphanages, poor houses, refuges, homes for the aged, homes for infants, and infirmaries—a type of institutionalized social service unknown to the pagan world. The great social achievement of the church, says Oliver, "is that during this transition time it had wellnigh captured for itself the leadership of agressive social endeavor in the civilized world."[6]

This does not mean, of course, that all social problems were solved. Slavery lingered on for many generations and only gradually passed into other forms of economic arrangement. War was accepted as a necessary evil. Christians had served in the imperial armies from early times, though no church father, so far as we are aware, approved the practice. Pacifism, however, died out after the Constantinian revolution, when Christians themselves became responsible for the defense of the empire. Augustine developed the idea of a "just war," which Christians for the most part have continued to hold to the present day. According to this theory, Christians have a right to fight in self-defense, but the war is to be fought as far as possible with respect to the laws of humanity, and mercy is to be shown to a fallen foe.

THE CHURCH INSPIRED SACRIFICIAL SERVICE

There were trends toward asceticism that seem unhealthy to our modern age. In the second and third centuries the idea grew that to spend one's time in contemplation, prayer, and fasting, to surrender one's property and give to the poor, to renounce marriage and live as a celibate, to withdraw from the world, was a holier life than to marry, beget children, and participate in normal human affairs. By accepting this higher morality one gained merit from God and became more certain of his final salvation.

After Constantine this ascetic trend led to the development of monasticism. An impetus was given to this movement by a young Egyptian named Anthony. Holding that Jesus' advice to the rich young ruler (Mark 10:21) applied universally, he sold his property and retired into the desert that he might live a life of complete devotion to God. The story of his life, written by Athanasius, was widely read and excited emulation. The earliest ascetics, like Anthony, were hermits who lived apart from men, appearing only infrequently in human haunts. Some, oddly, attempted to outdo their fellow ascetics in feats of austerity.

For example, Paul the Simple said daily three hundred prayers, counting them with pebbles which he carried in his bosom. The renowned Isidore of Alexandria touched no meat, never ate enough, and often burst into tears at table for shame that he who was destined to eat angel's food in paradise should have to eat material stuff like the irrational brutes. Macarius the Elder for a long time ate only once a week, and slept standing and leaning on a staff. Saints Anthony and Hilarion scorned to comb or cut their hair (save once a year at Easter) or to wash their hands or feet. Aksepsimas spent sixty years in the same cell without seeing or speaking to anyone and looked so wild and shaggy that he was once actually taken for a wolf by a shepherd, who assailed him with stones, till he discovered his error and then worshiped the hermit as a saint.

Most famous of these extremists was Simeon Stylites, who about A.D. 422, near Antioch, built himself a column, which finally rose to a height of about sixty feet, and was six feet across, and on which he lived for thirty-six years. Disciples provided for his needs, and crowds came to gape and to listen to his exhortations. His presumed piety created a fashion of "pillar hermits" which lasted for twelve centuries.

It was not long, however, before the ascetics began to live in communities, for which, of course, certain rules became necessary. Most significant for the western church were the rules drawn up by Benedict of Nursia, about A.D. 480. This Benedictine Rule, based on earlier rules drawn up in the East, became the basis of all further development of western monasticism.

Before Benedict every man had been a law to himself. He might retire from the world and then return to normal human society. He might live alone or in a community; and there was no uniformity among the various communities.

The Benedictine Rule, drawn up in the year A.D. 529 for his own monastery at Monte Cassino in Italy, made provision for an abbot to be elected by the monks themselves, who thereafter became the absolute head of the order, though bound to consult his brethren on all matters of importance.

A member was admitted to the monastery only after a year's novitiate. He then took a threefold vow (from which he could be released only by the hierarchy of the church), first to obedience, second to poverty (no private property was to be held by the monk, only by the monastery), and third to chastity (that is, celibacy).

Life in the monastery was carefully regulated, by general regulations set forth in Benedict's Rule and by specific direction of the abbot, taking into account the needs of the individual monk. Four hours a day were to be spent in worship, distributed through seven periods, some solitary, some communal. The remainder of the time, except that needed for rest, was to be spent laboring in the fields (the monasteries were self-sustaining) and in the library (the copying of books, and the like).

Charles M. Jacobs in his *Story of the Church* says:

> Monasticism was a way of life, but before it became a way of life, it was a way of thought. The hermit in his mountaincave, the pillar-saint, spending long years on the top of a column, the monk cut off from his fellow-men and passing his time in labor and study in a Benedictine house, all these were products of an idea. It was the belief that the world was hopeless and that the only escape from irresistible temptation was in flight from the allurements of the world. Insofar, it was a denial of the Saviour's teaching. Combined with that belief was the conviction that a man by undergoing special hardships could make himself peculiarly worthy to appear before the judgmentseat of God; and that was a flat contradiction of what St. Paul had taught. Of the two ideas the first was stronger in the earlier, the second in the later period of monastic development. But the second idea was not confined to the monks. It was the common belief of the whole Church, with here and there a rare exception. Therefore monasticism became the characteristic institution of the Church.
>
> But monasticism also had another side. It was the monks who were most deeply in earnest with their religious faith. It was they, rather than the bishops, who were the missionaries and the teachers, and the scholars of the following age, and who were the founders and the administrators of the Church's

work of mercy; and when Western Europe became a political and social chaos, it was the monks who kept the embers of Roman culture from dying and fanned them, by and by, into a new blaze. It is easy to criticize the monastic idea. It was a one-sided view of the Christian life, and because one-sided, it was false. The institutions it produced were frequently corrupt and the lives of the monks often accorded ill with the professions which they made. But the debt which later ages owe to the monks cannot be paid with criticism. They were the preservers of personal and practical Christianity in the dark days when the official Church seemed to have forgotten its true calling and to have become chiefly concerned with the things of this world.[7]

THE CHURCH PRESERVED CIVILIZATION

The empire in the West was now crumbling under the impact of the barbarian invasions. For two hundred years various Germanic tribes had been disturbing the peace of the empire, but they had been restrained and held behind two great rivers, the Rhine flowing north and the Danube flowing south. In the final quarter of the fourth century and throughout the fifth century, first one tribe and then another, impelled by vast movements of population in their rear and attracted by the wealth and growing weakness of the empire, breached these borders and settled with their families and other possessions within the empire itself. The Visigoths had sought shelter across the frontier of the lower Danube in 376. Two years later they annihilated a Roman army near Adrianople. They moved on slowly into Greece, then on into Italy, capturing Rome in 410, and nine years later settled in southern Gaul, later extending their conquests to include most of the Spanish peninsula. Vandals meanwhile had marched through the peninsula, and crossing the Strait of Gibraltar, had established themselves in northern Africa, carrying so much destruction in their wake that a new word, "vandalism," was coined and brought into the vocabulary. The Franks meanwhile conquered northern Gaul, and the Burgundians established themselves in that part of the province which still bears their name. Anglo-Saxons invaded England and drove the Celtic population back into the mountains of Wales and

Scotland. Italy meanwhile had suffered from a series of invasions. Alaric, leader of the Visigoths, captured Rome in 410; the Huns ravaged northern Italy but spared Rome at the instigation of Leo I; the Vandals crossed over from northern Africa and sacked the city in 455. In 476 Odoavakar, a German chieftain, deposed the last Roman emperor in the West and set up a kingdom of his own in his stead; his kingdom was succeeded by the kingdom of the Ostrogoths in 493. Nominally these various German chieftains ruled as dependents of the emperor in Constantinople; actually they were independent sovereigns. They did not intend to destroy the empire and its civilization; but such, so far as the West was concerned, was the outcome. Justinian, one of the stronger of the later emperors ruling in Constantinople (535–555), recovered possession of Italy and also brought an end to the Vandal kingdom in northern Africa. But shortly thereafter a new Germanic people, the Lombards, established a kingdom in northern Italy that was to continue for two hundred years.

Most of these Germanic people who thus broke into the Roman Empire of the West had been won to Christianity before the invasions began. They were Arians rather than orthodox Trinitarians. Nonetheless they had some respect for Catholic institutions. Otherwise the course of Christianity, as well as the history of western Europe, might have been very different.

In 496 Clovis, king of the Salic Franks (from the River Sale), himself a pagan, was converted to Catholic Christianity. He had married a Catholic princess who had endeavored in vain to win him to her faith. In a battle with the Alemans (ancestors of the modern Germans), Clovis, faced with defeat, prayed to "Jesus Christ, whom Chrotochildis [his wife] declares to be the Son of the living God, who says that Thou wilt help those in need and give victory to those who hope in thee . . . " The fortunes of battle thereupon turned, according to the ancient account, and Clovis, true to his promise, was baptized into the Catholic faith, along with three thousand of his followers. According to an old legend, as Clovis and his followers were immersed in the waters they carefully held their right arms—their sword arms—high above the water. The legend may not be altogether correct as to the facts, but it illustrates the truth. As a distinguished Catholic Frenchman quoted by Philip Schaff declares:

The Franks ... were sad Christians. While they respected the freedom of the Catholic faith and made external profession of it, they violated without scruple all its precepts, and at the same time the simplest laws of humanity. After having prostrated themselves before the tomb of some holy martyr or confessor; after having distinguished themselves by the choice of an ir-reproachable bishop; after having listened respectfully to the voice of a pontiff or monk, we see them, sometimes in out-breaks of fury, sometimes by cold-blooded cruelties, give full course to the evil instincts of their savage nature. Their incred-ible perversity was most apparent in the domestic tragedies, the fratricidal executions and assassinations of which Clovis gave the first example, and which marked the history of his son and grandson with an ineffaceable stain. Polygamy and perjury mingled in their daily life with a semi-pagan superstition, and in reading these bloody biographies, scarcely lightened by some transient gleams of faith or humility, it is difficult to be-lieve that, in embracing Christianity, they gave up a single pa-gan vice, or adopted a single Christian virtue.[8]

The conversion of Clovis and his followers did not mean that the Franks or their leaders had become good Christians, but only that the church had more opportunity to make them so. The Franks were now the strongest of the various Germanic kingdoms, and their conversion to Catholic Christianity induced the various Arian bodies to accept the same faith and so come under the tutelage of Rome.

In this period of strain and stress, the papacy gradually emerged as the one authority able to give the Western church its necessary unity and strength. Leo I (440–461) was credited with saving Rome from the Huns. He claimed, as we have seen, universal authority in the church, and in the West made this claim largely good. His author-ity was recognized not only in Italy, but also in Gaul, Spain, and northern Africa. Gelasius (492–496) advanced the claim that there are "two by whom principally this world is ruled: the sacred author-ity of the pontiffs and the royal power. Of these the importance of the priests is so much the greater, as even for kings of men they will have to give an account in the divine judgment."[9] In divine matters, Gelasius went on to claim, kings must "submit [their] neck[s] to the prelates." In 502 Bishop Ennodius of Pavia urged that the pope can be judged by God alone. So early were staked out claims largely realized by later popes.

It was Gregory I (Gregory the Great, A.D. 590–604), however, who more than any other laid the foundations of the medieval papacy. Gregory resigned a high civil post to enter the service of the church. The fortunes of the papal chair had reached a low ebb. The city of Rome had been sacked again and again and was greatly reduced in population; its aqueducts were no longer functioning, and many of the huge public buildings were falling into ruin. Gregory restored order; he utilized the vast fortunes of the church to succor the needy; his power exceeded that of the civil officials; the Lombards treated with him as an independent political power. He may be regarded as the first founder of the temporal power of the papacy on Italian soil. Gregory, who has been called "perhaps the greatest, probably the best man who ever occupied the papal chair," did not covet power: he exercised power because there was a vacuum that must be filled; and it was the church, and the church alone, which in the circumstances could fill that vacuum.

For the church not only served the empire; it also survived the empire. As one historian has written:

> Then when . . . the barriers of the Empire broke and a tide of barbarians poured in, the churches were the only islands amid that flood of barbaric life. For in that chaos that followed the Church was the only unified, stable, and authoritative institution. "It was the one upstanding thing in an order whose every other inheritance of the past had gone; the one continuing institution in chaos and change, the one unifying force through the wash of migrating populations, great and small, whose kingdoms, won or lost, were like dissolving pictures on the screen." The Church was the sole preserver of the classical culture, the schoolmistress of this rude barbarian horde. It was the largest property holder and took to itself the landed estates of the fleeing nobility. It was the one depository of wealth and so became the [guardian] of the poor. It had its law courts

which somewhat retained the majesty of Roman law and gave
to that world its only rude justice. So in this great crisis in human history the Church became the inheritor of civilization.[10]

FOR CONSIDERATION

1. "By their fruits ye shall know them" (Matt. 7:20, K.J.V.). What
fruit may we rightfully expect Christianity to bear in the world?
What fruit may we expect in individual lives; what in the social
life? How can this be illustrated in the early Christian centuries?

2. Do Christians really believe in the worth of the individual, of
every individual? If so, in what sense?

3. If the Christian conviction regarding the individual and his worth
became generally accepted, what practices or customs in our
modern life would it affect?

4. If the church were eliminated from modern life, what difference
would it make?

5. What does it mean to call Christians "the salt of the earth"? What
illustrations are found in the chapter just read?

*6. How does the example of the early church aid us in determining
our attitude on such questions as abortion, war, distinctions of
race and class within the church?

7. Some modern governments seek to destroy the church; some
men of good will in our own land dismiss the church as irrelevant
to the problems and needs of our modern world. Why can this be
said?

8. Is it possible or desirable for the church to take a stand on controversial social issues? Could the minister of your church take a
strong stand on any vital issue in opposition to influential members of the congregation and retain his position? Can a layman
take a strong stand opposite to that of his minister and still be accepted as a Christian brother?

9. Do Christian people have a responsibility to see that constructive
aid is given to underprivileged people of the world under government auspices? If so, how is the responsibility to be fulfilled?

10. What, if anything, can Protestantism learn from the life and work
of monks and nuns?

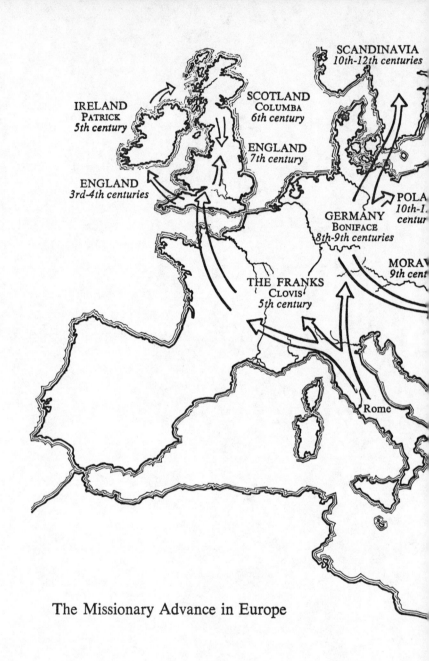

The Missionary Advance in Europe

Part II
IN THE
MIDDLE AGES

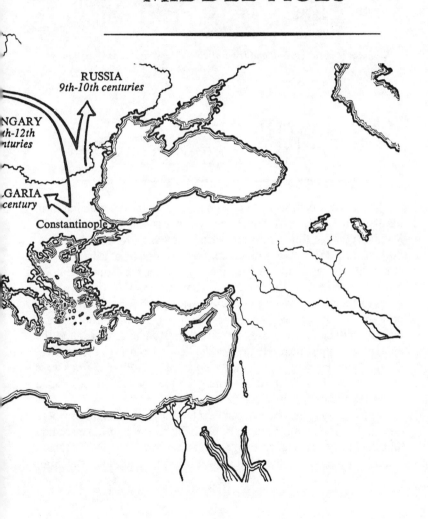

RUSSIA
9th-10th centuries

NGARY
h-12th
nturies

GARIA
century

Constantinople

King Aethelberht of Kent and His Followers Hearing About Christianity

8
THE CHURCH
GAINS AND LOSES

WE HAVE CONSIDERED to this point the fortunes of the church in the Roman Empire. We come now to what is commonly called the Middle Ages—a thousand-year period, stretching roughly from A.D. 500 to A.D. 1500. We will be concerned here primarily with the church in western Europe after the breakup of the Roman Empire down to the time of the Protestant Reformation. Historians sometimes distinguish between Early and Late Middle Ages. In the earlier period, often called the Dark Ages, there was civil disorder, no enduring political entity arose to replace the Roman Empire, and the light of learning flickered unsteadily, tended only by the church. Gradually order reappeared, the foundations of modern nations were laid, universities spread their learning, and a new culture developed under the banner of the church.

In this period the church won new territory, and lost lands where once it had the greatest strength. On balance it might have seemed that the losses outweighed the gains. In the fifth century the Roman Empire, with which the church was closely identified, was pre-

eminent both politically and culturally. A thousand years later the
situation was altered.

> In wealth, size, political power, and in some respects, civiliza-
> tion, Christian Western Europe in 1500 was inferior to Hindu
> India, the Ottoman Empire [Mohammedan], and the Ming
> Dynasty [China]. Europe was one of the smallest major cul-
> tural areas, containing only 10 to 15 percent of humanity.[1]

What could not have been foreseen at the time was that in the centuries that followed, the Western power would gain political domi-
nance and spread elements of its civilization throughout the world.
The territorial gains made by the church during this period were,
therefore, to prove of utmost significance.

THE CHURCH GAINS

First in order was the conquest of the British Isles. Christianity
was introduced into Celtic England in the third and fourth centuries,
probably by traders from the continent and, it may be, by soldiers
serving the Roman garrisons. As Roman power declined, the garrisons were withdrawn; after which (449–457) came the Anglo-
Saxon invaders. The older Celtic population was driven back into
Scotland and Wales. England became once more a pagan land.

From Wales the gospel was carried to Ireland. The great missionary here was Patrick (389–461). He had been taken to Ireland as a
slave; but managed to escape and later, despite the opposition of rel-
atives and friends, returned to win for Christ the land he had learned
to love. Patrick established monasteries, which became centers of
learning, as well as bases for evangelization. For a time these Irish
monasteries did more to keep learning alive than any other centers in
western Europe. From the Emerald Island, missionaries fanned out
over the continent. Here they introduced a practice which they had
found useful within their own fellowship—that of private (lay) confession, followed by absolution (assurance of God's pardon).[2] The
practice proved so valuable in the training of converts raw from heathenism that it spread widely; the time would come (A.D. 1216) when
such confession would be made obligatory upon all Catholics.
Christianity began to spread into Scotland by the end of the

fourth century. It came from Ireland, and also across the border from England. But the great missionary to Scotland was Columba (521–597). He had previously assisted in the founding of a number of monasteries in Ireland. Angered by a decision of King Diarmaid depriving him of a valued manuscript which he had laboriously copied from the monastery of St. Finnian, Columba helped to stir up a border war which resulted in much bloodshed. Conscience-stricken, under the censure of his church, and in order to make some reparation, Columba, now forty years of age, sailed for Scotland. He established a monastery on the little island of Iona off the coast. Missionaries sent out from this monastery won the Picts, the strongest tribe in Scotland. The Christianity that thus came into Scotland represented an early type of the faith that differed in some respects from that which had developed meanwhile in the older regions to the south. The episcopal system, for example, was not firmly established. Columba, though a mere presbyter, and his successors, as abbots of Iona, ruled not only the monastery but also bishops, serving without dioceses, on the mainland. There was no thought of papal authority. There were minor differences, regarding the form of the tonsure, for example, and one—regarding the date of Easter—which came in time to be a source of friction.

Christianity came into Anglo-Saxon England from both North and South. Aidan, a monk from Iona, established a similar monastery on the island of Lindisfarne, and from this center Celtic Christianity spread widely in northern England. Meanwhile Gregory the Great had dispatched a mission of great historical moment under the leadership of the monk Augustine, which reached Canterbury in the spring of 597. Aethelberht, King of Kent, who had married a Catholic princess from the continent, along with a number of his followers, soon accepted Christianity as it was held and taught by the bishops of Rome. It may be observed here that women, both as mothers and as wives, played a considerable role in the spread of Christianity throughout Europe.

In an important council, when Paulinus (later bishop of York) presented the claims of the gospel to Edwin, King of Northumbria, along with his "wise men," one of the king's chief men approved the missionary's presentation and added:

The present life of man, O king, seems to me, in comparison of that time which is unknown to us, like to the swift flight of a sparrow through the room wherein you sit at supper in winter, with your commanders and ministers, and a good fire in the midst, whilst the storms of rain and snow prevail abroad; the sparrow, I say, flying in at one door, and immediately out at another, whilst he is within, is safe from the wintry storm; but after a short space of fair weather, he immediately vanishes out of your sight, into the dark winter from which he had emerged. So this life of man appears for a short space, but of what went before, or of what is to follow, we are utterly ignorant. If, therefore, this new doctrine contains something more certain, it seems justly to deserve to be followed.[3]

The other elders and king's councillors, wrote Bede, the ancient chronicler, spoke to the same effect. Whence has man come, why is he here, whither is he going? To such questions Christianity alone had the answer; and in due time King Edwin and his nation had accepted the Christian faith. So a second important center of Christianity had been established in England, one in the South by Augustine (Canterbury), the other in the North (York) by Paulinus.

As Celtic and Roman Christianity both spread among the little English kingdoms conflicts arose, particularly regarding the date of Easter, which determined the Christian year, with its numerous holy days, as a whole. Finally in the year A.D. 663 Oswy, king of Northumbria, held a synod in Whitby in which representatives of the two forms of Christianity presented their respective claims. The Scottish spokesman based his claim for the date of Easter on the authority of the Apostle John. The Roman champion countered with that of Peter. "Your Columba," he said, "yes, our Columba too, may have been a saint and mighty in deeds of power, but can he be given the slightest preference above the most blessed prince of the apostles, to whom our Lord said, 'You are Peter, and I will give you the keys of the kingdom of heaven'?"

"Did our Lord really say that to Peter?" Oswy inquired.

When both parties assured him that this was the case, Oswy replied, " I am in no mind to go against this doorkeeper, but desire to obey his ordinances in everything . . . Otherwise when I come to the doors of the kingdom of heaven, I may find none to open to me."

So Roman Catholicism came to be the form of religion that prevailed in Northumberland, and soon afterwards in the rest of England. Southern Ireland had acknowledged the authority of the bishop of Rome as early as 630; but the papal authority was not accepted in northern Ireland until about 703. The Romanization of the church in Scotland began during the reign of Malcolm III (1073–1090), who had married an English Catholic princess, and was completed in the reign of David (1124–1153). So all the British Isles were finally brought in the expanding orbit of the Roman Catholic Church, which, as circumstances then were, was no doubt for the best. It meant that Christianity in Britain would not remain an isolated outpost, removed from the developing culture of the continent.

In the eighth and ninth centuries Christianity spread widely through the Germanic tribes beyond the Rhine and beyond the former borders of the Roman Empire. Its spread was facilitated by the conquests of the Frankish kings, especially Charlemagne, who imposed Christianity, or at least the forms of Christianity, on the lands and people whom he conquered by the sword. Missionaries from England, however, did far more to win the hearts of the people.

Most famous of these missionaries was Winifred, or Boniface (680–754), commissioned by Pope Gregory II to preach the gospel in Germany wherever he might find an opportunity. He found the task no easy one. Some of his converts remained firm in the faith, but the majority, fascinated by the spell of their old superstitions, blended the old and the new in wild confusion. Baptized in the name of Christ, they continued to worship groves and fountains, to consult augurs (fortune tellers) and cast lots, to offer sacrifices on the old altars. Boniface saw that he must take strenuous measures to convince them of the vanity of their old beliefs. About this time he received a letter from the aged bishop of Winchester, himself a German, who advised him to avoid all contemptuous and violent language, to cultivate rather a spirit of patience and moderation. In preference to open controversy, the bishop suggested that Boniface should rather put from time to time such questions as would tend to rouse the people to a sense of the contradictions which their superstitions involved; then, after a while, compare these superstitions with the Christian doctrines, and touch upon the latter judiciously, "that thy people may not be exasperated against thee, but ashamed of their foolish errors."

Boniface deemed, however, that the present juncture required sterner and more uncompromising measures. Near Geismar, in Upper Hesse, stood an ancient oak sacred to Thor, the god of thunder. It was regarded by the people with peculiar reverence and was the rallying point of the assemblies of all the tribes. Boniface had preached often against the senseless worship of a tree, but his sermons had fallen on deaf ears. Now he was determined to act. On an appointed day he advanced with all his clergy to cut down this monarch of the forest. The people assembled by the thousands, some infuriated, more confident that they would witness the immediate vengeance of the offended god. But the blows fell and the tree finally toppled, and with it went the spell of the ancient gods.

The gospel now spread more rapidly through Hesse and Thuringia: "heathen temples disappeared; humble churches rose amidst the forest glades; monastic buildings sprung up wherever [fertile] . . . soil and . . . running water suggested an inviting site; the land was cleared and brought under the plough." For with the gospel came the scientific cultivation of the soil and the many other advantages of a higher civilization. Boniface appealed for aid, and other missionaries came from England to work under his direction, including a number of women, who left the comforts of home to superintend the convents which Boniface established. So Germany gradually came under the influence of the Cross.

But paganism still prevailed in portions of Frisia, and Boniface could not rest content. When he was seventy-five years of age or upward he set out with a party of three priests, three deacons, four monks, and forty-one laymen for this unwon territory. For a time all went well. The venerable missionary was welcomed by several of the tribes and succeeded in laying the foundations of a number of churches. But on June 5, 754, he and his party were attacked by a large band of pagans. Some of Boniface's group counseled resistance, but the aged bishop would not permit it. "Let us not return evil for evil," said he; "the long-expected day has come, and the time of our departure is at hand. Strengthen ye yourselves in the Lord, and he will redeem your souls. Be not afraid of those who can only kill the body, but put all your trust in God, who will speedily give you an eternal reward, and an entrance into his heavenly kingdom."[4]

So died the man who did more than any other to bring the gospel, and with it, the first necessary elements of civilization, to central and western Germany. Boniface also did much to bring the church in both Germany and France under the authority of the pope.

Missionaries from Germany carried the Roman version of the gospel into the Scandinavian countries (ending the terrors which the pagan Norseman had long carried into the heart of the continent) and also into Poland and Hungary.

Meanwhile missionaries from the eastern wing of the church were carrying the gospel into Bulgaria, Moravia, and Russia. The work was firmly established in this latter country when Grand Duke Vladimir I (960–1015) received baptism and compelled his subjects to follow his example. A "metropolitan" nominated by the patriarch of Constantinople was placed at the head of the Russian Church, with his see in Kiev, ultimately transferred to Moscow. Russia was thereby brought into the cultural orbit of the Byzantine Empire, from which its own civilization was to be derived.

So by 1200 all of Europe had been nominally Christianized.

THE CHURCH DIVIDES

The church meanwhile had suffered its most serious cleavage—a rift not yet healed between East and West. The two sections of the church had been drifting steadily apart. There was no longer a common language, as in the days of the early church: the eastern scholars continued to write in Greek, the western scholars wrote now in Latin, and the thought of one became largely hidden from the other. There was also a vast difference in culture, the magnificence and decadence of the later Byzantine Empire in contrast with the rude vigor of the West. The political unity of Christendom was a thing of the past. Rulers of the new Germanic nations had long since asserted their independence of Constantinople, even though the memory of the old Roman Empire still lingered in the minds of men. The greatest obstacle to the unity of the church was found, however, in the advancing claims of the bishops of Rome to universal supremacy in the church.

These claims were increasingly realized among the newer churches of the West; they were steadily resisted among the older churches of the East.

In the eighth century (726–787) the church was racked by the so-called Iconoclastic Controversy. The question was: Is it right for a Christian to venerate pictures of Christ or the saints? Powerful emperors in Constantinople attempted to abolish "image-worship," which had gained a great hold upon the affections of the people, but which Mohammedanism, Christianity's bitter rival, charged—with some basis in fact—to be only a new species of idolatry. The Iconoclastic Movement, opposed to the use of images, finally failed, and the seventh and last ecumenical council to be accepted by both East and West declared that

> ... the venerable and holy images, as well in painting and mosaic as of other fit materials, should be set forth in the holy churches of God ... in houses and by the wayside ... For by so much more frequently as they are seen in artistic representation, by so much more readily are men lifted up to the memory of their prototypes, and to a longing after them; and to these should be given due salutation and honourable reverence ... not indeed that true worship of faith ... which pertains alone to the divine nature ... For the honour which is paid to the image passes on to that which the image represents, and he who reveres the image reveres in it the subject represented. ... [5]

In the course of this long controversy the popes turned to the rulers of the Franks for help, and their old relations with the emperor in Constantinople were never resumed. In the following century western theologians, with the approval of the pope, inserted a phrase (*filioque*) into the Nicene Creed, which asserted that the Holy Spirit proceeded not only from the Father (as in the original creed) but also from the Son. This change was vigorously opposed by Eastern leaders, not only on theological grounds, but also because it amended a sacred creed which had been approved by an ecumenical council. This inserted clause remains to the present day an obstacle to the reunion of the Greek Orthodox and Roman Catholic Churches.

In this same century the attempt of Pope Nicholas I to assert his authority over the Constantinopolitan see led to a breach between the two patriarchs. This rupture was finally healed, as were other minor rifts. The irreparable breach came in the eleventh century, in the year 1054. There came a clash between Leo IX, bishop of Rome, and Michael Cerularius, bishop of Constantinople, arising originally out of papal interference with the churches especially of Sicily, which still paid allegiance to Constantinople. The bitter quarrel ended when papal representatives laid on the altar of St. Sophia a sentence of excommunication, denouncing eleven evil doctrines and practices of Michael and his supporters and cursing them with the awful imprecation: "Let them be anathema [forever damned] . . . with all heretics: yea, with the devil and his angels. Amen, Amen, Amen." Michael replied with a similar condemnation of the bishop of Rome. From that day, July 16, 1054, the two branches of the church—one, the Greek Orthodox; the other, the Roman Catholic—have gone their separate ways.

THE CHURCH LOSES

The Byzantine Empire, vastly superior to the western states in learning, wealth, and power, had lost meanwhile a large part of its territory to the rising Mohammedan power. Mohammed, an Arabian merchant, had his first visions in the year A.D. 613. Seventeen years later the prophet urged his followers to extend their faith by the sword. In the Koran his words remain embodied:

> Let them . . . fight for the religion of GOD . . . for whosoever fighteth for the religion of GOD, whether he be slain, or be victorious, we will surely give him a great reward.[6]

There followed a remarkable series of military conquests. Arabia was conquered in two years, three years later Damascus fell to Mohammed's generals, and Jerusalem, three years later still; in three more years Antioch to the north and Alexandria to the south had been incorporated in the Mohammedan Empire. The Mohammedans continued their triumphal march across northern Africa, crossed the Straits of Gibraltar, and by A.D. 711 had conquered the whole of Spain. They crossed the Pyrenees Mountains and marched into

France, being finally turned back by the forces of Charles Martel at Tours, in the year A.D. 732. The territory lost to the Mohammedans, most of it permanently, included the lands where the ancient civilizations had risen, and where Christianity had won some of its earliest successes, and from which had come a number of its greatest theologians and leaders. The Mohammedans gave the conquered populace their choice—Mohammedanism, tribute, or the sword. Christianity survived, and for a time was permitted considerable liberty, but as time went on its life was increasingly stifled. In most of these lands a Christian minority remains even to the present day. But the church in these lands has long since ceased to play an important role in the ongoing movement of Christianity.

The Isaurian Dynasty (A.D. 717–1025) brought renewed strength to the apparently collapsing empire, which now recovered much of the territory lost to the Mohammedans in Asia Minor. But in the eleventh century came the Seljuk Turks, a new and more aggressive Mohammedan power. In the year 1070 they captured Jerusalem from the Fatimid rulers and the pilgrimages which the latter had permitted Christians to make to Jerusalem became difficult if not impossible. In 1071 a Byzantine army was annihilated, and the Turks proceeded to capture Antioch, Edessa, and Nicaea. They were hammering now at the gates of Constantinople; if this fortress fell all Europe would be in danger.

Under these circumstances the eastern emperor, Alexius, appealed to Pope Urban II for aid, and this vigorous pope, in what has been called the most influential speech in the Middle Ages, called upon the Christian princes in Europe to undertake a crusade for the rescue of the Holy Land from the infidels. Such crusades would engage the attention of Europe for the next two hundred years. Many considerations played a part. It was wise military strategy to sustain the eastern empire, which stood between the western states and this new threat to their safety; old trade routes were blocked and needed to be reopened; ambitious nobles longed to carve out new conquests in the fabulous East; for the common soldier there was always the hope of loot; the crusades appealed to the imagination of romantic youth; but the religious element was also strong, and to this motive Urban II and his successors made unabashed appeal. Christ himself,

ASIA MINOR
(Seljuk Turks)

LESSER ARMENIA   COUNTY OF EDESSA

ANTIOCH

CYPRUS   COUNTY OF TRIPOLI

SYRIA

Damascus

This short-lived kingdom was the most extensive realm the crusaders ever established.   KINGDOM OF JERUSALEM   Acre   Hattin

Alexandria   Jerusalem

The Crusades
There were eight crusades, the first beginning in 1096, the last ending in 1291.

CALIPHATE OF CAIRO   Cairo

Urban promised, would lead the advancing warriors across sea and mountains. And if any one of them fell in battle the glories of heaven would immediately open. To Urban's stirring appeal, playing on every emotion of the human heart, there came back from the whole throng, "Deus vult!" ("God wills it!") "It is," replied the pope, "it is the will of God. Let these words be your war-cry when you unsheathe the sword. You are soldiers of the cross. Wear on your breasts . . . the blood-red sign of the cross. Wear it as a token that His help will never fail you, as the pledge of a vow never to be recalled."[7]

The First Crusade was the most successful. The Christian warriors fought their way slowly across Asia Minor, and after three years of grueling campaign captured the Holy City. "Then," reports the priestly eyewitness, Raymond of Agiles,

wonderful things were to be seen. Numbers of the Saracens
were beheaded ... others were shot with arrows, or forced to
jump from the towers; others were tortured for several days,
and then burned in flames. In the streets were seen piles of
heads and hands and feet. One rode about everywhere amid
the corpses of men and horses.[8]

"Other contemporaries," as Will Durant points out,
contribute details: women were stabbed to death, suckling
babes were snatched by the leg from their mother's breasts and
flung over the walls, or had their necks broken by being dashed
against posts; and 70,000 Moslems remaining in the city were
slaughtered. The surviving Jews were herded into a synagogue
and burned alive. The victors flocked to the church of the Holy
Sepulcher, whose grotto, they believed, had once held the crucified Christ. There, embracing one another, they wept with
joy and release, and thanked the God of Mercies for their
victory.[9]

Instead of returning the territory regained to the Byzantine Empire as the emperor had expected, four independent Latin kingdoms
were established. Three military orders (Hospitallers, Templars, and
Teutonic Knights) also arose; their function was to safeguard pil-
grims and protect the holy sites.

The Second Crusade (1147–1148), occasioned by the loss of one
of the four Latin kingdoms, the Duchy of Edessa, was a complete
failure. Constantinople, now thoroughly disillusioned, sent the cru-
sading armies on their way, and then abandoned them to their fate.
Richard the Lionhearted was the hero of the Third Crusade, which
followed the capture of Jerusalem by the Mohammedans. Richard
succeeded in winning a toehold on the seacoast, the fortress of Acre,
which the crusaders managed to retain for a hundred years. The
Fourth Crusade was diverted from its original purpose, the invasion
of Egypt, by the hope of gain. The army turned against Constantinople at the invitation of Alexius, son of the deposed Emperor Isaac,
captured the city, which had long served as the West's great bulwark
of defense, and when the promised reward was not forthcoming, gave
itself over to unrestrained pillage and riot. Western rule was then extended over the city and its surrounding territory, and Roman Cath-

olic rites imposed on the subjugated populace. The eastern empire regained Constantinople a half-century later (1261) but it was left enfeebled and embittered.

Shortly after the Fourth Crusade came the so-called Children's Crusade (1218–1221). Thousands of youth made their way into Italy, hoping to succeed where the knights had failed, because their hearts were pure. Boats carrying them across the Mediterranean were wrecked by a storm; the children who managed to land were finally sold into slavery. Other crusades followed. Four more are ordinarily recognized, but none of them met with more than passing success. Acre, the last Christian stronghold in the Holy Land, fell in 1291. Crusades continued to be talked for two hundred years. Columbus, for example, signed an agreement April 17, 1492, to devote the proceeds of his undertaking beyond the western seas to the recovery of the Holy Sepulchre. But the European nations had had their fill. Crusades had gone out of fashion.

The crusades greatly affected the subsequent history of Europe— and of the church. The aggressive thrust of the Seljuk Turks had been checked, but the eastern empire, so long the shield of the West, had been seriously weakened. In the West a spirit of nationalism had been aroused, and the power of monarchs over their contending nobility strengthened. Trade between East and West had developed, and the growth of towns greatly stimulated. From the East the crusaders brought back new sciences, new arts, and many new inspirations— also new vices, diseases, and doubts. Morals deteriorated. Hatred for the Jew ("the infidel behind the lines") had been aroused. The division between Christians and Mohammedans, and between Orthodox and Catholics, had been deepened.

In the thirteenth and fourteenth centuries a new wave of Mohammedans swept in from the East—the Ottoman Turks, ancestors of our present Turks. In 1291 they captured Acre, the last stronghold of the crusaders. By 1354 they had encircled the eastern empire and occupied the various Balkan states. Constantinople itself fell in 1453. The Byzantine Empire, for so many centuries the stay and the support of western Europe, the wealthiest and most cultured Christian nation, was no more. Over against these losses to Mohammedans there were gains in Spain. Here the Moors were slowly driven back by the sword until finally in the thirteenth century the Mohammedans were confined to the kingdom of Granada; this was conquered in 1492, and Spain was now solely, and as a consequence of this long struggle, fanatically, Roman Catholic.

THE CHURCH FAILS

As we have suggested, the crusades opened a new chapter in the relations of Christians and Jews. Anti-Semitic legislation had begun with Constantine. By the middle of the sixth century (the age of Justinian), Jews were laboring under social, economic, civil, political, and religious disabilities. Relations between Jews and Christians, however, remained fairly cordial until, in the period of the crusades, hatred engendered against the infidel abroad reacted against the unbeliever at home. Occasional persecutions which arose from this time against the Jews culminated in their final expulsion from England in 1290, from France in 1394, and from Spain in 1492. From this latter country forty thousand Jews were plundered and then driven out. In 1495 an edict offered them the alternative of baptism or death. Children under fourteen were forcibly taken from their parents and the sacred rite was administered to them. Ten years later, two thousand of the alleged ungenuine converts were massacred in cold blood. In Italy and in the Holy Roman Empire (Germany) the Jews were allowed to remain, but here they were compelled to live in ghettos— situated usually in the worst part of the town, and too small always for the number of people confined in it. Alleys were dark and narrow, and sanitation was difficult. Outside of the ghetto Jews were compelled to wear peculiar peaked hats and yellow badges, which made them all too often the butt for the ridicule and assault of the town's ruffians. Trades once open to them were now forbidden. The descendants of those who had been Europe's merchants and then its bankers were now reduced to the lowest possible economic level.

Such in brief were the gains of the church, and such the losses, in the thousand-year period from A.D. 500 to 1500.

FOR CONSIDERATION

*1. What bearing do the following Scripture passages have on the material treated in this chapter? The book of Jonah; Matthew 28:19-20; Romans 11:13-32; 1 Corinthians 1:10-13.

2. What light does this chapter throw on the missionary enterprise of the church?

3. In the Middle Ages missions affected profoundly not only the history of the church, but also the history of western Europe. What future effects, if any, on history may be made by the present missionary work of the church, especially in the new countries of the world?

4. What in your estimation is the most compelling argument for world missions? How do you explain the prevailing indifference on the subject?

*5. In the Middle Ages the church was aided by the superior culture which it was able to mediate to the newer lands. Is this still true today? Is our western culture an aid or a hinderance to the expansion of the gospel? Why is this the case?

6. In the early centuries the church spread primarily through one man's telling his neighbor the gospel story. In the Middle Ages there was more reliance on "missionaries." Is too much reliance being placed today on one or the other? Why do you think so?

7. Which task was more important: to win the people of Europe to Christianity, or to teach them to live as Christians? How are these tasks related?

8. Relations between Eastern Orthodox and Protestant Churches have been more friendly in recent years. Should these warmer relations be further cultivated? If so, how?

*9. Today both Mohammedanism and Christianity are threatened by atheistic Communism. Is it desirable for them to develop a common front against a common enemy? Should leaders of these two religions seek mutual understanding, greater friendliness, and co-operation, or are our differences too great?

*10. What is the cause of continuing anti-Semitism, present even in America? What should be done to halt its further spread? Should we attempt to win Jews to the Christian faith? How can this best be done?

Emperor Henry IV Waiting in the Snow at Canossa for Pope Gregory VII

9
THE POPES
EXTEND THEIR POWERS

THE CHURCH AT ROME played an important role in the history of Christendom almost from the start. It was only in the fifth century, however, as we have seen, that bishops of Rome began to claim universal supremacy in the church. In the older churches of the East this claim was never allowed. But in the newer churches arising in the West, it was otherwise. Here, not at any definite date, but gradually, the claims of the bishops of Rome were accepted, and the early catholic, or universal, church, of which the Apostles' Creed speaks, became *Roman* Catholic.

In the previous chapter we recognized the contribution of missionaries to this end. Augustine in England, Boniface in Germany, and many others, proclaimed Jesus as the Son of God, and Peter and his successors, the bishops of Rome, as his vicars or personal representatives. We trace now the fortunes of the papacy, as reflected in the relation of the popes to the dominant European state.

THE PAPACY AND THE BYZANTINE EMPIRE, A.D. 323–739

Constantine became sole emperor of the Roman (or Byzantine)

119

Western Europe in Charlemagne's Time

Empire in the year A.D. 323. For four centuries after this event the bishop of Rome remained, nominally at least, a subject of the empire. When the crown exercised effective political control over the West, it dominated the church here, as it did also in the East. As its hold on the West relaxed, bishops in Rome became more independent. Gelasius (429–496) was able to claim, as we have seen, that there were two by whom the world was principally governed—the sacred authority of the pontiffs and the royal power—and that in divine matters kings "must submit their necks to the prelates." A century later the civil power in the West had well-nigh crumbled, and the Lombards pressing down from northern Italy dealt with Pope Gregory in preference to the representatives of the empire. The Iconoclastic Controversy (725–775) further estranged the churches of the East and the West, and snapped the ties that bound Rome (now identified with the church rather than with the empire) to Constantinople, which had succeeded Rome as the seat of empire.

THE PAPACY AND THE FRANKS, A.D. 739–885

In lieu of this eastern connection, the papacy now turned its face to the West, forming an "alliance" with the Franks, at this time the strongest of the new Germanic powers. As in all alliances there was something to be gained by both parties. The popes wanted protection from the Lombards, who had long occupied northern Italy and were now threatening Rome itself. Actual power among the Franks had been wielded for some time by "mayors of the palace," serving kings who were no more than figureheads. The former wanted the sanction of the church, and particularly of the popes as the most representative figures in the church, for assuming the kingly title. In the year A.D. 751 Pope Zacharias approved the coronation of Pepin (probably by Boniface) and three years later Pope Stephen II himself placed the crown on Pepin's head, and proclaimed him patrician (i.e., protector) of the Romans. "This participation of the pope," a careful historian has pointed out,

> brought about a very fundamental change in the theory of kingship. The kings of the Germans up to this time had been military leaders selected, or holding their office, by the will of the people, or at least of the aristocracy. Their rule had had no divine sanction, but only that of general acquiescence backed up by sufficient skill and popularity to frustrate the efforts of rivals. By the anointing of Pippin [Pepin] in accordance with the ancient Jewish custom, first by St. Boniface and then by the pope himself, "a German chieftain was," as Gibbon expresses it, "transformed into the Lord's anointed." The pope uttered a dire anathema of divine vengeance against any one who should attempt to supplant the holy and meritorious face of Pippin [Pepin]. It became a *religious* duty to obey the king. He came to be regarded by the Church, when he had duly received its sanction, as God's representative on earth. Here we have the basis of the later idea of monarchs "by the grace of God," against whom, however bad they might be, it was not merely a political offense, but a sin, to revolt.[1]

In the same year in which he had crowned Pepin, Stephen addressed a letter to the king, purporting to be a direct message from Peter:

> I, Peter the Apostle, of whom you are adopted sons, admonish
> you to defend the city of Rome, the people committed to my
> charge, and the Church in which my body lies, from the hands
> of enemies . . . Our Lady, the mother of God, the virgin
> Mary, joins with me in laying this obligation upon you.[2]

If Pepin does not act at once as the apostle admonished him, he is
told that he will be "lacerated and tortured, body and soul, in the
eternal and inextinguishable fires of hell with the Devil and his pes-
tilent angels."[3]

Pepin responded at once. The Lombards were roundly defeated,
and civil authority in Italy was placed in the hands of the papacy. So
began the State of the Church, and the popes became civil as well as
spiritual rulers.

From this period comes the so-called Donation of Constantine,
termed by Lord Bryce the "most stupendous of all the mediaeval
forgeries, which . . . commanded for seven centuries the almost un-
questioning belief of mankind."[4] In this document, which laid a legal
foundation for the stupendous claims of the medieval popes, the Emperor Constantine, who built Constantinople as the new capital of the
empire, is said to have recognized the rightful claims of the popes to
supreme authority over the church, and, further, to have bestowed on
them civil authority over Rome, Italy, and "the regions of the West."
As a token of this rule there was conveyed to the then reigning pope

> . . . our imperial Lateran palace, which is superior to and ex-
> cels all palaces in the whole world; and further the diadem,
> which is the crown of our head . . . the stole which usually sur-
> rounds our imperial neck; and the purple cloak and the scarlet
> tunic and all the imperial robes . . .[5]

It was some time yet, however, before this document now recognized
as a forgery, was used by the popes to advance their claims to universal supremacy.

Greatest of the Frankish rulers was Charlemagne (768–814). In
a series of successful campaigns (fifty-four in all) he extended the
boundaries of his kingdom in every direction, until finally it included
a large part of western Europe—what is now France, Italy, Spain, the
Low Countries, and much of Germany. He became the patron of culture and of education. He imposed the Christian religion on con-

quered German peoples. He regarded himself indeed as a second David, and like David ruled the church in his domain.[6] Europe had not seen such a ruler or experienced such hope since the breakup of the old Roman Empire.

On Christmas Day, in the year A.D. 800, while the great emperor was quietly worshiping in St. Peter's Church in Rome, Pope Leo III stepped down and crowned Charlemagne successor of the Caesars, ruler of what came to be known as the Holy Roman Empire.

> To the thinking of the Roman populace who applauded, as to the West generally, it was the restoration of the empire to the West, that had for centuries been held by the ruler in Constantinople. It placed Charlemagne in the great succession from Augustus. It gave a [divine] stamp to that empire. Unexpected, and not wholly welcome at the time to Charlemagne, it was the visible embodiment of a great ideal. The Roman Empire, men thought, had never died, and now God's consecration had been given to a Western Emperor by the hands of His representative. .... For the West and for the papacy the coronation was of the utmost consequence. It raised questions of imperial power and of papal authority that were to be controverted throughout the Middle ages. It emphasized the feeling that church and state were but two sides of the same shield ... and both closely related and owing mutual helpfulness. It made more evident than ever the deep-seated religious and political cleavage between East and West. To the great Emperor himself it seemed the fulfilment of the dream of Augustine's *City of God*—the union of Christendom in a kingdom of God, of which he was the earthly head.[7]

Charlemagne certainly could not have imagined that the time would come when successors of Leo III would claim that a pope had placed the imperial crown upon Charlemagne's head, and that they could withdraw what their predecessor had bestowed. But so in time it would prove to be.

THE PAPACY AND THE ITALIAN PRINCES, A.D. 885–955

Unfortunately, Charlemagne's heirs could not maintain the empire which he had constructed. Under his grandsons there came the trifold division which ultimately became the kingdoms of Germany, Italy, and France. But for many generations there was no centralized control in any of these lands. In a time when kings and so-called emperors could not protect their subjects from invading bands of Norsemen, when brigands were abroad and travel was unsafe, a decentralized form of government known as feudalism arose, and continued, longer in some parts of Europe than in others, for many centuries. According to this system an owner or lord of a piece of land, whether large or small, became the sovereign of all who dwelled on the land: He was their lord, and they were his vassals. Peasants gave their service and owed their allegiance to the baron, who occupied the castle on the hill; to him they looked in return for protection. The baron in turn had his overlord, and so it continued on up to the king at the top. Society was held together by such a system in which both vassals and lords had their respective obligations and rights. But nobles often found excuse to resist their lawful sovereign, and welcomed the opportunity to extend their power at his expense. They were greatly aided in such efforts if the church, particularly the papacy, released them from their sacred obligations, and thus gave religious sanction to their ambitions.

There was a period, however, lasting for nearly three quarters of a century (885–955), when the papacy suffered from a series of unworthy occupants. As Philip Schaff has written:

> The political disorder of Europe affected the church and paralyzed its efforts for good. The papacy itself lost all independence and dignity, and became the prey of avarice, violence, and intrigue, a veritable synagogue of Satan. It was dragged through the quagmire of the darkest crimes, and would have perished in utter disgrace had not Providence saved it for better times. Pope followed pope in rapid succession, and most of them ended their career in deposition, prison, and murder. The rich and powerful marquises of Tuscany and the Counts of Tusculum acquired control over the city of Rome and the papacy for more than half a century. And what is worse ... three bold and energetic women of the highest rank and lowest character, Theodora the elder ... and her

two daughters, Marozia and Theodora, filled the chair of St. Peter with their paramours and bastards. These Roman Amazons combined with the fatal charms of personal beauty and wealth, a rare capacity for intrigue, and a burning lust for power and pleasure ... They turned the church of St. Peter into a den of robbers and the residence of his successors into a harem. And they gloried in their shame. Hence this infamous period is called the papal Pornocracy ... [8]

Some popes of this period were almost as bad as the worst emperors of heathen Rome and far less excusable.

The Papacy and Germany (Holy Roman Empire), A.D. 955–1260

From such depths of degradation the papacy was rescued by the rise of the Saxon Dynasty in Germany. Otto I (936–973), the strongest ruler Europe had known since the days of Charlemagne, consolidated his kingdom through his control of bishops and abbots, whom he made temporal rulers and also his feudal dependents. Otto also conquered possessions in Italy and accepted from the hands of the pope the crown of the Holy Roman Empire. With him began the German domination of the papacy. Men appointed to this high office by Otto were prevailingly men of character and ability. The policies of Otto I were followed by his son and grandson, Otto II and Otto III. Henry II, the last ruler of this house, lost control in Italy, and for a short period the papacy again suffered as the pawn of Italian politics. It was rescued from this new degradation by the rise of another strong dynasty in Germany, the Franconian house. Henry III appointed as pope Leo IX, first of a series of reforming popes destined to give the papacy a new place in the history of Europe. A College of Cardinals was erected, to which able ecclesiastics were appointed from the whole of Europe, and to this body was given the responsibility of electing a new pope on the death of the old.

In 1073 Hildebrand, a monk who for some years had been the driving force behind the reforming party in the church, came to the papal throne, taking upon himself the name of Gregory VII. His view of the papal power was more far-reaching than that of any of his predecessors. As Vicar of Christ he claimed absolute power in the church—power to depose and reinstate bishops, to rule by edict, to accept or reject decisions of a church council, to hear and dispose all appeals from church courts; in other words, absolute power as administrator, legislator, and judge. He also claimed power over the state. To him all civil rulers were responsible, not only for their spiritual welfare, but also for their temporal government. He claimed power to depose kings and emperors, and to dissolve subjects from oaths of loyalty to their rulers. He judged all men, but he himself could be judged by no man, only by God himself. It was, in fact, a claim to world dominion.

Gregory was not an evil man grasping selfishly for power. Only through such power vested in the hands of the pope as the Vicar of Christ, it seemed to him, could Augustine's ideal of the City of God be realized. Only so could God's will be done on earth as it was in heaven. Throughout Europe there were those who listened to Gregory because only so, they agreed, could the continued clash of evil and selfish men be averted, and peace with justice return to a sorely troubled world. Gregory himself could not see—and many disposed to accept his claims did not yet understand—that the average pope was not good enough, and that the best of popes was not nearly wise enough to exercise the power that Gregory VII had claimed. It was in some ways a magnificent dream, but it was based on an illusion— that Christ had appointed Peter, and the bishops of Rome, as his successors, to rule in his name.

To achieve his goal Gregory developed a two-point program, involving, first, the abolition of clerical marriages, and second, the abolition of lay investiture (a procedure which enabled temporal rulers to bestow on all churchmen the powers and privileges of their office— actually to appoint them to office). Earlier popes had forbidden the marriage of the clergy, but the edict had not been enforced. So widely indeed was it disregarded that Gregory's stern decree to this effect broke upon the church like a sudden burst of thunder. Many of the clergy, particularly in Germany, vehemently denounced the decree of the pope as worthy only of a heretic; they expressed an intention, if the matter were pressed, to forsake the priesthood rather than their wives; and then the pope, who was not content with the service of men, might make shift as he could to secure the ministration of angels in the churches. Gregory, however, exhorted the people to have nothing to do with married priests, and instructed prominent laymen to prevent such priests by force if necessary from exercising the functions of their office.

- By such means Gregory finally achieved his end, and from that day to this the policy of a celibate (unmarried) priesthood has prevailed in the Roman Catholic Church. But this success was bought at a considerable price—the private morals of the clergy. Wives were no more, but concubines flourished, and misconduct became common. The records of the Middle Ages make it abundantly clear that sex license and drunkenness spread widely among the clergy of every rank, not excluding—at times—the papacy.[9]

The second step in Gregory's program brought him into open conflict with the state. The German emperors, as we have seen, maintained their power largely through appointment of bishops and abbots to their office, and this power was bound up with the practice of lay investiture. Gregory's decree that henceforth any cleric who received a bishopric or abbey from the hands of any lay person was excommunicate, as was the civil ruler (whether emperor, king, duke, margrave, count, or any other secular power or person) who presumed to invest him, was intolerable to Henry IV, one of the strongest rulers that the empire had known.

When finally the pope threatened to excommunicate Henry, the king retaliated by compelling his bishops to renounce their obedience to the pope, and then ordered Gregory—"not the pope, but a false monk"—to descend from his papal throne. Gregory then took the supreme step. Appealing to "Holy Peter, chief of the Apostles" for support, he boldly proclaimed:

> I deprive King Henry, son of the emperor Henry ... of the government of the whole Empire of Germany and Italy. I release all Christians from the oath which they have made, or yet may make to him, and hereby forbid any man to serve him as King.

Henry, to his dismay, discovered that his power was fading away. Finally in desperation he sought to make his peace with the determined monk, now ruling in St. Peter's chair. In the dead of winter, with snow on the ground, he waited barefooted, and in sackcloth, for three days before a castle high in the Alps (Canossa), asking audience of the pope. To him he finally made his humble submission, and from his hands received again the royal crown which he had forfeited by his opposition to the papal policy. Canossa dramatizes for all times the claims to temporal authority advanced, and at times exercised, by the medieval popes. But Canossa was not the end. Some years later Gregory again excommunicated Henry, but on this occasion the emperor was better prepared. He led an army into Italy, and the pope was compelled to flee. Henry himself was finally forced to abdicate, but the struggle continued between his son, Henry V, and the successors of Gregory. In 1122 there came a compromise, embodied in the Concordat of Worms. The church retained the right to elect its own popes. In Germany the emperor renounced the right of investiture with ring and staff (the symbols of spiritual authority) but retained the right to bestow temporal possessions such as real estate by touch of his scepter, which meant in effect that ecclesiastics in Germany must be acceptable to both church and state.

During the reign of the Hohenstaufens (1130–1295) the struggle between popes and emperors in Germany was renewed. There were times when the popes had moral right on their side; there were times when emperors championed the right of a secular government to be free from tyrannical ecclesiasticism. In large measure, however, it became a struggle for naked power. The story is too complicated for us to follow in detail. It was during this period, however, that the papacy reached the peak of its power. Innocent III (1198–1216) came nearer exercising the power that Gregory VII had claimed than any other pope who either preceded or followed him. It was his proud claim that the Lord had given to St. Peter and his successors the government not only of the church but also of the whole world, and the facts seemed to bear out this statement. As one historian has pointed out:

> ... in area and population his dominions compared favorably with the empire of [the Caesars]. The emperors of Old Rome might claim divine authorization, but they could not hurl interdicts that bore with them everlasting penalties, nor cite ancient

and revered scriptures an explicit divine commission to rule the states of the world ... Innocent reigned as a king of kings, directing national policies and making war and peace. But holding by inheritance from Peter the Keys of the Kingdom, he ruled also, as only a medieval pontiff could, through the discipline of the church, an empire in the thoughts of believing men.[10]

In Germany (the Holy Roman Empire) Innocent deposed and raised up emperors; he compelled a French king to take back his wife; he launched a crusade against princes in southern France who were too lax in their attitude toward heresy, and gave their domains to others more amenable to his will. In England he compelled King John to make humble submission and to acknowledge publicly that he held his kingdom only as a fief of the pope. Constance, widow of Henry VI, acknowledged that she held the kingdom of Sicily as a feudal dependent of the pope, and in her will left him the guardian of her son and the regent of the kingdom. In the little kingdoms of Spain (León, Aragon, Portugal), the pope's will was absolute. He received Peter's Pence (a token of dependency) from England, Ireland, Norway, Sweden, Prussia, and Poland. At his call there assembled in Rome representatives from all parts of Christendom in what is known as the Fourth Lateran Council. In addition to bishops and abbots there were present representatives of the emperors of both East and West, of the kings of England, France, Aragon, Hungary, Cyprus, and Jerusalem and many other potentates.

> The extraordinary personal ascendancy of the Pope was shown by the fact that though the states represented were vitally concerned with some of the business transacted, the vast assembly did not discuss, but simply endorsed, what the Pope decreed.[11]

Exhausted by its long struggle with the papacy, the Holy Roman Empire declined, and was succeeded by France as the dominant power in Europe.

THE PAPACY AND FRANCE, A.D. 1285–1417

The fortunes of the papacy now took a turn for the worse. In their struggle for power the popes had lost moral prestige. Meanwhile, modern states had begun to emerge. Kings, first in France, later in England, then in Spain, succeeded in curbing the power of their ambitious nobles and in establishing strong, centralized control in their dominions. Under such conditions popes could no longer exercise power as easily as their predecessors had done.

The changed situation was manifest in the struggle of Pope Boniface VIII with Philip the Fair, king of France (1285–1314). In the course of this dispute Boniface issued his famous bull *Unam Sanctam.* In this bull it was claimed

> . . . that there is one Holy Catholic and Apostolic Church, and . . . outside this Church there is neither salvation nor remission of sins. . . . Of this one and only Church there is one body and one head . . . namely Christ, and Christ's vicar is Peter, and Peter's successor . . .
>
> . . . in this Church and in her power are two swords . . . the spiritual sword and the material. But the latter is to be used for the Church, the former by her; the former by the priest, the latter by kings and captains but at the will and by the permission of the priest.
>
> If . . . the earthly power err, it shall be judged by the spiritual power; and if a lesser power err, it shall be judged by a greater. But if the supreme power [the papacy itself] err, it can only be judged by God, not by man . . . Furthermore we declare, state, define and pronounce that it is altogether necessary to salvation for every human creature to be subject to the Roman pontiff.[12]

This had been the theory of Gregory VII, of Innocent III, and of other occupants of the papal chair, but nowhere had it been stated more boldly and more succinctly. Philip, in reply, sent bold men to Italy who managed to secure the pope's person, place him under arrest, and start with him on the way to France. Boniface was rescued, but died shortly thereafter, partly, it may be, from the shock of this painful episode. A modern Roman Catholic historian has written:

> The outrage of Anagni, when "Christ himself was taken prisoner in his vicar," was the death of the medieval papacy, and

of all the theological and political ideas on which it was founded.[13]

At the time it seemed only a temporary setback. In retrospect it becomes clear that the peak of papal power had been passed. The papacy could not control the new world-forces now coming into being.

The humiliation of Boniface VIII was followed by what came to be known as "the Babylonian Captivity of the papacy." For nearly seventy years (1309–1377) the papal residence was transferred from Rome to Avignon in southern France, where the popes could be kept under the surveillance, if not the control, of the French monarchs.

The history of the papacy during this period is characterized chiefly by the popes' political activity in the interests of France (all of the popes during this period were French) and by their financial activity, which became an international scandal.

The partisanship of the Avignon popes aroused keen opposition. Some, like Dante and John of Paris, opposed their temporal pretensions; others like Marsilius and William of Occam questioned their spiritual claims. England and the Holy Roman Empire, disturbed by the intermeddling of a French pope in their internal affairs, adopted certain national measures of defense. The latter, for example, adopted the Declaration of Rense (1338), in which the pope's right to interfere in the election of an emperor was denied. The English Parliament adopted a Statute of Provisors which insisted that the church in England had a right to choose its own bishops without papal interference, and a Statute of Praemunire which limited appeals from English courts to the papacy. All these laws were largely dead from the start, but the handwriting on the wall had appeared.

It was during these same years that the papacy brought its financial system to the peak of efficiency. Money siphoned off to Avignon for various services and by various expedients became a major problem in almost every European nation. The pope's income far exceeded that of any sovereign in Europe, and one leading historian of the Middle Ages even claims that at the height of its power the income of the Holy See was greater than the combined revenues of all the secular sovereigns of Europe. The money so received was used to maintain the most luxurious court in Europe. Of the entire sum spent by the papal treasurer under John XXII, approximately two-thirds went for wars in which the pope had an interest.

Such political activity, such offensive taxation, such prodigal expenditure eroded rapidly the moral prestige on which the great influence of the papacy had so long depended.

Worse was to come. In 1378 the College of Cardinals assembled in Rome to elect a successor to Pope Gregory XI. Pressure was brought on the conclave by Roman citizens to elect a pope pledged to return the seat of the papacy to the Holy City. Urban VI, who gave such assurances, was elected. A tactless man, determined to end French influence over the papacy, he quickly alienated all of the cardinals (most of whom were French). Four months after the earlier election they reassembled and elected an Avignon pope who took the title of Clement VII. So began the Great Schism which continued for nearly forty years (1378–1417). During the whole of this period there were two or more popes, with the allegiance of the various nations of Europe divided between them. As one historian writes:

> Europe was pained and scandalized, while the papal abuses, especially of taxation, were augmented, and two courts must now be maintained. Above all, the profound feeling that the church must be visibly one was offended. The papacy sank enormously in popular regard.[14]

The solution of the Great Schism became the major problem in Europe. The search for means by which this end might be accomplished led to the development of a conciliar party, who held, as eastern Christians had always done, that a general council was a greater authority than the pope. With the growth of this feeling such a council, called by the combined College of Cardinals, finally gathered in Pisa (A.D. 1409). Popes of both lines were deposed, and a new pope elected. This election, however, was not recognized by the two incumbents nor by a number of the European nations. As a result there now came to be three popes instead of two. This was truly intolerable. A second council, called by the Emperor Sigismund, met in Constance during the years 1414–1418. It was probably the most imposing assemblage held in medieval Europe. In addition to the many cardinals, patriarchs, and bishops in attendance, there were numerous doctors of theology, doctors in both civil and church laws, and doctors of medicine; there were also 83 kings and princes represented by envoys, 38 dukes, 172 counts, 71 barons, and more than 1500 knights, besides writers of bulls, buglers, fiddlers, and players of other musical instruments.

The council began well, with a vigorous declaration of conciliar supremacy:

> ... representing the Catholic Church ... it has its authority immediately from Christ; and ... all men, of every rank and condition, including the Pope himself, is bound to obey it in matters concerning the Faith, the abolition of the schism, and the reformation of the Church of God in its head-and its members.[15]

It then accepted the resignation of the Roman pope (Gregory XII), deposed the Avignon pope (John XXIII, whose life was the most scandalous of any claimant of the papal chair to this time), isolated the Avignon pope (Benedict XIII) and elected a single new pope, Martin V. The long and disastrous schism was finally healed. The council then effected a few minor reforms in the machinery of the church, leaving further reformation to future councils, which, it ordered, were to be held at regular intervals, the first in five years, the second in seven, and another every ten years thereafter. Had this provision been carried out, the Roman Church would have become a constitutional monarchy; and a reformation, destroying the unity of the church, might have been averted.

But only one additional council was held: the Council of Basel in the year 1433. This council too began well, successfully reasserting the theory of councils as the superior authority rather than popes, and making provision for badly needed reforms intended to end some of the more grievous financial abuses, and further to limit the power of the papacy. Pope Eugenius, however, succeeded in dividing the council. The majority remained in Basel; the minority, in response to the pope's invitation, adjourned to meet first in Ferrara, later in Florence. Popular support gradually shifted to the council meeting in Florence, and when the remnant in Basel finally lost their heads and deposed the pope, thus threatening a new schism, its days were numbered. In the end no reforms were accomplished, and the pope had successfully reasserted his power over the church.

THE PAPACY AND THE ITALIAN RENAISSANCE, A.D. 1417–1521

Special interest attaches to the popes of the Italian Renaissance, the hundred-year period preceding the Protestant Reformation. The popes of this period were primarily temporal princes. Italy was now divided among a number of city-states, one of which, in the middle of the Italian boot, was the State of the Church, ruled by the pope. Each of these states sought to extend its domains at the expense of the rivals; and in this effort the pope was no less zealous, or any less scrupulous, than his rivals. As one historian has written: "They plotted and intrigued and fought and lied, according to the fashion of the times." The only difference was that in addition to the secular means at their disposal, the popes were free to call upon the spiritual weapons in their arsenal, particularly excommunication and the interdict. The last, the most dreaded of all weapons in the pope's armory, forbade the performance of some or all of the church's rites, on which it was thought the soul's eternal destiny depended. It stimulated popular pressure which few rulers could long resist.

Many of the popes during this hundred-year period were also patrons of the Renaissance. They used their not inconsiderable revenues to beautify the city of Rome. Rome became the artistic capital of the western world.

Many were indulgent uncles or fathers. Their chief interest was to advance the fortunes of their families.

Some were shameless profligates. Alexander VI has the notorious distinction of being the most corrupt pope of this period, and perhaps in the whole history of the papacy. Even in the judgment of Catholic historians, his dissoluteness knew no restraint; and his readiness to abuse the papacy for his own personal ends, no bounds.

The popes of the Italian Renaissance were also shrewd financiers. As Dr. Jacobs has written in his *Story of the Church:*

> The means with which to support their secular distinctions came to the popes from their official position as the head of the

Church. They were the "vicars of Christ on earth," and all the power of God for man's salvation was declared to be in their hands. They had the keys of the kingdom of heaven, to bind and loose, to pardon and condemn, as they saw fit. In the hands of men who were saturated with the ideals of the Renaissance, this awful power was prostituted to personal and official ambition. They excommunicated those who opposed their political plans and their own wars were always "crusades." They used their spiritual functions to provide them with the wealth they needed to support their temporal pretensions. Every device that could add to the papal revenues was held legitimate. Church positions and appointments were bought and sold; permissions to violate church laws were granted for money under the name of "dispensations"; indulgences were hawked about Europe; taxes were laid whenever an excuse presented itself or could be devised; in more than one country the drain upon the gold-supply caused by the constant flow of money into the Roman coffers was looked upon with apprehension. The wealth thus gained was used to support the most luxurious court in Christendom. Vast sums were spent on public buildings of every sort and on sumptuous palaces in which to house the men of the Church. The papal courtiers enjoyed the income of parishes in foreign lands which they had never seen, sometimes one man would have a dozen such. The lives of papal officials, and often of the popes themselves, were scandalous and vile. The papal court was "entirely emancipated from morality."

This condition could not exist at Rome without affecting the whole Church. It was most acute at the papal residence, but in a less conspicuous way the spirit of the Renaissance was the spirit of the whole Church. It was secularized in the extreme; its office-bearers were living for worldly ends and using their spiritual offices to secure them; immorality among the clergy was a condition so widespread that it was taken for granted; monasteries and nunneries were all too often homes of lust. Naturally among the many thousands of priests and monks, there were great numbers of beautiful exceptions, but the condition was general. Never was a Reformation of the Church "in head and members" more sorely needed than when the Renaissance was at its height.[16]

Not all of the popes during this period were evil men. One of the better of them, Leo X, was on the throne when the Reformation broke. Of him Paolo Sarpi, a Roman Catholic historian (1552–1623), wrote, not unfairly:

> Leo, noble by birth and education, brought many aptitudes to the Papacy, especially a remarkable knowledge of classical literature, humanity, kindness, the greatest liberality, an avowed intention of supporting artists and learned men, who for many years had enjoyed no such favour in the Holy See. He would have made an ideal pope had he added to these qualities some knowledge of the things of religion, and a little inclination to piety, both of them things for which he cared little.[17]

FOR CONSIDERATION

1. Are church people—people generally—informed regarding the development of the papacy? Is there need for such information? Can it be presented without prejudice? Has it been so presented in this chapter?
2. Does Protestantism have the right and the responsibility to counter Roman Catholic claims and to teach facts regarding the rise of papal power?
*3. Pope Pius IX in his famous Syllabus of Errors (1865) declared that no pope has ever exceeded his rightful claims. Not all Roman Catholic scholars would accept this statement—nor the further declaration of Pius IX, that no Roman Catholic can accept the idea of separation between church (i.e., the Roman Catholic Church) and state. But the claims of Pius IX have never been denied by papal authorities. Is it proper under the circumstances for non-Catholics to inquire of Roman Catholics running for office their views on current question involved?
4. Why is the freedom and independence of the Christian church in general something to be safeguarded? Are there dangers in our time to such freedom? If so, what are they?
5. "Hildebrand's goal was a Christian society. If you believe this

goal to be valid but disagree with the methods by which he sought to achieve it, what would you suggest are the proper means for the church to employ in seeking to Christianize society?"[18]

6. "Do you think that God's truth is more adequately represented by the whole company of the faithful than by any segment of the church? Why? What should the respective roles of the clergy and the laity be in the preservation of God's truth in the church?"[19]

7. What makes the reform of the church so difficult?

8. Read Matthew 16:13–24; 20:20–28. Does the history of the papacy as sketched in this chapter throw any additional light on these familiar Scripture passages? If so, what?

Thomas Aquinas Expounding His Theology

10
ROMAN CATHOLIC
THEOLOGY TAKES FORM

IN THE MIDDLE AGES Roman Catholic theology took form—much as it remains to the present day.

In the early part of this period there was little intellectual activity: Schools had vanished, libraries had been destroyed, learning had gone into eclipse. The church spent its energies in sustaining, transmitting, and extending the faith. Cathedral schools were maintained for the training of the clergy. Monasteries also had their schools, and much of the monks' time was spent in copying manuscripts which they had saved from destruction. As times grew better and it became safe for young men to travel, outstanding teachers, particularly in the cathedral schools, attracted increasing numbers of students from all over Europe. If news came of a fresh and more popular teacher the students might emigrate en masse almost overnight. Gradually universities arose, with teams of teachers or faculties, and the number of students multiplied.

These universities, it should be observed, arose under the auspices of the church; the teachers were friars, members of the various mendicant (begging) orders, and theology was regarded as "the queen of the sciences."

From these schoolmen came the theology of the Middle Ages—Scholasticism, as it came to be termed; the theology to which, with some additions, the Roman Catholic Church is still committed. Many able minds labored to construct this enduring edifice, but the most influential were Thomas Aquinas (1225–1274), recognized officially by the Roman Catholic Church today as its theologian par excellence, and John Duns Scotus (1265–1308). Disciples of these two masters, Thomists and Scotists, as they were called, differed in some respects, as we shall note, and some of these differences have had important consequences for the life and thought of the church.

A survey of this Scholastic theology introduces us to the theology of Roman Catholicism today.

REGARDING AUTHORITY

We begin with the question of authority. A place was found here for reason, revelation, and the church. The schoolmen placed great emphasis on reason, as does the Roman Catholic Church today. Anselm (1033–1109), one of the earliest of the great schoolmen, believed that reason could establish independently all the great doctrines of the church, and that this was the task of theology. He himself supplied arguments for the existence of God and for the fact of the Incarnation ("Why God Became Man"). Aquinas (1225–1274) made a more moderate claim. He held that while some truths could be established by reason—for example, the existence of God—there were others which come to us only through revelation; these, however, can be shown to be reasonable. This is the general position maintained by the Roman Catholic theologians at the present time. Duns Scotus (1265–1308), however, doubted that all Christian truth could be established as reasonable; this idea grew among theologians of the late Middle Ages, who then fell back upon the authority of the church as the necessary basis for belief. With the general acceptance of this latter point of view the Scholastic movement came to an end.

All the schoolmen accepted the idea of divine revelation. This revelation is preserved in Scripture, which is the final authority. The Scriptures included the Old and New Testament, as now recognized by Protestants, but in addition fourteen Apocryphal books of the Old Testament, found in the Septuagint translation of the Old Testament but not in the Hebrew canon as recognized by the rabbis. Jerome's translation of these Scriptures from the original languages into Latin (the Vulgate) was accepted, as it still is, as the authoritative version of the Scriptures. While supreme importance was attached to Scripture, it was agreed that Scripture was to be understood in the light of the interpretations of the councils and the Fathers (tradition). Tradition tended therefore, in actual practice, to become more important than Scripture.

But there was needed some authoritative interpreter of both Scripture and tradition. The Eastern (Orthodox) Church held and still holds that this authoritative voice comes only from an ecumenical council—the seven ecumenical councils of the undivided church. In the Western Church the papacy claimed to be that voice, and Aquinas, along with other schoolmen, agreed; the pope alone could issue new definitions of the faith, and in issuing such definition Aquinas apparently held that the pope was infallible. Not until 1870, however, did this become a dogma of the church.

REGARDING GOD

The schoolmen held staunchly to the Trinitarian faith (one God, three persons) and to the Chalcedonian Creed (Jesus Christ fully God and fully man), as does the Roman Catholic Church today. They believed that God could be approached more readily through the intercession of the saints, particularly the Virgin Mary. There was a difference of opinion regarding Mary's birth: Thomas Aquinas denied, and Duns Scotus affirmed, that she was born without original sin (the doctrine of the immaculate conception). This disputed dogma of the Middle Ages was finally declared to be essential Catholic dogma in 1854.

REGARDING MAN

In their view of man, the schoolmen held to the traditional views regarding original righteousness and original sin. Man was created, however, with both supernatural and natural gifts. The natural gifts are those which belong to man as such (conscience, reason, will); the supernatural gifts are those which enable him to seek the highest good and practice the three Christian virtues (faith, hope, and love). When Adam sinned, the supernatural gifts were withdrawn; the natural gifts, according to Aquinas, were perverted—sin tainted every faculty, he became "totally depraved" (the Augustinian view), and could do no good works or merit any reward until he had received the grace of God in baptism. (This grace is often called *prevenient,* because it precedes and makes possible man's first act of faith.) Once this saving grace had been received, however, man had full power to do good works, thus winning merit that could be put to his account, or if not needed, transferred to a Treasury of Merits on which the church could draw for the benefit of more needy sinners. Duns Scotus held that after Adam's sin the natural gifts remained unimpaired, only that, with the supernatural gifts withdrawn, they became inordinate, out of control. Man could therefore do good works and merit reward even before the reception of grace (the Semi-Pelagian view). This latter view placed much greater emphasis on man's effort, and tended more definitely toward a view of salvation by works. It was in this direction that Catholic theology was to move.

Regarding Salvation

How was man saved? Only by the grace of God, it was agreed—grace, which flowed, as it were, from the cross through the sacraments. All held to the necessity of an atonement. Anselm, archbishop of Canterbury about A.D. 1100, wrote a famous little book, *Cur Deus Homo?* ("Why was God made Man?"), in which he develops the theory that Christ's voluntary death was the "satisfaction" which God accepts, as a medieval knight might, in reparation for the dishonor which man's disobedience has wrought on God. Abelard countered with what came to be known as a moral influence theory: God's love manifested in Christ's death on the cross wins man's love in return, and so we who were formerly estranged become reconciled to God. Aquinas and Duns Scotus presented combinations of these two views.

On man's part there must be both faith and works—or faith working through love. Faith for Aquinas included not only acceptance of Christ as Savior and Lord, but also the acceptance-as-true of the doctrines of the church. This should be an explicit faith, in which one understands and accepts what the church teaches to be true. An "implicit" faith, however, will suffice: that is, acceptance of "what the church teaches," even without knowing *what* that is. The works which follow from faith, and which are necessary for salvation, include not only obedience to the laws of Christ, but also obedience to the laws of the church (such present requirements, for example, as attending Mass on Sunday, and refraining from meat on Fridays; these are not laws of Christ, but disciplinary requirements of the church). In addition there must be use of the sacraments, for only through them, under ordinary circumstances, can saving grace be received.

REGARDING THE SACRAMENTS

The word "sacrament" is not found in the New Testament. It had been brought into the church's vocabulary early in the third century, and was used loosely to describe various symbolic actions of the church which possessed an inner, spiritual significance; "a visible sign of an invisible grace," as described by Augustine. Baptism and the Lord's Supper were the most important of these sacraments, but other actions were included which later were dropped from the list of sacraments. In time the word came to be employed only for those rites which, it was supposed, had been instituted by Christ. For some time the exact number was in doubt. In the later Middle Ages the number was fixed at seven.

These sacraments, it was now agreed, were more than symbols; they were in some sense vehicles which *conveyed* saving grace, without which, indeed, such grace, ordinarily, could not be received. The reception of grace was not dependent on the faith of the recipient (though lack of faith might be an obstacle, blocking the reception of grace), but on the proper performance of the sacrament itself. Thus infant baptism wiped out original sin even though the infant was wholly unaware of what was being done on its behalf; so also extreme unction, in the case of a dying man who had lost consciousness. Grace might not be conveyed even where faith was present—if, for example, the officiating priest had not been properly ordained, or did not have the intention of effecting that which the sacrament was supposed to accomplish.

Baptism, first of the sacraments in order, was ordinarily administered in infancy. A child who died unbaptized, it was held, went into a special compartment in hell, where it suffered no physical torment, but where it lacked through all eternity the bliss of the heavenly state. A child (or adult) who was baptized received forgiveness for past sins (original and actual) and was reborn, receiving a new nature, one which enabled it now to fulfill the will of God. It could continue through life without sin, and so pass immediately after death into the presence of God. If a believer came to the end of life with more merit than demerit he went directly to heaven, becoming thus a "saint" to whom sinners on earth could direct their petitions. The surplus merit accumulated by the saint passed into a Treasury of Merits, on which the church could draw for the benefit of those who fell short. Since baptism was essential for salvation this sacrament was one which could be performed in an emergency by a layman, even a woman.

Confirmation, the second sacrament in order, was accomplished by the laying on of the hands of the bishop, in accordance with the proper form. Originally it marked the completion of the sacrament of baptism, and was performed as soon as possible after baptism. In the Middle Ages it became a second sacrament, and was postponed ordinarily until early adolescence. The young person thus confirmed received additional grace by which he might avoid sin, at a time when he became more fully responsible for his own actions and the temptations of life became more severe.

In spite of baptism, and in spite of the new additional grace bestowed through confirmation, the ordinary Catholic falls again and again into sin. These sins may be more or less serious. For the lesser (or "venial") sins, satisfaction must be given, either in this life or in the next. This final punishment, or cleansing, came in purgatory, from which the sinner finally passed into his heavenly bliss. Only an occasional "saint" would expect to escape purgatory altogether, but there were various means by which one's time in purgatory could be diminished. The more serious, or mortal, sins condemned one to eternal punishment in hell. Included among mortal sins were not only breaches of God's Commandments as revealed in Scripture, but also breaches of the church's commandments (willful failure to attend Mass on Sunday, or to observe the prohibition of meat on Friday, are modern examples).

The punishment visited upon mortal sins could be voided through the sacrament of *penance*. In this sacrament are four elements—sorrow for sin, confession to the priest, absolution by the priest, satisfaction offered by the sinner. First there must be sorrow for sin: According to Thomas Aquinas, this must be contrition, genuine sorrow for sin; according to Duns Scotus, attrition, regret based on fear of consequences, may suffice (Catholic theology has tended to accept this latter view). In addition there must be confession to a priest. Confession of all mortal sins is required at least once a year; neglect of this duty becomes a mortal sin. Confession is followed by the priest's absolution, given, it is held, by Christ through the powers of the keys (Matt. 16:19): "I absolve thee of thy sins ... " Absolution takes from the sinner the eternal penalty due to sin, but leaves the temporal penalty, which must be borne either in this life or in purgatory. To lessen this temporal penalty, satisfaction (sometimes termed penance) is imposed—ordinarily some form of spiritual discipline.

In this connection the theory of indulgences is best understood. An indulgence is defined as remission of the temporal punishment due to sin when the eternal guilt has been removed; in other words, relaxation of the penalty of sin, ordinarily suffered in purgatory. The schoolmen taught that the pope could draw on the Treasury of Merits (an inexhaustible treasure because in addition to the surplus merits of the saints and of the Virgin Mary, there were the merits of the Lord Jesus Christ) and bestow this merit on the needy Christian who fulfilled the proper conditions. In the Middle Ages popes discovered that much money could be raised through the sale of indulgences; and such sales became one of the greatest abuses of the papal privilege.[1]

At the heart of Catholic worship—in the Middle Ages as today—stood the sacrament of *the Eucharist,* or *Lord's Supper.* It was observed then, as now, under two forms—the Mass and the Communion. In the Mass, only the priest partakes of the elements, in the Communion (mandatory for every Roman Catholic at least annually) the worshiper partakes of the bread (not the cup, which began to be withheld from the laity in the Middle Ages). In the early church three views of the Lord's Supper had been held: a "realistic" view, which taught that Christ was really present in the bread and wine, though the nature of that presence was not defined; a "symbolic" view (held, among others, by Augustine), which taught that the bread and wine were symbols of the body and blood of Christ; and a "metabolic" (from a Greek word meaning "to change") view, which taught that at the words of institution the bread and wine were in some sense, not clearly defined, changed into the body and blood of Christ. In the ninth century the *theory of transubstantiation* was first advanced— the theory that the bread and wine were transformed into the *historic* body of Christ, the same body that had once hung on the cross. This theory was combated by theologians of the period. "Never," exclaimed Maurus, "have I heard such language, never have I met with such ideas." He claimed in opposition that Christ has three bodies: the first, born of the Virgin Mary; the second, formed of the Eucharistic elements upon which the blessing of the Holy Ghost has descended; the third, constituted by the church. A third theologian (Ratramnus) argued that the bread and wine are *figuratively* the body and blood of the Savior. By the eleventh century, however, the theory of transubstantiation had won the day, and it was elaborated and defended by the great schoolmen of the later Middle Ages. Attendance upon the Mass, and participation in the Communion were supposed to bestow additional grace upon the worshiper, enabling him thus to avoid sin; it also made satisfaction for the temporal penalty due to sins, thus cutting down the time that would otherwise be spent in purgatory. Masses could also be said for souls now suffering in purgatory, so hastening their release.

Extreme unction (*now called the anointing of the sick*), the fifth sacrament, was based on the exhortation found in James 5:14. Gradually the anointing of the sick became a sacrament performed only for those in danger of death. The priest touched with a special ointment the eyes, ears, nose, mouth, hands, and feet of the dying man, saying, "Through this Holy Unction and His most holy mercy may the Lord remit whatever sins you may have committed through your sight [or hearing, smell, taste or speech, touch and footsteps]." This sacrament, which brings spiritual strength and forgiveness of sins, may also bring restoration to health, although of this there can be no assurance.

The five sacraments so far enumerated follow the Christian from the cradle to the grave. The sixth sacrament, and the first which is not for all, is that of *marriage*. A marriage of Catholics outside the Catholic Church is no true marriage. A marriage which for a variety of reasons is not properly performed or truly consummated may be annulled or set aside; a valid marriage can be terminated only by death.

Finally there is the sacrament of *ordination*—the sacrament which through the laying on of hands of bishops in the line of apostolic succession gives the clergyman his special character, one which enables him in turn to bestow grace through the other sacraments of the church; the power of the keys to absolve or refuse to absolve.

REGARDING THE CHURCH

In the doctrine of the sacraments it becomes particularly clear that there is no salvation outside the church. This dependence of the sinner upon the church for his salvation was one of the factors which made reformation of the church difficult, if not impossible.

But how can we distinguish the true church from the false? What are its marks? In the fifth century Augustine had named four essential characteristics, as expressed in the phrase "one holy catholic apostolic church." In the later Middle Ages a fifth mark had been added. It was now "one holy catholic apostolic *Roman* church." There was only one visible church; it was holy because it possessed the sacraments, which bestowed grace, from which holiness was derived; catholic, because universal; apostolic, because the apostles' authority had descended to their successors, the bishops; and Roman, because all were subordinate to the bishop of Rome, successor of Peter, Vicar of Christ. The supremacy of the pope as proclaimed by Gregory VII and his successors was accepted by Thomas Aquinas, who recognized the pope's right to issue new definitions of the faith, thus implying his infallibility. Subjection to the papacy, Aquinas taught, was necessary for salvation. There was, as we have seen, an alternative theory which appeared in the late Middle Ages, which accepted indeed the pope's position as titular head of the church, but which placed final authority in the hands of a general council. There were those too who denied his claim to temporal authority. It was, however, generally agreed that it was the duty of the state to protect the church and to punish heresy.

Thomas Aquinas developed the classical theory, which theoretically is still held by the Roman Catholic Church. According to

Aquinas, no one may be compelled to enter the Church. But once baptized he must be compelled, by violent means if necessary, to remain obedient to its faith. The sin of heresy, since it completely separates man from God, is the worst of all sins and hence deserves the worst possible punishment.

FOR CONSIDERATION

1. What basic beliefs do Roman Catholics and Protestants hold in common?
2. On what distinctive beliefs do Roman Catholics and Protestants differ?
3. Which of these differences would you regard as vital?
4. If a Protestant marrying a Roman Catholic solemnly promises not to bring up children born of the union in his (or her) faith, is he being true to his faith, true to his Lord?
*5. We intercede for our friends here on earth through our prayers. Is it improper for us to pray to the saints in heaven, asking them to intercede for us who are still on earth? If so, why?
6. There are advantages in having a single head to speak for the church. What are the disadvantages?
*7. Do Protestants need a substitute for the Roman Catholic confessional? Is there such a substitute?
8. What in your estimation is the value of the sacraments?
9. Are Roman Catholics to be recognized as fellow Christians?
10. Read Romans 1:16–17; 3:21–26. Is the doctrine here given by Paul at all like the doctrine of the Roman Catholic Church sketched above?

Saint Francis of Assisi Caring for the Leper

11
NEW MOVEMENTS STIR WITHIN THE CHURCH

IN THE LATE MIDDLE AGES new movements stirred within the church, profoundly influencing both its life and its thought. Four such movements we consider in the present chapter.

MONASTICISM

From the fourth century on, monasticism was the most characteristic institution of the church. It had begun as a lay movement, spontaneous, without rule or direction. Benedict's famous rule (p. 94 ff.) drawn up for his own monastery at Nursia proved so wise, so adapted to its age, that it became in time the basic rule for all western monasticism. The tenth century witnessed another important development: the rise of the Cluniac Order. Hitherto, each monastery had been a single unit, and its influence had been largely local. The monastery organized at Cluny (in France) early in the tenth century adopted a more rigid discipline than had become the custom. Asked to reform a sister monastery, it brought this second institution under the rule of its own abbot, and so with another and another, until finally it developed into the Cluniac Order. At the height of its power there were hundreds of monasteries in this order, all under the absolute control of one man, the abbot of Cluny. From this order came the Reform movement in the church which led first to its freedom from secular control, and then to its claim of papal supremacy over both church and state in the days of Pope Gregory VII. In the twelfth century the Cistercian Order came to the fore. Its most representative figure, Bernard of Clairvaux, dominated his age—as few men have done—solely by moral persuasion. If bishops, nobles, princes, or popes had any arduous work to perform, Bernard was their necessary ally. Peasants, knights, sovereigns, emperors, and even popes bent before his wrath. He was one of the most active public figures of his day, and yet his own desire and the ideal of his order (preserved to the present day among the Trappists, or Reformed Order of Cistercians) was a life of poverty, withdrawal from the world, and meditation. We are pointed to one of the sources of his strength in the hymn attributed to him (No. 215 in *The Hymnbook*):

> Jesus, Thou Joy of loving hearts,
>> Thou Fount of life, Thou Light of men,
> From the best bliss that earth imparts
>> We turn unfilled to Thee again.

In the thirteenth century came another important development in the monastic movement, one which was to change the character of the movement as a whole. This new development was the rise of the mendicant (or begging) orders. The ideal now came to be not withdrawal from the world, but service in the world; not meditation, but action. Members of these new orders were not monks (coming from a Greek root meaning "alone," "a solitary"), but friars (drawn from the Latin word "fratres," or "brothers"). Owning at the outset no property, they lived off of the gifts of the people. Later, as the orders grew wealthy, begging was continued as a practice in humility.

Francis of Assisi

Inspiration for this new development came from the life of Giovanni Bernardone, better known as Francis, the son of a well-to-do cloth merchant of Assisi in Central Italy. In his early days Francis was worldly, gay, and irresponsible. Gradually he became more serious, with a particular concern for the poor. But Francis had a love for the beautiful, and he shrank instinctively from all that was ugly or loathsome. Encountering a leper one day he spurred his horse along a bypath, flinging back a bit of gold to ease his conscience. Suddenly a great wave of pity swept over him; he turned back, dismounted, took money from his purse, and placed it with a courteous greeting in the man's hands. Then overcoming his fastidiousness, he embraced the leper. From that day the victory over himself was complete. He shrank from no man; he went daily to the lazar house, where lepers were confined, and performed willingly the humblest service for any he found in need.

His father, disgusted with his unbusinesslike ways, prepared to disinherit him. "Up to this time," replied Francis, "I have called Pietro Bernardone father, but now I am the servant of God. Not only the money but everything that can be called his, I will restore to my father, even the very clothes he has given me." Then stripping himself of his fine apparel, and clad only in a hair shirt, he strode away; as he entered the frosty woods he burst into song.

Gradually Francis' purpose matured—to live as Jesus had lived, with no permanent abode and no certain support, preaching to those who would listen the Good News of the Kingdom of God, ministering as he was able to those who were in need. He wore the simple garb of a peasant; when he lacked food he asked for a morsel of bread at the nearest house.

Later, when Francis had begun to gather about him a band of men who imitated him in his poverty, the bishop sent for him and pointed out the unpractical nature of a rule which forbade men to make any definite provision for their bodily needs. Francis replied, "If we have any possessions we should need weapons and laws to defend them. This would sometimes prevent us from loving God and our neighbors."

No one could doubt Francis' love for men. As Gilbert Chesterton has written:

> He ... saw the image of God multiplied but never monotonous. To him a man was always a man and did not disappear in a dense crowd any more than in a desert. ... What gave

him his extraordinary personal power was this; that from the pope to the beggar, from the sultan of Syria in his pavilion to the ragged robbers crawling out of the wood, there was never a man who looked into those brown burning eyes without being certain that Francis Bernardone was really interested in *him*. . . . [1]

He loved not men only, but all of God's creatures. Legends multiplied of how he preached to the birds, and how they stopped their twittering as he spoke; of how a fierce wolf came under his spell. The simplest things of life he received as the gift of God with its own place in God's economy for man. He did not call nature his mother, but it was Brother Fire which warmed him, and Sister Water which quenched his thirst. There was nothing sad or sanctimonious about Francis. He regarded himself rather as a troubadour of the Lord, and a song seemed to be always on his lips. Best known is his "Song of the Creatures," composed in his later days, when bodily afflictions had come upon him, and he had begun to lose his sight (see No. 100 in *The Hymnbook*):

> Praised be my Lord God with all his creatures, especially our
>   Brother the Sun . . .
> Praised be my Lord for Sister Moon and for the stars . . .
> Praised be my Lord for Brother Wind and for the air and
>   clouds and calms and all weathers . . .
> Praised be my Lord for Sister Water . . .
> Praised be my Lord for Mother Earth:
>   Who doth sustain and keep us, and bringeth forth various
>   fruits and colored flowers and grass.
> Praised be my Lord for Brother Fire,
> Through whom Thou givest light in darkness:
> And he is bright and pleasant and very mighty and strong.
> Praise ye and bless the Lord,
> And give thanks unto Him and serve Him with humility.

Disciples meanwhile had gathered about him, and Francis gave them a rule. It was based on three passages of Scripture: Matthew 16:24-26 ("If any man would come after me, let him deny himself ... "); 19:21 ("If you would be perfect, go, sell what you possess and give to the poor ... and come, follow me"); and Luke 9: 1–6 ("And he called the twelve together and gave them power and authority over all demons and to cure diseases, and he sent them out to preach the kingdom of God and to heal. ... ").

Such was the rule and such was the practice of the early Franciscans. As the order grew, the church with its usual instinct for order imposed other rules (mendicancy as a requirement for all members; a fixed costume; irrevocable vows) much to the grief of Francis, who finally withdrew from active control.

The story is told of how Francis in these latter days withdrew with three of his disciples, and went on alone to pray that he might feel in his own body the pain which his Lord had endured for him. Suddenly there came a dazzling vision of the Christ, and then sharp, excruciating pain, after which Francis bore in his body the stigmata, the wound prints that Christ had borne in his hands, his feet, and his side. The miracle of how they came to be is a legend, as is much else about the life of Francis, but regarding the fact of the stigmata themselves, there is now little doubt. They were due, we may well believe, to Francis' prolonged meditation on the sufferings which Christ had undergone for him, and which in turn had become the wellspring of his own love. That, as Rufus Jones has pointed out, and not the nail prints in his hands and feet, is the main wonder of Francis' life.

> The great wonder is the living fountain of love and joy which Christ poured into and through this 'poor little man.' He always knew where the real miracle lay. It was not in things that happened to his body, though they were wonderful enough. It was not to be found in the fact that birds and beasts, even the wolf of Gubbio, felt the spell of his spirit. It was the radiance of light and love breaking across the darkness and hate of his world and his time. He loved lepers. He loved robbers and changed their lives. He loved beggars in their rags. He loved rich men, too, and members of the Church, who needed him as much as the robbers did. He brought Christianity out of forms and creeds and services into the open air, into action and into the movements of life. He changed the entire line of march of

religion in the Western World. Brother Masseo, half jesting, asked him once why the whole world was running after him, not very comely, not very wise, not of noble birth. "Why after thee?" "God chose me," Francis answered, "because He could find no one more worthless, and He wished by me to confound the nobility and grandeur, the strength and beauty and learning of the world." But the real answer is that here at last in this wonderful man was an organ of that Spirit which was in Christ, and a marvelous transmitter of it to the world. The divine *agapé* [Christ-like love] went out into men's lives through him. Here was a childlike lover of men, ready, if need be, to be crucified for love, but also ready in humble everyday tasks to reveal this love.[2]

Peter Dominic

The second of the great mendicant orders, whose formal organization was approved by Pope Innocent III in the same year, was that of the Dominicans. Peter Dominic, its founder, was a Spaniard, disturbed by the way the masses were leaving a church, which had grown worldly and corrupt, and by the rise of new sects, stressing rigid morality and extreme simplicity of life. To richly dressed representatives of the church Dominic exclaimed:

> It is not by the display of power and pomp, a calvacade of retainers and richly housed palfreys, not by gorgeous apparel, that the heretics win proselytes. It is by zealous preaching, by apostolic humility, by austerity. Zeal must be met by zeal, humility by humility, false sanctity by real sanctity, preaching falsehood by preaching truth. Sow the good seeds as the heretics sow the bad. Cast off these sumptuous robes. Send away these brightly caparisoned palfreys. Go barefoot, without money or scrip like the apostles. Out-labor, out-fast, out-discipline these false teachers.

With such ideals before him Dominic founded his order of poor preachers. Francis had feared books—they too could turn men's minds from service to their fellowmen. Dominic was convinced, on the other hand, that to preach well, men must have the most thorough training. As a later minister-general put it: "The end of the order is not study, but study is most necessary for preaching and the salvation of souls."

From these two orders—the Franciscans and the Dominicans—came not only popular preachers, but also most of the scholars of the Middle Ages, and also the earliest scientists; later, many of the most self-denying missionaries. They, with other mendicant groups (Carmelites and Augustinians), won back to the church many whose hearts had been alienated. And yet in time the orders deteriorated. Francis and Dominic, recognizing that wealth corrupts, had planned that not only individuals, but also that their orders, hold no property. In time, nonetheless, the orders became heavily endowed, and the earlier ideals were obscured. As Philip Schaff has written:

> They were at first reformers themselves and offered an offset to the Cathari [a medieval sect, critical of the church's wealth and corruption] and the Poor Men of Lyons by their Apostolic self-denial and popular sympathies. But they degenerated into obstinate obstructors of progress in theology and civilization. From being the advocates of learning, they became the props of popular ignorance. The virtue of poverty was made the cloak for vulgar idleness and mendicancy for insolence.
>
> The changes set in long before the century closed in which the two orders had their birth. Bishops opposed them. The secular clergy [parish priests, the hierarchy] complained of them. The universities ridiculed and denounced them for their mock piety and vices ... The time came in the early part of the fifteenth century when the great teacher Gerson, in a public sermon, enumerated as the four persecutors of the Church, tyrants, heretics, antichrist and the Mendicants.[3]

And yet it was from the ranks of the mendicants that there came Martin Luther and others who would finally effect the great Reformation.

MYSTICISM

A second movement of importance arising in the Middle Ages was in the realm of mysticism. Mysticism may be defined as the direct intuition or experience of God; and a mystic is a person who has, to a greater or less degree, such a direct experience. There was a decided strain of mysticism in Paul, as well as in the writer of the Gospel According to John. And there has been a stream of mysticism running through the history of the church. In certain periods, however, great mystics have arisen, whose writings have become classics in the field, and who have continued to influence countless others in succeeding ages. The late Middle Ages saw such a flowering of mysticism. Bernard of Clairvaux was one of the early mystics of this period, and not a little of his mysticism is retained in the great hymn which we still love to sing, the first verse of which was quoted earlier in this chapter. It appears even stronger in the later verses—for example:

> We taste Thee, O Thou living Bread,
> And long to feast upon Thee still;
> We drink of Thee, the Fountain-head,
> And thirst our souls from Thee to fill.

The moment of ecstasy, when the mystic lost himself in the presence of God, came only rarely and for the moment. The mystic longed for the time when he might have an abiding sense of God's presence:

> O Jesus, ever with us stay,
> Make all our moments calm and bright;
> Chase the dark night of sin away,
> Shed o'er the world Thy holy light.

It was the later mystics—particularly Meister Eckhart and John Tauler in Germany, and John of Ruysbroeck from Holland—whose writings fed hungry groups of worshipers here and there in Europe and have continued to find their readers until the present time. Those who found their needs met in the mystical writings of the Middle Ages did not withdraw from the hierarchical church, but their souls were fed through their intimate communings with God—and priests and sacraments became of little importance. Much of the best in this German mysticism is gathered up in a little book called, strangely enough, *German Theology*. It remains to the present day one of the classics of Christian devotional literature. Even more widely read is *The Imitation of Christ*, written, or at least edited, by Thomas a Kempis, which in similar fashion gathers up much that is best in the

Dutch mysticism. It has its defects—stressing the negative virtues more than the positive and resignation rather than active service for Christ, and yet throughout the ages it has been probably the most widely read Christian classic next to the Bible itself. It is the imitation of Christ that the book proposes as our goal in life; we are exhorted not to imitate the outward details of Jesus' life, but rather to reflect his spirit.

Says the author:

> Of a surety at the day of judgment; it will be demanded of us, not what we have read, but what we have done; not how well we have spoken, but how holily we have lived.[4]

And again:

> What doth it profit thee to enter into deep discussion concerning the Holy Trinity, if thou·lack humility, and be thus displeasing to the Trinity? For verily it is not deep words that make a man holy and upright; It is a good life which makes a man dear to God. I had rather feel contrition than be skilful in the definition thereof. If thou knowest the whole Bible, and the sayings of all the philosophers, what should all this profit thee without the love and grace of God? *Vanity of vanities, all is vanity,* save to love God, and Him only to serve. That is the highest wisdom, to cast the world behind us, and to reach forward to the heavenly kingdom.[5]

It is self-criticism the author demands, not the criticism of others:

> Look well unto thyself; and beware that thou judge not the doings of others. In judging others a man laboureth in vain; he often erreth, and easily falleth into sin; but in judging and examining himself he always laboureth to good purpose.[6]

Thomas a Kempis begins by urging us to follow Jesus, but he passes quickly from following Jesus to fellowship with him, a fellowship which transforms the hidden springs of life, turning bitter waters into sweet, foulness into purity, and death into life.

> Grant me, most sweet and loving Jesus, [he cries] to rest in

Thee above every creature, above all health and beauty, above all glory and honour, above all power and dignity, above all knowledge and skilfulness, above all riches and arts, above all joy and exultation, above all fame and praise, above all sweetness and consolation, above all hope and promise, above all merit and desire, above all gifts and rewards . . .[7]

It is in such fellowship that he finds strength to achieve.

Out of this mystical movement developed a group of men who called themselves Brethren of the Common Lot. They took no monastic vows, but they held all things in common; they preached in the language of the people and developed schools which became the best in Europe. Out of these schools, and under such influence, came men who would take the lead in the Reformation of the church.

CRITICISM AND DISSENT

A third important movement gathering strength in the Middle Ages was a movement of criticism and dissent. It represented a growing protest against the worldliness of the church, the wealth and dissoluteness of many of its clergy, and the efficacy attached to sacraments as administered by unworthy priests.

In the twelfth century the protest was voiced by individual critics, lowly men for the most part, and too far in advance of their age to develop a wide following. They came to a cruel end, sometimes at the hands of a mob.

In the following century the movement gained momentum. Antichurchly sects now appeared, and whole areas were disaffected. How many of these sects there were cannot be estimated with any accuracy. One writer in this century gives 19 as the number; another, 72; still another, 130. No doubt, however, many of these represented the same movement under different names.

Most important of these sects were the Cathari (or Albigenses) and the Waldensians. The Cathari were a dualistic sect, claiming the Bible as the basis of their religion, but departing widely from the Catholic faith. By 1200 their numbers had reached menacing proportions. The Dominican Rainerius gave four million as their number. Joachim of Flora stated that they were sending out their emissaries like locusts. Such statements are no doubt exaggerated, but they reveal a widespread religious unrest. Men did not know to what the heresy might lead.

The Waldensians were the disciples of Peter Waldo, originally a merchant in Lyons. He became convinced that the Bible was the supreme authority in the church, and that all men, and not merely the priests, were commissioned to proclaim its truths. When the church sought to silence him, Waldo and his followers refused to obey. The movement grew, becoming more and more hostile to Roman dogma. The Waldensians objected to the rites and sacraments of the church, the use of images, the doctrine of purgatory, and other elements of the hierarchical system. They set up a church of their own with a system of democratic rule. Their economic organization tended toward Christian communism. By the end of the fifteenth century the Waldensians had perhaps 100,000 members in France and Italy, with an equal number in Switzerland, Germany, and Moravia.

To win back the disaffected multitudes the church dispatched missionaries. It was largely for this purpose that Peter Dominic had organized his order of poor preachers. The princes were called upon to crush the movement, particularly in southern France, where the heretics were most numerous. When they delayed, first Alexander III, and later Innocent III, proclaimed a crusade against the disaffected area. Those guilty were to be shown no mercy, and if some who were innocent were slain along with the guilty, the Lord would know his own. Writes Schaff:

> The papal policy had met with complete but blighting success and, after the thirteenth century, heresy in Southern France was almost like a noiseless underground stream. Languedoc at the opening of the wars had been one of the most prosperous and cultured parts of Europe. At their close, its villages and vineyards were in ruins, its industries shattered, its population impoverished and decimated. The country that had given promise of leading Europe in a renaissance of intellectual culture fell behind her neighbors in the race of progress.[8]

The Cathari as an organized movement were completely destroyed; Waldensians, however, survived, particularly in the Swiss mountains; and exist today in Italy and the United States, as a branch of the Reformed or Presbyterian Church.

A synod which met in Toulouse in 1229 took steps to prevent such heresies from arising in the future. One step was to prohibit laymen from reading the Scripture. This prohibition was a local one, applying specifically to the areas where the danger had arisen. But it became a policy of the Roman Catholic Church to discourage or forbid the reading of the Scriptures in the vernacular by laymen. They could learn what was necessary from the clergy, and the danger of heretical interpretation might thus be avoided. At this synod also steps were taken to establish the Papal Inquisition. Heretofore each bishop had a responsibility for rooting out heresy in his own diocese. This procedure had proved ineffective. Now the machinery for ferreting out and punishing heresy was concentrated in the hands of the pope, who placed responsibility in turn on the Dominicans. Under their administration the Inquisition became one of the most dread agencies of repression that history has known. A man accused of heresy was not permitted to face his accusers, torture was habitually used to extract confession, those convicted were commonly burned at the stake. By such means reform was postponed, and the immediate danger to the church was averted.

In the fourteenth century, however, as we have seen, the abuses of the Avignon papacy (see chapter 9, especially pages 132 ff.) and the scandals accompanying the Great Schism raised up stout opponents of papal pretensions—such men as Dante, who rejected the temporal claims of the papacy, and Marsilius, who questioned his claims to spiritual authority. Also there were Conciliarists, who advanced the views endorsed by the great reforming councils that supreme authority was vested in a general council rather than in the pope. In the end these claims came to nought, and men came to see that the needed reformation of the church could not be effected by a general council.

In the fourteenth and fifteenth centuries came other men, now popularly known as "Reformers before the Reformation." The first of these was John Wycliffe (1324–1384), a professor in the University of Oxford. He advanced the theory that the church was the body of the elect (rather than the hierarchy as taught by the earlier schoolmen), that Jesus Christ was its only head, and that the Bible was its only law. He became more and more critical of the papacy, which finally he denounced as anti-Christ; he also condemned other institutions and practices of the church. Under his auspices the Bible was translated from the official Latin into English, and an order of poor preachers (taking no monastic vows) was instituted to circulate copies of this Scripture among the people.

Wycliffe was forced out of his position in the university but was protected from further persecution by the government, because of services rendered. Wycliffe's translation of the Scripture, however, was repudiated by the church, and in 1408 an ominous act was passed that no man by his own authority should translate the Bible into English or any other tongue, until such translation was approved by the bishop. Six years later the reading of the English Scriptures was forbidden upon pain of forfeiture "of land, cattle, life, and goods from their heirs forever." The following year a committee of four appointed by the Council of Constance to examine the heresies of Wycliffe and his disciple John Hus brought in an interim report. Wycliffe was condemned on no less than 260 different counts. His writings were ordered to be burned, and his bones to be dug up and cast out of the consecrated ground. In the spring of 1428 this was done. Wycliffe's bones were disinterred, burned to ashes, and then cast in the little River Swift, "to the damnation and destruction of his memory." "His vile corpse," wrote Netter, "they consigned to hell and the river absorbed his ashes."

Wycliffe's teachings were given wider circulation by John Hus, who thus became the second of the "Reformers before the Reformation." Hus, professor in the University of Prague, was not so radical as Wycliffe, but he was excommunicated first for spreading Wycliffe's doctrines, and later for opposing a sale of indulgences to finance one of the pope's personal crusades. The teachings of Hus continued to spread through Bohemia (modern Czechoslovakia), and Hus was finally invited to appear before the Council of Constance, under promise given by the Emperor Sigismund that he would be allowed to return in safety to his own people. This promise was conveniently ignored (the council ruled that a promise given to a heretic was not binding) Hus was not allowed to speak in his own defense. When he refused to recant, the council ordered that he be burned at the stake. Before the torch was applied he was given a final opportunity to recant, but this also he declined. "In the truth which I have proclaimed, according to the gospel of Jesus Christ and the expositions of holy teachers," he affirmed, "I will, this day, joyfully die." As the flames arose about him, Hus began to chant the Catholic burial prayer, "Christ, Thou Son of God, have mercy upon us." At the third line of the chant a gust of wind dashed the smoke and sparks into his face. His lips moved faintly in silent prayer, but the last words had been spoken. The agony fortunately was short.

Third of the "Reformers before the Reformation" was Savonarola, a Dominican friar in the city of Florence. Savonarola did not question the doctrines of the church; he was, rather, a preacher of righteousness. He became involved in the political life of the times, but his fatal mistake was his castigation of the notorious Borgian pope, Alexander VI. On his account the pope placed the city of Florence under an interdict. The tide of popular favor turned against the great preacher. Giving way under torture, he was hanged, mutilated, and burned.

It had become quite clear that anyone who opposed the ecclesiatical "system" did so at peril of his life.

THE RENAISSANCE

The Renaissance has been defined by Webster as a transition movement between the medieval and modern world. Included in the wider movement was a literary phase, which, particularly in Italy, the land of its birth, was based on a new appreciation of the classical literature of Greece and Rome. This in turn led to freedom from the intellectual bondage to which individuals had been subjected by the theology and hierarchy of the church, and to a new emphasis on present life, its beauty and its satisfactions. The Renaissance scholars became known as humanists.

North of the Alps where the Renaissance bore its more enduring fruits, the humanists were more interested in the early Christian literature. This in turn stimulated a desire for the reformation of the church in accordance with the Scriptures and the writings of the church fathers.[9]

Most influential of these humanists, and the dominating literary figure of his age, was Erasmus. Some of his most popular writings were those which ridiculed the many superstitious beliefs of the church. Erasmus had no desire to become a martyr; he did not openly attack. He only intimated—delicately, with keen irony and gentle wit; a course which afforded the Inquisition no opportunity to silence him. More important were his editions of various church fathers—edited, with notes; more important still was his Greek New Testament, brought out in 1516, also with footnotes, and with a preface, which expressed the hope that the Bible would be translated from the original language into the vernacular of every land, so that in time even the plowboy would become better acquainted with the Scriptures than then were even the priests.

When the Reformation broke there were those who charged that Erasmus laid the egg which Luther hatched. "Yes," Erasmus replied, "but I laid a hen's egg, Luther hatched a game cock."

There are some, even today, who think it would have been better if the Reformation had come as these humanists desired—slowly, gradually, by a process of education, without destroying the unity of the church. But something more was needed: a religious revival, in which men's dependence upon a hierarchical priesthood for salvation would be broken, and common people would be led to understand that they could come to God directly in penitence and faith and so find pardon for their sins.

This was the work, not of Erasmus and his fellow humanists, though they put essential tools into the Reformers' hands, but of Martin Luther, an Augustinian friar in the city of Wittenberg.

FOR CONSIDERATION

1. Is it possible or desirable to live a life in exact imitation of Christ (the ideal of Francis)? What would you suggest as an alternative?

2. Is it possible and desirable to have Protestant orders similar to those of the Catholic Church? Consult an Episcopal minister for information about Anglican orders, or a Lutheran friend regarding deaconesses.

3. What value is there in accepting a specific discipline for the

cultivation or expression of the religious life? What are some of the items which might well be included in such a discipline?

4. What mystical experiences are recorded in the Scriptures? Where?

5. Is the mystical experience desirable for the average Christian today? Is it possible, do you think, for all Christians to have such experiences? Do you know any mystics?

6. Does Protestantism give sufficient encouragement to mystical religion?

7. Consider carefully Bernard of Clairvaux's great hymn, "Jesus, Thou Joy of Loving Hearts." Can you paraphrase the thought of this hymn in meaningful prose? What does it mean to you?

*8. Is there danger that the modern church, our own denomination, will fail to heed the critics to whom it should listen, as did the church in latter Middle Ages? In what areas of church life is criticism most needed?

*9. What are the dangers of censorship? Can censorship in any form be defended? How can the church encourage the reading of the best religious literature?

10. How is error in the church to be repressed? In society as a whole?

*11. Consider the Scripture passages chosen by Francis as the basis of his order—Matthew 16:24–26; 19:21; Luke 9:1–6. What meaning do these verses have for us today?

Part III
THE
REFORMATION

IN WHICH PROTESTANTS

SEEK TO REFORM THE CHURCH

ACCORDING TO

NEW TESTAMENT IDEALS

The Christian Church in Europe About 1565 A.D. Boundary line separates predominantly Protestant from Roman Catholic countries. Horizontal shading indicates Catholics; vertical shading indicates Protestants. Pockets of Protestantism existed in Catholic areas, such as France, and Catholicism in Germany and England.

PROTESTANT

SCOTLAND
Edinburgh
Glasgow

Belfast
IRELAND

WALES ENGLAND
London

Brussels

Paris
FRANCE

CATHOLIC

Geneva

PORTUGAL

SPAIN

NORWAY

SWEDEN

DENMARK

Leyden Wittenberg
Cologne
GERMANY
Worms

Basle
SWITZERLAND

PAPAL
STATES
Rome

SARDINIA

FINLAND

ORTHODOX

Warsaw
POLAND

AUSTRIA
Vienna

HUNGARY

Salzburg

MOSLEM

SICILY

Martin Luther Burning the Papal Bull and Other Books

12
LUTHERAN CHURCHES ARE ESTABLISHED

THE REFORMATION which finally shattered the unity of western Christendom came as the climax of the long movement of criticism and dissent which we have briefly traced. The "Reformers" continued to regard themselves as Catholic Christians, but when the hierarchy sought to silence and finally excommunicated them, they repudiated the authority of the pope; they did not seek to found a new church but rather to reform the existing church in accordance with New Testament ideals.

MARTIN LUTHER

This new Reformation movement appeared first in Germany, under the leadership of Martin Luther.

Luther came from peasant stock, but his father accumulated enough worldly goods to send his son through the university. Martin took his bachelor's and his master's degrees and was about to enter upon the study of law when suddenly, to his father's great distress, he entered a monastery. His rise here was rapid. He was ordained as a

166

priest, returned to the university that he might take his doctor's degree, became a professor of theology in the newly established University of Wittenberg, a popular preacher, and a district vicar of the Augustinian Order with eleven monasteries under his care. *wm. Booth!*

Meanwhile he was undergoing an intense religious experience. Luther had entered the monastery that he might become certain of salvation. "I was a good monk," he later recalled, "and I kept the rule of my order so strictly that I may say that if ever a monk got to heaven by his monkery it was I. All my brothers in the monastery who knew me will bear me out. If I had kept on any longer, I should have killed myself with vigils, prayers, readings, and other work."[1] But according to the ideas of the time, a man was not "justified"— that is, finally forgiven and accepted by God—until he was actually righteous or just in the eyes of God; and that, Luther knew he was not. In his commentary on Galatians 2:18 Luther recalled that when he confessed his sins to a fellow monk (as he did, so he was told, with unnecessary frequency) absolution was pronounced in the following form:

> God forgive thee my brother. The merit of the passion of our Lord Jesus Christ, and of blessed S. Mary, always a virgin, and of all the saints: the merit of thine order, the straitness of thy religion, the humility of thy confession, the contrition of thy heart, the good works which thou hast done and shall do for the love of our Lord Jesus Christ, be unto thee available for the remission of thy sins, the increase of merit and grace, and the reward of everlasting life. Amen.[2]

Luther found that he could not love the God who forgave men on such terms and feared that he had committed the unpardonable sin. Relief came at long last when he discovered through intense Bible studies the true meaning of the Pauline doctrine of *justification by faith*—that God freely forgives and receives us into his fellowship, as though we were righteous, through faith in Jesus; that we are not accepted because of our good works, which always fall short of what God desires, but that good works follow from the new relationship established with God through faith. Luther did not suspect that this newly understood truth (which was to become the first basic Protes-

Principle of Protestant #1 Faith

faith: Luther Wesley Booth

Innocence of His Belief

tant belief) would end in his expulsion from the official church of his day. He taught joyously the Bible as he had come to understand it, and students were drawn to the university in increasing numbers by his growing fame.

MARTIN LUTHER'S PROTESTATIONS

In the year 1517 Pope Leo X ordered a sale of indulgences, that funds might be secured for the building of a great cathedral (St. Peter's) in Rome. These indulgences offered some unusual advantages—among others it was promised that by using them, souls could be released immediately from purgatory, and that those securing indulgences for the dead need not themselves be contrite and confess their sins. This service for departed loved ones was strongly emphasized by Tetzel, a dynamic salesman who hawked his wares in Luther's territory. Cried he:

> As soon as the coin in the coffer rings,
> The soul from purgatory springs.[3]

Distressed by the effect of such high-pressure salesmanship on members of his parish, Luther preached against indulgences, and on October 31, 1517, posted on the university bulletin board (the church door) ninety-five Latin theses which, according to customary academic procedure, he was prepared to defend in public debate. In these theses Luther maintained that the church could impose and relax its own discipline, but that it could not extend its discipline beyond the grave—that was in God's hands alone. Forgiveness for sins could not be bought; it could be secured, and secured only through repentance and faith.

Enterprising printers scattered a translation of Luther's theses throughout Germany. Luther's propositions were plain and to the point. The sale of indulgences dropped sharply. Luther had assumed that the pope would sustain him in his contention, but soon learned otherwise. This led him to investigate the sources of papal authority; he found to his surprise that it had no historical basis. In the year 1519 in Leipzig, he met in debate an erstwhile friend, Professor Eck of Ingolstadt, who forced Luther to acknowledge that he could accept neither the authority of the pope on this question, nor that of a gen-

NOTE

eral council, since both in the past had erred. Luther took his stand rather on the sole authority of the Scripture (which came to be accepted as the second basic principle of Protestantism).

#2
Artie le
of
Protestant
Faith

A papal bull (special decree) excommunicating Luther and sentencing him to be punished as an obstinate heretic (i.e., burned at the stake) was issued the following year. All princes, magistrates, and citizens were exhorted on threat of excommunication and promise of reward to seize Luther and his followers, and to turn them over to the proper authorities. Places which harbored them were threatened with the interdict (see p. 134). Christians were forbidden to read, print, or publish any of his books and were commanded to burn them.

Luther retaliated by publicly burning the pope's bull—a fiery signal of his absolute and final separation from Rome. Such open defiance helped to free multitudes from the fear that long kept them in bondage to the church. In this same year (1520) Luther issued a number of important treatises, in which basic principles of the Reformation were clearly set forth. The first of these treatises, addressed "To the Christian Nobility of the German Nation," stressed, among other things, the priesthood of all believers. In accordance with this #3 doctrine all believers have the right of immediate access to God; the claim that they are dependent upon a mediating priesthood for salvation is false; in others words, there is no essential difference between clergy and laity, except that each has his own office and work in the household of faith.

The second of these great Reformation treatises had to do with "The Babylonian Captivity of the Church"—i.e., the sacramental system of the church; the theory that saving grace was available only through the sacraments as administered by the priests of the church. Sacraments Only two sacraments, Luther taught, were to be accepted as coming from Christ himself: baptism and the Lord's Supper. The value of key these sacraments depended upon one's faith in the promise which they embodied. Somewhat inconsistently, however, Luther retained his belief in the baptismal regeneration of infants—not, of course, through their own faith, but through the faith of their parents. In regard to the Lord's Supper Luther rejected the theory of transubstantiation but fell back on an alternative view which had appeared in the late Middle Ages, that at the words of institution the physical body of

Christ came to be in, with, and under the elements of bread and wine, so that the communicant partook of both bread and the physical body of Christ. This theory, still retained in Lutheran confessional statements, was to have important historical consequences.

NOTE A third treatise appearing this same year, "On Christian Liberty," developed twin theses. "A Christian man is a perfectly free Lord of all, subject to none. A Christian man is a perfectly dutiful servant of all, subject to all." It is, in fact, a devotional tract, based on the principles set forth in Paul's Letter to the Galatians, particularly chapter 5. Through faith a Christian is free from obedience to law as a means of salvation; through faith he is bound in love to serve God and man.

Another treatise issued this year was "On Good Works." In this important work, Luther developed the idea of Christian vocation: that there is no superior merit in entering monastery or convent; that one may serve God acceptably in his own vocation, whether that be important or unimportant in the eyes of men. As Williston Walker has said,

Read

> This vindication of the natural human life as the best field for the service of God, rather than the unnatural limitations of asceticism, was to be one of Luther's most important contributions to Protestant thought, as well as one of his most significant departures from ancient and mediaeval Christian conceptions.[4]

Luther's prince, Frederick the Wise, refused to surrender Luther as demanded in the papal bull, until he had had an opportunity to appear before the German Diet. This opportunity came in 1521, when Luther was summoned to appear before the Diet meeting this year in the city of Worms (pronounced "Vormss"). Luther knew that his safe conduct might be disregarded, as had been the case with Hus a century earlier. Friends urged him not to risk his neck. Luther replied that he would go to Worms if there were as many devils there as tiles upon the rooftops. He was willing to take the risk that he might present his case before a court of his nation. But he was given no opportunity to speak in defense of his beliefs; he was simply ordered to recant. He asked for twenty-four hours to consider his reply.

On the next day the atmosphere was tense with excitement.

"Do you wish to defend the books which are recognized as your work? Or to retract anything contained in them?" asked the court official.

Luther replied that his books were not all of the same kind. Some were simple works of piety, which not even his adversaries had condemned. These he certainly could not retract.

In a second category were works attacking various papal abuses which were evident to all. Said Luther:

> If then I recant these, the only effect will be to add strength to such tyranny, to open not the windows but the main doors to such blasphemy, which will thereupon stalk farther and more widely than it has hitherto dared. . . .
>
> The third kind consists of those books which I have written against private individuals, so-called; against those, that is, who have exerted themselves in defense of the Roman tyranny and to the overthrow of that piety which I have taught. I confess that I have been more harsh against them than befits my religious vows and my profession. For I do not make myself out to be any kind of saint, nor am I now contending about my conduct but about Christian doctrine. But it is not in my power to recant them, because that recantation would give that tyranny and blasphemy an occasion to lord it over those whom I defend and to rage against God's people more violently than ever.[5]

It might be, Luther went on to indicate, that here and there he was in error. If any such errors could be pointed out to him, proven to be such from Scripture, he would be the first to cast his writings into the fire.

The "Orator of the Empire" replied that his answer was not to the point: He was being asked for a simple reply, without beating about the bush, to the question: "Was he prepared to recant, or no?"

Replied Luther then:

> Your Imperial Majesty and Your Lordships demand a simple answer. Here it is, plain and unvarnished. Unless I am convicted of error by the testimony of Scripture or (since I put no

trust in the unsupported authority of Pope or of councils, since it is plain that they have often erred and often contradicted themselves) by manifest reasoning I stand convicted by the Scriptures to which I have appealed, and my conscience is taken captive by God's word, I cannot and will not recant anything, for to act against our conscience is neither safe for us, nor open to us.

On this I take my stand. I can do no other. God help me. Amen.[6]

So Martin Luther, in the name of conscience, taken captive by the Word, took his stand against the highest authority of both church and state.

THE PEASANTS' REBELLION

After his departure from the Diet, Luther was placed under the ban of the empire, and so, excommunicated by the pope and banned by the empire (a double sentence of death), he remained until the close of his days. He had been protected from the beginning, and remained protected until the end, by his prince, Frederick the Wise. Other German rulers were won to the cause of the gospel. For a time, indeed, it seemed as if the whole nation might rally behind Luther. In 1524, however, there occurred a disastrous Peasants' Rebellion. The peasants, who suffered under many grievous disabilities, looked to Luther for support. He sympathized at the first, but when they resorted to violence, turned bitterly against them. "It is better that the peasants be killed," he wrote, "than that the princes and magistrates perish, because the rustics took the sword without divine authority." The uprising was put down, and the final condition of the peasants was worse than the first. Luther had lost the sympathies of the peasants; many of the rulers, previously inclined toward the evangelical gospel, drew back, convinced that the new religious movement carried within it the seeds of revolution. Germany from this time was divided into two camps, Protestant and Roman Catholic, drawing ever closer to armed conflict.

THE DEVELOPMENT OF THE EVANGELICAL CHURCHES

Evangelical churches meanwhile had been formed in the states whose rulers followed Luther. Distrusting the common people (because of the Peasants' Revolt), Luther was content for the government of these churches to fall into the hands of the princes. They ruled absolutely in civil affairs; they now assumed responsibility for the churches as well. So began a union of church and state in Germany that further alienated the people and would cost the church dear in the years that were to come.

In worship Luther approved only those changes necessitated by *worship* the gospel. He introduced the use of everyday German in place of the traditional Latin; gave new importance to the sermon; sponsored congregational singing (heretofore confined to the choir loft), and himself wrote both words and music for hymns (the best known of which is "A Mighty Fortress Is Our God"); reduced the number of church festivals, but preserved those connected with the life and work of Jesus, the Advent, Christmas, Epiphany, Easter, Ascension, Whitsuntide, and the Festival of the Trinity, for example. He retained also many elements of the traditional service, particularly portions of the ritual which were not opposed to the gospel.

The earliest doctrinal statements of the new movement were drawn up as confessions of faith—on which rulers and people were willing to stand, even at the cost of their lives. First and most important of these was the Augsburg Confession. It was written by Melanchthon, Luther's younger colleague on the university faculty, and presented to the Diet of Augsburg (1530) as a statement of the truths for which the Lutheran princes were prepared to contend. It remains the basic confession of world Lutheranism to the present day.

Luther made a major contribution to his cause when he translated *Bible* first the New Testament and later the Old Testament from the origi- *TRANSLATION* nal languages into German. This great translation remains the Bible of the German people. Luther also prepared a smaller and a larger catechism, which were used to train members of the Lutheran churches, and particularly their children, in the tenets of the faith.

The word "Protestant" became attached to the evangelical movement without premeditation—by what might be termed an historical accident. Lutheran princes at the Diet of Speyer (1529), confronted with hostile legislation intended to restrict the Reformation movement, declared that if their plea for redress was not heard they must protest and testify publicly before God "that they could consent to nothing contrary to His Word." Gradually the name "Protestant" came to be applied to all of those who protested against Roman Catholic departure from scriptural truth.

In his forty-second year Luther married a former nun, Catherine von Bora, for whom the Reformer had failed to find a husband. As many convents were closed or closing, many nuns had no homes to which they could return, and Luther felt responsible to find husbands for them. Miss von Bora, hard to please, finally suggested that she would consent to marry Luther himself, and so it happened. A very happy marriage it turned out to be (there were six children). According to his biographer, Roland H. Bainton, Luther did more than any other person to determine the tone of German domestic relations for the next four centuries. It was based on the patriarchal idea of the home, of which the father was undeniably the head.

By 1546 (the year of Luther's death) the emperor of Germany, also king of Spain and ruler of the Netherlands, felt that he was strong enough to crush the Reformation in Germany by force of arms. In the earlier phase of the struggle—the first Schmalkaldic War (1546–1547)—he appeared to have succeeded in this effort. In the second Schmalkaldic War (1552), however, the Protestant princes recovered freedom of action. Three years later the Peace of Augsburg brought the first stage of the Reformation struggle in Germany to an end. Two religions were recognized as legitimate: the Roman Catholic and the Lutheran (not the Reformed); each prince was to determine the religion of his own state.

There followed an uneasy truce which culminated finally in the Thirty Years War (1618–1648), when once again a Roman Catholic ruler, with the aid of Spanish troops, sought to crush Protestantism in Germany. This war ended with the Treaty of Westphalia, which recognized three religions as legitimate (Roman Catholicism, Lutheranism, and the Reformed or Presbyterian faith). The princes might still determine the religion of their state, but toleration was granted to adherents of the other faiths (except that no privileges were granted to Protestants in Austria or Bohemia). So ended the effort to crush the Reformation by force in Germany.

The Lutheran faith, meanwhile, had penetrated the Scandinavian countries, which remain officially Lutheran to the present time.

FOR CONSIDERATION

*1. What is the heart and center of Paul's gospel as set forth in Romans 1:1–17; 3:9–26; Galatians 5:1—6:10?

*2. How would you explain simply to a Roman Catholic the Protestant understanding of justification by faith, the sole authority of Scripture, the priesthood of all believers?

 3. "What other implications are there in the affirmation that we must place our trust in Christ alone? To what extent, from day to day, are we tempted to place our trust in ourselves rather than in Christ?"[7]

*4. What do you believe the job of the minister is? On what grounds are certain functions restricted only to those who are ordained (e.g., why does he alone baptize)?

 5. What is the meaning of the "priesthood of all believers"? Can it be said that every believer is his own priest?

 6. Should we make more of the great days of the church year: Christmas, Good Friday, Easter, Pentecost?

*7. What, as you see it, is the significance of infant baptism? the Lord's Supper?

 8. What light does Luther's own personal experience cast on his great hymn, "A Mighty Fortress Is Our God?"

*9. How would you explain to a Roman Catholic the distinctive Protestant views of the sacraments as over against the Roman Catholic view?

10. What distinctive values does the Lutheran Church have to offer to ecumenical Christianity?

11. The Roman Catholic Church claims that an infallible Bible has little value unless there is also an infallible church. What can the Protestant say in reply?

John Calvin Explaining His Reforms to the City Council of Geneva

13
REFORMED AND PRESBYTERIAN CHURCHES SPREAD

TWO MAJOR REFORMATION MOVEMENTS developed on the continent of Europe: one, under the leadership of Martin Luther, gave rise to the Lutheran Churches, whose nominal membership remains the largest of any family of churches within the Protestant fold; the second, under the leadership first of Ulrich Zwingli and then of John Calvin, gave rise to the Reformed Churches on the continent of Europe and the Presbyterian Churches in Great Britain and its colonies —the most widely distributed family of Protestants, and perhaps the largest in bona fide membership.[1]

IN SWITZERLAND

This second movement arose in democratic Switzerland, officially a part of the Holy Roman (German) Empire, but actually independent.

Ulrich Zwingli

Zwingli, a contemporary of Luther, had been trained as a student to regard the Scriptures as the final source of authority. In Zürich,

176

one of the leading cities in Switzerland, he preached through the various books of the Bible in order, noting the church's departures from its teaching as he went. Certain citizens of the town broke the Lenten fast, citing Zwingli's views of Scripture as their authority. Zwingli spoke and wrote in their defense, and was upheld by the city council, which thereby in effect assumed control of the church. Three years later (1525), after a series of debates in which the council accepted Zwingli's interpretation of Scripture, the Reformation in this city was complete. There was no separation of church and state, but Zürich was a free city, and church and state were governed jointly by a council chosen by citizens who were also members of the church.

The Reformation here was more thorough than that under Luther. Worship, for example, was freed from all traces of medieval superstition; the churches were purged of pictures, relics, crucifixes, altars, candles, and other ornaments; the frescoes were effaced and the walls whitewashed. Luther, as later John Calvin, favored a weekly observance of the Lord's Supper. Zwingli introduced the custom of quarterly observance. On these occasions he took his place at the head of a simple table which was covered with a white linen cloth and on which were placed communion cups and plates of wood. After praying and reading in German the "words of institution" (i.e., 1 Cor. 11:23–26), with other pertinent Scripture passages, Zwingli and his assistants partook of the bread and wine and then distributed these sacred symbols among the people.

Luther and Zwingli agreed on major evangelical doctrines—justification by faith, the sole authority of Scripture, the priesthood of all believers—but differed in their conception of the Lord's Supper. Luther, as we have seen, believed that our Lord's physical body came to be in, with, and under the bread, so that in the sacrament the worshiper partook of both bread and body of Christ. Zwingli, on the other hand, looked upon the rite as a simple memorial feast, in which bread and wine were only symbols of the body of Christ. To Luther this was a fundamental difference, and at an important conference held at Marburg in 1529 he refused to give Zwingli the hand of brotherhood, saying, "Your spirit is different from mine." From that time the two movements (Lutheran and Reformed) went their separate ways.

There were also differences in outlook between the two great Reformers, differences which perpetuated themselves in their respective movements. Dr. McGiffert draws the lines too closely, but indicates the difference in emphases:

> Instead of giving the controlling place in Christian thought to a personal religious experience—the consciousness of divine forgiveness—[as Luther had done, Zwingli] gave it to a theoretical doctrine—the absolute and unconditioned will of God. Instead of viewing the Christian life as the free and spontaneous expression of gratitude to God [Zwingli] conceived it as obedience to the divine will revealed in the Scriptures. Instead of finding the significance of the Bible in the proclamation of the gospel of God's forgiving love in Christ, he found it in its revelation of the divine will, and made it an authoritative code for the government of Christian life and thought, rather than a means of grace. In all these matters the Reformed wing of Protestantism followed (Zwingli) rather than Luther . . . [2]

Zwingli's influence spread beyond Zürich, in six of the thirteen Swiss cantons (districts) and down the Rhine country, as far as Strassburg. In 1531 he was killed in an armed struggle between Protestant and Roman Catholic cantons, and leadership of the Reformed movement passed into other hands.

John Calvin

Most important of these later leaders was John Calvin. Calvin was born in a middle-class home in Noyon, a town in northern France, in the year 1509. He received his bachelor's degree from the University of Paris, continued his studies in the Universities of Orléans and Bourges, graduated in law, though he never practiced, returned instead to Paris, where he became one of a little group of humanists, interested in the production of literature. His first book, a commentary on Seneca, established his reputation as a scholar. In 1533 he became a Protestant. We know little of his conversion experience. Something of its significance, however, was pictured later in his personal seal—a flaming heart on the palm of an extended hand, symbolizing his whole-hearted commitment to the living God. A decision to become Protestant was not without its dangers. In 1533, the same year in which Calvin was converted, his close friend, Nicholas Cop, delivered his inaugural address as rector of the University of Paris. In this address Cop championed Protestant positions. As a consequence, both he and Calvin were compelled to flee. Three years later Calvin, still a young man only twenty-seven years of age, issued the first edition of his famous *Institutes of the Christian Religion*, a book which placed him at once in the front rank of the Reformers. The *Institutes* was a handbook of the Christian faith intended for both ministers and laymen. It was by far the ablest statement, the clearest exposition of evangelical principles, yet to appear. As such it became Protestantism's most effective weapon, defensively and also offensively. Calvin's great service here was not that of an original thinker, but that of a systematic theologian, able to set forth the Protestant positions more clearly, systematically, and persuasively than any other. Though he agreed generally with Luther and other Reformers who preceded him there were some distinctive positions of his own. With Zwingli he put great emphasis on the sovereignty of God—God's sovereign power exercised in history, God's sovereign grace experienced in redemption, God's sovereign will revealed in Scripture. He rejected Luther's doctrine of baptismal regeneration, but held that children of believing parents were included in the covenant promise and entitled therefore to the sacrament of baptism. The Lord's Supper was more than a symbol as Zwingli had taught; Christ was really present in the sacrament, but spiritually, not physically, as Luther contended. Calvin agreed with Luther that the church existed wherever the gospel was truly preached and the sacraments rightly administered, but he taught, as Luther did not, that the church ought to draw its pattern of worship, organization, and discipline from the Bible. All the elect, he held, are knit together as the different members of a Body of which Christ is the sole head and are called not only to the same inheritance of eternal life, but to a participation of one God and of one flock. We are under obligation, he declared, to cultivate the communion of the universal, visible church. " . . . There are not several churches," he insisted, "but only one, which is extended throughout all the world."

Calvin also put more emphasis than Luther had done on the necessity of "good works": we are not saved, he taught, by good works, but neither are we saved without them; the church, through its instruction and through its discipline, had a responsibility to see that these good works were performed. Calvin also taught, as Luther did not, that church and state must labor together to build a Christian society.

Shortly after the publication of the *Institutes* Calvin passed through Geneva on his way to Basel, where he hoped to find freedom to write. Geneva was not a large city, possessing a population of only twelve thousand, but it was a free city and on the crossroads of Europe, a strategic city, therefore, for the spread of the gospel. William Farel, an older Reformer, who had persuaded the city fathers to accept the evangelical gospel, induced the younger man, very much against his will, to remain in the city as his assistant. Calvin's strict measures induced a reaction, and after three years he and Farel were banished from the city. Calvin became pastor of a church of French refugees in the city of Strassburg. Three years later he returned to Geneva at the urging of the city council, who had come to realize their need of the strong leadership that only he could give. Calvin remained in Geneva for the rest of his life, the leading pastor of the city. And from Geneva his influence spread far and wide. He became indeed the one international Reformer whose personal leadership extended far beyond the domains of his own country.

Calvin belonged, it will be observed, to the second generation of Reformers. He came to the fore at a time when a revived and aggressive Roman Catholicism threatened to wipe a weak, divided, and struggling Protestantism from the face of the earth. He did more than any other to organize, save, and extend the Reformation. He also founded an enduring church, and left his stamp upon Protestantism as a whole.

His influence, then and later, was due to a number of factors.

1. *Institutes of the Christian Religion*: This great work, which received its final revision in 1559, was printed in seventy-four full editions, fourteen partial editions, and in nine different languages before 1630. Calvin's Geneva Catechism, designed as an aid to instruction in the doctrines of the *Institutes,* meanwhile had gone through seventy-four editions and might be had in nearly all the languages of Europe. Calvinism remained the dominant theology in both Great

Britain and America until sometime in the nineteenth century, when it was replaced by Arminianism (page 189), a modification of the original Calvinism.

2. Calvin wrote commentaries on most of the Old Testament books, and all of those in the New Testament except 2 and 3 John and the book of Revelation (which he confessed he did not understand). He was without doubt the greatest interpreter of Scripture of his own day, and one of the greatest of all time.

3. He was the foremost defender of the faith in his day, defending the evangelical doctrine and enabling his followers to give a reason for the faith that was in them.

4. Calvin drew from Scripture that form of church government which we know today as Presbyterianism. It was unique, among other things, in that it admitted laymen to a place in the government of the church along with the clergy and that it preserved the unity of the church through a series of ascending courts—a system of representative democracy, similar in some ways to that of our own national government. In its stand for religious freedom, modern democracy had its birth.

5. Luther, followed by Anglicans, retained those forms of worship which had proved their value in the past. Calvin, on the other hand, returned to the Bible for his basic principles, and sought to ground his worship in a theology of the Word. He rejected the special days set aside in the church year (including Christmas and Easter), retained liturgical forms as a model for worship, introduced free prayer, placed high value on the sacraments, emphasized the singing of the Psalms. Thrilling congregational singing was one of the striking features of Calvinist worship and "the most seductive aspect generally of the Reformed Churches in their expansion."

6. Calvin placed great emphasis on education. He arranged for a complete school system in Geneva, reaching its culmination in the founding of the Academy (actually a university), which in its first year attracted nine hundred students from all parts of Europe. Students returned from the university to become leaders of the Reformation in their own land. Calvin imparted such interest in education to his followers that some historians have spoken of him as "the father of modern education."

7. Calvin influenced his own and subsequent ages by the system

of discipline which he imposed upon all the inhabitants of Geneva. The consistory, composed of both ministers and elders, kept close watch on the morals of church members. Spiritual penalties only (culminating in exclusion from the Lord's Supper) were inflicted by the consistory, but serious offenses were turned over to the civic authorities for further punishment. To our modern age such exercise of discipline seems extreme, as it did to some men of his own day. But it met a need. Luther believed that when men came to know that their sins had been forgiven in Christ the Christian grace would spontaneously follow. When instead the loosening of old loyalties led to the spread of moral laxity, he grew discouraged and longed for the end of the world. The discipline which Calvin introduced helped to save the Reformation; it drew men to Geneva and made it for many the showplace of Europe. It was Calvin's discipline, as taken over and exercised by Presbyterians, Congregationalists, Baptists, Methodists, and others, that gave these evangelical bodies much of their strength in America, especially upon the advancing frontier.

8. Calvin emphasized even more strongly than Luther that every man must serve God in his own vocation. One must not only accept his lot in life, but make it a medium through which God's will was to be done on earth as in heaven; in other words, he must serve God not only in his calling, but by his calling.

9. Calvin believed that the church must be interested in the total life of the community. In Geneva he and his fellow ministers exercised spiritual leadership; teachers (also officers in the church) were responsible for education; elders took oversight of the city's morals; deacons, who cared for the finances of the church, also looked after the poor, the sick, and the aged. Calvin believed that church and state must labor together to build a Christian society. To implement this program in Geneva he insisted on the restriction of interest, supported civil legislation bearing upon trade and consumption, and labored for the establishment of a church system of poor relief and social welfare. At his instigation the manufacture of cloth, velvet, and watches was introduced into Geneva to give work to the poor and unemployed. His letters deal constantly with the interests of finance, trade, and industry. From his pulpit he fought for the rights of the common man. He and his successor Beza were in fact the tribunes or champions of the people.

As a historian of Christian social ethics has declared:

> Here then—for the first time in the history of the Christian ethic—there came into existence a Christian Church whose social influence, as far as it was possible at that period, was completely comprehensive. . . . It [sought to mold] in a corporate way the whole of life in the State and in Society, in the Family, and in the economic sphere, in public and private, in accordance with Christian standards. It took care that every individual member should receive his appointed share of the natural and spiritual possessions of the community, while at the same time it sought to make the whole of Society, down to the smallest detail, a real expression of the royal dominion of Christ.[3]

10. Calvin was concerned not only with the church in Geneva, and not only with the churches which accepted his own ideas regarding worship, doctrine, and polity, but with the whole of Protestantism, in fact with the church universal. Young men came to Geneva to be trained by him and his aides and returned to their own lands to become the shock troops of the Reformation. Through his correspondence he kept in touch with men of every rank, princes and reformers, scholars and common people, and helped to give direction to the Reformation in every land.

No one labored more strenuously than he to overcome the divisions which had arisen in the Protestant ranks.

Calvin faced opposition in Geneva. It came from two sources: (1) from libertarians, who disliked his strict discipline; and (2) from older citizens who resented the fact that control tended to pass into the hands of newcomers whom Calvin had attracted to Geneva. At times his enemies controlled the city council, and it seemed as though he might once again be forced to flee. This opposition to Calvin reached its climax in the Servetus affair. Servetus was a unitarian—a man who denied the deity of Christ. As such, his life was in jeopardy all through Europe. If one who destroys the body deserves to die, men argued, how much more one who endangers the immortal souls of countless numbers. The presence of Servetus in Lyons was revealed to the Roman Catholic authorities, and he was sentenced to be burned. He escaped from his captors and for some reason came to

Geneva, where he was arrested, prosecuted by Calvin, and condemned by the city council, then in the hands of Calvin's enemies, to die at the stake. (Calvin, though pressing for a death sentence, had requested a more humane execution.)

There were a few in Calvin's day who opposed sending a heretic to his death, but not many. Calvin in this respect was no worse than other men in his day, but unfortunately he was no better. The fact that Servetus had sought to make common cause with the Council, then dominated by Calvin's enemies, threw control of the city back into the hands of Calvin's friends. From this point until his death, Calvin's influence in the city was undisputed.

In France

The Reformed movement under the leadership of John Calvin became the growing cutting-edge of Protestantism, particularly where there was strong government opposition.

This opposition became increasingly severe in France. Lutheran teaching was penetrating this nation by 1522, five years after Luther had nailed his ninety-five theses on the university bulletin board. Calvin, however, soon became the recognized leader of the growing Protestant movement. In 1547 Henry II came to the throne. He established a new court of justice to deal with heresy, which from its habit of sending its victims to the stake soon became known as the Burning Chamber. If the heretic recanted on the scaffold he was strangled before the fire was lit; if he refused to recant his tongue was cut out. Those who were merely suspected were cast into dungeons from which many never came out alive. Torture was habitually used to extract confession.

Writes a secular historian:

> In the face of this fiery persecution the conduct of the Calvinists was wonderfully fine. They showed great adroitness in evading the law by all means save recantation and great astuteness in using what poor legal means of defence were at their disposal. On the other hand they suffered punishment with splendid constancy and courage, very few failing in the hour of trial, and most meeting death in a state of exaltation. Large numbers found refuge in other lands.[4]

Continues the same careful historian:

> Of all the fine types of French manhood, that of the Huguenot [as the French Protestants came to be called] is one of the finest. Gallic gaiety is tempered with earnestness; intrepidity is strengthened with a new moral fibre like that of steel. Except in the case of a few great lords, who joined the party without serious conviction, the high standard of the Huguenot morals was recognized even by their enemies. In an age of profligacy, the 'men of the religion,' as they called themselves, walked the paths of rectitude and sobriety.[5]

In spite of such fiery persecution the church continued to grow. By 1559 it claimed a membership of approximately 400,000 and according to Calvin's estimate held the allegiance of approximately one-tenth of the nation. In this year the church was organized on a national basis, with a confession drawn up by the disciples of Calvin, and a series of ascending courts, corresponding to those found in Presbyterian Churches at the present time. This was the first Presbyterian Church in which the full Presbyterian system, as conceived by Calvin, was exhibited.

Recognizing the growing strength of Protestantism Catherine de' Medici, ruling as regent for her young son, granted it limited rights of worship. The fanatical Roman Catholic party, led by the Duke of Guise, opposed such concessions. A group of the duke's armed retainers attacked a congregation, worshiping as the law permitted, outside the town of Vassey. This inspired similar attacks in other parts of the nation. The Huguenots took arms in self-defense. There followed a series of wars which convulsed France for a generation and more (1562–1598). They became wars for both religious and political freedom.

After the third so-called Huguenot War, Catherine, fearing that France would bleed to death, arranged a truce. It was to be sealed by the marriage of her daughter, Margaret, to young Henry of Navarre, scion of one of the leading Huguenot families, with royal blood in his veins.

Huguenot leaders gathered in Paris for the event, under promise of safe conduct. Fearing the growing influence of the Huguenot leader, Admiral Coligny, over her son, Charles IX, Catherine arranged for his murder. It failed to achieve its object, and Catherine, aided by the Guises and their followers, found it necessary to proceed further. On St. Bartholomew's Day, August 24, 1572, while the church bells were issuing their call for early mass, armed ruffians fanned through the city slaying Coligny and his fellow Protestants. Contemporaries estimated that eight thousand were slaughtered in Paris, and many times that number outside the city. Henry of Navarre saved his life only by renouncing Protestantism. He later escaped, and gathered the Huguenots for renewed resistance. There followed a fourth, a fifth, a sixth, a seventh, and an eighth Huguenot War. Time and time again Henry had victory snatched from his hand by the intervention of Spain. The war finally ended when Henry, now the legitimate successor to the throne, renounced Protestantism for a second time that he might secure the necessary Roman Catholic support. "Paris," he declared somewhat cynically, "is well worth a Mass."

The new ruler did not, however, turn his back on members of his former faith. In 1598 he issued the Edict of Nantes, which granted the Huguenots fuller toleration than they had previously received, and which left them in possession of a number of armed cities as a safeguard.

So long as Henry lived, this edict was faithfully observed. During the reign of his son and grandson (Louis XIII and XIV), however, the rights of the Huguenots were restricted, and finally persecution was resumed. Schools were closed; churches were destroyed; Huguenots, drawing largely from the prosperous middle class, were forbidden to enter certain professions or to engage in particular trades; children on various pretexts were taken from their parents and raised as Roman Catholics; troops were quartered in Huguenot homes, with the intention of ruining them financially, and making their life as miserable as possible. In 1685 the Edict of Nantes was revoked. Protestants were left with no rights of worship: if they did not renounce their faith, their property was confiscated, their children were taken from their care, and their men were sentenced to serve in the galleys, a grueling punishment, which after two years ended ordinarily in death. Borders were sealed; hundreds of thousands, however, by one stratagem or another managed to make their escape. Directly or indirectly many of these came ultimately to the American Colonies.

Repression of Protestantism in France continued for more than a hundred years. Not until 1789 was there complete freedom of religion. The Reformed Church in France, weaker comparatively than it was in Reformation days, remains as one of the important branches of the Reformed and Presbyterian family.

In Holland

The Lowlands (including modern Belgium and Holland) in the Reformation period were a part of the Spanish Empire. The policy of the Spanish rulers (Charles V, followed by Philip II) was to destroy the political liberties of the Low Countries, to exploit them economically, and to crush the growing Protestant movement; the War for Dutch Independence that finally resulted was in part a war for political freedom, in part a war for economic freedom, and in large part a war for religious freedom. Lutherans, Anabaptists, and Calvinists were all present in the Netherlands, but it was the latter who were the more numerous and aggressive. The Inquisition, with all its paraphernalia of torture, was early introduced to destroy this growing movement—the only land in northern Europe where this was the case—all to no avail. Finally Philip sent the Duke of Alva, one of the most efficient and cruel of all Spanish soldiers, to stamp out the Protestant heresy. To accomplish this purpose he was prepared, if necessary, to make the Netherlands a desert. A judicial chamber was established, soon to be known as the Bloody Tribunal, which sentenced men to death for even the suspicion of treason, without bothering with the formality of a trial. According to Alva's edict, it was treason to have presented or signed any petition against the new bishoprics or the Inquisition; to have tolerated public preaching under any circumstances; to have omitted to resist field preaching; to maintain that the council did not have the right to override all the laws and privileges of the Netherlands. Commissioners were sent through the land to search for any suspected of treason so defined. Informers were bribed to come forward, and soon floods of denunciations and evidence were flowing in. The accused were brought before the council and sentenced in batches—thirty-five, forty-six, eighty-four, ninety-five at a time. On one occasion eight hundred were taken, and on still another, fifteen hundred. In each case, Alva wrote to Philip, "I have ordered them all to be executed." In view of these records the language of a contemporary chronicler does not appear exaggerated:

> The gallows, the wheel, stakes, trees along the highways, were laden with carcasses or limbs of those who had been hanged, beheaded, or roasted; so that the air which God made for the respiration of the living, was now become the common grave or habitation of the dead. Every day produced fresh objects of pity and of mourning, and the noise of the bloody passing-bell was continually heard, which by the martyrdom of this man's cousin, and the other's brother or friend, rang dismal peals in the hearts of the survivors.[6]

The total number put to death during the six years of Alva's administration has been variously estimated at from 6,000 to 18,000. Within the next thirty or forty years 400,000 are estimated to have left the country.

In opposition to such policies came the War for Dutch Independence, under the inspiring leadership of William of Orange. Comments Preserved Smith:

> The rise of the Dutch Republic is one of the most inspiring pages in history. Superficially it has many points of resemblance with the American War of Independence. In both there was the absentee king, the national hero, the local jealousies of the several provinces, the economic grievances, the rising national feeling and even the religious issue, though this had become very small in America. But the difference was in the ferocity of the tyranny and the intensity of the struggle. . . . The one is decent and familiar, the other lurid and ghastly. With true Anglo-Saxon moderation the American war was fought like a game or an election, with humanity and attention to rules; but in Holland and Belgium was enacted the most terrible frightfulness in the world; over the whole land, mingled with the reek of candles carried in procession and of incense burnt to celebrate a massacre, brooded the sultry miasma of human blood and tears. On the one side flashed the savage

sword of Alva and the pitiless flame of the inquisitor Tapper; on the other were arrayed, behind their dykes and walls, men resolved to win that freedom which alone can give scope and nobility to life.[7]

William was assassinated in 1584, but the struggle continued until independence was assured.

Long before this was accomplished the Reformed Church of Holland had been organized—with a Calvinistic creed (the Belgic Confession) and a Presbyterian organization. Holland remains predominantly Reformed (or Presbyterian) and Calvinistic to the present day.

The Arminian Controversy

In seventeenth-century Holland occurred the Arminian controversy which was to have significance for the further development of Calvinistic thought. Arminius, professor of theology in the University of Leyden, sought to modify the rigorous Calvinism which had arisen in the second generation of the Reformed movement—a generation which placed far more emphasis on the doctrine of predestination than had Calvin himself. Arminius taught that God elected those who he foresaw would accept the offer of salvation; that Christ died for all men and not simply for the elect; that man was saved through the prevenient (preceding) grace of God, which he was free to accept or reject; and that those thus elected and saved might eventually fall from grace and be eternally lost. To counter this Arminian modification of rigid Calvinism there was held the Synod of Dort (1618), attended by Reformed theologians from other lands, as well as from Holland. This synod reaffirmed the doctrines against which Arminius and his followers protested: God's election was not conditioned on his foreknowledge; Christ's death was sufficient for all, efficient only for the elect; grace was irresistible, though man's responsibility remained; those elected and saved could not finally perish. From this pronouncement came the five so-called Points of Calvinism (actually the five *disputed* Points of Calvinism): total depravity, unconditional election, limited atonement, irresistible grace, and the final perseverance of the saints.

Those who could not accept the canons of the Synod of Dort were deprived of their place in the church; a number were fined; a few were sentenced to life imprisonment; about eighty were banished from the land. It was, however, more than a matter of theology. Remonstrants, as they were called, were opposed to the political control of Maurice, son of William, who had overthrown the states' rights party, supported by the Arminians.

The Reformed Church in Holland, under William, had been far more tolerant than other churches of the same period and was to become so again after the short Arminian interlude.

Insistence on the five disputed Points of Calvinism, however, was to cost Presbyterianism heavily, particularly in America on the advancing frontier where "predestination" (in exaggerated form) became a most unpopular doctrine.

IN SCOTLAND

Scotland, on the eve of the Reformation, was economically undeveloped, socially backward, "four hundred years behind the rest of Europe," and educationally retarded. Much of the country's wealth was in the hands of the church, but the standards of the clergy were low, judged even by pre-reformation standards. No country was in greater need of reformation.

John Knox

Nine years after Luther's ninety-five theses (1526), Tyndale's English New Testament began to circulate in Scotland. In 1528, Patrick Hamilton, a young Scot who had accepted Lutheran teachings in Germany, perished after six long hours of torture on the stake, as the first Scottish martyr. A few years later George Wishart brought into Scotland the more radical Reformed movement from Switzerland; he too was burned at the stake. The leader in the Reformation struggle, however, was John Knox. Wrote one of our leading historians:

> No figure stands out more sharply in Reformation story than that of the powerful man just named. Far from possessing the originality and genius of Luther or of Calvin as a thinker, he was like Luther in his capacity to sway men, in his love for

the vernacular of his native land, and in his passion. He had something of Calvin's gifts of organization, and he was also, to the utmost fibre of his being, typical of the land of his birth. Intense, religious, argumentative, democratic, fearless, intolerant, forceful, he led Scotland as no other man in its history has done. He influenced the character and religion of his nation as no other.[8]

We know little of Knox's early life. He was born probably in 1514 (five years younger than John Calvin). Ordained as a priest, he served for a time as bodyguard and defender of George Wishart, by whom, probably, he had been won to the Reformed faith. After Wishart's martyrdom a group of his friends took revenge by assassinating Cardinal Beaton, who had been responsible for his death. Though not directly implicated in this bloody deed, Knox, with others, took refuge in St. Andrews Castle. Here, after strong insistence, he began to preach; he proved to be one of the most powerful preachers that the Reformation produced. Regent of Scotland at this time was a French woman, Mary of Guise, mother of the infant Mary, Queen of Scots. A French fleet sent at the request of the regent captured the castle, and Knox and others were sentenced to serve as galley slaves. Released after two years through an exchange of prisoners with Protestant England, Knox became one of the six court preachers in this land, laboring in this capacity for five years. When England came again under Roman Catholic control (with the accession of "Bloody" Mary to the throne), Knox with others fled to the continent of Europe, where ultimately he became pastor of an English congregation in Calvin's Geneva. In the ten years that Knox labored in England and on the continent among English refugees he helped to mold the thorough- *Puritans* going Protestant group later to be known as Puritans.

In the meantime Knox continued in touch with the growing Protestant movement in his native land. He returned for a brief visit in 1555, and encouraged the Protestant nobles to break openly with Rome; shortly thereafter a group of them solemnly covenanted "to renounce the congregation of Satan with all the superstitions, abominations and idolatry thereof, and to defend the whole congregation of Christ and the members thereof." In 1559 the Queen Mother took positive steps to crush the Reformation movement; at this critical juncture John Knox landed at Leith, the port of Edinburgh. From this time he became the soul of the Protestant movement, winning recruits, sustaining morale, inspiring resistance as no other could do. As Thomas Randolph, English ambassador, reported to Queen Elizabeth, Knox's voice could "put life into them more than five hundred trumpets." The following year Mary of Guise died, leaving Parliament, now predominantly Protestant, in control.

In this and the following years the Reformation of the church was carried out under John Knox's direction. Papal jurisdiction was abolished. A confession of faith was drawn up—solidly Calvinistic, but with "election" only barely mentioned. A form of government was provided in the *First Book of Discipline* (though never accepted by Parliament). Ministers, elders, deacons, and teachers—the four officers regarded by John Calvin as scriptural—were recognized, and in addition, readers and superintendents. This was the most democratic of all Presbyterian organizations coming from the Reformation period: Ministers were elected by the people, as were the elders and deacons, these last two for only a year at a time, "lest by long continuance of such officers men presume upon the liberties of the Church." Knox believed with Calvin that education was a function of the church; where local congregations could not support teachers, primary education was to be undertaken by the pastor. Children were to be examined in the catechism every Sunday afternoon; at least annually the ministers and elders were to inquire into the religious knowledge of every adult. Readers were provided because as yet there were not enough educated ministers. Superintendents served about like home mission executives. There was a series of courts: session, presbytery (in germ only), synod, and general assembly. The last became the most representative body in Scotland, and was able to speak for the nation as a whole more authentically even than Parliament. The *Book of Discipline* as drawn up by Knox provided for a complete system of free public education for the entire nation (the first such in history: beside every church, a school; in every notable town, a college; in three important cities, a university) and also for a system of national charities in which all unable to earn a living should be supported out of public funds, and all able to work should be compelled to do so. These two farsighted proposals were to be financed out of the properties of the church. Due to the selfishness of the Scottish nobility, however, they were never put into effect. Much of the property of the Roman Catholic Church finally found its way into private hands.

Knox also caused to be drawn up for the church a Book of Common Order. As in other Reformed systems there was provision for both free and set prayers; there was place for a general confession of sin, for the Apostles' Creed, and for the Lord's Prayer. Forms for the sacraments were suggested, but not made mandatory. The Communion was to be observed at long tables set in the nave of the church. To participate in the Communion one must have a token, given by the kirk-session as an indication of his spiritual readiness. Marriages were performed before the congregation as a part of the regular service.

Even while the organization of the church was being perfected, a new struggle had begun with the young Queen come to claim her throne. Mary as an infant had been sent to France for safekeeping, where she was reared in a strongly Catholic atmosphere. She had been married to the dauphin of France, and ruled for a few brief months as queen by his side. After the death of Mary of Guise, she returned to Scotland, a young widow, nineteen years of age. "She was a lovely creature," writes T. M. Lindsay, "and was, besides, gifted with a power of personal fascination greater than her physical charms, and such as no woman of her time possessed; she had a sweet caressing voice, beautiful hands; and not least, she had a gift of tears at command."[9] This attractive young woman returned to Scotland determined to crush the democratic liberties of Scotland (she had accepted the continental view of the divine right of kings) and to restore Scotland to its Catholic faith.

> In Knox [now minister of St. Giles Church, Edinburgh] and in the spirit which he had nurtured she met the chief stumbling blocks. The battle which he fought was waged with weapons of invective on his part that seem coarse and often brutal, his bitterness and intolerance are repulsive to our altered age, but that battle was none the less one for popular sovereignty and

religious freedom. It was self-governing Scotland against an unrepresentative sovereign.[10]

Despite Knox's vigorous opposition Mary might well have won her battle had it not been for a certain weakness in her character. She managed to fall in love repeatedly and always with the wrong man: first, with Lord Darnley, whom she married but soon ceased to respect; then with her Italian secretary, David Rizzio, who was murdered by order of her jealous husband; and finally with Lord Bothwell, an unprincipled Protestant nobleman. Darnley was assassinated, and Bothwell was charged with the deed. Mary managed to win his acquittal; Bothwell kidnapped Mary, it was suspected with her consent; after he had secured a divorce from his wife, Bothwell and Mary were married. This was too much for the Scottish people. They rose in their wrath, deposed Mary, placing her infant son, James VI, on the throne. Protestantism once more was in the ascendancy.

Andrew Melville

As James came to manhood the struggle was renewed—with Andrew Melville now defending the liberties of the church. Bishops without power had been appointed to hold legal possession of the properties of the church; King James and his advisers (believers in royal absolutism) sought to strengthen the power of these bishops through whom the monarch might control the church. Melville prepared a *Second Book of Discipline,* in which episcopacy was declared to be illegal and the parity of the ministry was strongly stressed. Presbytery took its place as the fourth Presbyterian court. Presbyterianism was declared to have been ordained by divine law (the *jure divino* theory).

The king's attempt to control the church was stoutly resisted. On one never-to-be-forgotten occasion, Melville seized the monarch by the sleeve of his robe and said,

> Sir, as divers times before I have told you, so now again I must tell you, there are two kings and two kingdoms in Scotland: there is King James, the head of the Commonwealth, and there is Christ Jesus, the King of the Church, whose subject James

VI is, and of whose kingdom he is not a king nor a head, but a member . . .

This struggle was continuing when Elizabeth, queen of England, died, and James VI of Scotland became James I, king of England and of Scotland. From this time the history of the Scottish Reformation is bound inseparably with that of the Reformation in England, and to this story we shall soon turn.

We observe, in the meantime, that the Reformed faith had taken strong hold in Germany (from which came the important Heidelberg Catechism, Calvinistic, though without mention of predestination), in Hungary, in the Italian Alps (where it had been accepted by the ancient Waldensian Church), and in Bohemia (present Czechoslovakia) where it had been accepted by the followers of John Hus. It also took temporary root in Spain and in Poland, where it was finally overthrown by the forces of the Counter-Reformation.

FOR CONSIDERATION

*1. What in your judgment are the vital differences, if any, between the Lutheran and Reformed traditions? What can each learn from the other?

2. What, if any, distinct contribution do Presbyterian and Reformed Churches have to make at the present time to ecumenical Christianity?

3. Calvin is not at present a very popular figure. Why, do you think, is this the case? What can those who are in the Calvinistic traditions say in Calvin's defense?

*4. What is there in Calvin's ministry with which you agree? disagree? What can the church of today learn from his ministry? In other words, what should the Calvinistic tradition mean to us today?

*5. Is the doctrine of predestination a comforting one or a disturbing one? Why? What does the doctrine actually mean to you?

6. Are the so-called five Points of Calvinism vital points of doctrine at the present time?

7. Was the decision of the Synod of Dort regarding Arminianism a wise one?

8. Do you agree with Calvin that the church must be interested in the total life of the community?

9. In your judgment, would it be wise for the church to attempt to discipline members who fall below accepted Christian standards?

10. What is your judgment of John Knox as a man and as a Reformer?

11. Are there any reasons, in your judgment, why we should pattern our church government on that of Scripture?

*12. In what sense can the Presbyterian form of church government be said to be scriptural?

13. What are the particular values of Presbyterian Church government?

14. What are the values and the significance of infant baptism?

15. Calvin labored to unite all of Protestantism in one workable organization. Should we seek the same objective in our own day?

Dutch Mennonites Suffering Persecution for Their Interpretation of the Bible

14
"RADICAL" MOVEMENTS APPEAR

THE TWO IMPORTANT REFORMATION MOVEMENTS on the continent of Europe, so far as numbers are concerned, were those leading to the formation of Lutheran and Reformed Churches. There were other movements, however, considered more radical at the time, which attained less imposing proportions, but which have had more or less influence on the subsequent history of the church.

ANABAPTISTS

Most important of these "minor" movements was that of the Anabaptists. This movement arose in Zürich, in the year 1525, and was an offshoot of the Zwinglian Reformation. Zwingli assumed with the men of that day generally that all citizens were members of the church and accepted the authority of the city council over both church and state. Conrad Grebel and Felix Manz, young disciples of Zwingli, maintained on the other hand that the church was composed of conscious believers who voluntarily chose to accept its discipline (a "gathered" church) and that this church should recognize only the

197

authority of the Word. Baptism came to be the focal point of dispute. Grebel and Manz rejected the baptism of infants as unscriptural. They held that only professing Christians should be baptized and counted as members of the church—so breaking with a tradition which had prevailed for more than a millennium. To Zwingli and others this seemed a revolutionary doctrine, one that would undermine the basis of both church and state and their long and fruitful relationship.

In a disputation called to consider the matter, Zwingli pointed out that baptism under the new covenant took the place of circumcision under the old covenant (see Col. 2:11–12); as children were members of the Old Testament church, so should they be recognized as members of the New Testament church. He also appealed to 1 Corinthians 7:14 which implies the church membership of the children of Christian parents and to the example of family baptism in Acts 16: 31–33; 18:8; and 1 Corinthians 1:16.

The city fathers agreed with Zwingli, ordered Grebel and Manz to desist from their agitation, and expelled from the city families who refused to present their children for baptism. Grebel and Manz, who declined to follow this ruling, were later arrested and sentenced to life imprisonment. Grebel escaped and died a few months later; Manz, who also escaped, was arrested and drowned—the punishment decreed for those who dared to rebaptize by immersion.

The movement continued to spread, however, outside of Zürich —in Switzerland, in Germany, and in Holland, especially among the common people.

Most of the leaders of the new movement were evangelical Christians, agreeing with Zwingli and other Reformed leaders that the Bible was to be accepted as the foundation of one's faith and as the guiding principle of one's life. They interpreted the Bible, however, more legalistically, and also more literally. This led in turn to their distinctive doctrines regarding (1) the church, and (2) the Christian life.

First, as to the church: They taught, as we have seen, that only conscious believers should be recognized as members of the church, and only those who agreed to separate from the world and accept the church's conception of the Christian life. They held that only such believers should be baptized, since this was the rite of admission into the church. The scriptural mode of baptism (understood by them to be immersion) came to be stressed, but was not so significant as the subjects of baptism. They taught that each church was an independent, self-governing unit (congregational church government). They became the earliest advocates of complete separation of church and state. Since magistrates were compelled to act at times in ways that were opposed to scriptural injunctions, no member of the church was to hold office in the state.

Second, in regard to the Christian life: They found the essence of Christianity in discipleship, in strict obedience to the commands of Christ, as set forth in Scripture. These commands they tended to interpret with strict literalness—no violence, readiness on the other hand to turn the other cheek; no oaths; footwashing as preliminary to the observance of the Lord's Supper; strict separation from a world whose standards were opposed to the standards of Christ. Such separation was to be enforced by rigid discipline, including the practice of "shunning" those excommunicated by the church. Shunning was defined by one of the early Anabaptist leaders (Balthasar Hubmaier, formerly a professor in the University of Ingolstadt) as follows:

> It is exclusion and separation to such an extent that no fellowship is held with such a person by Christians, whether in speaking, eating, drinking, grinding, baking, or in any other way, but he is treated as a heathen and a publican, who is bound and delivered over to Satan. He is to be avoided and shunned, lest the entire visible church be evil spoken of, disgraced and dishonoured by his company, and corrupted by his example, instead of being startled and made afraid by his punishment, so that they will mortify their sins. For as truly as God lives what the Church admits or excludes on earth is admitted or excluded above.[1]

Conrad Grebel had proposed the erection of "a church without sin," in which all goods should be held in common. This was later interpreted by Anabaptists generally to mean that the church should allow no one to suffer from physical want, but followers of Jacob Hutter did establish among themselves a community of goods, an experiment which has continued among his followers (the Hutterians) to the present day.

To Zwingli the idea of a church of approved saints made sinless by regeneration as proposed by Grebel, seemed utterly unrealistic as well as unscriptural (see Matt. 13:14–30). It also appeared to him and others in authority to be a subversive movement—one which pointed to anarchy, communism, and revolution.

Unfortunately, a few extremists, in no wise typical of the movement as a whole, helped to confirm this suspicion in the minds of sober-minded men in both church and state. Some of these extremists were premillennarians who taught the early return of Christ, to be followed by the establishment of an earthly kingdom in which justice would be at last secured for all. Some indicated that this consummation might be hastened by a judicious use of force. Two such, Jan Mattys and Jan of Leyden, claiming to be prophets, declared that Münster (in Germany) was to be the center of this new kingdom. They and their followers seized control of the city, and introduced the practice of communism and free love. The town was recaptured; the leaders were cruelly tortured, and their bodies hung in the tower of Lambert Church, where they remained until as late as 1881. Johann von Battenburg attempted to organize some of those who escaped from Münster and their sympathizers. The Battenburgians, as they were called, defended polygamy and held that those who refused to fight with them would finally be destroyed by the sword. David Joris, another of these fanatics, taught that he was the messiah of a better kingdom than Christ's, in which members were no longer bound by the laws of morality.

Such extremists brought the whole Anabaptist movement under suspicion and intensified the persecution which had begun on other grounds. Innocent men and women were tortured on the rack, scourged, imprisoned in dungeons, drowned, buried alive, roasted to death before slow fires.

As a consequence of unremitting persecution, the Anabaptist movement was largely stamped out. But not altogether. A former Catholic priest, named Menno Simons, representing the gentler and far more numerous wing of Anabaptists, gathered up the broken remnants, organized them, put upon them the stamp of his personality—

to such an extent that they took the name Mennonites. A smaller, and even more conservative group, carrying the practice of shunning to its furthest length, became known as Amish. A still smaller group, practicing Christian communism, are the Hutterians. The total number of Mennonites (to use the more inclusive term) today is approximately one-half million, one-third of whom continue in Europe, two-thirds of whom are now found in North and South America. Approximately 75,000 are in the United States.

Though small in number, they have remained a sturdy and conscientious folk, and some of their principles (congregational church government, baptism of conscious believers only, baptism by immersion, separation of church and state), hurdling the British Channel and later the Atlantic Ocean, have gained massive support.

"SPIRITUALISTS"

A second radical group growing out of the Reformation period, sometimes confused with the Anabaptists, are better described as "Spiritualists." They differed from other Reformed movements in that they valued immediate illumination by the Holy Spirit more highly than God's revelation in his word. The roots of this movement are to be found in late medieval Catholic mysticism, mingled with ideas borrowed from the Reformation. Some of these "Spiritualists," like some of the fanatical Anabaptists, advocated the establishment of an earthly millennium by the use of force. One of the most radical of these demagogues was Thomas Münzer, who proposed the establishment of the kingdom of God on a communistic basis. His rabid oratory helped to bring on the Peasants' Revolution of 1524–25. Others, like Sebastian Franck and Casper Schwenkfeld (some of whose followers brought the Schwenkfeld Church to America) were quietists (people who stressed personal, inner faith) who set up independent congregations, apart from the organized churches of their day. Much of what was best in this movement was later to find a home in the Society of Friends (the Quakers).

SOCINIANS

The third of these Radical Reformation groups were the Socinians, who may be described more exactly as not believing in the church's doctrine of the Trinity.) (See chapter 6.) In the Reformation period there were a number of rationalists, men of reason rather than faith, who found themselves unable to accept the orthodox doctrine of the Trinity. Some of these were to be found in the Anabaptist movement; some, particularly in northern Italy, could trace their roots back to the medieval schoolmen who discovered that there was opposition between Catholic doctrine and reason; the majority of these schoolmen fell back on the authority of the church; the early Anti-Trinitarians came to put more emphasis on reason. The man to whom the movement owes most was the Spaniard, Michael Servetus, who was burned at the stake in Geneva. His execution led Lelio Socinus, an Italian, regarded as an evangelical, residing in Zürich, to examine the writings of Servetus and ultimately to accept his views. Having no desire to be martyred he kept his opinions to himself. After his death, however, his nephew, Fausto Socinus, reading some of his uncle's manuscripts, was himself brought to the Anti-Trinitarian position. He removed to Transylvania and later to Poland, where it was possible at that time to preserve some freedom of thought, and there taught "Socinian" views, later embodied in the Racovian Catechism.

Socinus accepted the inspiration of Scripture, but held that there was nothing of value in it contrary to reason. God was Creator and Judge. Jesus was a man who lived a life of such complete obedience that he was raised from the dead and rewarded with a kind of delegated divinity. The Holy Spirit was only another name for the divine influence in the world. Eternal life was the consequence of a good life. There was no need for atonement. Christ's death on the cross was an example. There was no vital personal relationship between the believing soul and God through Jesus Christ.

Socinianism survived in Transylvania (now in Communist hands) at least as late as World War II, though it was never a movement of any great size. Some of its ideas took root among the Arminians in Holland. From Holland these ideas spread to England and later to the United States, where they became embodied in Unitarianism. To these movements we shall later return. It may be observed, however, that no movement in Christian history denying the deity of Christ has attracted any large following.

note

FOR CONSIDERATION

1. What do you find of value in the Anabaptist vision?
2. Baptist bodies insist upon baptism by immersion only. What should be the non-Baptist response to this insistence?
3. Baptist bodies insist upon baptism of conscious believers only. What should be the non-Baptist response to this insistence?
*4. Calvin believed that church and state should co-operate in the building of a Christian society. Luther believed that church and state moved in different realms: the mission of the church was confined to the salvation of souls. The Anabaptists abandoned all ideas of a Christian social order and sought to realize a perfected Christian society within the church itself. Which view is the more nearly correct?
5. What are the dangers of looking to the Spirit for guidance apart from Scripture?
6. What are the dangers of tying oneself too exclusively to the words of Scripture?
7. Do Protestants generally make it too easy to join the church?
8. Would the Protestant churches benefit by a return to the practice of discipline?
*9. What are the values and weaknesses of a congregational form of church government, in which each congregation is a law to itself?
*10. Socinians held that there is nothing of value in Scripture which is contrary to reason. Is this a proper approach to Scripture?

Archbishop Cranmer Being Imprisoned in the Tower of London

15
REFORMATION
COMES TO ENGLAND

THE THIRD MAJOR REFORMATION MOVEMENT—one destined to have particular significance for America—was that in England. Much dissatisfaction with Roman domination had developed here before Luther gave the signal for separation from Rome, so that Protestant teaching (first in Lutheran, later in Calvinistic, forms) fell on fertile soil. Particularly fruitful was Tyndale's translation of the New Testament into English from Erasmus' edition of the Greek (1524). Royal and ecclesiastical authorities sought in vain to suppress it. Tyndale himself fled to the continent and began a translation of the Old Testament, which he did not live to finish. Betrayed by a friend, he was arrested, tried, convicted, strangled, and burned by emissaries of the emperor. Much of the charm of the King James and later versions of the English Bible derives from Tyndale's amazing mastery of the English language.

REVOLT (Henry VIII, 1509–1547)

England's ruler, Henry VIII, had taken a strong stand in opposition to Martin Luther, as also to William Tyndale and his work. But when the pope steadfastly refused to annul his marriage with Catherine, a Spanish princess whom he had married sixteen years earlier, Henry, supported by Parliament and the clergy of his church, repudiated the authority of the pope and secured his own recognition as head of the church in England. The nation as a whole was ready for the break.

REFORMATION (Edward VI, 1547–1553)

Real reformation of the church began in the reign of his son, Edward VI (1547–1553). A brief statement of faith, the Forty-Two Articles—mildly Calvinistic in tone—was drawn up by Archbishop Cranmer and approved. More important by far was the Prayer Book, also prepared by Cranmer, who had the same gift for matchless prose that had been granted to Tyndale. Some of the prayers in this book were drawn from the old Roman Breviary (or liturgy), some were taken from earlier Reformed books of worship, some were original with Cranmer—but on all he put the magic of his pen.

As one historian has pointed out:

> Although Protestantism generally aimed to found itself upon a book, the *Bible,* it was upon quite another book that the Church of England was to be founded; their *Book of Common Prayer.* In general, uniformity of faith was sought, not by defining a faith as to leave it as much as possible free of precise definition; whereas what was more and more definitely sought (in England) was *uniformity of worship* ... Its oft-repeated prayers embedded themselves in the temper of the people, helping to mould the graciousness and kindliness of England's neighborly and more intimate social intercourse ... Something more, and very far-reaching was also accomplished by this book. Its phrases wove themselves into the language, during a period when the English language as we know it to-day was being formed and polished. It has been said that the authorized translation of the Bible, dating from the beginning of the seventeenth century, together with the Book of Common Prayer, have influenced more than any other literary work,

Shakespeare's included, the diction and phrasing of the English language.[1]

REACTION (Mary, 1553–1558)

Unfortunately Edward, after a short reign of less than six years, sickened and died. He was succeeded by Mary, the daughter of Henry and Catherine, like her mother a loyal Roman Catholic. Under her reign the reforming measures of Edward were revoked, papal supremacy was restored, the persecution of Protestants was resumed. Many of the Protestant leaders, among them John Knox, fled to the continent, particularly to Geneva. A number of those who remained —perhaps three hundred in all—were burned at the stake. Two of the more notable of these were the former Bishops Latimer and Ridley. Englishmen long remembered Latimer's words on the way to execution: "Be of good comfort, Master Ridley, and play the man. We shall this day light such a candle by God's grace, in England, as I trust shall never be put out." His words proved prophetic. Archbishop Cranmer was not cast in the heroic mold. Hoping to save his life he renounced his former faith. But Mary had no intention of sparing the man who had pronounced her mother's marriage invalid. Condemned to die, Cranmer's courage returned. He renounced what he had written "for fear of death and to save my life, if it might be . . . As for the Pope," he added, "I refuse him as Christ's enemy and Anti-Christ, with all his false doctrine." He was immediately hurried to the stake. As a sign that this unexpected retraction was final he stretched out his right hand and held it in the flame, crying with a loud voice, "This hand has offended." A few moments later he was dead.

THE ELIZABETHAN SETTLEMENT
(Elizabeth I, 1558–1602)

Mary's early death brought the persecutions to an end. They had served to make England truly Protestant. As someone said, the people of England have never got the fires of Smithfield out of their nostrils.

Mary was succeeded by her sister Elizabeth, under whom England returned to its Protestant moorings. According to "the Elizabethan settlement" the monarch was recognized as the Supreme Governor of the Church (rather than Supreme Head, as formerly); the Forty-Two Articles of Edward, reduced to thirty-nine were approved as the Church's statement of faith; bishops, ordained by Edwardian bishops, who had been retired by Mary, were charged with the administration of the church; the Second Prayer Book of Edward was revised and made the basis of the church's worship; a new law of uniformity required that it only could be used.

Opposition arose to this settlement from two quarters: first, from Roman Catholics, a small minority in the island; and second, from "Puritans" who felt that it represented only a halfway reform.

At this time a seminary was established at Douay in Belgium for the purpose of training priests to rewin England for Roman Catholicism. From the seminary came the first approved Roman Catholic translation of the Bible into English—the Douay version, still used by modern Roman Catholics in England and America. A rebellion against Elizabeth by loyal Catholics in the north of England was suppressed. Jesuit priests, fanning through England and suspected of disloyalty, were apprehended and punished. In 1570, too late to have much effect, came a papal bull rejecting Elizabeth as the rightful sovereign of England and releasing all Roman Catholics from their allegiance to her throne. There followed a number of plots to assassinate Elizabeth. With her out of the way, Mary, Queen of Scots, a strong Roman Catholic, was expected to succeed to the throne. In 1588 Spain, regarded at the time as the world's mightiest power, a nation which had taken the lead in suppressing Protestantism in Europe, sent her fleet, the "Great Armada," against the British Isles. Had it been successful, Protestantism in England and on the continent would likely have been suppressed. Defeat of this ambitious effort to subdue stout little England seemed to be truly providential. Consequences of this varied Roman Catholic resistance to Elizabeth and her religious settlement made England even more fiercely Protestant.

But opposition to the Elizabethan settlement came also from Puritans—a term given originally in scorn to a group who wished a more thorough Reformation in accordance with their understanding of the Scriptures. The leaders of this movement returned to England from the continent where they had been exposed to the teachings of

Calvin. His theology was at this time generally accepted in England, so that there was no difference on this score between the Puritans and those who upheld the principles of the Elizabethan settlement. Puritan opposition first arose in the field of worship. Puritans opposed the use of vestments which had been associated with the Mass, and favored in lieu thereof a simple cassock with bands—"the Geneva gown," as it is termed. They opposed kneeling in the Communion service, for this too (they felt) smacked of the superstition of the Mass, adoring the physical body of Christ. They wished to bring the table out from the chancel, where it had served as an altar, into the midst of the worshiping congregation, where it might once again become a symbol of the congregation's communion with one another and with their risen Lord. They opposed making the sign of the cross, for about this also many superstitions had arisen. Use of the ring in the wedding ceremony was rejected because it was associated with erroneous notions regarding the sacrament of marriage. Puritans did not at first oppose the use of liturgy as such; but as time went on they came to take an extreme view, rejecting the use of all read prayers, even the Lord's Prayer, the use of the Gloria Patri, and the Apostles' Creed in public worship. The barren unadorned worship that came to prevail in many Protestant churches in America was due in large measure to the Puritan modification of early Reformed worship.

More fundamental was Puritan opposition to the government of the church, as provided by the Elizabethan settlement. With Calvin, Puritans were strenuously opposed to state control of the church; they were opposed also to government by bishops, because it was through the appointment of bishops that monarchs were able to control the church, and because they had come to believe very strongly in the parity (equality) of the clergy. In the beginning the majority of the Puritans looked forward to the establishment of a presbyterian government in the Church of England. Thomas Cartwright, professor in Cambridge University, advocated *jure divino* presbyterianism—the theory that presbyterianism is *the* system of church government laid down by divine law in Scripture. Other Puritans, however, believed that congregational church government was more in accord with Scripture, and this party was to grow in influence as time went on.

Puritan insistence on the Bible as a guidebook for life was to have profound influence on English minds. As J. R. Green wrote in his famed *Short History of the English People:*

> No greater moral change ever passed over a nation than passed over England during the years that parted the middle of the reign of Elizabeth from the meeting of the Long Parliament. England became the people of a book, and that book was the Bible.[2]

It was the Puritans more than any other group who made them so.

As the religious struggle advanced, the Puritans became more stern and rigid. As Green has written again:

> Humor, the faculty which above all corrects exaggeration and extravagance, died away before the new stress and strain of existence. The absolute devotion of the Puritan to a Supreme Will tended more and more to rob him of all sense of measure and proportion in common matters. Little things became great things in the glare of religious zeal; and the godly man learned to shrink from a surplice, or a mince-pie at Christmas, as he shrank from impurity or a lie. Life became hard, rigid, colorless, as it became intense.[3]

Worldly amusements, in particular, came under the condemnation of the Puritans. Their opposition to the theatre, to card-playing, to the dance, spread to America—and in some conservative religious bodies, lingers on to the present day.

Luther had thought the injunction to rest on the seventh day a bit of Jewish ceremonial done away with by the new dispensation, so that after attending church the Christian might devote the day to what work or pleasure he thought proper. Calvin forbade all work and commanded attendance on sermons, but did not insist on the strict observance of any particular day, either the first or the seventh day of the week. The Puritans interpreted the Fourth Commandment more rigidly than any who had gone before them. As summarized in the Westminster Shorter Catechism, questions 60 and 61:

> The Sabbath is to be sanctified by a holy resting all that day, even from such worldly employments and recreations as are lawful on other days; and spending the whole time in the pub-

lic and private exercises of God's worship, except so much as is
to be taken up in the works of necessity and mercy. . . . The
fourth commandment forbiddeth the omission, or careless performance, of the duties required, and the profaning the day by
idleness, or doing that which is in itself sinful, or by unnecessary thoughts, words, or works, about our worldly employ-
ments or recreations.

The large majority of the Puritans remained in the Church of
England, hoping in time that it might be made to conform more nearly
to their desires. A tiny minority in Elizabeth's reign lost all hope that
this might be accomplished, and withdrew—"separated"—from the
Church of England to form a church of gathered saints; those who
followed their example came to be known as "Separatists."

What policy was the Crown to adopt in the face of this Puritan
and Separatist opposition? What was to be the attitude of Anglican
leaders?

The policy approved by Elizabeth and her successors on the
throne was one of enforced conformity. Everyone must worship according to the Prayer Book, and no one was to worship outside the
Church of England. Cartwright, leader of the Presbyterian wing, was
imprisoned in 1585, and Robert Browne, leader of the Separatists,
suffered a similar indignity for his convictions. Other leading separatists were to pay for their beliefs with their lifeblood.

As over against the Puritan insistence on the Bible as the one rule
by which all worship and all organization were to be tested, Richard
Hooker developed the moderate Anglican position that the Bible,
tradition, and reason all were to be taken into account. In matters of
faith, Hooker contended that the Bible alone should be followed, but
in the sphere of government and worship the church might adopt such
forms as she pleased, and might change them when she saw fit, provided she did not contradict the principles of religion laid down in
Scripture. He did not maintain that bishops—as distinct from presbyters (elders)—existed in the New Testament church; but episcopacy
was the historic form which had continued in the church for fifteen
hundred years, and therefore should be preserved as from God himself.

A more extreme position was developed by what came to be

known as the High Church party. Hooker argued that bishops were necessary for the well-being of the church; the High Church group insisted that bishops in succession from the apostles were necessary to the very being of the church, without which salvation is quite impossible. Baptism itself is not effectual to salvation unless administered within the unity of this church. Presbyterian and Independent bodies are not the true church because they lack apostolic succession. The Roman Catholic body, on the other hand, is a true and Catholic church, within which salvation may be obtained; but it is corrupt and its abuses are so great that salvation is made difficult; the Church of England's separation from it is, therefore, abundantly justified.

This view of the church was to have its ups and its downs in the Reformation period; in the Church of England and in the Protestant Episcopal Church in our own land it is known today as Anglo-Catholicism.

Enforced Conformity (James I, 1602–1625)

With the death of Elizabeth the reign of the Tudors came to an end, to be followed by that of the Stuarts. James VI of Scotland now became James I, ruler of the United Kingdom—England and Scotland. What would be his religious policy? Puritans presumed that one reared in Presbyterian Scotland would favor their cause; Roman Catholics hoped that, having escaped Presbyterian control, he would revert to the religion of his mother, Mary, Queen of Scots; Anglicans were quietly confident that one who believed as strongly in the divine right of kings as did James would maintain an Episcopal establishment which he could control through the appointment of bishops. So it happened. At the famous Hampton Court Conference, called to consider Puritan grievances, James finally blurted out: "You are aiming at a Scots presbytery, which agreeth as well with monarchy as God and the devil. Then Jack and Tom and Will and Dick shall meet and at their pleasure censure me and my council. Then Will shall stand up and say, 'It must be thus.' Then Dick shall reply and say, 'Nay, marry, but we will have it thus'; and therefore I say, the King shall decide." Then turning to his courtiers he added, "I will make them conform or I will harry them out of the land, or else worse—hang them."

This became the policy of James and his successors in the Stuart line—a policy of enforced conformity that went far beyond the comparatively moderate measures of Elizabeth, who was a far wiser monarch. Puritanism, however, continued to grow, not only as a religious movement, but also as a political movement, strongly opposed to the autocratic claims of the Crown. Some of the more radical Puritans now despaired of reforming the Church of England and formed "Separatist" congregations at Gainsborough and Scrooby. The restrictive measures of James induced members of these congregations to migrate to Holland. Some here came in contact with Mennonites and adopted Baptist views. In 1611 Thomas Helwys led a small group (eight or ten) back to England and founded the first Baptist church on English soil. Five years later another portion returned to England and founded the first Congregational church. In 1620 still another group, under the leadership of William Brewster and John Bradford, sought asylum in what came to be known as New England—the Pilgrim Fathers, as we have termed them. Presbyterians, Congregationalists, Baptists, it will be observed, were all part of the larger Puritan movement; and all except a minority of the Baptists (who accepted Arminian views in Holland) were Calvinists.

James' policy was more unpopular in Scotland than in England. Here there was a Presbyterian Church, with titular bishops (bishops by title only), appointed originally that the church might retain legal possession of its property. James sought to strengthen the power of these bishops at the expense of presbytery and general assembly; when he died the land was seething with bitterness and resentment.

James's one great gift to the church was the King James Bible. At the Hampton Court Conference reference was made to the Geneva Version of the Bible—a revision of Tyndale's great work, made by English refugees in Geneva during the reign of Queen Mary. It had become the popular version in England, but was detested by James because it had footnotes strongly opposed to the divine right of kings, to which James was committed. James cried he would have a new Bible. He proceeded to appoint forty-seven scholars, the leading scholars in the realm, to make the new translation. They labored for seven years and brought forth a version of the Bible, actually a revision of Tyndale and other earlier revisions, which James accepted, and so became known as the Authorized Version of the Bible. For beauty of rendition this great version has never been surpassed. Unfortunately, however, the ink on its pages was hardly dry when in some sense it became out of date. The oldest manuscript on which the ⸜ translators relied went back to approximately A.D. 1000. A few years after 1611 Cyril Lucar, patriarch of Constantinople, sent the king a gift—an early New Testament manuscript dating from the fifth century, a more reliable text, therefore, than the one on which the King James scholars had been forced to depend.

ENFORCED CONFORMITY (Charles I, 1625–1649)

James I, who had experienced Presbyterian opposition in Scotland before he came to England, and had proceeded with some caution in religious affairs, was succeeded by his son Charles I, who showed far less discretion. He believed, as did his father, in the divine right of kings. His policy, politically, therefore, was one of royal absolutism. Pressure for some effective checks on the monarch's powers, for an approach to real democracy, came from the Puritans.

Charles's evil genius was William Laud, archbishop of Canterbury. The Church of England, despite its bishops, had been regarded hitherto as a branch of the Reformed family of churches. Ministers from the continent, without Episcopal ordination, had been received into the ministry of the church, and had indeed played a prominent part in the English Reformation. Laud, however, regarded the Church of England as Catholic rather than Protestant—Catholic, but not Roman Catholic, though Laud dreamed of bridging over the gulf. Ties with the Reformed Churches of the continent were broken; for to Laud, Lutheran and Reformed Churches were not churches at all. On Puritanism he waged merciless war. He did not use the stake; only such "gentle persuasives" as the scourge, pillory, prison, cropping of ears, and splitting of noses. Ministers who refused to conform were deprived of their posts; their positions were filled with ministers who denounced Calvinism and declared passive obedience to the sovereign to be a part of the law of God. A similar policy was followed in Scotland and in the north of Ireland.

Ireland as a whole remained staunchly Roman Catholic. During the reign of Elizabeth lands of the rebellious Lords of Tyrone and Tyrconnel had been confiscated by the Crown; James I had opened these lands in northern Ireland to settlement; the majority of those who came in were Lowland Scots, who after their settlement in Ireland came to be known as the Scotch-Irish. They worshiped in the parish churches, but were allowed by Archbishop Ussher, a tolerant Anglican, to do without the hated Prayer Book, and to follow instead their accustomed Presbyterian forms. Now, under Thomas Wentworth, lord deputy of Ireland under Charles I, this toleration came to a sudden end. Presbyterians were required to take an oath "upon the Holy Evangelists" that they would give full allegiance to King Charles I and not oppose at any time in any way anything he might command. Those who refused to take this Black Oath were severely punished. Wentworth was making his plans to deport all Presbyterians back to Scotland when the situation sudden changed.

A considerable number of Puritans (Independents or Congregationalists for the most part) migrated to New England during the reign of Charles. Religion was not the sole motive for their departure, but it played a large part, probably the largest part so far as the leaders of the movement were concerned. They went in order that they might worship God freely in accordance with their conscience; not to separate from the Church of England, but to establish the purer worship, which now seemed impossible in the motherland. They were in great part men of the professional and middle classes—some of them men of large landed estates, some zealous clergymen, some shrewd lawyers, and some young scholars from Oxford. The majority were God-fearing farmers.

In Scotland there was revolt. It began in Edinburgh, in St. Giles Cathedral, on the Sunday in which the new Prayer Book imposed on the Scotch churches was introduced. A riot ended the service, and that afternoon in Grayfriars Churchyard Scotch Presbyterians signed a solemn covenant "to defend the doctrine and discipline of the Church of Scotland." Charles, faced by armed revolt in Scotland, called what came to be termed "The Long Parliament" to raise necessary funds for the prosecution of the war. This Parliament proved to be overwhelmingly Puritan in sentiment, and Charles soon found himself engaged in civil war in England in addition to the struggle in

Scotland. Laud in England, Wentworth in Ireland, were arrested by order of Parliament, tried, convicted, and executed. The forces of Charles were finally defeated, and he himself beheaded by order of Cromwell, most successful military leader in the civil war.

It was in this troubled period that a Presbyterian Church was organized in Ireland. Troops sent by Parliament to suppress the rebellion of Roman Catholics against its authority were mostly Scots, each regiment of whom had for its chaplain a Presbyterian minister. Churches were organized among the troops and among the Presbyterian settlers in the north of Ireland. In 1642 five ministers and four elders came together in Carrickfergus, a little north of Belfast, and organized the first presbytery in Ireland. By 1660 there were in the northern part of Ireland 80 Presbyterian churches, 70 ministers, 5 presbyteries, and 100,000 communicants.

Parliament meanwhile had called an assembly of "divines" to meet in Westminster Abbey, London (whence the name "Westminster Assembly"), to advise them regarding a religious establishment to replace the Laudian regime and with it the Prayer Book, use of which was now declared to be illegal.[4]

One hundred and fifty-one men were invited to participate in this gathering. Of these a hundred and twenty-one were clergymen, the rest laymen. John Selden, a member of Parliament, explained that "there must be some laymen in the assembly to overlook the clergy, lest they spoil the civil work; just as when the good woman puts a cat into the milk house to kill a mouse she sends her maid to look after the cat, lest the cat eat up the cream."

Two of those named to membership in the assembly were Anglicans, five were Independents or Congregationalists, some were Erastians (believers in government control of the church), the rest were Presbyterian in sentiment. In addition there were eight Scots who were invited to attend the assembly as advisers; their influence proved to be greater than their numbers would indicate.

The labors of the Westminster Assembly culminated in the drawing up of the so-called Westminster Standards; a Directory of Worship, adopted by Parliament in 1644; a Confession of Faith, with Longer and Shorter Catechisms, adopted by Parliament in 1648; a Form of Government (Presbyterian), approved by Parliament in

1648. As G. J. Slosser has stated:

> These Standards represented, for at least 250 years after their formulation, the most widely accepted and therefore the most influential body of Christian teaching within the English speaking world.[5]

With some changes they remain the standards (or constitution) of most Presbyterian churches in English-speaking lands today.

These standards having been adopted by Parliament, the Church of England became for a short period legally Presbyterian. A few presbyteries were actually established. But the Presbyterian establishment failed to materialize, partly because Parliament alienated the mass of Englishmen by their intolerance (Milton, himself a Puritan, wrote, "Presbyter is only priest writ large"), but chiefly because Oliver Cromwell and his army of Independents, Baptists, and Sectaries, were determined that it should not be.

LIMITED TOLERATION (Cromwell, 1653–1658)

Cromwell first purged Parliament of its Presbyterian opposition and finally dissolved it, ruling the kingdom autocratically as lord protector. During his regime (1653–1658) all except Anglicans and Roman Catholics were allowed to worship as they liked. Innumerable sects had now appeared—left-wing Puritanism, it might be called—including Levellers, led by John Lilburne, who demanded full equality for all men before the law, and a real share of the whole people in the work of government; Diggers, whose spokesman, Gerrard Winstanley, held that "all mankind ought to have a quiet subsistence and freedom to live upon earth; and there be no bondman nor beggar in all his holy mountain"; Fifth Monarchy Men, who expected Cromwell's regime to be followed by the fifth world empire or full dominion of Christ, characterized by the complete Christian anarchy of love; and Seekers, who held that no true church had existed since the spirit of "Antichrist became uppermost in the Church, and that God would in his own time ordain new Apostles or Prophets to found a new Church."

Most important of these new religious groups, and most enduring, were the Quakers, or Friends, founded and organized by George Fox.

As a young man Fox sought desperately for religious reality and found it at last, as he was convinced, through direct revelation of the Spirit. Out of this experience came his basic doctrine regarding the Inner Light: that the Light of the Spirit—the same Holy Spirit who inspired the Scriptures—is available to every man, and reveals to him the way of Christ, in following which he may find salvation. This Inner Light, rather than the Holy Scripture, is the highest authority. This doctrine Fox felt called upon to proclaim to gatherings of church people, as well as to individuals by the way. Again and again he was jailed for disturbing religious meetings; meanwhile he was gathering disciples—within eight years the movement had spread not only on the continent of Europe, but also in Asia, Africa, and North America. Under the supposed inspiration of the Holy Spirit many foolish and obnoxious things were done, which invited opposition and also persecution. Gradually Fox gave form to the growing movement; Quaker meetings imposed the restraints of the group upon individual eccentricity; the Quakers took on something of the placidity and amiableness which now characterizes them, whereupon they ceased to grow.[6]

Many of the Quaker peculiarities have now disappeared; some worshiping congregations still wait for the Spirit to move them, while others depend on a regular ministry. Their distinctive dress has vanished; their distinctive speech is now seldom heard. They continue, however, in the forefront of benevolent activity, and they contribute to ecumenical Christianity a strain of mysticism from which many non-Quakers continue to learn.

ENFORCED CONFORMITY (Charles II, 1660–1685)

Oliver Cromwell died in 1658. His son Richard was not able to continue his regime, and in 1660 Charles II, son of Charles I, came to the throne, with the combined support of both Anglicans and Presbyterians. Puritanism, whose ideals regarding worldly amusements and Sabbath observance had been enacted into law under Cromwell, was now thoroughly discredited among the upper classes, who for a time wallowed in an excess of indulgence. The middle class, however, retained much of its former sobriety.

J. R. Green reminds us:

> As soon as the wild orgy of the Restoration was over, men be-

gan to see that nothing really worthy in the work of Puritanism had been undone. [It left them] what Puritanism had made them, serious, earnest, sober in life and conduct, firm in their love of Protestantism and freedom ... Slowly but steadily it introduced its own seriousness and purity into English society, English literature, English politics. The whole history of English progress since the Restoration, on its moral and spiritual sides, has been the history of Puritanism.[7]

Under Charles, however, there was no place for Puritanism within the church. Two years after his accession to the throne a new Act of Uniformity was adopted. Each clergyman was required to make an oath of "unfeigned assent and consent to all and everything contained and prescribed" in a revised and more obnoxious Prayer Book, and also "that it is not lawful, upon any pretense whatever, to take arms against the King." This conscientious Puritans could not do. As a consequence some eighteen hundred rectors were compelled to surrender their posts. As J. R. Green has written:

It was the definite expulsion of a great party which from the time of the Reformation had played the most active and popular part in the life of the church. It was the close of an effort which had been going on ever since Elizabeth to bring the English communion into closer relations with the Reformed communions of the Continent. ... The Church of England stood from that moment isolated and alone among all the churches of the Christian world. The Reformation had cut it off from the Catholic Church. By its rejection of all but Episcopal orders the Act of Uniformity (of 1662) severed it as irretrievably from the general body of the Protestant churches whether Lutheran or Reformed.[8]

Parliament was not content, however, merely to expel Puritan ministers from the Church of England: Dissenters were not permitted to engage in religious services outside the church. In 1664 a Conventicle Act was passed imposing fines, imprisonment, and ultimate transportation (banishment) on those who attended a service not in accordance with the Prayer Book, if five or more persons not of the same household were present. The following year a Five Mile Act was passed forbidding any dissenting minister to come within five miles of an incorporated town, or within the same distance of the place of his former ministry. Such persons were also forbidden to teach school (about the only occupation readily open to a former minister). Though such laws could not be perfectly enforced, there was much persecution, and consequently much suffering. One popular Baptist minister, a tinker by trade, named John Bunyan, spent altogether twelve-and-a-half years in prison through the execution of these laws. And it was in prison that he wrote his immortal allegory, *Pilgrim's Progress,* perhaps the most widely read of all Protestant classics. In 1673 a Test Act was passed which prevented Roman Catholics and dissenters from holding military or civil office unless they took the Lord's Supper according to the rites of the Church of England. This act was not finally repealed until 1828.

Episcopacy meanwhile had been re-established in Scotland, along with a series of restrictions similar to, but even more drastic than, those enacted for England. All office holders were required to disown the Covenants of 1638 and 1643, looking to the establishment of Presbyterianism. Fines were levied against those who failed to attend the services of newly appointed Episcopal rectors; if payment was not forthcoming, troops were quartered in their homes. As Presbyterian ministers continued to hold services in open fields apart from the towns, troops were sent to disperse their gatherings. Ultimately it became a capital crime to attend such a conventicle. Women and children were tortured to reveal the whereabouts of husbands and fathers, whose lives were forfeited because of such attendance. In the old churchyard at Stirling a monument has been erected to Margaret Wilson, a young girl of eighteen, drowned in Solway Inlet because she would not renounce her Presbyterian faith. In 1666 a revolt of Covenanters in Pentland was ruthlessly crushed, as was a more serious uprising thirteen years later in the Battle of Bothwell Bridge. Numerous prisoners taken in this last struggle were deported to the American Colonies.

THE KILLING TIME (James II, 1685–1688)

The more uncompromising Presbyterians were now a proscribed and hunted folk, known as Cameronians (from one of their leaders, Richard Cameron).

The persecutions begun under Charles II were continued during the reign of his brother James II; in fact, became more severe. The first year of his reign became known as "the killing time." James II, however, was a Roman Catholic; he was ready to grant indulgence to dissenters in both England and Scotland in order that he might remove all penalties from his coreligionists. His ill-concealed efforts to restore Roman Catholicism as the established church of the British Isles united all parties against him, and in 1688 he was driven from the throne. He was succeeded the following year by joint sovereigns, William, Stadholder of the Netherlands (a Dutch Calvinist) and Mary, his wife, daughter of James.

TOLERATION (William and Mary, 1689–1702)

At the beginning of this new reign a Toleration Act was passed which brought the long Reformation struggle in England and Scotland to an end. In England, the Church of England (Episcopal) remained established by law; but the dissenting bodies (Presbyterian, Congregational, Baptist, and Quakers), representing now only a minority of the population, were permitted to worship as they pleased. In Scotland, the Presbyterian Church, accepting the Westminster Standards, became the established religion, with toleration granted to Episcopalians and others. The Cameronians, who had resisted all efforts to compel them to conform, continued their opposition to any control of the church by civil authority and condemned the failure to renew the ancient covenants, organizing finally as the Reformed Presbyterian Church of Scotland. Out of this long struggle for religious and political freedom came constitutional monarchy in England and the great principles which are the pride of the Anglo-Saxon democracies (representative government, freedom of speech and worship, the right of habeas corpus, for example). And it was during this period that the Thirteen Colonies were settled—many dissenters coming to the new lands that they might worship God freely, according to the dictates of their own conscience.

FOR CONSIDERATION

1. Were the Puritan objections to the Elizabethan settlement justified at the time?

*2. What are the advantages and disadvantages of a liturgical form of worship, such as that which is found today in the Protestant Episcopal Church? Would it be wise for our own church to use additional liturgical elements? To make fuller use of the church year?

 3. Episcopalians, through the use of their Prayer Book, become as familiar with the great prayers of their church as we do with our favorite hymns. Prayers offered in nonliturgical churches are apt to be more heartfelt and adaptable to changing circumstances. Which type of prayer is preferable for the present day?

 4. What justification was there for the Puritan attitude toward "worldly amusements"? What should be the Christian attitude toward such things today?

 5. How would you evaluate the puritan conception of the Sabbath? How, in your estimation, should the Sabbath be observed today? Consider in this connection Exodus 20:8–11; Mark 2:23–28; Luke 14:1–6; 6:1–10; John 7:21–23; Colossians 2:16–17; Romans 14:5–12.

 6. What can we learn from Puritanism today?

 7. What is the evangelical objection to Anglo-Catholicism?

*8. The question of "apostolic succession" is an important one for Episcopalians. It is a stumbling block to the reunion of Anglican and non-Anglican bodies. For Presbyterian ministers to accept reordination by bishops in the line of apostolic succession would discount the ministry of their fathers. Is this a vital point of difference?

 9. In what sense can Presbyterianism be termed a scriptural form of government?

10. The Presbyterian Church has a detailed written constitution. What are the values of such a constitution? What are the dangers?

11. Is it true, as James indicated, that autocratic civil government and democratic ecclesiastical government are incompatible? Why?

*12. Consider the relative merits of the King James and later translations of the Bible. Which version should we give to our young people? Why?

13. What can we learn from the Inner Light of the Quakers?
14. John Bunyan could have been released at any time, if he had agreed not to preach. Was he wise in declining to give such assurance? What was the principle involved?
15. Episcopalians and others, following the Prayer Book, pray, "Forgive us our trespasses." Presbyterians and others, following the Bible, pray, "Forgive us our debts." How should the two get together in public prayer?

Ignatius Exhorting His Fellow Jesuits to Purify the Roman Catholic Church

16
COUNTER-REFORMATION DEVELOPS

"THE EXTRAORDINARY THING about the Protestant conquests," says Preserved Smith,

> was their sudden end. Within less than fifty years the Scandinavian North, most of Germany including Austria, parts of Hungary, Poland, most of Switzerland, and Great Britain had declared for the 'gospel.' France was divided and apparently going the same road; even in Italy there were serious symptoms of disaffection. That within a single generation the tide should not only be stopped but rolled back is one of the most dramatic changes of fortune in history. The only country which Protestantism gained after 1560 was the Dutch Republic. Large parts of Germany and Poland were won back to the church, and Catholicism made safe in all the Latin countries.[1]

This reversal of fortunes was one effect of the so-called Counter-Reformation—a transformation of the Roman Catholic Church, stimulated by the Protestant Reformation. It included administrative reform, educational reform, moral reform (but no doctrinal reform), combined with an attempt to crush Protestantism and to compel all dissenters to return to the Roman obedience.

There had been at the outset a moderate party within the Roman Catholic hierarchy, prepared to make some concessions, hoping to win back the Protestants. Differences regarding the Mass, veneration of the saints, papal supremacy, and other matters could not however be reconciled; and finally in 1542 Pope Paul III approved a rigid uncompromising policy, which was followed by his successors. In accordance with this policy the *Inquisition* (see page 159) was re-organized and made more effective. By it, promising Protestant movements in Italy and Spain were entirely wiped out. It claimed a multitude of victims in other lands. (Back of the attempts to crush the Reformation in Germany, Holland, France, and Great Britain [which we have briefly surveyed] was the might of *Spain,* then enjoying her brief hour of glory.) To prevent heretical notions from being planted in Catholic minds there was established the *Index,* a list of prohibited books which no Catholic was permitted to read without official per-mission. Regulations to prevent any seepage of wrong ideas into Ro-man Catholic circles have since been greatly extended.

THE SOCIETY OF JESUS

Meanwhile (1540) the Society of Jesus had been organized—an aggressive Roman Catholic order formed to oppose Protestantism. It succeeded perhaps better than any other agency in checking the growth of the Reformation. Founder of the Jesuits was Ignatius Loyola, a Spaniard, who originally sought glory on the field of battle but after a crippling wound underwent a profound religious experi-ence which led him to devote his life to the service of Christ. A true Christian, he had come to believe, is led to submit wholly to God and to become an utterly disciplined member of the church. Realizing that he must have an education to accomplish his purpose, Loyola entered a boys' class in Barcelona, made rapid progress, and finally graduated from the University of Paris. Here he gathered about him a devoted group of able men, who became the nucleus of the Society of Jesus, a new species of monastic order.

The Jesuits, as they came to be called, were a body of picked men

—carefully selected and highly trained, subject to strict military discipline according to which the member was obligated to obey his superior "like a corpse which can be turned this way or that, or a rod that follows every impluse, or a ball of wax that might be molded in any form." In order that members of the order might be free to serve the church in any needed capacity, they were given freedom from previous monastic restraints regarding abode, dress, hours of devotion, or particular type of service. All underwent the remarkable "Spiritual Exercises" developed by Loyola, which serves the order as a Manual of Arms, and helps to impress upon them something of a distinctive character.

Under Loyola's leadership the Jesuits gave themselves first to works of charity, which won for them the affections of the people. They developed outstanding preachers who did not hesitate to preach to out-of-doors assemblages, by which means many were won back to their former faith. They put great emphasis on schools, which came to be regarded in some areas as the best schools of their day, and which succeeded in enrolling and winning scholars from Protestant families. Polished, cultivated men of the world, the Jesuits became the favorite father confessors of the rich and powerful, and transformed the confessional into a power instrument of moral and spiritual guidance for the benefit of the church. In this endeavor it seemed to many, Roman Catholics as well as Protestants, that the Jesuits debased the ethics of Christ. They were criticized especially for accepting attrition (sorrow for sin based on fear of the consequences) in place of contrition (godly sorrow) in the sacrament of penance; for accepting the theory of probabilism (that a not absolutely certain law does not bind the conscience); for teaching that the sinfulness of an act depends upon the intention of the doer rather than upon the act itself—tending, so it was charged, toward the doctrine that the end justifies the means (though this accusation was strenuously denied by the Jesuits); and for upholding the right of mental reservation, by means of which one could make statements or give answers which he recognized at the time would be definitely misleading. The Jesuits gave to the church a host of devoted missionaries, men who carried the gospel to the Orient (India, China, Japan) and to North and South America, long before Protestants had become awakened to their missionary responsibilities. They also developed a remarkable capacity for political intrigue.

"Immediately upon their confirmation by the Pope," summarizes an article in the *Concordia Encyclopedia,*

> the Jesuits opened their campaign against the Reformation. They were a controlling influence in the Council of Trent and determined the severely anti-Protestant position of that body. They were largely instrumental in suppressing the Reformation in Italy, indeed in all Southern Europe. In Germany they worked with marked success from various centers, instigating Catholic princes to exterminate Protestantism by force. They were active in Austria ... Hungary, Tyrol, Silesia, Poland, Moravia, and even entered Russia in an attempt to convert the Czar. They were a powerful force in Spain and Portugal. Belgium was saved for Catholicism through their labors. Their entrance into France (1561) though exciting the jealousy and suspicion of the *Parlement* of Paris and the French clergy, was soon followed by a marked change of popular sentiment in favor of Catholicism. The horrors of St. Bartholomew-tide and the assassination of Henry IV are laid to their charge. They denounced the Edict of Nantes, which granted a measure of toleration to the Huguenots, and they were in hearty accord with, if not actually responsible for, its revocation (1685) and all the horrors that followed. In England they kept up a secret propaganda for more than a century. They made repeated attempts on the life of Queen Elizabeth ... [2]

THE COUNCIL OF TRENT

During the years 1545–1563 (with interruptions) there met in the German Tyrolean town of Trent, on the border of Italy, a general council, called by Pope Paul III to undertake seriously a work of reform within the Catholic Church, and to draw up a definitive statement of its faith in opposition to the various Protestant confessions. In this confessional statement—the Decrees and Canons of the Council of Trent— tradition was recognized as a co-ordinate authority with Scripture; justification by faith was rejected; the Roman

Catholic sacramental system was affirmed; purgatory, the veneration of the saints, the use of relics and images, were defended. It was admitted that the sale of indulgences had led to abuses; such sales were therefore forbidden for the future; but the theory of indulgences and their proper use was defended. Interestingly enough, there is no statement regarding the authority of the pope. There was as yet no final understanding regarding the relative authority of pope and council.

The Council of Trent also took action correcting many of the abuses which had crept into the Roman Catholic system (absentee bishops drawing income from benefices—or dioceses—which they never visited, for example). Provision was also made for the better education of the clergy, more preaching, more pastoral care of the laity, more constant and helpful oversight of the clergy by the bishops.

By the middle of the sixteenth century a change had come over the papacy itself; abuses in the curia were corrected; the popes continued to exercise temporal power, but they were mostly men of strict life and deep religious earnestness. Along with this development came a renewal of zeal and devotion within the church.

> So it came about that the Roman Church [forty years after Luther] presented a very different spectacle from that exhibited when [he] had begun his work. Its principles were essentially unchanged, but it had had a thorough awakening. The revival of piety and of theology, the formulation of its doctrines, its missionary zeal, above all the enthusiasm and activity of its new order, the Jesuits, and the support of able princes, were all manifestations of vigorous life. It had renewed its strength and was ready to contest the right of Protestantism to exist in Christendom.[3]

The struggle to crush Protestantism and rewin lost territory continued, as we have seen, in Holland until approximately 1587, in England till 1588 (the Great Armada), in Germany till 1648 (the Peace of Westphalia), in France till after 1685 (revocation of the Edict of Nantes). By this time the religious map of Europe had been drawn much as it has remained to the present time.

FOR CONSIDERATION

*1. What is your evaluation of the Roman Catholic Counter-Reformation? Where was it right? Where wrong? Where incomplete?

2. What can Protestantism learn from the Counter-Reformation?

3. The Roman Catholic Church has never officially given up the idea that error in religion and morals should be suppressed by force. Can Protestants call attention to the dangers which they fear from this attitude, without risking the charge of bigotry?

4. When and how should error be suppressed?

*5. What is the danger of censorship?

6. Should Protestant churches imitate the Roman Catholics and attempt to give more guidance to their members in regard to unwholesome literature, films, and other media of mass communication?

*7. How in your estimation does Protestant piety and zeal compare with that of Roman Catholicism? Why the difference?

8. Would you accept or modify Ignatius Loyola's definition of a true Christian? (See page 224.)

9. Should the discussions now developing between Protestants and Roman Catholics be encouraged or discouraged?

10. In the face of mounting opposition to all Christian truth, should Protestants and Roman Catholics now seek to develop a common front, to co-operate (as far as possible) rather than keep attacking each other?

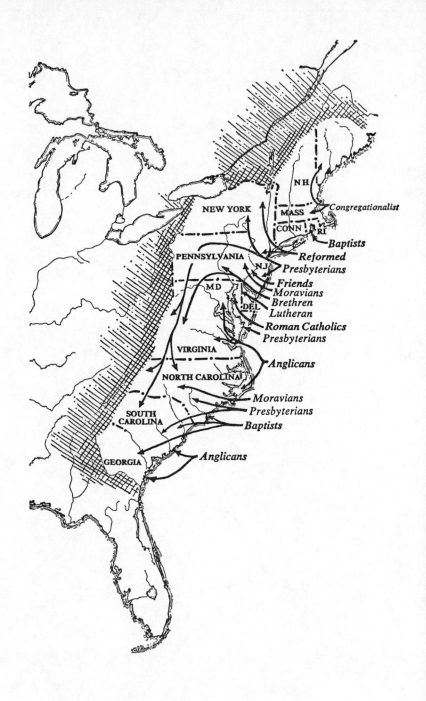

NEW YORK

N.H.

MASS

CONN

RI

Congregationalist

Baptists

Reformed

PENNSYLVANIA

N.J.

Presbyterians

Friends

Moravians

MD

Brethren

DEL

Lutheran

Roman Catholics

Presbyterians

VIRGINIA

Anglicans

NORTH CAROLINA

Moravians

Presbyterians

SOUTH
CAROLINA

Baptists

GEORGIA

Anglicans

Part IV
IN
MODERN TIMES

The Thirteen Colonies

The map indicates where early religious groups predominantly settled during colonial period.

Dutch Reformed Christians Coming to Worship in New Amsterdam, 1650

17
THE CHURCH
COMES TO THE AMERICAS

"IN 1492 COLUMBUS sailed the ocean blue," opening up a new world for eventual colonization. Martin Luther was then a lad of nine years. In the years that followed, both Roman Catholicism and Protestantism were brought to the Americas. Roman Catholicism led the way—naturally, for Protestantism was still struggling for the right to exist, and it was some time before Protestant governments were strong enough to support colonies in distant lands. In order of priority came . . .

THE ROMAN CATHOLIC CHURCH

In 1493, the year following Columbus' great discovery, Pope Alexander VI published a bull in which he drew an imaginary line from the North Pole to the South Pole, a hundred leagues west of the Azores, bestowing on Spain all the territory lying to the west of that boundary, while all to the east was confirmed to Portugal. As a consequence of this decision, Portugal ultimately established her authority and planted her religion in what is now the Republic of Brazil; Spain took over the rest of South America, Central America, the West Indies, and portions of North America (Florida, Texas, New Mexico, Arizona, and California).

The Spanish conquerors, "conquistadores" they were called, had come in search for gold. There was in consequence much heartless exploitation. They had also come to save souls.

> In a form deliberately drawn up and prescribed by the civil and ecclesiastical counselors at Madrid, the invader of a new province was to summon the rulers and people to acknowledge the church and the pope and the king of Spain; and in case of refusal or delay to comply with this summons, the invader was to notify them of the consequences in these terms: "If you refuse, by the help of God we shall enter with force into your land, and shall make war against you in all ways and manners that we can, and subject you to the yoke and obedience of the church and of their Highnesses; we shall take you and your wives and your children and make slaves of them, and sell and dispose of them as their Highnesses may command; and we shall take away your goods, and do you all the mischief and damage that we can, as to vassals who do not obey and refuse to receive their lord; and we protest that the deaths and losses that shall accrue from this are your own fault."[1]

Along with the conquistadores, however, came devoted missionaries, particularly Jesuits, who sought, with some success, to protect the Indians from every type of injustice. Through their zealous labors primarily, the natives were won to a nominal Catholicism which has remained the dominant religion of these areas, except in the United States, to the present day.

France began her bid for empire in North America in 1608, moving up the St. Lawrence, then on to the Great Lakes and down the Mississippi. In the southern hemisphere the Spanish conquests had opened the way for the Cross; in the northern hemisphere, daring missionaries preceded the explorers. Jesuits risked their lives to win the ferocious Iroquois to the Christian faith.

One of these, Father Jogues, venturing into hostile territory, was captured along with Huron companions, and cruelly tortured to the limits of human endurance. He passed up opportunities to escape from his tormentors to minister to the Christians among his fellow captives. Learning, however, that the Iroquois planned to kill him, he found his way to a friendly settlement and then home to France. He soon returned, however, to Canada, again ventured out among the Iroquois, and this time paid the penalty with his life.

The imperial hopes of France collapsed under the growing power of England, but the French influence (strongly Roman Catholic) remains in Canada (particularly around Quebec) and also in southern Louisiana. Little knots of French Roman Catholics were engulfed by the pioneers moving into the Mississippi Valley after the Revolutionary War.

THE CHURCH OF ENGLAND

England began its colonizing activities along the Atlantic Seaboard in 1607. The charter issued to the Virginia Company provided that "the Word and services of God be preached, planted and used, not only in the said colonies, but also as much as might be among the savages bordering among them, according to the rites and doctrines of the Church of England." The earliest ministers to come to Virginia were Puritans (inclined toward Presbyterianism) with little regard for the Prayer Book; but after 1624, when the colony came under the control of the Crown, laws were passed to make sure that services would be conducted only by episcopally ordained ministers, and in conformity with the canons of the Church of England. No rival body was permitted in this colony until after 1689, when the British Toleration Act was enacted. Some Presbyterian ministers were licensed after this date; Baptists, who refused to apply for license, were persecuted up to the eve of the Revolution. In five other colonies (New York, Maryland, the Carolinas, and Georgia) the Church of England became in time the established church (supported by public taxation, recognized, and granted privileges by law). In all save Virginia it represented only a minority of the population; generally speaking, the governing, aristocratic class.

The Congregational Churches

The second Protestant communion to be brought to American shores was Congregationalism. The Pilgrim Fathers (Separatists), fearing that their children might marry out of the faith, left Holland and disembarked at Plymouth Rock in 1620. Puritans, insisting that they were not separating from the Church of England, began to come to New England by the thousands eight years later. They came from mixed motives, but foremost among the leaders at least was the desire to worship God according to their own understanding of Scripture, and the resolve to build a covenant or holy community in "the wilderness." The dominant Presbyterian majority among the Puritans preferred to remain in England, where a few years later they would grasp at the reins of government. A number of Presbyterians were included in the migration, but they were overwhelmingly outnumbered by the "Independents."

The churches which they set up in the new land were congregational in government, Calvinistic in their theology. Puritans at this time—whether Congregational or Presbyterian—did not believe in the separation of church and state. As a consequence, the two were united in the three New England colonies (Massachusetts, Connecticut, and New Hampshire). The franchise was restricted to church members in Massachusetts until 1691, and citizens were taxed for the support of the church in all three colonies until after the Revolutionary War. There was no toleration for dissenters in New England, as there was none in Virginia, until after the enactment of the English Toleration Act in 1689. In both sections there were strict laws regarding Sabbath observance, though these were more strictly enforced in New England. (Many of the so-called "blue laws" of the New England Puritans are, however, fabrications.) The government here was not a theocracy, as often called, "for the influence of the clergy was entirely unofficial and without the sanction of law. They never did more than offer opinions and present communications, either unasked or on request." Clergy and magistrates co-operated, however, in their effort to create a Christian society, and New England was the most religious portion of the land.

THE DUTCH REFORMED CHURCH

New Amsterdam was founded as a Dutch colony in 1624. A church was organized four years later, with the full support of the colonial authorities, who, except for a short period, tolerated a diversity of faiths. The Dutch Church was the third Protestant church to be organized in America, and the first in the Reformed or Presbyterian tradition. In 1664 this colony was taken over by the English and renamed "New York." The Church of England now became the established church in the area around New York, but the Dutch Reformed (now the Reformed Church in America) retained its strength in this area, as it has done until the present day. In 1687 Governor Dongan wrote:

> New York has first a Chaplain belonging to the Fort of the Church of England; secondly a Dutch Calvinist; thirdly a French Calvinist; fourthly a Dutch Lutheran. Here bee not many of the Church of England; few Roman Catholocks; abundance of Quaker; preachers ... Sabbatarians; Anti-Sabbatarians; some Anabaptists; some Jews; in short, of all sorts of opinions there are some, and the most part of none at all.[2]

THE ROMAN CATHOLIC CHURCH IN THE COLONIES

Lord Baltimore, proprietor of the Colony of Maryland, was a Roman Catholic. Depending on Protestant immigrants for the success of his financial venture, and wishing at the same time to make Maryland a haven for his fellow religionists laboring under legal disabilities in England, Baltimore opened Maryland to "all liege subjects of the king." In 1649 a predominantly Protestant legislature at the suggestion of the proprietor passed a Law of Toleration permitting freedom of worship to all who acknowledged the Deity of Christ. Maryland thus became the first colony providing for real, though limited, religious toleration. In 1692 Maryland became a Crown colony, and shortly thereafter a law was passed continuing toleration for all except Roman Catholics. The Catholic Church, limited from the beginning to a small minority of the population, continued its existence, however, until all restrictions were removed after the Revolutionary War.

THE BAPTIST CHURCHES

Roger Williams, a Puritan clergyman, came to Massachusetts in 1631. He refused to settle in Boston because the church here had not officially separated from the Church of England. His insistence on complete separation of church and state in Massachusetts, and his claim that the land had not been properly bought from the Indians, led to his banishment from the colony. Before he could be returned to England he fled into the wilderness, and later with friends founded the town of Providence, which became the heart and center of the new colony of Rhode Island. The charter which Williams secured for the colony provided for the complete separation of church and state—the first such state in the modern world. Williams' tract on "The Bloody Tenent of Persecution" has been called the ablest statement and defense of the principle of absolute liberty of conscience that had appeared in any language.

Two years after founding Providence, Williams became a Baptist and organized the first Baptist church on American soil. Rhode Island soon became a haven for Baptists and other dissenters; Roger Williams himself left the Baptist Church and died a "seeker," despairing of all churches and all ordinances. Other Baptists, meanwhile, were appearing in New England (where for a time they were severely persecuted) and later in the Middle Colonies. The first Baptist association composed of five ministers was organized in Philadelphia in 1707. At this time there were twenty Baptist churches in the colonies with a total of approximately five hundred members. Baptist growth came with the revival known as the "Great Awakening," beginning about 1740. Pressing into the South where the masses of the people were out of touch with the established (Episcopal) church, they gained by the end of the Colonial period that numerical superiority in this region which they have retained to the present day.

THE PRESBYTERIAN CHURCH

Presbyterianism in America drew from many sources. Puritans inclined toward Presbyterianism, as we have seen, came to Virginia;

others were lost among the mass of Congregationally-inclined Puritans in New England. Some removed to Long Island where a Presbyterian church was organized as early as 1640. Nine years later a group of Puritans, no longer welcomed in Virginia, migrated to Maryland around Annapolis, where later some of the earliest Presbyterian churches were organized. From 1660 on, Presbyterians came from Scotland and the north of Ireland, some to escape the religious difficulties there, settling in various spots along the Atlantic Seaboard. Huguenots began to arrive after 1685, fleeing France after the revocation of the Edict of Nantes. The majority of these in the South ultimately found their way into the established (Episcopal) church, but many elsewhere entered the Presbyterian Church, as did some Dutch and Welsh settlers. Puritans and Scots founded an Independent Church in Charleston sometime after 1680. A large colony of Highland Scots began to settle along the Cape Feâr River in North Carolina in 1747.

Francis Makemie, the apostle of Presbyterianism in the new land, arrived from the north of Ireland in 1683. He organized important churches (especially Snow Hill and Rehoboth) on the Eastern Shore of Maryland, and in 1706 joined with six other ministers to form the first presbytery. Eleven years later a synod was organized, with four presbyteries; the churches were all in the Middle Colonies. An independent presbytery was formed in South Carolina sometime after 1722. In 1725 the great Scotch-Irish immigration set in, continuing to the eve of the Revolution. These sturdy settlers, who contributed more to the growth of the Presbyterian Church in the colonies than any others, came to America largely on account of economic difficulties in the Old Country, but also in part because of political and religious restrictions from which they suffered.

They came in three streams: one to New York; a second to the South Carolina Piedmont; a third, the largest, to Pennsylvania, and then on into the back country of Virginia and the Carolinas. As a consequence of this Scotch-Irish migration, the Presbyterian Church by 1776 had become the second largest church in the colonies, surpassed only by the Congregationalists, whose strength was confined to New England. Presbyterian strength was in the Middle Colonies and along the frontier, where they constituted "a shield of sinewy men thrust in between the peoples of the Seaboard and the red warriors of the wilderness." Associate and Reformed Presbyterians coming to the colonies shortly before the Revolution united in 1782 to form the Associate Reformed Presbyterian Church.

THE SOCIETY OF FRIENDS (QUAKERS)

Quakers began to come into the colonies after 1656. Feared as troublemakers, they were unwelcome in both Massachusetts and Virginia. In the former colony a number were whipped, and others were imprisoned; four who persisted in returning to the colony were hanged. Quakers were soon found in all the colonies, but most were congregated in the three "Quaker colonies"—New Jersey, Delaware, and Pennsylvania. William Penn organized the colony which bore his name on democratic lines, with complete religious toleration from the beginning. Advertisement of this fact brought a mass of settlers from Europe, with the result that Pennsylvania soon became one of the most important colonies, with a heterogeneous population, chief of whom were Quakers, Scotch-Irish Presbyterians, and a variety of German bodies. By 1700 the Quakers were the most widely spread and the best organized of all the churches in the colonies as a whole. After this period, however, their missionary zeal subsided, and they ceased to grow.

VARIOUS GERMAN BODIES

Various German groups came to America, particularly to Pennsylvania, beginning in 1683, and continuing to the Revolution. They came partly because of economic reasons (the dire poverty resulting from the Thirty Years War); partly also for political reasons (the devastations of the Palatinate by the armies of Louis XIV); and partly for religious reasons (continuing persecutions by their Catholic rulers). Lutherans were in the majority, but there were also many German Reformed; a number of Moravians, some of whom came for missionary purposes (their major settlements were in Bethlehem, Pennsylvania, and Salem, North Carolina); a handful of Schwenkfelders; and groups of Mennonites (including the Amish) and Dunkards (a pietistic sect of German Baptists now known as the Church of the Brethren, and the Brethren Church).

As we glance back over the beginnings of the churches in America, it is clear that not all of the pioneers by any means came for religious reasons; but there were many who did. The multiplicity of churches in America stems in considerable part from the fact that here was a land of political, economic, and religious freedom. Many peoples have brought their particular religious traditions to enrich the whole; here more than anywhere, we do well to recall the words of Paul: "All things are yours, whether Paul or Apollos or Cephas ... all are yours; and you are Christ's, and Christ is God's" (1 Cor. 3: 21–23).

FOR CONSIDERATION

1. Is it true that our forefathers came to America to worship God according to their own conscience? Give reasons for your answer.

*2. Consider in turn each of the various religious bodies treated in this chapter that you know something about. What, in your estimation, has been the contribution of each to our religious heritage?

3. How does 1 Corinthians 3:21–23 (quoted above) relate to the Colonial period of our history? To the current American scene?

Proving the Copernican Theory / Deciphering the Dead Sea Scrolls

18
THE CHURCH
ABSORBS NEW KNOWLEDGE

THE REFORMATION was inspired in large part by the recovery of two great biblical truths: the doctrine of justification by faith, and the sole authority of Scripture. This led inevitably to a period of profound theological reconstruction.

By the end of the second or third generation, elaborate systems of theology had emerged, which, it was insisted, must be held in their entirety by members of the church, particularly by ministers. In the Lutheran Churches it was the Formula of Concord, approved after a generation of bitter struggle, in the year 1577. In the Reformed Churches it was the Second Helvetic Confession (1566), the Canons of the Synod of Dort (1618), the Westminster Confession (1649). Theologians of this period regarded the Bible

> as the literal word of God in all its parts, having been dictated by the Holy Spirit to men acting only as amanuenses [stenographers]. . . . Not simply is the Bible as a whole, or the truths which it contains, from God, but every phrase, word,

and letter, including even the vowel points of the Hebrew Massoretic text. It is infallible, not alone in the sphere of religion and morals, but in history, geography, geology, astronomy, and every other field upon which it touches.[1]

THE CHALLENGE TO THE CHURCH

These dogmatic systems, including this doctrine of Scripture (still regarded by many as the test of orthodoxy), had hardly been completed before new intellectual movements had arisen which threatened to destroy the foundations of all Christian belief.

The New Science

The first of these was the new cosmology or world view. The old cosmology was that of Aristotle and Ptolemy (second Christian century), accepted by Thomas Aquinas (thirteenth century), and woven into the theology of the Catholic Church. Included in this conception was the belief that our world was the physical center of the universe, and a belief in special providences—the theory that every event, or at least every important event in nature and in public and private life, is contrived by God for the warning, help, or edification of his own.

Prime architects of the new world view were Copernicus (1473–1543), who advanced the hypothesis that the earth revolved around the sun rather than vice versa; Galileo (1564–1642), who proved by the use of a telescope that the Copernican theory was correct; and Sir Isaac Newton (1642–1727), who formulated the law of gravitation, which explains why an apple falls to the earth rather than into space, and why the heavenly bodies move as they do. According to this conception, the universe is governed by law, and the earth, so long the center of the universe, is only a tiny speck lost in the infinities of space.

The Copernican hypothesis was at first denounced by both theologians and scientists. Luther referred to its author as "an upstart astrologer, who strove to show that the Earth revolves, not the heavens or the firmament, the Sun and the Moon. This book," he went on, "wishes to reverse the entire science of astronomy; but sacred scripture tells us that Joshua commanded the Sun to stand still and not the Earth." Turretin (not Calvin, as frequently charged), appealing to

Psalm 93: 'The world also is established that it cannot be moved,' said, 'Who will venture to place the authority of Copernicus above that of the Holy Spirit?'

"It is easy to condemn these men as narrow-minded and bigoted" (writes Hector MacPherson),

> it would be more accurate to censure them for not realizing that men like Copernicus did know something about astronomy. But the struggle of the Reformation had driven the Reformers to assert with particular vehemence the infallibility of the Holy Scriptures, and they were unable to distinguish between the spirit and the letter, or to realize that the Scriptures could not be authoritative in regard to purely material things. In addition, the Reformers were totally ignorant of the subject under discussion.[2]

The new scientific point of view—the idea of a world governed by law—was to have great significance for the church. It challenged the authority of the Bible (only because theologians regarded it as a scientific textbook); it emphasized the insignificance of man (now a tiny creature on an insignificant planet); it weakened the sense of God (no longer needed, it seemed to many, since man had discovered the unvarying law of cause and effect); it exalted scientific method (all knowledge to be tested by observation and experiment); it began the long conflict between science and theology, which has continued, though with decreasing intensity, down to our present day (the most serious of these later conflicts was that over evolution).

The New Philosophy

A second intellectual movement, growing out of the first, was the new philosophy, of which Descartes (1596–1650), Spinoza (1632–1677), and Leibnitz (1646–1716), were the chief exponents. These men—profound thinkers all of them, intoxicated by the new scientific discoveries—accepted as true only that which could be proven by reason. Reason was interpreted in the narrowest sense and equated with logical demonstration, leading, to the kind of certainty attainable in mathematics. Though it became evident in time that little or nothing (save perhaps mathematics) could be "proved" by reason so understood, authority in every realm was challenged, and increasing numbers of men turned away from all religious truth which struck them as unreasonable. At about the same time, British empiricism was developing into a form which together with rationalism led to a mechanistic view of the universe, in which all of nature, including man, was a machine—without purpose and without spiritual significance. This remained the prevailing view of man in intellectual circles until the beginning of the present century, when at first slowly and then more rapidly men came to be recognized again as creative individuals.

The Historical Study of the Bible

The third of these new intellectual movements which threatened to undermine the foundations of Christian belief was the rise of the historical study of the Bible—including the so-called lower criticism (which was an attempt to recover the original text of the Bible), and the so-called higher criticism (which was a careful study of the documents themselves, in an attempt to discover who the author was, when he wrote, and for what purpose). Textual criticism has given us a more accurate text of the Bible; it is, we can be sure, a reliable text in all essential respects; at the same time—since the earliest manuscripts differ in particulars—it has become unmistakably clear that there is no infallible text. Higher criticism proved more damaging to traditional views of inspiration. It came to be widely agreed, for example, that Moses was not the author of the Pentateuch. Scholars are now generally agreed that there are four major documents (JEDP) back of the present work, the earliest of these composed a century or more after the reign of David; and that these four major documents were combined into one sometime after the Exile. Other traditional ideas have been challenged. Isaiah is seen to be a composite work. Daniel, for the great majority of scholars, has lost its strictly historical character and become a prophetic work, written to inspire the Jews to heroic resistance during the days of Antiochus Epiphanes. Such conclusions have made it difficult for increasing numbers of men to accept the older views of inspiration. Because it had been affirmed over and over again that inspiration depended on absolute inerrancy, for many the Bible ceased to be inspired at all. It became only a book among other books.[3]

Deism

The new science, the new philosophy, the beginnings of the new historical study of the Bible, along with an awakening interest in, coupled with much misunderstanding of, the new field of comparative religions, gave rise to Deism, a religious movement which, originating in Great Britain, spread rapidly to France, America, Germany, and other lands. The Deists rejected all supernatural religion and advocated in its stead what they termed natural religion, what they understood, falsely, to have been the religion of mankind before the various supernatural religions appeared—i.e., a simple belief in God, in morality as the service of God, in immortality as the reward of the good life. Deists in England unleashed a slashing attack on Christianity: on the arguments advanced for its supernatural aspects (prophecy and miracles), on the content of Christianity (including most of the worn-out objections which are still advanced by our "village atheists"), and on the bases of Christian morality (future rewards and punishments rather than experience). In England able champions appeared to defend Christianity, and within a generation Deism as a movement had disappeared—partly because of this intellectual defense, partly because of its own inherent weakness, and partly because of an evangelical movement (the Methodist Awakening) which enabled the church to prosecute its mission with new vigor and success.

In place of Deism, however, skepticism arose in certain intellectual circles: It has continued among many of the intelligentsia, philosophers, scientists, and literary figures to the present day. Another result was Unitarianism, retaining a belief in God, and in Jesus Christ as a moral teacher, but rejecting all belief in the Deity of Christ or in the inspiration of Scriptures.

Deism spread from England to France, where its effects were still more devastating. "So many of the most eminent men of letters in France joined in the attack on Christianity and the [Roman Catholic] Church that they might almost seem to have entered into a conspiracy of irreligion." This irreligion reached its height in the French Revolution, when reason was officially enthroned in the place of Christ. The French Revolution spent its fury, but religion has never recovered its old strength in this land, once so strongly Catholic.

From France, Deism spread to America—especially in the Rev-

olutionary period, when French thought came to be the vogue. Tom
Paine, Benjamin Franklin, Thomas Jefferson, and others shared
Deistic views, though few entered the lists against the church.

In Germany, there developed a rationalistic movement known as
the Enlightenment. It diffused the view that Scripture was to be
valued only for the truths of natural religion and its morality, divested
of miracle or the supernatural. Though there were still many who
preached Christ and many who followed them, the general tendency
of the educated and still more of the half-educated was to turn away
from Christ.

To many intellectuals, not only in Germany but also in England,
France, and the United States, it seemed as though Christianity's days
were numbered; in another generation, they boasted, no intelligent
man would accept its supernatural claims.

But Christianity did not die. Instead, the next century was to witness the most massive expansion that the church had known in all its
history.

THE RESPONSE OF THE CHURCH

This recovery of Christianity, this expansion, was due in part to
the intellectual vigor of its chief representatives—particularly in Germany, where "modern" theology had its birth—and to the great evangelical movement which originated in Germany, spread to England,
to America, and then "to the end of the earth." To this movement we
will turn shortly. We will attempt here to sketch very briefly the rise
of "modern theology," to which the rationalistic movement, particularly in Germany, gave birth.

Liberalism

Most important of the early theologians who sought to stem the
rationalistic assault was Friedrich Ernst Schleiermacher (1768–
1834). Born in a pious evangelical home, he developed a warm devotion to Jesus Christ which remained with him to the end of his days.
In Berlin he became an intimate of a little coterie of brilliant intellectuals, most of whom found no value in Christianity. To them he directed his first significant theological work: "Addresses on Religion
to the Educated Among Its Despisers." Religion, he held, was based

on feeling—the feeling of absolute dependence on God—what he referred to more frequently as the "God-consciousness." Christianity in turn was based on the feeling of absolute dependence on God through Jesus Christ. In accordance with this view the Scriptures became a record of vitalizing Christian experiences which could awaken like experiences in us. Doctrine was an attempt (always inadequate) to describe these experiences in words. All religions were to be judged by their success in reconciling man with God. Christianity was the truest religion because it succeeded more perfectly in this endeavor than any other.

Schleiermacher founded no school, but he succeeded in turning the tide of intellectualism, running so heavily against the church. The data of religious experience, he emphasized, are as valid as any other data, and must be taken into account in any attempt to understand ultimate reality. This emphasis, however, led many theologians to look to themselves, rather than to Scripture, for a true knowledge of God.

Albrecht Ritschl, Schleiermacher's most important successor (1822–1889), insisted that the source and norm of all true religion is to be found in the historic revelation of God in Jesus Christ. To get at this revelation, he taught, we must follow ordinary methods of historical research (hampered by no particular view of inspiration).

The Ritschlian School became the dominant school of theology in Germany, England, and the United States in the period preceding World War I. Adolf Harnack, the most influential disciple of Ritschl, more liberal than his master or many of his disciples, reduced Christianity to a belief in the Fatherhood of God, the infinite worth of the individual, righteousness and love as the requirements of God. Jesus became little more than a moral teacher. Followers of Ritschl, exponents of the "social gospel," were optimistic that God's Kingdom—the reign of righteousness and peace on earth—was close to realization.

Neo-Orthodoxy

The First World War, followed by the Great Depression, and then the Second World War, shattered this easy optimism and led to far-reaching theological reconstruction.

According to an excellent recent survey:

> The mood of recent Protestant thought is one of renewed appreciation of traditional Christian modes of thought. It is a mode of increased sympathy with the biblical point of view, with the creeds and doctrines of the church, and with the principles of the reformers. Thus, in one sense the newer theological emphases can be described as a return to the past, a reaction against liberal interpretations and a revival of "classical patterns of thought." So such terms as "neo-orthodoxy" and "neo-Protestantism" have been used to refer to the new theology. . . . [4]

Some of the distinctive motifs of this present-day theology are:

(a.) The Sovereignty of God. If the divine immanence was a primary concern of the liberal conception of God, recent Protestant thought has emphasized the transcendence, the otherness, the sovereignty of God. . . .

(b.) Revelation. The emphasis on the sovereignty of God is intimately related in the Protestant thinking of today with a profound concern for *revelation* as the source of the knowledge of God and as the basis for all Christian thinking. This may be approached by way of what is frequently called the "I-Thou" relationship, which means simply that the relation of God and man is one of personal confrontation. . . . In the personal encounter with God, a decision must be made—for or against, obedience or rebellion, faith or unfaith. . . .

(c.) Christ the Word. One of the great gains of liberal theology was its rediscovery of the humanity of Jesus. From the point of view of more recent Protestant thought, however, the liberal concern with the "historical Jesus" left little room for the recognition that he is also more than man. Thus it is felt that liberalism departed both from the Christian tradition and from the biblical witness at a crucial point. For if we are to be fair to the New Testament, we must see that its very center is the confession that Jesus is the Lord, that God was truly in him. Whatever is said about his life and his teaching is there only because of the faith that in him God was present to men, and that in his life and death and resurrection God was reconciling the world to himself. Jesus as man is significant for the New Testament writers just because in this man "all the fullness of God was pleased to dwell" (Col. 1:19). . . .

(d.) Man the Sinner. The most widely discussed aspect of contemporary Protestant thinking has doubtless been the conception of man as sinner. Here the revolt against liberalism has been most obvious, and has been reinforced by the course of recent historical events and by discoveries of the new psychology. The result has been a quite conclusive repudiation of the optimism of the late nineteenth century, and an explicit and thoroughgoing recognition of the tragic aspects of human existence, of the precariousness of human achievements, and of the depths to which man can and does descend. . . .

(e.) History and the Kingdom of God. The chastening of the liberal faith in man has inevitably had a profound effect on the social gospel, particularly as regards its confidence in the possibility of "building the kingdom of God upon earth." This has not meant a denial of the church's obligation to speak to the social orders as well as to individuals. That central concern of the social gospel has continued. But the confident assumption that the social order might be progressively transformed into the kingdom of God has been rejected. Its place has been taken by a more vivid sense of divine judgment upon all human history and by a new understanding of the hope of the kingdom of God. . . .

. . . the hope of Christians is [now] seen to point beyond history.

To put this in other words, the kingdom of God is not the end product of a progressive "Christianizing" of the social order. That notion of the kingdom was more the reflection of a nineteenth-century evolutionary outlook than of the New Testament hope. The kingdom of God, in the New Testament hope, is wholly *God's* kingdom, not to be established by any human effort but solely at the divine initiative. The responsibility of man is not that of "building" the kingdom but of "readiness" for its coming, by repentance and faith. Moreover, the kingdom is not a continuation of historical development. It symbolizes the end of the present age; but stands "beyond" this history.[5]

Liberalism Today

It will be understood, of course, that there still remains a wide range of theological opinion. Liberalism continues as a living force in the ongoing church. It is not characterized by particular ideas so much as by method. It emphasizes the importance of free inquiry in religious truths without previous decision as to what the outcome might be. It stresses the vital importance of experience, and relies heavily on reason for the apprehension and understanding of the divine revelation. It includes influential theologians of the present day, such as Bonhoeffer, martyred under Adolf Hitler, who suggests that religion should be freed from its institutional forms; Bultmann, who contends that the message of the Bible must be loosed from the mythological trappings in which it is now imprisoned; and Paul Tillich, who attempts—with what success is debatable—to be a Christian philosophical theologian. There are many shades of liberalism, from Bishop J.A.T. Robinson, who in his amazingly popular *Honest to God* sought to popularize certain aspects of the three theologians named above, on the one hand, to the more evangelical type of theology presented by L. Harold De Wolf (see his "Theology for the Living Church" and "Theology in Liberal Perspective"), on the other.

Conservatism ("Orthodoxy") Today

Conservatism also remains a living force, and is represented probably even more widely than liberalism among both clergy and laity. As with liberalism, this term—conservatism—covers a variety of groups and viewpoints. In general, it describes those forms of Christianity retaining standards of belief which developed in the Reformation period and became embodied either in tradition (the Baptist churches) or in historic creeds such as the Formula of Concord (Lutheran), the Canons of Dort (Reformed), or the Westminster Confession of Faith (Presbyterian). At one end of the conservative spectrum are churches and teachers who accept the modern scientific point of view and have absorbed much of the historico-literary approach to the Bible, once identified with "liberalism." At the other end of the conservative spectrum are churches and teachers who hold to a very rigid interpretation of whatever creed they profess and have not moved intellectually out of the seventeenth century.

Fundamentalism

Identified by some with conservatism, yet severely criticized by leading conservatives, fundamentalism is marked by three characteristics: (1) a belief that the Bible contains no errors whatever, (2) a strongly literal interpretation of the Bible, (3) antagonism to other groups and refusal to co-operate in ecumenical life; and sometimes (4) an excessive interest in the future (e.g., the Second Coming and the millennium), often with the result of becoming totally uninterested in doing anything for the improvement of this present world. (These various viewpoints will be dealt with more at length in a later year's CLC study of Christian doctrines; see also page 276.)

The Present Outlook

It is plain that there still remains a wide range of theological opinion. Extremists on the right (fundamentalists) and on the left (modernists), however, are in the minority; orthodox (retaining the traditional view) and neo-orthodox are now in the vast majority. The bitter conflict that racked the churches in the latter part of the nineteenth and the early portion of the twentieth century is all but forgotten. Theological debates will continue, but it has become clear that faith in God as revealed in Jesus Christ will not be discredited by further advances in science, or by the increased knowledge of the Bible which comes to us through the careful labors of our scholars.

FOR CONSIDERATION

*1. Does modern science make it more or less difficult to believe in God? Why is this the case?

2. How far can reason be accepted as a test of religious truth?

*3. Does belief in the inspiration of the Bible require us to believe that it is free from all error? Study carefully in this connection 2 Timothy 3:13–17.

4. Can we look to the Bible for truth regarding scientific questions?
5. Does the truth of Christianity depend upon any particular view of inspiration?
6. Does the acceptance of the newer theories regarding the authorship and composition of various books of the Bible (see page 244 for example) destroy or make stronger the credibility of Scripture? Why?
7. Should young people be informed of the various views of Scripture held by Christian scholars?
8. How can we safeguard our young people against the skepticism and rejection of Christian truth which is so widespread among molders of public opinion in the present day?
9. Should young people be taught that Christianity stands or falls with the particular view held by the teacher himself, or by a particular school of Christian thought?
10. Is it possible for orthodox and neo-orthodox to live peaceably within the same church?
11. Which of the positions outlined on pages 246–251 are you prepared to accept? Which would you question?
12. Is the final judgment expressed on page 251 too optimistic? How would you sum up the situation?

Missionaries Bring the Bible to the American Frontier and to China

19
THE CHURCH
EXTENDS ITS BORDERS

THE EIGHTEENTH CENTURY closed, as we have seen, with the church, in the judgment of its enemies, facing an uncertain future. In the century following, however, its expansion was greater than at any other time in its history. This expansion was due in large measure to the evangelical movement which arose in Germany and spread from Germany to England, America, and then throughout the world.

IN GERMANY

The evangelical movement (pietism) arose in Germany shortly after the Thirty Years War, which spread physical devastation and human degradation through most of the land. Religious life was low and the ministry generally ill-equipped to stir it to new vigor. The awakening came through the labors of Philipp Jakob Spener (1635–1705) and his disciple and successor as leader of the movement, August Hermann Francke (1663–1727).

Pietism stimulated a revival of personal religion. According to Spener, every true Christian must have an independent religious life of his own, a life of direct communion with Christ, not dependent up-

253

on the ministration of a priest or the mediation of a church. Pietism emphasized the necessity of a conscious conversion. (Francke had experienced a very sudden conversion, preceded by a great spiritual struggle and a conviction of sin; this for many became the standard whereby all real conversions should be tested.) It encouraged laymen to take a more active part in the work of the church; it promoted Bible study, in which laymen participated along with their pastor (a revolutionary step which aroused much opposition); it inspired efforts for the religious training of the young (leading to the establishment of Sunday Schools); it promoted practical benevolence; it insisted on a renunciation of the world, including under this head the theatre, card-playing, dancing, and all use of tobacco; it overemphasized Christian experience at the cost of the intellectual element in Christianity; it had little concern for social reform; some paid inordinate attention to a study of the second coming of Christ (encouraging the rise of premillennarianism and of the later dispensationalism [see Glossary]); there was a tendency to withdraw into little associations of the "truly awakened," critical of all who held opposing views, and thus to weaken the power and significance of the church as a whole.

Such was pietism in its weakness and in its strength. Some of these same tendencies have appeared and reappeared in the evangelical movement in every land.

An offshoot of pietism was our present Moravian Church. Beginning in 1722, a few refugees from the long-continued persecutions of Protestants in Bohemia and Moravia crossed over into Germany and began to settle on the estates of a German nobleman, Nikolaus Ludwig, Count von Zinzendorf. This gifted and spiritually sensitive young man, reared under pietistic influences, became more and more interested in these humble exiles from their own land and soon became accepted as their spiritual leader.

The Moravians had wished to maintain their own separate church. Zinzendorf desired them to become a pietistic association within the established Lutheran Church. The compromise was a unique community centering at Herrnhut, on Zinzendorf's estates, serving somewhat as a church within a church, endeavoring to build an international association of zealous Christians with membership in all Christian churches.

Despite Zinzendorf's wishes, the Moravians, joined by a group of German pietists, became in time a distinctive denomination, with their own rich liturgy and hymnology. There were bishops, preserving continuity with the Unitas Fratrum (Unity of the Brethren) or Bohemian Brethren, a pre-Reformation movement drawing its inspiration from the life and teaching of John Hus, but the polity was more presbyterian than episcopal. The Moravians continued their efforts to build up the cause of Christ rather than their own particular denomination. It was in a Moravian prayer meeting, carried on within an Anglican church, that John Wesley had the heartwarming experience which transformed his ministry and gave birth to the Methodist Church.

The group at Herrnhut became the first Protestant community to accept responsibility for carrying the gospel to other lands. Their first missionary was sent to the West Indies in 1732. The following year they were in Greenland. In 1735 their missionaries came to America, seeking to minister to the growing number of German colonists, at the time largely sheep without a shepherd. A year later their missionaries were laboring in Guinea, Egypt, South Africa, and Labrador. Within ten years this little village of exiles, about six hundred in number, had established missions in the West Indies, in South America, Surinam, Greenland, among the American Indians, in Lapland, Tartary, Algiers, Guinea, South Africa, and Ceylon. In two decades the little "Brother" community had called into life more missions than the whole Protestant church in Germany had done for two centuries.

Zinzendorf died in 1769, living in the memories of those who had known him as a man of singularly impressive and commanding personality, devout, earnest, and warmhearted, who gave his great endowments with a single mind to the furtherance of the gospel of Christ. He stirred up the missionary spirit in Protestantism, and his society became a witness to real and heartfelt piety in the midst of rationalism and indifference. He is one of the few men in history who could truthfully say, "to me to live is Christ."

In England

In England the evangelical movement advanced under the leadership of John and Charles Wesley and their friend George Whitefield. The situation here was similar to that which had prevailed earlier in

Germany—spiritual destitution among the masses, skepticism and indifference on the part of the educated (a consequence of the Deistic movement), accompanied by spiritual lethargy within the church. There were indeed some leaders (William Law, whose *Treatise on Christian Perfection* and *A Serious Call to a Devout and Holy Life* remain as two of our devotional classics, and Isaac Watts, founder of English hymnody) and some movements (particularly missionary societies for spreading the gospel in America) that held spiritual promise, but it was the Wesleys and Whitefield who really awakened the church. All three of these men, clergymen in the Church of England, had had conversion experiences on the pietistic pattern (the Wesleys were greatly influenced by the Moravians). Forced out of the churches they began to preach to the unchurched in the open fields. John Wesley, the most durable of the three, traveled incessantly—by horseback or in chaise—never less than 4,500 miles a year (an imposing record for the roads of that day), and preached an average of two times a day for fifty years. He organized his converts into societies, and these societies in time under his guidance became The Methodist Church—the largest religious body in England, outside the Anglican (state) Church. George Whitefield's influence was perpetuated more fully in the evangelical party within the Church of England (still strong, especially among the laity). Charles Wesley wrote hymns that carried the revival message and continue to be sung by Christians throughout the world ("Love Divine, All Loves Excelling"; "Hark, the Herald Angels Sing"; "O for a Thousand Tongues to Sing"; "Jesus, Lover of My Soul"; "O for a Heart to Praise My God!"; and many others).

The first Methodists reached America just ten years before the outbreak of the American Revolution. It was here on the frontier that their church was to have its greatest growth.

IN THE UNITED STATES
The Great Awakening

The Great Awakening, as it was called, reached the American colonies early in the eighteenth century. There was the same need here as in the older lands—a noticeable spiritual decline from the piety of the earlier generations. The awakening began in the Middle

Colonies, where it was carried largely by Presbyterian ministers. It flared up more spectacularly in New England under the preaching of Jonathan Edwards, and was carried through the length and breadth of the land by George Whitefield, who in all made seven trips to the colonies, the first in 1738, the last in 1769–70. Presbyterian evangelists brought the evangelical gospel into the Southern Colonies, particularly among the Scotch-Irish settlements stretched along the frontier, but also in eastern Virginia. As a consequence of their labors, Hanover, the first southern presbytery, was formed in 1755. But the Presbyterians lacked ministers, because of the high educational qualifications which were demanded. Baptist ministers, without having to meet any educational qualifications, came in far larger numbers, and within a single generation, after the Presbyterians had had their opportunity, the Baptists laid the foundations for that numerical superiority in the South which they have retained to the present time.

The Great Awakening brought growth to the American churches —Congregationalists benefiting most in New England, Presbyterians in the Middle Colonies, and Baptists in the South. It also brought divisions. Among the Congregationalists there appeared Old Lights (who opposed the revival message and the revival methods) and New Lights, some of whom became Baptists. It was these Separate Baptists (Calvinists) rather than the Regulars (Arminians) who preached the evangelical gospel, and it was they who registered the large numerical gains. Presbyterians also split into two parties—the Old Side and the New Side—who formally separated in 1741, but reunited, fortunately, in 1758. It was during the course of this revival that Presbyterians began to realize their need of educational institutions for the training of their ministers. A "Log College" had been founded in Pennsylvania in 1728; the College of New Jersey, now Princeton University, was founded in 1746.

The Great Awakening was not only a tremendous quickening of the Christian life: It changed the conception of entrance on that life in a way that profoundly affected the majority of American churches until comparatively recent times. It emphasized the conception of a transforming regenerative change, a conversion, as the normal method of entrance into the Kingdom of God. It gave general diffusion to the Baptist or Congregational view of the church as a company of Christians who had undergone a "conversion" experience. It laid little weight on Christian growth within the family. It promoted an ascetic theory of the Christian life.

The Revolutionary War, strongly supported by most Christian bodies, brought demoralization and loss to the American churches. Not only were buildings destroyed, and congregations scattered; morals had been shattered, and French infidelity or Deism encouraged. With war came separation of church and state. The decisive victory was won in Virginia, where Jefferson and Madison received essential support from Presbyterians and Baptists. The principle was later written into the Federal Constitution. The separation of church and state in America compelled each denomination to rely upon its own efforts if it was to maintain itself and grow; revivalism became a means to this end; churches which failed to make evangelistic efforts registered little gains.

Never was greater effort required. Before the Revolution, the colonists had been confined to the territory east of the Alleghenies. The war over, the mass migration into the Mississippi Valley was quickly under way. As one historian has indicated, few migrations in history can compare with the exodus from the East, and the supplementary migration from Europe to the West, in America. The story of the settlement of the West is one of the epics of history.

This vast movement of population came at a time when the churches in America were at their lowest ebb. Not more than five or six individuals out of a hundred were members of the church; skepticism and unbelief were on the increase; enemies of Christianity predicted its early death. To follow the hurrying throngs in search of new lands under these circumstances and in face of all the difficulties was the greatest challenge that the American churches have ever faced. They responded magnificently.

As one historian has written:

> The story of American home missions is one of the great chapters of church history. It has never been told adequately. Its significance for the nation has never been realized fully. It is as thrilling as the story of the pioneer settlers, as dramatic as the tales of Indian battles and buffalo hunts on the plains, as consequential as anything that three centuries of national progress have produced.[1]

Most successful in this missionary endeavor were Methodists, Baptists, and Presbyterians—in the order named. Within a single generation, Methodists, only a handful when the Revolutionary War began, became the largest church numerically in America. They still have one of the largest white memberships of any denomination in America and are more evenly distributed than any other. Their success was due to their zeal and their organization (admirably adapted to frontier conditions: circuit riders under the direction of their bishops). Baptists were second only to the Methodists in numbers, but their gains were registered mostly in the South—due to the fact that they migrated mostly from the South to the South and that their ministers, who farmed for their living, were unable to travel as extensively as the Methodist itinerants. Presbyterians held the strategic place on the frontier when the westward movement began. As a consequence of the first Great Awakening and the massive Scotch-Irish immigration, they were at the time the second largest denomination in America. In 1801 they entered into a plan of union with Congregational Churches (the largest denomination), so that actually Presbyterian and Congregationalist evangelists labored to build up the Presbyterian Church in the West.

They made extensive gains in Tennessee, Kentucky, Pennsylvania, and in all the states north of the Ohio. But they fell far behind the Methodists and Baptists, primarily because high educational qualifications drastically limited the number of their ministers. There were compensations, however. The educated Presbyterian ministers who believed church and school belonged together did far more for education in the South and West than any other denomination, and far more than the state, which had not yet awakened to its educational responsibility. They also collected about themselves in every community which they entered a large proportion of the better educated and more influential citizens. By 1837 the Presbyterian Church had become, not the largest, but the most influential denomination in America.

The Great American Revival

The growth of the churches in the early part of this period was aided immeasurably by what has been called the Second Great Awakening or the Great American Revival. This revival began in the East shortly after the Revolutionary War and spread to the West. In the East it was comparatively quiet and unspectacular, progressing for the most part under the preaching of faithful men in churches and in schools. In the West it was otherwise. It began here on the Kentucky frontier under the preaching of Presbyterian ministers in connection with their stated Communion services. The number attending these Communion services increased until thousands gathered in great camp meetings which continued as long as food could be preserved. Ministers of all denominations took part. Physical manifestations occurred: Strong men were stricken to the ground; they shouted, jumped, hopped, and rolled. Presbyterians gradually withdrew, and the camp meetings were taken over by the Methodists, who reaped the largest gain.

From Kentucky and Tennessee the great revival spread throughout the West, and also into the South. It continued at high intensity until about 1810, then with diminishing frequency and with less intensity in some parts of the country till about 1840. It brought great growth to the American churches; also, as we shall see, divisions, especially among Presbyterians, and the rise of new denominations. It led to the organization of most of our benevolent activities—foreign mission societies, home mission societies, Bible societies, tract societies, Sunday School associations, women's societies, church papers, and many others. It also helped to make revivalism one of the characteristic features of American Christianity. "Through it probably more than any other channel," writes Peter J. Mode,

> our evangelical Christianity has brought the impact of the Gospel to bear upon the problems of American society . . . It would not be difficult and by no means unsatisfactory to write the history of American Protestantism from the standpoint of its periodic awakenings.[2]

The last nationwide revival in the United States occurred in 1857, on the eve of the Civil War. Since that time there has been a series of great revivalists (and a host of imitators): Dwight L. Moody (1837–1899), B. Fay Mills, J. Wilbur Chapman, William A. Sunday (1863–1935), and more recently Billy Graham. Old-style revivalism remains a primary method for the recruitment of new members in many of the more emotional groups. In the older churches it has given way to other types of evangelism. It is clear, however, that the evangelical movement in America has not yet spent its force.

THE MODERN MISSIONARY MOVEMENT

Out of the early evangelical movement came the worldwide missionary endeavor. In the sixteenth and seventeenth centuries the Roman Catholic Church was laying the foundation of its present strength in what is now called Latin America, and in the Far East. The Protestant churches moved much more tardily. This was due in part to the fact that for some time they were struggling for the right to exist; in part to the fact that it was the Roman Catholic powers who first conquered possessions in the New World and made contacts with the older civilizations of the Far East; in part also to the fact that Protestants were slow to awaken to a sense of their missionary responsibility.

It is true that some missionary activity was carried on in the seventeenth century following the Dutch conquests in Ceylon, Java, and Formosa. An English "Society for the Propagation of the Gospel in Foreign Parts" in New England was organized in 1649. Pietists from Germany sent missionaries to India and Greenland early in the eighteenth century. By 1732 Moravians had become aflame with missionary zeal. But Protestantism as a whole still slumbered, lulled to sleep by the comfortable conviction that God's plans for the heathen would be accomplished without human effort.

William Carey

It was William Carey, a Baptist minister, cobbling shoes for a livelihood, who more than any other finally awakened Protestantism to its responsibility. In 1792 he published a pamphlet entitled "An Enquiry into the Obligations of Christians to use means, for the Conversion of the Heathens . . . ", which the *Encyclopedia Britannica* (Eleventh Edition, Article "Missions") rightly declared marked "a distinct point of departure in the history of Christianity." Shortly thereafter he preached on this same theme at a meeting of his Baptist Ministers Association. His text was, "Enlarge the place of thy tent, and let them stretch forth the curtains of thine habitations: spare not, lengthen thy cords, and strengthen thy stakes; For thou shalt break forth on the right hand and on the left . . . " (Isa. 54:2–3, K.J.V.). His message was summed up in two unforgettable phrases: "Expect great things from God. Attempt great things for God." This sermon led to the formation of a Baptist missionary society which sent William Carey as one of its first missionaries to India. He proved to be one of the greatest missionaries of all times, opening up lines which foreign missionaries have continued to follow till the present day. He was first and foremost an evangelist, not of hellfire, which he does not mention in his *Enquiry,* but of God's love for all mankind. He laid the basis for a system of modern education in India, beginning with the primary grades and culminating in a great university. He advocated all possible co-operation with other Christians. He pioneered in the use of literature—almost created the Bengali language, published a Chinese Bible, published Asia's first newspaper. He grappled with cruel customs and degrading social conditions, opposed the slave traffic, helped to end the sacrifice of infants in the Ganges, and the burning alive of widows on their husbands' funeral pyres. He founded the Agricultural and Botanic Society of Bengal, hoping to improve the productiveness and therefore the standard of living of the poverty-stricken Indian peasant.

The breadth and depth of Carey's missionary service is well illustrated in the principles laid down for themselves by the Serampore Brotherhood to be read three times a year in each station in their charge. Here is a summary:

"1. To set an infinite value on men's souls.

"2. To abstain from whatever deepens India's prejudice against the Gospel.

"3. To watch for every chance of doing the people good.

"4. To preach Christ crucified as the grand means of conversions.

"5. To esteem and treat Indians always as equals.

"6. To be instant in the nurture of personal religion.

"7. To cultivate the spiritual gifts of the Indian brethren, ever pressing upon them their missionary obligation, since Indians only can win India for Christ." . . .

For forty years Carey lived in India without a furlough home, the centre and inspiration of a far-reaching and many-sided work: perhaps the greatest and most versatile missionary of modern times and certainly one of the great names in Christian history.[3]

It was Carey, who, by his labors and his letters, finally aroused the Protestant churches as a whole to undertake the task of world missions. Within a single generation (1792–1835) practically every important Protestant church in Europe and America had within it an organized foreign-mission society.

We cannot follow the further progress of world missions in any detail, but K. S. Latourette, our most eminent historian in this area, describes the period 1815–1915 as the Great Century. During this period Christianity spread more rapidly than at any other period in its history, and became for the first time a world movement.

We must not overestimate the strength of this movement. In many lands the proportion of Christians remains pitifully low. In Asia and in Africa the church faces formidable opposition, contending ideologies, some of which are the exact opposite of Christianity, and none of which have the answer to human needs. Nonetheless the church continues to make impressive gains in many parts of the world, and in almost every land a native church has arisen, independent of all foreign control, with its own institutions and its own trained leadership. These newer churches are now producing some of our keenest, most penetrating evangelical leaders and theological minds. These churches will continue to need financial aid for many generations, but they have much to give in return. If necessary—if the churches in Europe and America were to perish—they could sustain the Christian witness alone.

FOR CONSIDERATION

1. Read Matthew 28:18–20; Acts 1:8; 2 Corinthians 5:16–20; Romans 10:1–15. What is their bearing upon the matter of this chapter?
2. What, in your judgment, is the strength and the weakness of the pietistic movement as sketched above?

3. To what extent are pietistic elements found in the evangelical churches today?

4. Consider the so-called gospel hymns, growing out of the revival movement inspired by Dwight L. Moody, Billy Sunday, and other popular revivalists of the last two generations. Is there a place for these hymns in the modern church?

5. Look up the missionary hymns as they are listed in your hymnbook. They spoke powerfully to our fathers. Have they lost their appeal? Why?

6. Has the evangelical movement, as traced in this chapter, disappeared?

7. What is the central evangelical message for the present day?

8. Should there be more or less hellfire preaching?

9. Is yours an evangelistic church?

10. What are the most compelling reasons why the American churches should support the foreign mission enterprise?

11. Is your church's interest in world missions rising or falling at the present time? Why is this the case?

12. What in your judgment is the major responsibility of the church in the "home field"?

*13. What are the advantages and what are the disadvantages of the separation of church and state as set forth in our national Constitution?

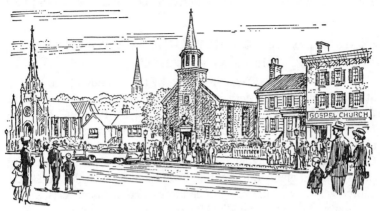

*Contemporary American Christians Gathering for
Worship on Sunday Morning*

20
THE CHURCH IN AMERICA
GROWS AND PROLIFERATES

THE WORD "proliferate" in the title is important. It means to grow—in a special way: namely, by putting out buds, as do many living things. So the church has grown through the ages, and will continue to grow. And so in America, a variety of denominations have sprouted.

As we have seen, a number of denominations were brought to America in the Colonial period from the older countries in Europe. At the end of this period the four largest churches in order of size were the Congregationalist, confined almost entirely to New England; the Presbyterian, with its greatest strength in the Middle Colonies; the Baptist, numerically first in the South; and the Anglican, scattered up and down the Seaboard, with its greatest strength in Virginia. Other denominations fell far behind, the larger groups being those of the Quakers, the Lutherans, the German and Dutch Reformed. Methodists, as we have previously noted, were only a handful.

AFTER THE REVOLUTIONARY WAR
Formation of National Organizations

The Revolutionary War, followed by the erection of the United States of America, led Methodists and Anglicans to form independent (national) organizations, the former in 1784, the latter in 1789. The Methodist societies had been gathered by lay preachers unauthorized to minister the sacraments; members were expected to receive the Communion from Anglican ministers. But most of these rectors had sided with England during the Revolutionary struggle, and their church was now on the verge of collapse; Methodist converts, meanwhile, were increasing rapidly. Under these circumstances John Wesley (a priest, or presbyter, in the Church of England) ordained ministers and sent them to America to ordain others. On Christmas Eve, 1784, ministers so ordained organized the Methodist Episcopal Church in America. The bishops (not John Wesley's idea) had not been ordained by bishops in the line of apostolic succession, and were not therefore recognized by the mother church.

Five years later, survivors of the Anglican Church, having finally, after much difficulty, secured bishops in the desired succession, organized the Protestant Episcopal Church in the United States. It had lost heavily in the Revolutionary struggle and only slowly regained something of its former strength.

In this same period the Presbyterian Church organized its first General Assembly. This church, wholly independent of foreign control since its first presbytery had been organized in 1706, was now too widely spread and growing too rapidly to expect representatives to meet annually in a single synod. In the new assembly were four synods, those of New York, Philadelphia, Virginia, and the Carolinas.

The Revolutionary War brought an end to the Anglican Church establishments.[1] The great principles emerging from the struggle in Virginia were written into the Constitution of the new nation. The withdrawal of all state support from any religious body—the constitutional provision for separation of church and state—was a novel and revolutionary experiment in the history of civilization. It meant not only that the church was free to conduct its mission as itself deemed best, but also that no single church could expect to enjoy a favored or dominant position in society, that all must recruit their membership on a purely voluntary basis, that "denominationalism" or religious pluralism would become and long remain the pattern of American Christianity.

In the new nation, where individualism was encouraged and where no particular sacredness was attached to traditional organizations, the number of denominations increased rapidly.

Offshoots of Rationalism

Two denominations, Unitarianism and Universalism, were offshoots of the more liberal religion incited by the rationalistic movement in England and America. Both drew chiefly from New England Congregationalism. Unitarians, organized nationally in 1825, rejected belief in the Deity of Christ. Without formal creed they believed generally in the fatherhood of God, the brotherhood of man, the leadership of Jesus Christ, salvation by character. In more recent times, extremists have appeared who disclaim belief in God and deny they are a "Christian" body. Unitarians as a whole put great emphasis on humanitarian endeavor. Universalists at first differed from orthodox bodies only in their denial of eternal punishment. They came ultimately to acceptance of Unitarian positions. In 1961 Unitarians and Universalists—both small bodies which have grown little through the years—united to form a single denomination.

Products of the Frontier

As we have seen, Methodists, Baptists, and Presbyterians were the groups which grew most rapidly on the expanding American frontier. But in each of these groups there were minorities which withdrew to form separate organizations. In 1792 James O'Kelly, a prominent Methodist minister in Virginia, dissatisfied with the appointing power of the bishops, withdrew together with a number of his followers and eventually organized a denomination called the Republican Methodists. In 1830 a more serious dissatisfaction on much the same grounds led to the formation of the Methodist Protestant Church. Meanwhile, Methodist influence had led to the organization of two denominations among the German-speaking population, particularly of Pennsylvania—the Evangelical Association and the United Brethren in Christ.

In 1946 these two bodies united to form the Evangelical and United Brethren.

Baptists formed their first National Convention in 1814 to support two foreign missionaries who had been sent out originally under the American Board of Commissioners for Foreign Missions. But an anti-mission movement arose among the Baptists, giving rise to Primitive or Hardshell Baptists, and to Two-Seed-in-the-Spirit Predestinarian Baptists, both now dwindling bodies. Numerous other Baptist groups arose on the frontier.

Presbyterians suffered heavy losses in the new West. When the Synod of Kentucky took disciplinary action against Cumberland Presbytery for ordaining ministers without proper educational qualifications, three ministers withdrew to form the Cumberland Presbyterian Church, which grew rapidly in Kentucky, Tennessee, and the neighboring states. A few years later a group of revival ministers in northern Kentucky, faced by disciplinary action because of their dissatisfaction with rigid Calvinism, withdrew from the Presbyterian Church. Two of these later joined the Shaker movement, which forbade marriage and flourished for only a short period. One, Barton W. Stone, became the leader of the Christian Church, a church which in their view was organized on the New Testament model, and which was without a written creed. It adopted Baptist principles and a Congregational church polity. James O'Kelly and his Republican Methodists became absorbed into this movement. In 1929 the Christian Church united with the Congregational Church to form the Congregational-Christian Church.

Thomas Campbell, a Presbyterian minister from Scotland, and his son, Alexander Campbell, rebelled against the divisiveness of human creeds as they had seen it on the frontier and organized the Disciples of Christ. The Campbells, like Stone, had no desire to form another denomination or sect. They hoped rather that all Christian people might be induced to unite upon the broad platform of the Scriptures. Nevertheless, the Disciples of Christ did become another denomination, baptizing only conscious believers by immersion and following a strictly congregational pattern. Barton W. Stone led a large portion of his following into the large movement initiated by the Campbells. Since there was no central body to adopt an official name for the combined body, both names, "Christians" and "Disciples," have been retained.[2] In 1849 some of the more conservative followers of Campbell began to separate from their brethren and ultimately took the name "Churches of Christ." They reject all musical instruments in the worship of God, are opposed to missionary societies and ecclesiastical boards, do not fraternize with other churches or affiliate with any interdenominational agency.

In the 1830's the Presbyterians suffered the most serious division which they had known to this time. At the turn of the century (1801), Presbyterians and Congregationalists (then the two largest religious bodies in America) had entered into a Plan of Union, whereby they agreed to combine their efforts for the winning of the West. As a consequence, large numbers of Congregationalists came into the Presbyterian Church; members of the two churches supported joint benevolent operations; and for a time each church had representatives in the highest governing body of the other. But theological differences appeared: Congregationalists accepting a modified Calvinism, Presbyterians tending to retain old-line Calvinism. "Old" and "New" Schools developed within the Presbyterian Church: The Old School opposed Congregational representation in Presbyterian courts, joint benevolent operations not controlled by the Presbyterian Church, and particularly the new theology seeping into the church through Congregational channels. The New School party took the opposite stand.

Differences over slavery were also beginning to emerge, the New School becoming increasingly critical. Southern conservatives, strongly Old School, insisted that the church could not condemn an institution recognized in Scripture. In 1837–8 came the division, the Presbyterian Church being split into two nearly equal divisions, each claiming to be the constitutional assembly. Southern churches were largely Old School, but there were New School minorities, particularly in the border states. Before this division, the Presbyterian Church had been the most influential (not the largest) church in the land. This position of leadership was now lost and has not since been regained.

Premillennial Bodies

The frontier also spawned some strange new movements, looking for the early return of Christ and the establishment of his millennial reign on this earth. One of these was the Church of Christ of Latter-Day Saints, popularly known as the Mormons. Founder of this body was Joseph Smith, who claimed that the angel Moroni had directed him to a spot where he found the Book of Mormon written on plates of gold in reformed Egyptian hieroglyphics, which he was enabled to translate into English through the aid of "transparent peep-stones" like lenses set in a silver frame. This book claims to describe the history of America from its first settlement by a colony that came from the Tower of Babel to the beginning of the fifth century of the Christian era. Those who accept the revelation as given to Joseph Smith become members of the one true church, now reconstituted on earth.

Troubles between the Mormons and their neighbors, especially after rumors arose about the plural marriages into which Joseph Smith had entered, led the Mormons from New York into Ohio, then into Missouri, and then into Illinois. Here Smith was slain by a mob. Brigham Young then organized the mighty trek of the Mormons across the western plains into what is now the state of Utah, where the desert was made to blossom as the rose. Here polygamy became the accepted practice of the sect, until finally in order that Utah might be received as a state of the Union, a new revelation to the then president of the Mormons ordered that the laws of the state opposing polygamy should be obeyed.

The Mormons are now one of our most rapidly growing sects. They believe that God revealed himself through Jesus Christ, Mohammed, Joseph Smith, and Brigham Young, and that he continues to reveal himself through the president of the Mormons. Salvation is for them through faith, repentance, and baptism by immersion, followed by obedience within the church. But baptism may be performed for the dead, who retain in the spirit world the normal powers of individuals and may at their option accept the work done vicariously for them in the Mormon temples here on earth. To give the dead such opportunity is an important part of the church's mission. Those who are sealed in marriage according to the Mormon rite (and only those) will be advanced to the dignity of gods in the afterlife. The Ten Lost Tribes, it is held, will be gathered, and Zion will be built on American soil. Christ will come to reign upon the earth, and the Mormons, or Latter-Day Saints, will be rulers over the world. They claim to be the heirs to all the material promises of the Old Testament.

Mormons were only one of numerous sects springing up at this time in the United States and other lands who set their hopes on the imminent return of Christ. Most important of these bodies was the Seventh-Day Adventist. William Miller, a Baptist in New York, interpreted Daniel 8:13–14 to mean that Christ would return to earth sometime in the year beginning March 21, 1843. When Christ failed to appear in the appointed period, the movement as a whole collapsed, but a handful of his original followers organized the Seventh-Day Adventist Church, which continues to emphasize the imminent return of our Lord, along with their insistence on the seventh day, instead of the first day of the week, as the proper day for religious worship.

Slavery Schisms

In the generation preceding the Civil War slavery became the all-absorbing issue. Increasing tension over the morality of slave-holding had played a minor role, as we have seen, in the division between Old and New School Presbyterians.

Methodists and Baptists divided into northern and southern bodies solely over the issue of slavery in 1845. New School Presbyterians divided on the same issue in 1857.

AFTER THE CIVIL WAR
"War-Inspired" Developments

Old School Presbyterians divided in 1861, after the War Between the States had begun and as an indirect consequence of that bloody conflict. Southern presbyteries claimed that the resolution pledging the allegiance of Presbyterians to the Federal Government made it impossible for them to remain. Meeting in Augusta, Georgia, on December 4, 1861, they organized the Presbyterian Church in the Confederate States of America, now the Presbyterian Church in the United States.

"Race-Inspired" Developments

Before the war, the majority of Negroes had been gathered into Methodist and Baptist Churches (almost equal in number); Presbyterians and Episcopalians fell far behind. Independent Churches were frowned upon. After the war, Negroes, unwilling to remain in a position of inferiority, left the white churches en masse. Baptist Churches encouraged them in this effort and garnered the greatest fruit. Methodists delayed and lost the larger part of their Negro constituency. Those remaining were organized into the Colored Methodist Episcopal Church. Meanwhile, two independent Negro churches pressed in from the North: the African Methodist Episcopal Church and the African Methodist Episcopal Church, Zion. Southern Presbyterians dallied too long and lost their total Negro constituency, though a portion was salvaged by the northern branch of the church.

Growing Out of the New Immigration

Immigration from Europe halted by the Civil War now increased rapidly; by the end of the century, the number entering averaged 800,000 a year. In 1924, when our present restricted immigration law went into effect, one-third of our total population was foreign-born or the sons of foreign-born.

Before 1890 most of the immigrants had come from northern and western Europe—kin to the earliest immigrants in religion and also in culture. After 1890 the largest proportion came increasingly from southern and eastern Europe, drawn to America primarily for economic reasons, differing from the early settlers in both religion and culture. The Roman Catholic Church, representing a small minority of the population in the Colonial period, increased by a large Irish emigration in the Antebellum period, now grew rapidly—becoming in time the largest single denomination. Lutherans also made extensive gains, finally passing Presbyterians to become the third largest Protestant denomination. They tended to organize in national groups, representing at times different layers of immigration from the same country. The Eastern Orthodox Churches (eleven major bodies, now totaling more than five million members) for the first time became a sizeable group. Largest of these churches is the Greek Orthodox, now numbering more than a million. Somewhat smaller are the Russian Orthodox Churches, three in number, differing in their attitude toward the Moscow patriarch. Jews, divided into three bodies (Orthodox, Reformed, and Conservative), became numerous. This new immigration into America also greatly increased the number of the unchurched. Some had become hostile to the church in the old countries; others were unshepherded or unreached in the new land to which they came.

Arising on the New Urban "Frontier"

America's old frontier—new land for the asking—was officially closed in 1890. But by now a new frontier was appearing: cities, growing rapidly, with their slums, changing neighborhoods, and ever expanding suburbs. City missions arose to meet the new need; the Salvation Army, seeking to evangelize inhabitants of the slum areas, all who were down and out, developed their extensive social activities; the Y.M.C.A. and the Y.W.C.A. offered a Christian environment to young men and young women in the cities, and expanded their activities to serve a variety of individuals in other areas.

Changing conditions of life, changing theological and ethical views, changing cultural patterns, new stresses, anxieties, and needs encouraged the rise of more denominations, and also of some strange new cults. These new bodies, too numerous even to enumerate, can be arranged in a number of categories, suggesting one at least of their distinctive emphases.

First, there are *premillennial* sects, which build their hopes around the imminent return of Christ. ("Any day now!") The Seventh-Day Adventists (see page 271), an older body, but entering on a new period of growth, fall into this category. A more recent sect, drawing some of their original inspiration from the Seventh-Day Adventists, are the Jehovah's Witnesses. They believe that the seventh trumpet (Rev. 11:15) has blown, and that the great battle between the forces of Jehovah and of Satan (the battle or Armageddon) will take place now at any time. Satan will marshall all his visible forces, commercial, ecclesiastical, and political, against Jehovah. They will come with tanks, planes, guns, from every nation. Only Jehovah's Witnesses will be secure. Weapons of war will be consumed, all political and ecclesiastical organizations will be destroyed. Satan will be bound; the millennium will begin. Jehovah's Witnesses will rule over the world.

Second, there are *perfectionist* sects. Most perfectionist sects are premillennial; but their emphasis is on Christian perfection—a state in which man is free from all conscious sin—which comes to one as a

second blessing (after justification). Largest and most rapidly growing of the perfectionist sects is the Church of the Nazarenes; another
is the Church of God headquartered in Anderson, Indiana.

In the *third* category come the *Pentecostal* sects. They are all premillennial bodies, and perfectionist as well; they put particular emphasis, however, on the pentecostal gift of the Spirit, evidenced only
by speaking in tongues. Many of them also give large place to faith-
healing. Most popular evangelists who include faith-healing as a part
of their technique belong to this group.

Perfectionist sects drew from the older churches, particularly the
Methodists, beginning about 1880; the Pentecostal churches, of
which the Assemblies of God and the Church of God headquartered
in Cleveland, Tennessee, are the largest, developed after the turn of
the century. They drew originally, and do still to a very large extent,
from economically depressed classes in both city and country. As Dr.
John B. Holt of the United States Department of Agriculture wrote
(in 1940),

> This religious movement is largely the natural product of the
> disorganization and cultural conflict which have attended the
> overrapid ... urbanization of an intensely rural and among
> other things, religiously fundamentalist population.[3]

To put the same idea more simply: They draw from a population
which no longer feels at home in the older churches, emotionally, economically, socially, theologically, morally.

Perfectionist and Pentecostal churches are strongly fundamentalist in their theology. Most of them inculcate the old Puritan morality—opposing dancing, card-playing, theatre-going (including the
movies), the reading of novels and other "light" literature; decrying
also the use of tobacco and intoxicating beverages.

Pentecostal churches are growing rapidly, not only in America,
but also in other lands, particularly on the mission fields (as are the
Seventh-Day Adventists), where they appeal particularly to those of
the lower economic classes.

Egocentric churches constitute a *fourth* category, into which a
number of our newer sects may be placed. Such churches have physical comfort, personal exhilaration, and freedom from pain, disease,

and boredom as their objectives. Here belong a large number of cults attached to the "New Thought" movement and emphasizing the influence of mind over body. For them God is essentially impersonal, and man essentially divine; salvation is defined as harmony, wholeness, health, happiness, mental peace, poise, and well-being; Jesus is the man who best exemplifies the truth (i.e., the Christ) which sets us free.

Most successful of these cults is Christian Science. According to its founder, Mary Baker Eddy, God is good, God is all: Therefore there is no evil, i.e., any such thing as matter, the material senses, sickness, pain, or death. All we need to do to get rid of sin, suffering, and death is to deny that it exists.

The Unity School of Christianity ("Unity" for short) is a kind of streamlined Christian Science. According to Charles Fillmore, its founder, all men are sons of God in the same sense that Jesus was the son of God. Recognition of this fact will banish sin, sickness, ignorance, and poverty. All we need to do is pray—and to pray is to affirm that God has already given what we wish. In the Foreword of his book *Prosperity* Fillmore wrote:

> What we need to realize above all else . . . is that God has provided for the most minute needs of our daily life and that if we lack anything it is because we have not used our mind in making the right contact with the supermind and the cosmic ray that flows from it.[4]

The New Thought religions, not recognized as orthodox Christian bodies, appeal to the well-to-do and the cultured—very different from those reached by the premillennial, perfectionist, and Pentecostal bodies.

Communal groups, of which there were many in the period preceding the Civil War, have continued to arise. Most widely publicized was the one revolving around "Father" Divine, composed largely of underprivileged Negroes, but including also a number of whites. Missions spread to many centers in America and in other lands. Peace centers included recreational facilities, homes for the aged, orphanages, employment agencies, schools. Father Divine encouraged his followers to regard him as God Incarnate.

✓There are also *esoteric* cults (see Glossary), with ideas drawn from Hindu religions, and *theosophy* (such as Bahaism; see Glossary); these, however, attract only a scattering of followers.

Developments Based on Fundamentalism

Denominations of a totally different type came out of the fundamentalist movement. In the 1890's acceptance of new views regarding the Scriptures brought a number of heresy trials, particularly in the Presbyterian Church in the U.S.A. About 1910 a series of little books began to be published called: *The Fundamentals—A Testimony to the Truth*. Emphasized as fundamental to the faith were the virgin birth of Christ, the physical resurrection, inerrancy of Scripture, penal, substitutionary atonement, and the imminent, physical second coming of Christ. In the next decade (1919–1929) a controversy arose over these or other "fundamentals" in a number of northern churches. For a time it seemed as if they might divide over the issue. The conflict finally subsided with a victory for those willing to tolerate differences in theological viewpoint. But a number of fundamentalist sects did appear, including the Orthodox Presbyterian Church, the Covenant Presbyterian Church, and the Bible Presbyterian Church (all stemming from a group of ministers disciplined by the Presbyterian Church in the U.S.A.), and the Methodist Protestant Church (a splinter sect which refused to come into the merger of the three major Methodist groups), and some others. Most of the premillennial, perfectionist, and Pentecostal churches, as we have noted, also retain fundamentalist ideas.

In 1963–64, as reaction from the older liberalism continued in the major denominations of America and as former fundamentalists (repudiating the term) adopted a more scholarly approach, tensions between the two theological points of view seemed to be abating. A small group of bitter-enders—mostly associated with the American Council of Churches—however, continued the attack on all other churches than their own, branding them as apostate.

FOR CONSIDERATION

*1. Does Christianity gain or lose by the variety and multiplicity of American religious sects?

2. Which of these religious bodies are making unique or distinctive contributions to the cause of Christ?

3. What is the distinctive contribution of your own denomination?

*4. Which, if any, of these religious bodies are divisive or harmful to the Christian enterprise? What harm can you point out?

5. In what sense can the church truthfully sing: "We are not divided, all one body we, one in hope and doctrine, one in charity" (from "Onward, Christian Soldiers").

6. In Colossians 3:11 Paul wrote: "Here there cannot be Greek and Jew, circumcised and uncircumcised, barbarian, Scythian, slave, free man, but Christ is all, and in all." What does this verse have to say regarding our present divisions?

7. Would you agree with those who hold that denominational divisions are actually sinful?

8. What church unions, if any, would you like to see?

9. The "newer sects" tend to draw from the less privileged classes. Is this a reflection on the older bodies? Give a reason for your answer.

10. To what extent is your local church, your denomination, a "class church"? Why is this the case? Ought it to be otherwise? If so, how can it move in that direction?

11. In the light of this chapter, read and consider the meaning of Jesus' words in John 17:20–23.

The Church Ministering to the People of the West Side Slums of New York

21
THE CHURCH BECOMES CONCERNED ABOUT SOCIETY

FOUR SIGNIFICANT MOVEMENTS have helped to shape Protestantism since the Reformation: first, an intellectual movement in which the church absorbed new knowledge and readjusted its theology in the light of modern science, modern philosophy, and the new historical study of the Bible; second, an evangelical movement, which appeared first in Germany, spread to England and America, and culminated in the modern missionary movement, which in the last one hundred and fifty years has led to the greatest expansion of Christianity in all its history; third, an ethical movement in which the church has recovered its concern for society and sought to carry the gospel into every aspect of life; and finally, the ecumenical movement, in which the church seeks to recover its lost unity in Christ.

We look at this time at the third of these movements. To understand the rise of the so-called "social gospel" two major factors must be taken into account: first, the industrial revolution, with its extremes of poverty and wealth; and second, the growing alienation of the working class from the church.

THE BACKGROUND

The Industrial Revolution

The Industrial Revolution arose in England during the latter part of the eighteenth and the early part of the nineteenth centuries. The United States passed through a similar experience a generation or so later.

By the Industrial Revolution we mean very simply that profound transformation of society which took place when men learned to harness first the power of steam and then later the power of gasoline and electricity. It involved the substitution of machines for human hands, for many human hands; the transfer of the ownership of the means of production from artisans to capitalists; the rise of the factory system, vast numbers of people moving from village or country-side to factory town or city, and dependent now on the machines in the hands of capitalists for an opportunity to earn their livelihood. It was marked also by an amazing increase in wealth, in material goods and services, such as man had never known before—but very un-evenly distributed. In short, the rich became richer, while the poor, cut off from the means of production, remained poor or became even poorer.

To understand why this was so we need to recall that the Industrial Revolution was accompanied by an economic doctrine of laissez-faire, which meant very simply a policy of hands-off by the state. Men believed, to begin with, that they had an absolute inherent right to private property. They might do what they liked with their own. Economists taught, and their theories were accepted by businessmen and also by political leaders, that if free competition prevailed and every man sought his own interests the highest good would be achieved for all—that these were natural laws, of the same sort that Newton and his associates had proved to rule the universe, and with which men interfered at their own peril.

It seems strange to us now that such men did not realize how heavily the dice were loaded in favor of the industrialists; that there is no freedom of contract when a factory owner, for example, has so much surplus wealth that he can close his factory for an indefinite period or move it to another town, while workers who are dependent on their daily wage for a chance to eat compete with those out of work for the barest pittance that the owner chooses to offer.

Failure to realize this fact exacted a heavy toll of human life. As one historian has declared:

> In all the bloodstained annals of the ravages of Mammon on Christendom, few chapters can compare in lurid horror with those that record the ruthless exploitation of child-life, of youth and womanhood, during the opening decades of the Industrial Revolution in Great Britain. ... The fortunes made in the textile trades were very largely coined out of the blood of little children.[1]

What, under such circumstances, was the role of the church? The prevailing theory was that the gospel was concerned only with individual and family ethics, not with evils of the social order. This was not the concept which had prevailed during the Middle Ages, when the church was greatly concerned about the matter of a just price. It was not the concept of John Calvin, who labored so strenuously to establish a Christian community in Geneva. It was not the concept held by Puritans in the early days of the English Reformation. It was a concept which had come to prevail during the seventeenth century in England as modern capitalism developed and the problems of society became more complex.

"In the eighteenth century," as R. H. Tawney has indicated,

> it is almost superfluous to examine the teaching of the Church of England as to social ethics. For it brings no distinctive contribution, and, except by a few eccentrics, the very conception of the Church as an independent moral authority, whose standards may be in sharp antithesis to social conventions, has been abandoned.[2]

What were the consequences?

> It was ... in the sphere of providing succor for the noncombatants and for the wounded, not in inspiring the main army, that the social work of the church was conceived to lie. Its characteristic expressions in the eighteenth century were the relief of the poor, the care of the sick, and the establishment of

schools. ... The fundamental brain-work of criticism and construction [it abandoned] to the rationalist and the humanitarian.

Surprise has sometimes been expressed [Tawney observes] that the Church should not have been more effective in giving inspiration and guidance during [the so-called] Industrial Revolution. It did not give it, because it did not possess it. There were, no doubt, special conditions to account for its silence— mere ignorance and inefficiency, the supposed teachings of political economy, and, after 1790, the terror of the humanitarian movements inspired by France. But the explanation of its attitude is to be sought, less in the peculiar circumstances of the moment, than in the prevalence of a temper which accepted the established order of class relations as needing no vindication before any higher tribunal, and which made religion, not its critic or its accuser, but its anodyne, its apologist, and its drudge. It was not that there was any relapse into abnormal inhumanity. It was that the very idea that the Church possessed an independent standard of values, to which social institutions were amenable, had been abandoned. The surrender had been made long before the battle began. The spiritual blindness which made possible the general acquiescence in the horrors of the early factory system was, not a novelty, but the habit of a century.[3]

Alienation of the Masses from the Church

The church's recovery of its social vision was brought about not only by the shocking spectacle of human misery accompanying the Industrial Revolution, but also by the sudden realization that the lower classes had been largely alienated from the church.

The first indication of a changed attitude toward religion on the part of the masses, perhaps, is found in the French Revolution, which occurred only a few years after our American War of Independence. In the French Revolution, peasants and city proletariat, led by liberal intellectuals, for the first time turned against the church, which they numbered among their oppressors, and sought to replace the worship of God in Jesus Christ by the worship of human reason.

The French Revolution was followed in time by the development of what came to be known as scientific socialism and then by Communism, both of which received their classic formulation in the writings of Karl Marx and his friend and collaborator, Friedrich Engels. The family of Marx was Jewish, but like many other such families in Germany, had accepted Christianity. Karl Marx grew up, then, in a Christian home, in the land where Protestantism had its birth, and where it was still the dominant religion. Exiled from his homeland, Marx moved to England, and it was here, at a time when laissez-faire capitalism was exacting its heaviest toll in human blood, that he wrote his great work *Das Kapital.* Friedrich Engels' father was a wealthy industrialist in the Rhine Valley, with factories also in England. He was a strong evangelical, in fact a pillar of the church. It was the degradation of the workers—men, women, and children—occasioned by laissez-faire capitalism which Engels had witnessed in his father's factories that turned him against both capitalism and religion.

In 1848 these two men issued their *Communist Manifesto,* ending with the stirring call which broke upon Europe like a clap of thunder:

> The Communists disdain to conceal their views and aims. They openly declare that their ends can be attained only by the forcible overthrow of all existing social conditions. Let the ruling classes tremble at a Communistic revolution. The proletarians have nothing to lose but their chains. They have a world to win.
>
> Working men of all countries, unite![4]

Religion was dismissed by these men as being not only worthless in the necessary struggle for justice, but positively harmful. It taught men, so they charged, to be content with their lot, to accept unjust living conditions as divine providence, to look for their compensation in a future life—pie in the sky, by and by. Religion, in a word, was an opiate, a stratagem utilized by the ruling classes to keep the lower classes in helpless subjection.

This view has since spread through the world. The organized working class not only in Europe, but also in Asia and in Latin America, is largely indifferent, if not actively hostile, to the church.

It was a growing realization of this fact, along with the wretchedness of the many victims of the industrial process, that led finally to a recovery of social concern on the part of the church.

The story is best followed in England, where the Industrial Revolution and the "social gospel" both had their birth. There were three stages in the development, overlapping stages, each of which continues to the present.

HISTORICAL DEVELOPMENT
RISE OF SOCIAL CHRISTIANITY IN ENGLAND
Efforts on the Part of Individual Christians to Secure Isolated Reforms

This was inevitable. The church does not awaken to new responsibilities, and, as a matter of fact, cannot awaken to such responsibilities, until, first, individuals have been aroused, and ordinarily these individuals emerge apart from the official leadership. In this case they were not ministers but laymen, who had been touched by the great evangelical awakening inspired by Wesley and Whitefield, men who were grateful for their redemption through the blood of the Lamb and who believed the Master's words, "As you did it to one of the least of these my brethren, you did it to me." *Booth*

One of these great Christian laymen was John Howard, who inspired a movement for prison reform, first in England, and then throughout the world. A second was William Wilberforce, the man who more than any other was responsible for the abolition of the nefarious slave trade through the British Empire. Wilberforce did not, however, work alone. He was the leader of the "Clapham Sect," as it was called, a group of dedicated evangelicals, men of wealth, members of a church in the suburbs of London, which spearheaded the so-called Reform movement in England around the turn of the eighteenth century.

These "saints in politics," as they have been termed, working tirelessly as a team, not only ended the slave traffic and freed the slaves in the British Empire; they also sparked the movement for foreign missions, for the organization of the British and Foreign Bible Society, for popular education, for a more enlightened Colonial policy, for penal reform, for the improvement of morals and manners (temperance, the abolition of dueling, and the like), for religious toleration, and for what would now be called ecumenicity.

There has been no comparable group of "saints in politics," and seldom, if ever, has such a small group of Christians exerted such worldwide influence for the betterment of human relations.

A third great reformer who arose from the ranks of the evangelicals was Lord Shaftesbury (1801–1885), through whose initiative was enacted the first of a series of laws to protect men, women, and children in industry, a series of laws which mark the beginning of the end of laissez-faire, not only in England, but in other lands as well.

A second stage in the church's social concern is marked by . . .

The Growing Interest in Social Service

By social service we mean, very simply, ministrations of various sorts other than purely spiritual, rendered to those for whom society has not adequately provided. A few illustrations will suffice.

Thomas Chalmers, evangelical leader in the Church of Scotland, accepted a call to a church in whose parish were some of the most squalid slums in Glasgow, and that means in all the world. He divided his parish into twenty-five sections and placed an elder and a deacon in charge of each, the elder to concern himself primarily with the spiritual life, and the deacon with the material needs of its inhabitants. Under his personal supervision, plans were made for the systematic care of the poor, including the weeding out of those who were unworthy. Out of this effort came the beginnings of what we call organized charity, the scientific distribution of relief. Another illustration of the same movement is found in the rise of the Salvation Army, with its program of soup, soap, and salvation.

A second type of social service was exhibited in what is called the Institutional Church, the first of which was opened by Canon Barnett in London in 1880. To put it briefly, an Institutional Church is a church, ordinarily in an underprivileged area, which seeks to minister to the physical, the mental, and the social, as well as the moral and spiritual, needs of the people of its community—on weekdays as well as on the Sabbath.

The need for isolated reforms and for some type of social service persists, but as time went on church leaders came to see that isolated reforms accompanied by relief for the victims of our social disorder was not enough. So we come to a third phase of the development of the so-called social gospel.

3

The Growing Realization on the Part of the Church That It Must Seek to Christianize the Social Order

First it was individuals who were seized by this larger vision. Then organized efforts arose within the various denominations. A landmark in the development of the social gospel is found in the Copec (Christian Order of Politics, Economics, and Citizenship) conferences held in Great Britain in the years 1921 and again in 1924. These conferences, attended by leading pastors, theologians, and Christian laymen in Great Britain, made it clear that leaders in all the churches in that land were now committed to the establishment of a Christian order in these three important fields. To work for a Christian structure of society was now at last a recognized function of the churches.

The Basis of the Copec Union sets forth very clearly the nature of the "social gospel" as it had come to be accepted by leaders of the church in Great Britain and also in America:

"The basis of this Conference," runs the statement,

> is the conviction that the Christian faith, rightly interpreted and consistently followed, gives the vision and the power essential for solving the problems of today, that the social ethics of Christianity have been greatly neglected by Christians with disastrous consequences to the individual and to society, and that it is of the first importance that these should be given a clearer and more persistent emphasis. In the teaching and work of Jesus Christ there are certain fundamental principles—such as the universal Fatherhood of God with its corollary that mankind is God's family, and the law "that whoso loseth his life, findeth it"—which, if accepted, not only condemn much in the present organization of society, but show the way of regeneration. Christianity has proved itself to possess also a motive power for the transformation of the individual, without which no change of policy or method can succeed. In the light of its principles the constitution of society, the conduct of industry, the upbringing of children, national and international politics, the personal relations of men and women, in fact all human relationships, must be tested. It is hoped that through

this Conference the Church may win a fuller understanding of its Gospel, and hearing a clear call to practical action may find courage to obey.[5]

Development of the Social Gospel in America

Abandonment of the theory that religion is concerned with individual salvation alone, acceptance of the counter-theory that the churches have a social responsibility which cannot be evaded, came to churches in the United States, it may be noted, from a variety of causes, including a series of violent labor convulsions, in the closing decades of the nineteenth century: the discovery that a large portion of the laboring masses had been alienated from the church; the poverty, misery, and vice of our great cities; the abandonment of laissez-faire theory by economists; the influence of the British social movement, which we have briefly traced; and the recovery of the social message of the Bible.

Of prime importance also were the writings of such men as Walter Rauschenbusch, an evangelical, who, in his first parish ("Hell's Kitchen" in New York City) soon discovered that the slums of New York destroyed souls much more rapidly than the church was able to save them, and who did more than any other at the beginning of the present century to arouse the church-at-large to its social responsibility. The most powerful recent voice has been that of Reinhold Niebuhr. As a consequence of this growing social concern, most major denominations in America have now set up Departments or Councils of Christian Relations or Social Action. It was this interest that in large measure inspired the formation of the old Federal Council of Churches, whose functions have since been taken over and enlarged by the National Council of Churches. To these organizations we shall return in a later chapter.

Acceptance of Social Responsibility by Ecumenical Christianity

The interest in social Christianity had now leaped all national bounds. In 1924, for example, the Universal Christian Conference on Life and Work met in Stockholm. It had grown out of the sufferings and agony of the First World War. Five hundred delegates were present from thirty-seven countries, representing practically all the larger non-Roman churches throughout the world. Ignoring underlying differences of faith and order, the conference addressed itself to the practical problems which then pressed upon the consciences of men. It expressed the conviction that the gospel of Christ had relevance for every realm of life, and members consecrated themselves to the effort to make it prevail in every area of human experience.

"Responding to his call, 'Follow Me'," they said, "we have in the presence of the Cross accepted the urgent duty of applying his Gospel in all realms of human life—industrial, social, political, and international."

In 1938 a great missionary conference, representing both sending and receiving countries, was held in Madras, India. The question was raised as to whether missions should center upon individual conversion or upon social change. The conference answered emphatically, "We must do both."

The three conferences sponsored by the World Council of Churches, meeting in Amsterdam, Holland, in Evanston, Illinois, and in New Delhi, India (1961), have taken these insights for granted.

The first and primary function of the church in this area, said the Amsterdam Conference, is to renew its own life in faith and obedience to Christ. A second social function is to declare on occasion the will of God for public decisions of the hour. And finally the church is to inspire its members to carry Christian influence into all of life.

There are those within the churches who are opposed to this growing concern of the church with social issues. But it does not seem likely at this moment that the church will ever again—at least in those lands where it retains its freedom—accept the contention that any area of human life is exempt from the royal dominion of Christ and therefore from the searchlight of the gospel.

FOR CONSIDERATION

1. Is there a "social gospel"? How would you define it?
2. Why does the church have a concern for social issues? How can this concern be manifested?
3. Should the minister deal with social issues? If so, under what conditions?

4. Is it proper for church courts to issue deliverances on social issues? Why or why not?
5. What are the major social issues which challenge the interest of
   the church today?
6. What basis is there for the Communist charge that religion is the
   opiate of the people?
7. Are the factors which encourage the rise of Communism active in
   America today?
8. Should Bible classes give more time to a discussion of vital issues
   in our contemporary life? Should controversial issues be included?

*The World Council of Churches Meeting for the
First Time in Amsterdam, 1948*

22
THE CHURCH SEEKS
TO RECOVER ITS LOST UNITY

A glance back over the history of the church during the last half-millennium reveals two movements, one centrifugal, the other centripetal; first, a tendency to fly apart, to separate; second, a tendency to come together, co-operate, unite.

THE CENTRIFUGAL MOVEMENT

At first glance the centrifugal movement seems to dominate. Five hundred years ago there was one great church in western Europe, to which all but a handful of Christians gave allegiance; a church that was truly supranational and united under the control of a single man, the pope. Then came the Protestant Reformation which divided the church between Roman Catholics and Protestants. But the Protestants themselves were not united. Lutherans predominated in Germany and the Scandinavian countries; the Reformed or Presbyterian Churches in Switzerland, Holland, Scotland, and the north of Ireland; Anglicans in England. Mennonites and Socinians, in smaller numbers, were found here and there. Protestant churches were in no sense

289

supranational. The bounds of a church were the bounds of its nation, or the bounds of political subdivisions within the nation (in Germany and in Switzerland, for example), which meant that churchmen tended to think in national rather than in international dimensions. But Protestants within a single nation did not coalesce. Lutheran, Reformed, and a number of lesser bodies were found in Germany. As we saw, in England there came to be an established church and a number of dissenting bodies—Presbyterians, Congregationalists, Baptists, Quakers, Unitarians, and Methodists. Denominations within a single nation divided and subdivided. In Scotland, we find the Church of Scotland (Presbyterian), but also Reformed, Associate (or Secession), Relief, and Free Presbyterians. There were other subdivisions. The Associate Church, for example, divided into Burgher and Antiburgher groups, and each of these again into Old and New Light bodies. But it was in the United States of America that divisions became most numerous. This was due in part to the fact that practically all churches in Europe ultimately reproduced themselves in America; in some cases different waves of immigrants established their own separate churches. Denominations in America, as we have seen, tended to divide and subdivide for a variety of reasons: New bodies arose on the frontier; strange sects appeared, the lengthened shadow of some charismatic individual (Joseph Smith and the Mormons; Mary Baker Eddy and Christian Science, for example); Negro and white churches became separate after the Civil War; churches arose to meet the needs of social and economic classes which no longer felt at home in the older churches; fundamentalism drew off a number of splinter bodies.

In 1880 there were 145 distinct denominations in America. Since this time the number has steadily increased. There were 186 bodies in 1905; 202 in 1916; 213 in 1926; and 256 in 1936 (the last religious census). There are more, not less, at the present time.

At first glance, therefore, it may seem as though in Protestantism there is an inherent tendency to fly apart, to disintegrate. We observe, however, that 97 percent of all American Protestants are found in fifty-two denominations, and most of these are gathered into a few great families of churches—particularly Baptist, Methodist, Lutheran, Reformed, Congregational, and Episcopal.

The Centripetal Movement

In addition, a second look reveals that there is a centripetal movement, a tendency to coalesce, to co-operate and to unite, and that this movement, whose roots run back into the Reformation period, has been gathering momentum and in the last fifty years has accelerated. One keen observer is confident that

> future historians, looking back upon the troubled times in which our lot is cast and seeking to discover the most significant single feature of the Christian Movement in the first half of the twentieth century, are almost certain to fasten upon one fact. All through the first decades of this century, Christian leaders in every land where the Church has penetrated and of every major Communion (except the Church of Rome) have been coming increasingly to think of their Churches as members of a World Community.[1]

This centripetal movement includes a growing readiness to co-operate, an increasing desire to unite.

Co-operation

First there is the movement toward co-operation. In the United States this manifests itself on four distinct levels: in the local community, within the state, within the nation, throughout the world.

At the Local Level

It is on the local level, at the grass roots, probably, that the ecumenical movement as a whole (including the tendencies both to co-operate and to unite) is most important, and yet least active and evident. The average Christian, (particularly the layman), it would seem, thinks almost entirely in terms of his local congregation—its program and needs. He is compelled to think at times of his denominational program. But the relation that his church, or he himself, bears to the universal church is rarely or ever in his mind. In recent generations, however, there has been an increase of co-operation among churches in a community or within a rural area. In nearly every community there is at least a ministerial association (increasingly within the South these associations include Negroes as well as whites), which promotes fellowship and plans for some common religious activities. Often there are other interdenominational organizations; United Church Women, for example. Y.M.C.A. and Y.W.C.A. are lay organizations cutting across denominational lines. In most cities of the North and in a few southern cities there are local councils of churches, including not only ministers, but also lay representatives from each local church, and with a paid executive. In such communities co-operation of the church becomes more general and far more effective. Usually in such cases some "rules of comity" are accepted, which tend to prevent duplication of buildings within the same community, and therefore wastage of effort.

At the State Level

The pattern of co-operation varies from state to state, particularly in the South. All states out of this area, however, and some within, have State Councils of Churches, whose members (ministers and laymen) are elected by the constituent denominations, and which employ a full-time staff of workers. The work entrusted to such co-operative bodies is that which a single denomination cannot handle alone—for example, work among migrants, weekday religious education on a community basis, religious activities within various state institutions, comity plans for the state as a whole.

At the National Level

Co-operation on the national level arose because it was found to be desirable, or necessary, in this area and that, if the church was to carry on its mission. There came to be co-operative bodies in almost every phase of the church's work. A number of these were concerned with the youth of the nation—the Y.M.C.A. and the Y.W.C.A., both of which crossed from Britain to America before the Civil War; Christian Endeavor, developing in the 1880's, at a time when there were no denominational youth organizations; the Student Volunteers, which for some decades served to recruit most of our foreign missionaries; later the Interseminary Movement, and the United Christian Youth. To co-ordinate and serve the growing foreign mission activities of the various churches, there was organized the Foreign Missions Conference of North America and the Missionary Education Movement; for our own land there was the Home Missions Council. In the field of religious (or Christian) education, guidance was furnished by the International Council of Religious Education (among many other services, it sponsored the International Sunday School Lessons). The United Stewardship Council enabled one denomination to learn from another, as they sought to raise the level of giving within their respective bodies. The women's work in every denomination was aided and strengthened by the United Council of Church Women. Most of these and other organizations of similar nature were founded and kept alive by boards within the denominations because of the practical help which they afforded them.

In 1908 representatives of the leading denominations came together to organize the first co-operative organization representing the denominations as such—the Federal Council of Churches. Its service was rendered in fields not already occupied by earlier co-operative bodies organized for some particular service, particularly those mentioned above. Its major activity was in the church's new field of interest, the controversial "social gospel." It helped to arouse popular sentiment against the twelve-hour day in the steel industry, and stirred up criticism from the powerful which has not ceased to the present day.

Gradually, it became clear to churchmen that it was better to have all co-operative activities gathered under the care of a single organization—and one that was directly amenable to the denominations themselves. So finally in 1950 eight major co-operative agencies (including the Federal Council, the International Council of Religious Education, the Foreign Missions Conference, the Home Missions Council, the United Stewardship Council, the United Council of Church Women) were done away with, and in their stead was organized the National Council of Churches.

At the time of writing, this council is supported by thirty-four denominations, including most of the older and larger denominations in America. Thirty-nine other denominations share some of its activities. These activities are carried on in seventy-five departments, distributed among four major divisions and two other more general categories.[2] Within the Division of Christian Education we have such departments as children's work, youth work, adult work, weekday religious education, religious drama, camps and conferences, vacation church schools, campus Christian life, faculty Christian Fellowship, the Student Volunteer Movement, International Sunday School Lessons. The Division of Foreign Missions includes a number of Area Commissions (Africa, Asia, Latin America, for example); a Christian Medical Council for Overseas Work; a Bureau of Missionary Research. In the Home Missions Division are departments on the urban church, the town and country church, church buildings, and migrant work. The Division on Christian Life and Work has departments on social welfare, the church and economic life, religious liberty, stewardship, and benevolence. There are in addition Service Units on broadcasting and films, on councils of churches, on research and survey; also a Washington office which keeps denominations informed regarding legislative proposals in which they have an interest. Among the General Units are Church World Service, Evangelism, United Church Men, and United Church Women.

Though the National Council of Churches has the continuing support of the major denominations (without which, indeed, it could not exist), opposition to the council has arisen within various denominations, especially on the part of laymen, primarily because of some of the social deliverances of the council itself, or of some of the conferences which it has sponsored. Two major denominations are not officially represented in the National Council of Churches or generally in co-operative bodies on any level—the Missouri Synod of the Lutheran Church and the Southern Baptist Convention. Southern Baptists do support, however, certain activities of the council, and individual Baptist leaders are active in interdenominational efforts. Forty denominations, including many of the perfectionist and Pentecostal bodies, with very conservative theology, are represented in a rival organization, known as the National Association of Evangelicals (N.A.E.). A few splinter bodies are associated in the American Council of Churches, which spends most of its energies in vehemently denouncing both the N.A.E. and the National Council of Churches.

At the World Level

Co-operative organizations on the world level—twenty or more, altogether—arose, as did those on a national level, to aid the church in the conduct of its world mission, particularly in the all-important foreign missionary enterprise. In 1960 the two most important of these were the World Council of Churches and the International Missionary Council. The roots of both went back fifty years earlier to a missionary conference held in Edinburgh in 1910—the first such conference composed of official representatives of the churches themselves. Many of its leaders had learned to work together in organizations such as the World Student Christian Federation.

The first of these was the *International Missionary Council,* whose membership was drawn from various national missionary councils. In 1921 when the International Missionary Council was organized (the delay was due to the First World War), there were seventeen of these—thirteen representing the sending lands, and four represeñting the receiving lands; in 1960 there were thirty-eight national councils represented, and only fourteen of these were in the older sending bodies. In 1921 most of the representatives from mission lands were missionaries; in 1960 they were representatives of the indigenous churches. The work of the council was to study, to counsel, and to co-ordinate. In 1960 attention was being given to the training of a native ministry, to the relation between Christian and non-Christian religions, and to the relation of older and younger churches. Closely related to the International Missionary Council was the East Asia Christian Conference, organized in 1957–58 with its own full-time secretariat. Through the agency of this conference, churches in East Asia were for the first time becoming acquainted with one another and taking action to reinforce their common witness. In 1958 an All-African Church Conference appointed a provisional committee to explore ways and means of furthering African Christian solidarity with the worldwide fellowship of Christians. A similar All-Latin America Conference was in the planning stages.

The two other movements growing out of the Edinburgh Missionary Conference in 1910 were those on *Life and Work* and *Faith and Order.* Two world conferences on *Life and Work* were held—at Stockholm in 1925, and at Oxford, England, in 1937. The Stockholm Conference was the first world conference to be attended by representatives of the Orthodox Churches and marks the beginning of a new relationship between Protestantism and Orthodoxy. It also constituted a landmark in the recognition by the churches of their social responsibility. The declared objective of the council was to perpetuate and strengthen the fellowship between the churches in the application of Christian ethics to the social problems of modern life. After the Oxford Conference the "social gospel" began to have a new orientation. The church now came to be viewed not as an instrument for social welfare and the reform of secular society, but as a God-given community, transcending divisions of nation, race, and class, and providing visible evidence of what God means society as a whole to be.

Two world conferences on *Faith and Order* were also held—at Lausanne in 1927 and at Edinburgh in 1938. The purpose of both was to explore areas of agreement and disagreement among the participating churches, that they might exhibit to the world more of the unity for which Christ prayed.

Participants in these two world movements were now agreed that there was need of a *World Council of Churches* which would carry on and extend the work of both. Organization of such a Council was delayed by World War II, but a Provisional Committee of the World Council in Process of Formation rendered invaluable service in providing maintenance for the orphaned missions of the central powers and in maintaining contacts between churchmen of the various warring countries. Due to such reconciling activities of the provisional committee, the World Council, including representatives from the churches in Germany and also from the Orthodox Churches, was organized shortly after the close of the war (1948) in Amsterdam. It was a fellowship of churches accepting "our Lord Jesus Christ as God and Saviour." At New Delhi in 1961 the theological basis was amended to read:

> The World Council of Churches is a fellowship of churches which confess the Lord Jesus Christ as God and Saviour according to the Scriptures and therefore seek to fulfil together their common calling to the glory of the one God, Father, Son and Holy Spirit. . . . [3]

As the Evanston Council (1954) declared:

> The World Council of Churches is an instrument at the service

of the churches which enables them to enter into fraternal conversation with each other, to co-operate in various fields, and
to render witness together to the world. It is not a new church
(even less a super-church) and does not perform ecclesiastical
functions.[4]

At Amsterdam there were 147 churches represented; by 1961 the
number had come to be more than two hundred. Protestant and Orthodox Churches were included from both sides of the Iron Curtain.

The work of the council in 1960 was carried on by three divisions: one on Studies (Evangelism; Missionary Studies; Faith and
Order); the second on Interchurch Aid and Service to Refugees; the
third on Ecumenical Actions. In addition there were two commissions. The first, on *Faith and Order*, provided for a wider representation than that offered by the division of the same name, and arranged
for periodic conferences on questions of faith and order. The second
commission, on *International Affairs*, gave attention to international
affairs affecting missions, and to the issues of war and peace.

At the third meeting of the World Council at New Delhi in 1961
the International Missionary Council became a division within the
World Council of Churches. Provision was also made for a Commission on World Missions, which will provide for wider representation
than does the division, which in effect will serve as the commission's
executive agency.

At New Delhi for the first time official observers were present
from the Roman Catholic Church. This is one of a number of signs
that betoken a more conciliatory attitude on the part of this body.
There is no indication that barriers between Roman Catholicism and
Protestantism will disappear, but it does suggest that there will be increasing opportunities for open discussion, and perhaps to some extent and in some areas, for a limited amount of co-operation.

UNION

The ecumenical movement is marked not only by increasing
readiness to co-operate, but also by increasing desire for amalgama-
tion or union. Approximately ninety such unions have been achieved
in the last century and a half—the most important of these, in the last

fifty years. Still others are in prospect. These unions have occurred in all parts of Christendom.

Quite naturally the greatest impatience with denominationalism has been manifest in mission lands where the church remains a small minority surrounded by a sea of pagans, and where divisions within the church weaken the Christian witness. In many lands, national churches have been formed by the union of two or more denominations—in most of these Presbyterian and Reformed Churches have been included. The United Church of Japan (Kyodan) includes most of the Protestant denominations working in that land. The United Church of South India marked a notable advance, including for the first time Anglican, Presbyterian, and Congregational elements. Other such unions are in process in North India and in Ceylon.

On the continent of Europe there have been unions, particularly in France and in Germany. In this latter country, Lutheran and Reformed Churches are bound together in a loose confederation. In England, various Methodist bodies have reunited, and there is a far more friendly spirit between the Anglican Established church and the dissenting bodies. In Scotland, most of the Presbyterian bodies have come together in the Presbyterian Church of Scotland. In Canada, Congregationalists, Methodists, and most Presbyterians came together to form the United Church of Canada. In the United States, the important church unions include the following:

1906 Presbyterian Church U.S.A. (out of Cumberland and Presbyterians U.S.A.)

1918 United Lutheran Church

1931 Congregational-Christian Church

1934 Evangelical and Reformed Church

1938 The Methodist Church (out of three major Methodist bodies)

1946 Evangelical and United Brethren

1958 United Presbyterian Church in the U.S.A. (out of United Presbyterian Church and Presbyterian Church in the USA)

A number of other unions are in the offing, some problematic but under discussion.

What is the goal of the ecumenical movement: further co-operation, or ultimate union of all or most major Protestant bodies? On this question there is no agreement.

At least five views regarding the meaning of Christian unity, and therefore of the good to be attained, can be distinguished.

1. *Spiritual fellowship,* including mutual appreciation of other bodies, and good will toward them. All acknowledge the need of such unity, but for many this is not enough.

2. *Co-operation,* as exhibited, for example, in the National and World Councils of Churches, though such co-operation can be greatly extended.

3. *Mutual recognition*—involving a freely transferable membership, and ministry and sacraments accepted by all. Until there is such recognition Christians cannot sit down together about the table of the Lord, and the scandal of their division remains.

4. *Co-operation and mutual recognition*—a combination of the two preceding ideals. This for some is the most desirable ideal, and therefore the proper goal of the ecumenical movement.

5. *Organic union.* Most all will agree that there is need for more such unions within like-minded bodies; but there are others who desire a single great church, with a common doctrinal basis and a single administrative structure.

If this be the goal, its realization lies in a future so far away it cannot now be seen.

FOR CONSIDERATION

1. How do you interpret Jesus' prayer for his disciples, "that they may all be one . . . that the world may believe . . . " (John 17:21)? What type of unity is suggested here?
2. Is it good to have so many denominations? Give your reasons.
3. How does our divisiveness affect the witness of the church?
4. What are the values of a World Council of Churches?
5. Are there other religious bodies with which your own denomination might consider uniting?
6. What in your estimation is the proper goal of the ecumenical movement? (See above.)

*The Second Vatican Council Under Pope John XXIII
Convening in Rome, 1962*

23
ROMAN CATHOLICISM
MEETS NEW CONDITIONS

WITHIN CHRISTIANITY today are three major divisions: Eastern
Orthodoxy, Roman Catholicism, and Protestantism. The Orthodox
stem from the earliest churches founded in New Testament times in
lands traversed by Paul on his three missionary journeys. Their doctrine, polity, and worship is essentially that of the undivided church
(at the end of the fifth century). Roman Catholicism developed, as
we have seen, in western Europe, after the breakup of the Roman
Empire, among peoples accepting the claims of the bishop of Rome
to be the successors of Peter, Prince of the Apostles and Vicar of
Christ. Protestantism includes the churches which descend directly
or indirectly from the sixteenth-century Reformation. The Christian
population of the world for the year 1960 is estimated as follows:
Eastern Orthodox, 129,952,249; Roman Catholic, 527,643,000;
Protestant, 212,957,571; which means that approximately three
Christians out of every five are Roman Catholic. The Catholic majority is not so great as these figures show, as that church counts as members all who have been baptized, thus including tiny children. Most

Protestant churches count on their membership rolls only those who have made a profession of personal faith. On the other hand, it might be argued that Roman Catholicism is even stronger than bare figures report; for Protestantism is badly split; Orthodoxy has no organic unity; while Roman Catholicism has come to be increasingly integrated under the leadership of one man—the pope.

In the Reformation, as we have seen, the Roman Catholic Church suffered heavy losses; Germany, Switzerland, Holland, the Scandinavian countries, England, and Scotland became predominantly Protestant and have so remained till the present day. In the Counter-Reformation the gains of Protestantism in Europe were halted, and in many areas the tide even rolled backward. In the same period, missionaries were laying the basis of Roman Catholic strength in the Far East and also in Latin America.

A PERIOD OF DEPRESSION, 1643–1814

There followed a period of comparative weakness, beginning with the reign of Louis XIV in France (1643–1715) and ending with the career of Napoleon Bonaparte (1795–1814). Louis XIV, the "grand monarch" who brought France to its pinnacle of earthly glory, ruled as an absolute monarch over both church and state, and other Catholic sovereigns adopted the same policy, greatly restricting the prerogatives of the papacy. In France itself a Gallican party arose which sought to transform the church into something like a constitutional monarchy, with states' rights for national hierarchies. Catholic princes compelled the weakened papacy to abolish the Jesuit Order, whose political machinations had become intolerable.[1] During the French Revolution radicals sought to drag God out of the skies and to enthrone Reason in his stead. Napoleon, himself without religious feeling, hoped to use the church, which claimed the allegiance of a majority of Frenchmen, and so entered into an agreement with the papacy which enabled the government to control the church. Protestants, for the first time since the revocation of the Edict of Nantes, were granted freedom of worship. Napoleon soon quarreled with Pius VII, who had crowned him as emperor, annexed the State of the Church, and held the pope as a prisoner from 1809 until his fall in 1814.

A Period of Recovery, Since 1814

With the downfall of Napoleon came a conservative reaction in Europe as a whole, which included a return of many to the old church which seemed to hold up a standard for reaction. This in turn brought about increasing tensions between clericals and anticlericals in various lands in Europe, and also in Latin America.

The Church Gains and Loses

In the last century and a half there have been both gains and losses. In 1870 Victor Emmanuel captured Rome, and the inhabitants of the papal state, centering about Rome, voted 133,000 to 1,500 for annexation to the newly established Italian nation. So ended the State of the Church, the oldest secular sovereignty then existing in Europe. Though guarantees of papal freedom had been offered, the pope refused to acknowledge the change of sovereignty, and proclaimed himself a prisoner within the Vatican. The changed situation, though outwardly a defeat for the papacy, was actually a benefit.

> It aroused sympathy for the Pope, and the contributions that flowed in from the Catholic world more than made up for the financial loss. It removed from the papacy a secular task which it was ill-adapted to meet, and the attempted accomplishment of which laid it open to well-grounded charges of maladministration. It gave to the papacy unhindered scope for the development of its spiritual function and ultimately increased papal moral prestige.[2]

The problem created by the pope's refusal to accept the unification of Italy was not finally solved until 1929, when Pius XI entered into an agreement with Mussolini which resulted in the establishment of the Vatican State (approximately one hundred acres), of which the pope is now the sole ruler. It upholds the principle for which the papacy has long contended, that the head of a world church must be free from all civil control.

In 1870 the second German Reich (Empire) came into existence. The attempt of Bismarck, its chief architect, to limit the strength of the Roman Catholic Church in that land led to the so-called Kulturkampf (battle of cultures), which ended with an admission of defeat on the part of Bismarck and a consequent strengthening of the church. Increasing tensions led to the separation of church and state in France in 1904 and in Portugal in 1911. Once again the church gained by being freed from its secular ties.

The First World War led to a dissolution of Austria-Hungary, one of the strongest Roman Catholic powers; but in the weakened states set up after the end of the war—Austria, Hungary, Czechoslovakia, and Poland—the status of the church was enhanced.

A revolution in Mexico toppled the reactionary Díaz, who had been strongly supported by the Roman Catholic Church, and led in 1924 to the establishment of a new socialist government, which adopted oppressive anti-Catholic legislation (which also affected the comparatively weak Protestant missions). Many of these laws have been kept on the statute books but have become more and more a dead letter. The Roman Catholic Church has recovered much of its former power; and at times, and in certain areas, Protestants have suffered from the violence of Roman Catholic mobs. There has been similar persecution of the Protestants in other portions of Latin America, notably Colombia, though in recent years the tension has eased. (See current World Mission Reports.) Throughout Latin America generally Protestants are tolerated. Growth of Protestantism throughout this region has been rapid in recent years, particularly in Peru and in Brazil. The Roman Catholic Church remains the dominant church, but in most Latin American lands it has lost its hold on influential classes of the population. It has never been able to recruit an adequate native ministry and remains dependent on missionary priests coming from abroad.

In 1931 revolution broke out in Spain, resulting in the establishment of a democratic regime which disestablished the Roman Catholic Church and granted religious freedom to Protestants (a tiny minority of the people) for the first time in its history. Five years later the Republic was overthrown by General Franco, who had the blessing of the Roman Catholic Church and the active support of the two fascist powers, Germany and Italy. Protestant privileges were withdrawn, and the Roman Catholic Church re-established under the fascist dictatorship that followed.

The Roman Catholic Church has made its most important gains

in the United States of America. In the Colonial period, Roman Catholics were in a decided minority. Fearful of Roman Catholic power, under which so many of the immigrants had suffered, most of the colonies had restricted the rights of the members of this body. These restrictions were eased after the Revolutionary War, in which Roman Catholics had proved their loyalty to the new Republic. In the 1830's–40's the strength of the church was greatly increased by heavy immigration from Ireland and also from Germany. It was the "shanty-Irish" in particular who furnished the labor needed by the growing industries of America. But the increasing political power of the new immigrants, used, it was charged, at the behest of the priests, added to the fear of Protestants that the growth of Roman Catholicism jeopardized their religious liberties; this, together with the demands made by Roman Catholic prelates for state support for their schools, gave rise to a number of anti-Catholic movements, culminating in the American or Know-Nothing Party that came into short-lived but national prominence in the elections of 1855. As Professor W. E. Garrison has summarized:

> there has been an element of hysteria in all of these anti-Catholic organizations which has robbed them of any considerable influence upon thoughtful minds. Whatever may need to be done—if anything—to prevent the Roman Catholic church from exercising an undue influence in American politics, and especially in the determination of those "mixed" questions over which it undoubtedly claims jurisdiction but which the government of this country, under its present laws, reserves for civil control, it is historically demonstrated that the thing *not* to do is to organize a political party or a secret society. For further confirmation of the last item in this judgment, consider the tragi-comic futility of the American Protective Association, which rose and fell in the nineties, and of the Ku Klux Klan [following World War I].[3]

The greatest growth of the Roman Catholic Church, however, came, as we have seen, after the Civil War, particularly during the forty-year period of unrestricted immigration (1880–1924), when vast hordes, mostly from Roman Catholic lands, streamed to our lands. The present strength of the Roman Catholic Church in America stems from this immigration, not from conversions made at Protestant expense.

For some time the Roman Catholic Church did not exert the influence in America that its numbers made possible; growing influence became inevitable when foreign-born and sons of foreign-born were followed by generations fully at home in the American scene. Really effective organization of Roman Catholicism in our country came after World War I with the establishment of the National Catholic Welfare Conference, which now co-ordinates the church's many varied efforts to win the United States for the Catholic faith. Under the direction of the N.C.W.C. the church has developed a successful program of religious education, with schools at every level; its own ably edited press which parallels the secular press as the Catholic schools parallel the public schools; and its own system of hospitals. Under the direction of the N.C.W.C. the church is extending its efforts among Negroes. It has taken careful steps to preserve and extend the interests of the church among the armed forces. It keeps a watchful eye and seeks with considerable success to maintain an effective censorship on the press, movies, and other media of communication. It has developed an intelligent and comprehensive plan for converting the workers and converting rural America to its faith. The Executive Committee of the N.C.W.C., according to its own official report,

> keeps in direct personal touch with the officials of the Government from the President and Cabinet members to members of Congress. It is a medium of communication, of information, and of action between these officials and departments of government on all matters that affect Catholic interests and Catholic rights.

This new, vigorous, and many-sided policy of the Roman Catholic Church designed to win America to its own religious faith, coupled with its numerical size, its strongly disciplined membership, its growing political and economic strength, and its peculiar and basic conception of the relation of church and state, has aroused fears and created tensions from time to time with Protestants and others which —whether they are justified or no—cannot be ignored by Protestants or by Roman Catholics.

The Church Further Defines Its Beliefs

During the modern period, as we have just indicated, the Roman Catholic Church has suffered losses and made gains. During this same period it has further defined its beliefs.

Two dogmas (official doctrines) in particular have received definitive statement—first, the doctrine of the papacy; and second, the doctrine regarding Mary. During the Middle Ages, as we have seen, two theories regarding ultimate authority in the church were prevalent—one, the theory that the will of the pope was supreme; two, the theory that a general council had an authority superior to that of the pope. The Council of Trent, which gave an authoritative statement regarding Roman Catholic beliefs on most matters of controversy with Protestants, issued no statement on this point. Not until the First Vatican Council met in 1870 was this issue finally decided. According to this council, the papal authority is unlimited and immediate in every part of the church. Such claims had been made from the days of Gregory VII on, but not until recent times have they been fully realized. In France, as we have observed, there arose a Gallican party, which believed in states' rights for the Roman Catholic Church in France. Over against the Gallican party there arose an ultramontane ("over the mountains") party which contended for the centralization of all authority in the hands of the pope. The First Vatican Council sealed the victory of the ultramontane party. But it did more; it enunciated a doctrine of papal infallibility: that when the pope speaks officially as head of the church regarding matters of faith or morals, he is indeed infallible. It is this dogma, perhaps more than any other, that now stands as an insuperable barrier to the reconciliation of Protestants and Roman Catholics.[4]

Also tending to widen the breach between the two is the growing Mariolatry (worship of Mary) of the Roman Catholic Church. The cult of Mary has grown steadily within this latter body, but at no time more rapidly than in the last one hundred years. A great stimulus was given to this further development in 1854 when Pope Pius IX declared that it was a dogma of the faith (i.e., like all dogmas, this must be believed on penalty of mortal sin) that Mary had been born without original sin (the doctrine of the Immaculate Conception). In 1950 Pope Pius XII declared it to be a dogma of the faith that Mary's body never saw corruption but was taken up into heaven. Four years later, Mary was declared to be Queen of Heaven. Roman Catholic theologians now speak of her as our co-redemptress from sin, and as the Mediatrix (dispenser of all grace). More and more the piety of Roman Catholics has centered in the "worship" of Mary; closer and closer she has drawn to the Godhead itself.

Present-day tensions between Roman Catholics and Protestants, in the United States as in other lands, stem more from claims made by the former and the policies to which they give rise than to theological differences, important as they are. In his famous Syllabus of Errors issued in 1864, Pope Pius IX set forth these claims more explicitly than is found in any other single source. In this document Pius IX declared that separation of church (meaning the Roman Catholic Church) and state, freedom of worship, and freedom of expression were errors which no Roman Catholic could accept. He further asserted that in all cases of disputed jurisdiction between church and state the judgment of the church must prevail; that education and marriage (and all related questions) come under the jurisdiction of the church; that the clergy are not subject to civil courts; that the state has no right to tax the property of the church; that the church has a right to use force against nonbelievers; that no pope has ever exceeded the limits of his powers; that the Roman pontiff cannot and ought not to reconcile himself to and agree with progress, liberalism, and civilization as lately introduced; and that for any Catholic to hold otherwise is a grievous error. In accord with such principles the Roman Catholic Church in America has opposed the publicizing of any information regarding birth control; has claimed the right to public funds for the support of its vast educational system; has followed other policies which excite the concern of such organizations in our own land as Protestants and Other Americans United (POAU). Apprehensions have also been aroused by the frank declaration of some Roman Catholic theologians that, if the time ever came when Roman Catholicism was the dominant religion of America, Protestants could expect only the right of private worship in their homes—or at best the system now prevalent in Roman Catholic and fascist Spain.

The Church Begins to Move in New Directions

In the modern period the Roman Catholic Church has begun to

move in some new directions. During the reign of Leo XIII (1878–1903), for example, it received new intellectual, political, and social orientation. The new intellectual orientation has led to a theological revival, and to an impetus to scholarship in general—though the fact that underlying assumptions cannot be questioned subjects this revival to serious limitations. The new political orientation has led the papacy to develop its diplomatic corps and to seek concordats with nations which grant as many of its claims as possible. The new social orientation has Leo and his successors to recognize the rights of the workingman and to align the church on the side of those seeking social justice.

The church has also begun in recent years to encourage its members to read the Bible (in contradiction to its policy in previous years)—not Protestant versions of course, but Roman Catholic translations, with footnotes which safeguard the reader from what the Roman Catholic Church regards as error.

Notable has been the lay movement within Roman Catholicism. There are now numerous associations of Catholic laymen, under the leadership and control of the clergy, for a variety of benevolent, social, economic, and political purposes.

The liturgical movement within the church has attracted considerable attention—particularly the tendency to increase the participation of the worshiper in the services. There has been a vast expansion of missionary activity.

In Europe, as a consequence of the two world wars, there has been an improvement in Catholic-Protestant relations, and conversations between Catholic and Protestant theologians have become commonplace, and are now extending to America. The Roman Catholic Church has also begun to take a growing interest in the ecumenical movement, sending at first unofficial observers, and more recently official observers, to important gatherings under the auspices of the World Council of Churches.

Particularly hopeful in our land is the appearance of outstanding Catholic churchmen arguing that the separation of church and state—including religious toleration and freedom of expression—as found in the United States and written into our constitution is in accord with Roman Catholic tradition and serves the best interests of the church. This is the view of many, if not the majority of, Roman Catholic laymen, including politicians.

All of these tendencies were greatly strengthened by the geniality and good will of Pope John XXIII (1959–1963). The progress made in the Second Vatican Council, in session as these lines are written, indicates that a more moderate group, opposing the ultraconservative outlook and policies of the curia (the Roman bureaucracy), is now in the ascendancy among the bishops of the church generally. It appears not only that there will be some decentralization in the church's administration, but also that better relations with Protestantism will be cultivated and that the Roman Catholic Church, rid of some of the barnacles of the past, will be in better shape to commend its version of the gospel to the modern mind.

FOR CONSIDERATION

1. Do Protestants need to be informed of developments within the Roman Catholic Church? If so, why?
*2. What do you think can be done, or ought to be done, to improve relations between the two groups?
3. In your judgment, is there any possibility of ultimate reunion between Roman Catholics and Protestants? Why or why not?
4. What further developments have there been in the modernization of the Roman Catholic Church and in Protestant-Roman Catholic relations since the death of Pope John XXIII and the accession of Pope Paul VI?
*5. A few years ago there was much argument pro and con over the proposals of Roosevelt and Truman to send an ambassador to the Vatican State. What are the arguments for and against?
*6. Is the Roman Catholic Church a political force in our own land? If so, what, if anything, should be done to combat it?
7. What are the chief points of tension between Roman Catholics and Protestants at the present time?
8. Should federal aid be given to parochial schools?
9. Is it proper for Protestants to send missionaries to Latin America where the vast majority of the people are nominal Catholics (that is, baptized, but without active life in the Catholic Church)?
10. Is it bigotry to call attention to Roman Catholic pressures and

intolerance? Do you agree with Garrison's statement on page 304?

11. What significance do you think should be attached to the newer trends and developments in the Roman Catholic Church as sketched on pages 307–309? And as subsequently made manifest in the Second Vatican Council?

12. Should discussions between Protestants and Roman Catholics be encouraged? If so, why and how?

13. Read Mark 9:38–40. Does this passage have anything to say on the matter of this chapter?

The Berlin Wall at the Brandenburg Gate Separating East and West

24
THE CHURCH FACES
A CHANGING WORLD

THE COMMUNIST THREAT

The church has always confronted opposition, and at various times, in various lands, and in various ways, it has suffered persecution. In the twentieth century, however, it encountered a new phenomenon—militant atheism, entrenched in powerful states, seeking to eradicate all religion from the minds of men.

For Karl Marx and Friedrich Engels, who together formulated the Communist philosophy, religion, as we have seen, was regarded as an opiate with which Communism could not be reconciled. It was inevitable that it would seek to destroy religion in any nation in which it came to power. That was doubly true in Russia, for there, in a land where feudalism had lingered longer than elsewhere in Europe, church and state had been closely intertwined. Since the days of Peter the Great (1689–1725), the church had served indeed as an agency of the government, inculcating absolute subjection to the czar as a matter of religious obligation. When Communists took control of the government in March, 1917, they moved decisively against the church as one of the major obstacles in their way. All the property of the church was confiscated and all of its former privileges rescinded. Ruthless persecution followed. Hundreds of priests were "liquidated" —80 percent of all the clergy in some provinces. Those who remained were deprived of their civil rights. Not only were they denied employment, unless they renounced their clerical profession, and not only was the support of the clergy by their parishioners hedged about with various restrictions, but the discrimination was also extended to their children. They were excluded from schools, debarred from hospitals and other institutions open to workers. In addition, the church buildings were demolished and church organizations disrupted.

The constitution adopted in 1929 permitted "liberty of religious confession and of anti-religious propaganda." Under this provision Christians were permitted to gather for public worship—in the few buildings which had been spared—but were not permitted to give any religious instruction out of the home, or to seek in any way to win adherents (especially children) to the church, or to engage in any kind of propaganda or agitation. Meanwhile, the government enlisted all its resources—the press, radio, army, trade unions, collective farms, anti-religious demonstrations, museums, literature, the stage, and above all the schools—to destroy religious sentiment, and to inculcate in its stead atheistic materialism. More vigorous action against believers was taken by a Union of Militant Atheists, whose organization was encouraged by the government.

After 1936, however, the attitude of the government slowly moderated. The open persecution gradually ceased. The anti-God organizations were disbanded. The civil disabilities of the clergy were partially removed. The church was allowed to complete its organization, to open some new churches, to print some copies of the Scripture, and to resume the training of its clergy. But important limitations still remain. The church, for example, is not permitted to carry on any charitable work, to give any instruction to its youth, to engage in any sort of religious propaganda. No member of the Communist or governing party is permitted to be a Christian, and no member of the church is allowed to belong to the youth society or komsomol, from which all future leaders of the Communist state are recruited. And atheistic education continues in the schools.

How is this altered attitude on the part of the government to be explained? There is no evidence of any changed attitude toward religion—quite the reverse. It may have been due in part to the fact that the people clung to their religion more strongly than the government had expected; in part to the fact that the power of the church had been thoroughly broken—it was no longer a danger to the state; in part to the fact that the church proved its usefulness in World War II (though the changed attitude predated the war). In the estimation of some careful observers it is due largely to the fact that the church can be useful to the government at home and abroad: at home, in teaching submissiveness to the new government; abroad, in extending Communist influence among those whose minds would otherwise be closed.

The same general attitude toward religion, with variations, has prevailed in other Communist-dominated lands—in the Baltic republics absorbed into the Russian state; in Poland, Rumania, Bulgaria, Albania, Hungary, Czechoslovakia, and East Germany; more recently in China, and to some extent in Cuba.

In all these lands there is little or no persecution of religion as such. Leaders of Roman Catholic and Protestant churches, however, have been arrested and punished, on alleged political grounds, and the churches have finally been brought under the control of the state. Partial exceptions to this last statement are found in Poland, where the Roman Catholic Church still offers some resistance to the government; and in East Germany, where Protestants have done likewise.

This is one aspect of a changing world, in which the church now finds itself, but only one. The twentieth century, it has become plain, is facing revolution, the first truly worldwide revolution in history.

THE WORLD REVOLUTION [1]

This worldwide revolution is accompanied and in part caused by what is truly a "population explosion." In 1830 the world, after *fifty centuries* of economic and social development, reached a population of *one billion. One hundred years* later, in 1930, the *second billion* was reached. The *third billion,* it is expected, *will be reached in 1965;*

in a period, that is, of less than thirty-five years. The greatest share of this increase is in less developed lands where the pressure of population on resources is already at its heaviest.

The current world revolution, triggered in part by the population explosion, affects almost every phase of our lives.

It has *political repercussions.* The half-century following World War I has witnessed "the disappearance of ancient kingdoms and the rise of new nations; the earth-shaking Russian revolution; the coming of Soviet Russia and communism as world forces; convulsions of the East productive of such mighty phenomena as Red China and free India; the swift decline of the British, French, [Dutch], German, Japanese empires; the forced transfers of populations; the enslaving and slaughtering of tens of millions of people; the shattering of channels of commerce built up through centuries; and—a phenomenon of the first magnitude—the emergence of the United States from isolationism to world leadership."[2]

The rise of these new nations, and what is more important, the rise of a nationalistic spirit in these and other lands, which often takes the form of anti-Westernism, has not brought stability or even the promise of peace. Instead have come uncertainty, unrest, and a new struggle for power or independence that reaches beyond all national barriers.

The world revolution of the twentieth century has also its *economic aspects.* The mass of the world's population live in poverty and misery, but they have come to realize that they do not have to live this way, that science and technology have made a better life possible for all. They turn—many of them—to Communism because it seems the quickest way to realize their hopes.

Accompanying the political and economic revolution now sweeping the world is also a *social revolution.* The belief is widespread that only through technology can the economic problem be solved. Industrialization therefore becomes the nation's primary goal. With industrialization comes urbanization; and with urbanization, the disruption of old family patterns and established community relations. Out of the chaos two important groups emerge: first, the new urban proletariat, a population of factory workers apt to be the spearhead for further change; and second, the student group, trained in the ideals of our modern secular society but with limited hopes of personal advancement, pressing, therefore, together with the industrial proletariat, for radical experimentation. On these two groups, marked for leadership in the world of tomorrow, the church so far has made little impression.

Involved in this social revolution also is a new sense of worth, of human dignity, a demand for recognition, for prestige and power. Another aspect of this same movement is seen in the pressure for racial change in our own land. It has become clear that no ideology, religious or otherwise, based on racial discrimination has any possibility of acceptance by the masses of Asia and Africa today.

Involved in this world revolution is also a *religious revolution,* or as it sometimes seems, an anti-religious revolution. For the first time in history large masses of the world population have turned away from all recognized religions, in part through indifference, but in part also from hostility, under the impression that religion stands in the way of human progress.

Describing the cleavage in Europe, long the stronghold of Christianity, Denis de Rougemont reports: "There is no common language any more, no vision or ideal common to both worlds concerning the purposes of life and of society . . . Not a single authority exists today in Europe which could say anything that both sides would agree to accept as 'the truth.' . . .

"The vast majority of Europeans are guided neither by religious faith nor by ethical principles.

"The result—as may be guessed—is a profound sense of anxiety, loneliness of spirit, absence of roots in soil, church, or family."[3]

Not only in Europe, but also in Asia, Africa, and Latin America, many are turning to new substitute religions—Communism, fascism, and nationalism. And there is a still more dangerous foe, what the Germans called the Zeitgeist (or spirit of the times). "We are all familiar with its characteristics," writes Paul Hutchinson: "secularism; 'scientism' (by which I mean the almost blind worship of the supposed authority of physical science); the loss of objective standards of morality under the impact of world wars. . . . Religion today is being challenged to prove, not so much that it is intellectually respectable as that it is morally relevant . . ."[4]

THE CHURCH'S RESPONSE

Faced by such challenges, what has been the church's response?

For one thing, behind the Iron Curtain, behind the Bamboo Curtain, where the strongest opposition has arisen, the church still exists. For two generations now it has endured here the most severe persecution, the most relentless pressure that it has known in all of its history. We have no exact figures. But the Church of Russia, to take one example, entering the World Council of Churches in 1961, claimed a membership of fifty million. The number may be exaggerated. But there can be no doubt but that millions of believers remain and bear their witness under circumstances by no means easy.

In every European land active Christians have become a definite minority of the population; in every land also the church shows signs of continuing vitality. It may be indeed that the proportion of informed Christians actually committed to the Christian Way is as large as it ever was.

Kenneth Scott Latourette closes his mammoth survey of *The Twentieth Century in Europe* with a summary in which he states:

> In the half century which was ushered in by the fateful summer of 1914 Christianity was confronted with greater threats than it had known for many centuries ... As a result of these threats and challenges, Christianity was losing whatever hold it had possessed on many millions in what had been known as Christendom. .... This however was only a part of the picture. By a seeming paradox Christianity was very much alive. It was giving birth to new movements or strengthening old ones.[5]

This was true, he indicates, in the Orthodox Churches, and to a much greater degree in Roman Catholicism and Protestantism.

Particularly significant in these two latter was the new role assumed by laymen. In Protestant Europe, centers were being established where laymen might be trained in the life and doctrine of the church (best known of these is the Ecumenical Institute established at Chateau de Bossey in Switzerland); "communities" were operated where ministers and laymen could be enlisted in a disciplined effort to take Christianity again into the main currents of daily life (the Iona Community in Scotland is the best known example); more significant, perhaps, were the evangelical "academies," springing up thickly in Germany and to a lesser extent in other European countries, in which channels of approach were opened to circles with which the church had lost all contact, and in which Christian laymen were being trained to bear their witness in their daily vocations in a new and vital way. Dramatic witness was born to the strength of this growing lay movement by the annual "Kirchentag" (Church Day) held in Germany to which were drawn hundreds of thousands of participants.

In no land perhaps was the church so strong as in America. Here there had been rapid growth in membership. Thus in the fifty-year period 1906–1956, the population of the United States increased almost 100 percent; church membership during the same period increased 190 percent. Sixty-three percent of the total American population were enrolled in the church in this latter year, the largest proportion of people affiliated with religious bodies in the history of the nation. Four years later it had reached the two-thirds mark. True, there were many uncommitted members, but this has always been the case.

Other statistics indicate vigorous life pulsing within the churches —for example, the amount of money spent for new buildings, and the rising totals and percentages given for other religious purposes.

Laymen (men, women, and young people) have long been active in the American churches. These activities by mid-century were being intensified. The women, superbly organized, were taking more interest in the large issues confronting the church and affecting women as Christian citizens. There were signs that the lay movement in Europe would stir a similar interest among the laymen of the American churches. Interest had increased among young adults, and among young people at every age level.

More interest was being taken in worship; in Christian education, as indicated in the new curriculums of religious education being prepared by some of the larger denominations, and in the increased support given to Christian higher education.

A theological renaissance within the American churches, stimulated by currents of thought coming from abroad, had resulted in a new interest in religion in intellectual circles, and often on the campuses of our great universities. "Theologians," one historian declares, "have come to occupy the place in American life that during the half century after James and Royce was occupied by secular philosophers or almost secular liberal theologians."[6]

There have been notable advances in biblical scholarship.

The social concern of the American churches has matured and become, less optimistic it may be, but far more realistic and deeply rooted.

The interest in world missions remains at a high level, though a larger proportion of men sent and money contributed comes now from some of the newer sects, the more conservative bodies not identified with ecumenical Christianity.

THE WORLD COMMUNITY OF CHRISTIANS

This brings us to what is perhaps the most encouraging development within Christendom in the last fifty years: the growth of a Christian world community.

As a consequence of the missionary movement of the last 150 years, there has come into existence for the first time in history a family of God distributed through the earth, to which all men hungry for God can belong, and in which all men may truly be at home. To a casual observer, it is true, the church is badly rent; yet beneath the many divisions there is God-given unity; and increasingly these scattered bodies are being drawn into a conscious fellowship which stands above all national barriers and which recognizes its mission to all mankind.

We must not overestimate the strength of the Christian world community. In some countries Christians are not permitted to bear their witness; in many, the proportion of Christians is pitifully low. In the world as a whole, because of the population explosion—particularly in non-Christian lands—the proportion of Christians to non-Christians is rapidly diminishing. In Asia and in Africa, as well as in Europe, the church, as we have seen, faces formidable opposition, contending ideologies (systems of ideas), some of which are the very opposite of Christianity, none of which possesses the answer to human needs. Ancient religions, once thought to be dying, have taken on new life and in some areas are growing more rapidly than is Christianity. More dangerous to Christianity—and the peace of the world —is Communism, a declared enemy of all religions. The dominant passion in the newer nations is nationalism, not necessarily an enemy to Christianity, but tending to become such. A still greater danger is one which comes from the West, secular materialism, that sickness of the soul, which, arising in the Christian West, now threatens to engulf the world.

Recognizing all this and more that might be said, it must still be recognized that the rise of independent native churches in most of the countries of the world within the last half-century is something of a miracle. And during recent years there have been some very impressive gains. Thus in the twenty-five-year period 1925–1950, a troubled era in world history, it is estimated that the Christian population in China and Korea increased three times; in Indonesia, five times; in Argentina and in India, six to eight times; in Puerto Rico, ten times; in the Congo, eleven times; and in Brazil, twenty-four times. In 1916 there were only twelve thousand evangelicals in all of Latin America. In 1960 there were nearly five million.

In all of these countries, too, the influence of Christianity was greater than mere numbers would indicate. As an influential Tokyo daily put it: "The Christians weigh more than they count." It proceeded to point out that among the 600,000 Christians in Japan (out of a total population of 88,000,000) there were influential statesmen, scientists, scholars, judges, and businessmen.

The point is that in Asia, Africa, and Latin America native ("indigenous") churches have arisen, independent of all foreign control, with their own institutions and trained leadership. These churches have their weaknesses (as do our own); they face opposition; but they are here to stay. And these churches are now producing some of out most penetrating evangelical leaders, some of our keenest theological minds. As Bishop Manikam of India has stated: "Christianity is now in process of becoming domesticated in the East."

As never before, Christianity is in process of becoming worldwide.

FOR CONSIDERATION

1. Can the Russian Church, limited and largely controlled by an atheistic government, be regarded as a true church of Christ?

*2. What reasons can you advance for admitting or not admitting the Orthodox Church of Russia into the World Council of

Churches? Are there churches in other lands whose outlook is determined by their national interests?

3. What aid, if any, can we give to our fellow Christians in Communist-dominated lands?

4. Do you agree that we are now facing a world revolution? What items would you add or omit from those given in this chapter?

5. How does the "population explosion" affect the church in America?

6. Many Protestant bodies have endorsed the principle of "planned parenthood." Should information regarding the method of planned parenthood be made generally available in the United States? Should the United States aid in making such information available in other lands?

*7. What interest does the church have in the United Nations? Why should Christians seek to strengthen this organization as so many Christian bodies have urged?

8. Why should the church be concerned with the fact that the mass of the world's population live in poverty and misery?

9. Do Christians have a concern that their government give constructive aid to backward countries? What form should such aid take?

*10. Consider the statement on page 315: "On these two groups [the industrial population and the student generation], marked for leadership in the world of tomorrow, the church so far has made little impression." Do you think this is so? What does it suggest regarding the world strategy of the church? To what extent would this statement be true in our own land?

11. Is there any basis for the charge that religion stands in the way of human progress?

12. What evidences can you cite of the church's continuing vitality? Is its influence greater or less than it was ten, twenty, thirty years ago? Why do you think so?

13. What are the signs of life, or its reverse, in your own local church? denomination?

14. Consider God's eternal purpose for the universe as set forth in Ephesians 1:10. When and how will this purpose be realized? Can we expect to make progress toward the goal within our own lifetime?

Part V
THE
PRESBYTERIAN CHURCH
IN THE UNITED STATES

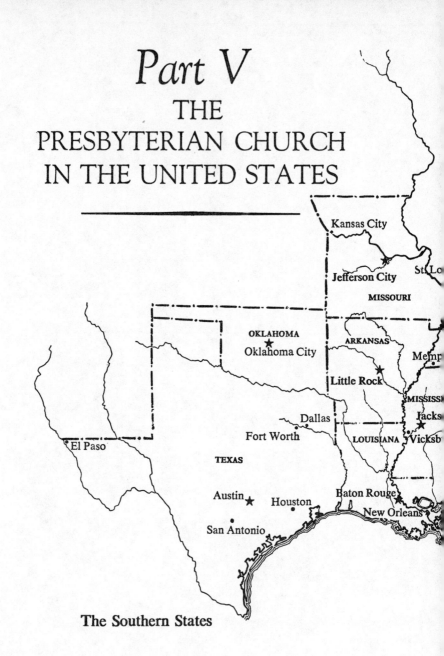

Kansas City

Jefferson City   St. Lo

MISSOURI

OKLAHOMA   **ARKANSAS**
Oklahoma City   Memp

Little Rock

MISSISSI

Dallas   Jacks

Fort Worth   **LOUISIANA** Vicksb

El Paso   **TEXAS**

Austin   Houston   Baton Rouge
New Orleans
San Antonio

The Southern States

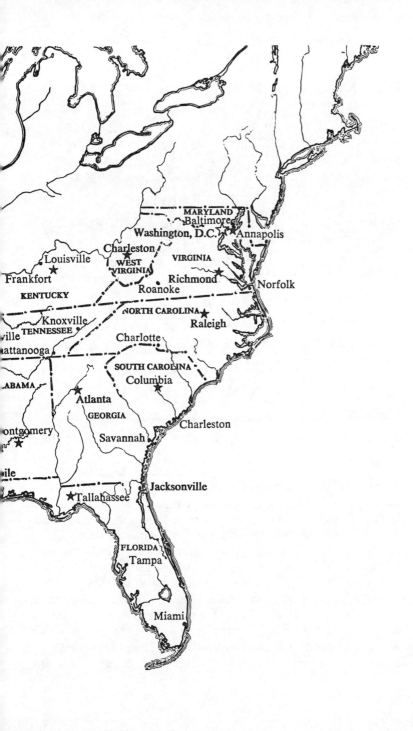

Presbyterian Church, U.S. Organizing at First Church,
Augusta, Georgia, 1861

25

YESTERDAY AND TODAY: A REVIEW AND A LOOK AHEAD

WITNESS

In the preceding chapters we have seen how the church, as the People of God, sought to carry out the Great Commission laid on them by their crucified and risen Lord (Matt. 28:18–20; Acts 1:8). Within a generation the gospel had spread throughout the Roman Empire. In the fourth century, Christianity became the state religion, and in a short time all were compelled to be baptized. Meanwhile, missionaries were carrying the gospel beyond the confines of the empire, winning peoples destined to lay the foundations of modern Europe. By A.D. 1200 all Europe was nominally Christian. A pattern is discernible. A people who received the gospel produced missionaries who recognized their obligation to carry it to others. So soldiers or traders brought it into Celtic England; a Celt (Patrick) carried it to Ireland; an Irishman (Columba) brought it to Scotland; Scottish

324

monks took it into Anglo-Saxon England; an Anglo-Saxon missionary (Boniface) became the great missionary among the Germans; German missionaries carried it to Scandinavian lands.

Meanwhile, Nestorian missionaries had planted churches in the Far East. In the seventh century, however, Mohammedans overran lands where Christianity had found its early strength; churches here were weakened; those in the Far East withered on the vine. Missionary efforts were brought to a temporary halt.

In the sixteenth century, following the discovery of America and of new trade routes to the East, the missionary expansion of Christianity was resumed. Devoted Roman Catholic missionaries planted their church in India, China, and Japan; the foundations of their present-day strength in South America, Central America, and the West Indies were laid. Protestant churches awakened more slowly to their missionary responsibility. Around the turn of the nineteenth century, however, missionary societies were formed in all major Protestant bodies. There followed the "Great Century" (1815–1915), in which Christianity spread more rapidly and more widely than ever before in its history. Today, as we have seen, there are national churches in almost every land.

Meanwhile, new difficulties have risen in the world: a population explosion, excessive mobility, secularism, militant atheism. The missionary task remains one of our most vital responsibilities.

What responsibility does our particular denomination have in this enterprise? How is it attempting to fulfill this responsibility? With what success?

What is the role of the local congregation in planting and sustaining new churches at home in the needier areas of the South? In aiding churches which we have helped to establish in other lands, and which remain dependent on us for financial support? How can the resources of the local church be utilized most efficiently in collaboration with the resources and efforts made by others to carry out the Great Commission which our Lord has laid upon us, for which so many have labored and suffered? These questions we shall need to consider.

ORGANIZATION

The loosely-knit Christian fellowship, assembled originally under the leadership of the apostles, was organized in New Testament times under two administrative officers—elders or bishops (the two terms being used interchangeably), and deacons (Acts 14:23; 1 Tim. 3: 1–10).

As the church grew, faced opposition, and confronted heresies, it evolved into a tightly articulated organization under the control of bishops, patterned ever more closely on the autocratic principle embodied in the Roman (Byzantine) Empire. The churches in the older East accepted an ecumenical council as the final authority in the church, as does their successor, the Orthodox Church, to the present time. The newer churches in the West, on the other hand, gradually came under the domination of the bishop of Rome, the pope, thus becoming *Roman* Catholic. Not until 1870, however, was it authoritatively declared that absolute power (as well as infallibility) was concentrated in the pope's hands. Protestant churches necessarily repudiated papal authority (after popes sought to suppress the preaching of the gospel). Lutheran Churches came under the control of civil rulers, with superintendents in place of bishops; so also the Anglican Church, though here the episcopal system was maintained. Anabaptists, turning to the Scriptures for their model, recognized no authority beyond that of the local congregation. Reformed and Presbyterian Churches, on the other hand, also looking to the New Testament for their model, organized churches controlled by presbyters (ruling and teaching elders), seeking to preserve the unity of the church by a series of ascending courts—a system of representative democracy as over against the pure democracy of the Anabaptist Churches. The three major systems of church government—episcopal, congregational, presbyterian—have all been maintained to the present day. But each order tends in some measure to incorporate some aspects of the rival systems into its own tradition. Thus some churches have accepted bishops without claims to apostolic succession; and all churches tend to bestow something like episcopal authority on some of their officials. So congregational independence becomes increasingly a fact in the life of all denominations. And both Congregational and Episcopal Churches have tended to take over the presbyterian principle of ascending courts in which final authority is shared by both clergy and laity.

Some form of church government is inevitable. What are the values of our particular tradition? How far is this tradition to be maintained, to what extent modified, as we face the changing times? These are questions which we will need to explore.

DOCTRINE

Christ had warned his disciples against the danger of false prophets, as did later the Apostle Paul (Matt. 24:24; Acts 20:28–30; 2 Tim. 4:1–4). The danger was quick to appear.

As the church moved out of its New Testament environment, as it met the inquiring Greek mind, as heresies arose (some of which seriously threatened the faith), it became necessary to define certain doctrines more exactly, to go beyond the simple scriptural language which heretics could twist to their own advantage. So councils met and adopted creeds which came to be accepted as standards of orthodoxy—particularly the Nicene Creed (which safeguarded the Deity of Christ), and the Chalcedonian Creed (which defined the Person of Christ, fully God and fully man). False beliefs such as Pelagianism, which minimized man's need of saving grace, were outlawed. But some beliefs that departed from the evangelical gospel as presented in the New Testament were gradually incorporated into the common faith—among them the view that saving grace was available only through sacraments administered by a mediating priesthood, that God could be more easily approached through the intercession of the saints, particularly that of the Virgin Mary, and that the pope, as successor of Peter, was Vicar of Christ. Roman Catholic theology, in almost its modern form, had come to be generally accepted, or imposed, by the end of the Middle Ages, and, because it made eternal salvation dependent on the ministrations of the church, was one of the factors which enabled abuses to accumulate, and for generations held back the growing call for reformation.

The Protestant Reformation came only as Martin Luther enabled men to understand the significance of Paul's teaching regarding justification by faith. Opposition from the Roman hierarchy led Luther to fall back on the sole authority of Scripture, which thereafter took its place alongside justification by faith as twin Protestant theses. But if Protestantism was to be maintained, fuller systems of belief had to be developed, articulated systems which could be placed alongside the imposing Catholic structure which had been slowly reared through the centuries. Two such systems arose, Lutheran and Calvinistic: the Lutheran theology centering in the forgiveness of sin, the Calvinistic system putting more emphasis on the sovereignty of God. Both systems became embodied in confessions of faith, for which men were prepared to contend; for which, if need be, some were prepared to die. Some of these confessions, such as the Augsburg Confession (Lutheran) and the Westminster Confession (Calvinistic) have come down to the present day and—though cast in the somewhat archaic language of another age and concerned with some problems whose significance is no longer recognized—are still accepted by many as standards of orthodoxy. In the generations after the Reformation elaborate systems of belief emerged, based on a rigid view of biblical inerrancy which made the Scriptures an absolute authority on matters of history, geography, science, and philosophy as well as religion.

In the course of time various modifications of the older systems had appeared. Arminianism (characterized by its reinterpretation of predestination), for example, is a modification of rigid Calvinism in a few of its more difficult aspects. Episcopalians developed their own view of the church; Baptists rejected the Calvinistic view of infant baptism; Quakers took over a distinctive view of the Holy Spirit.

Meanwhile new movements of thought had arisen which for a time threatened the whole structure of Christian faith: the new science, with its emphasis on observation and experiment; the new philosophy, insisting that no truth be accepted unless it could be logically demonstrated as valid; the new historical approach to the Bible, challenging traditional views of inspiration. Deists, rejecting an inspired Scripture and all belief in the Deity of Christ, anticipated the early collapse of Christian faith.

Able scholars, arising in the church, averted this threatened danger. In so doing they abandoned some of the older positions as no longer tenable, and offered new theologies, taking different forms in different lands. Echoes of the old controversies still continue—even in our own denomination—but in general their force has abated. Conservatives have tended to become more scholarly, and the more liberal have inclined to become more biblical. Luther and Calvin are studied more today perhaps than for many generations, not primarily for dogmatic purposes, rather, for their deep biblical insight. Scholars of all denominations are now embarked on an attempt to build a truly biblical theology, based on God's revelation in Christ. As they carry on their task, new questions emerge on which there will inevitably be, for a time at least, differences of opinion. Old questions meanwhile are relegated to the background. Some, no doubt, will in time again claim attention.

The skeptical attitude of many of the world's leading thinkers, however, has never been overcome. The prevalence of this attitude in intellectual circles, among many who have the ear of the public, must be taken into account as we seek to maintain and inculcate the faith in our own day.

What should be our attitude toward the confessional statements of our own particular church? What freedom should there be in the understanding and interpretation of the Bible? To what extent should a church insist on uniformity of belief? These are practical questions which we cannot completely disregard.

WORSHIP

In the course of history, changes have come not only in organization and doctrine, but also in worship. The early church built a Christian superstructure on the synagogue foundation, adding distinctively Christian elements such as the Lord's Supper (see Col. 3:16, Eph. 3:14–21; 1 Cor. 11:23–28). The Lord's Day replaced the Jewish Sabbath, and in addition there was an annual observance of the Resurrection and the great events that followed. Gradually the worship grew more elaborate, based on the re-offering of Christ's body by a mediating priest. Popular piety developed around the veneration of Mary, the Mother of God. Festivals in her honor took their place alongside those in honor of Christ. The church calendar became crowded with days set aside for commemoration of the "saints." Their relics became repositories of supernatural grace.

The new understanding of the gospel that accompanied the Protestant Reformation necessarily brought about fundamental alterations in the traditional pattern of worship. Lutherans, followed later by Anglicans, retained much of the old ritual, discarding only those elements which were plainly contrary to the gospel. Reformed and Presbyterian Churches, on the other hand, attempted to go back to a simpler worship, more in accordance with scriptural teaching. Emphasis was laid on word and sacraments; some liturgical elements were retained, and Zwingli also retained some of the great days of the church year. In their long struggle against Anglicanism and its attempt to impose the Prayer Book with its elaborate liturgy, Puritans came to oppose all liturgical elements in worship, including even use of the Apostles' Creed and repetition of the Lord's Prayer. Worship in churches of the Puritan tradition was further simplified—made more intensely personal, more sermon-centered—in the course of the evangelical awakening and particularly on the American frontier.

In recent days there has come a reaction against the drabness of Puritan worship. Vestments, though of a simpler sort, have returned, liturgical elements have been introduced, provision has been made for greater participation by the congregation. Elements of the church year are being recovered, more through popular pressure than by clerical leadership. Catholic and non-Catholic churches are re-examining their traditional modes of worship: We have entered upon a period of experiment and flux. The pattern of worship followed by various Presbyterian churches is a varied one, ranging from the simple worship of former days to highly liturgical services where the sermon has been reduced to a brief homily, similar to that found in a "high" Episcopal service.

What changes, if any, should we make in our traditional pattern of worship? By what principle should suggested innovations be tested? Have we discarded elements in our traditions which should have been retained? Are elements from other traditions now being introduced for purely aesthetic reasons which detract from the preaching and the hearing of God's word for our present day? Questions such as these cannot be safely evaded.

CONDUCT

In proclaiming the gospel throughout the world, the church has had to face numerous ethical questions. Some it has answered forthrightly in accordance with its understanding of the gospel; with others it has struggled, accepting unhappy compromises because no Christian solution was apparent. Still others have been ignored, because the church has been too blinded by this present age even to recognize that a problem exists. Again and again prophetic voices have been raised only to be ignored or opposed. Slowly at first, more massively in time, the Christian conscience has been aroused.

Thus in the early centuries church fathers took a strong stand against divorce, abortion, child exposure, gladiatorial combats, and gradually these were outlawed after the state had become Christian. War and slavery were recognized as evils but for them no solution was available: The church fell back on the theory that wars were justified under some circumstances, but must be fought for proper ends and in proper ways; consideration for the slaves as persons was emphasized, an attitude which in the end would undermine the system of slavery which, at that stage of society, seemed unavoidable. In the Middle Ages, the church opposed lending money on interest, advocated the principle of a just price, accepted the idea that the torture and extermination of heretics was justified. In the Reformation period, various attitudes were developed. Lutheran Churches tended to accept the idea that the provinces of church and state were distinct; the church's mission was confined to purely "spiritual" affairs, concern with the nurture of souls, with individual and family ethics, but not with larger social issues. Anabaptists carried the separation of church and state a step further. Literal obedience to Christ's commands was required. Since a magistrate could not carry on the duties of his office in accordance with the Sermon on the Mount, no true Christian could serve as a magistrate. Let the church, by strict discipline, erect a true Christian society in the face of a world abandoned to the Devil. The Reformed or Calvinistic conception was different. Church and state were to strive together to erect a Christian society: The church was to set forth God's will as revealed in Scripture for both the individual and society. The state was to implement the scriptural principles through appropriate legislation.

But as time went on, as modern capitalism developed, as the industrial situation became more complex, there was a reaction against church interference in economic affairs. Too often the clergy—the only accepted spokesmen for the church—were uninformed regarding the deeper issues involved, and continued to insist on traditional solutions that were no longer applicable; in addition, there was the inevitable human reaction against any interference with economic interests. There came a time when Protestant churches generally accepted the idea that the church was concerned only with the individual and his salvation, not at all with society and its problems.

The mounting horrors of the Industrial Revolution, at a time when laissez-faire (a policy of hands-off) was accepted as a natural law with which men interfered at their peril, and the widespread alienation of the working masses from the church caused the church to re-examine its mission. There emerged a so-called social gospel, some of whose principles are now accepted generally by church bodies, though not by all church members. Increasingly it is coming to be recognized that if the church is to speak on such issues—and on some it can hardly be silent—then the voice of the church must be not that of clergymen alone, but that of clergy and Christian laymen meeting in responsible exchange of ideas.

How can this be accomplished? How can the church today help men in the problems of their workaday world? How can the church avoid dangers of the past—of offering no guidance, of taking no part in overcoming deeply entrenched social evils, on the one hand; and on the other, of speaking in areas where it has no competence? These and other questions call for an answer in our own day.

THE ROLE OF THE LAITY

What is the place of the laymen (including women) in the church? This question has never been faced squarely or given any definitive answer. In New Testament times there was no distinction between clergy and laity (see 1 Cor. 12). But a clergy emerged, almost of necessity. Officers there had to be from the beginning; and as false prophets (laymen claiming inspiration) arose, responsibility for the mission of the church fell more and more on these duly appointed leaders—bishops, presbyters, and deacons. Laymen found new opportunities for service in monasteries and convents, though these too in time were worked into the official apparatus.

The Reformation emphasized the priesthood of all believers and recovered the doctrine of Christian vocation—that every Christian is called upon to serve God in his own particular occupation. Nonetheless, the role of the layman remained largely a passive one. The great evangelical movement which spread through Protestantism in the seventeenth and eighteenth centuries gave a far larger place to the laity. They were to become active participants in gatherings for Christian nurture, in winning souls, and in transmitting the faith. The Methodist Church was in its beginnings largely a lay movement—lay preachers operating under the supervision of an Anglican clergyman, John Wesley. In England and in America a host of voluntary societies grew up apart from any ecclesiastical control, supported by clergy and laity in fruitful co-operation.

In these voluntary societies most of the great benevolent work of our church had its birth: organized home missions, foreign missions, Sunday schools, educational societies, and the like. Only gradually were these organizations taken over by the denominations as a part of their normal operations. They have continued to give laymen a sphere of larger service in the life of the organized church. Meanwhile, organizations have been formed of men, women, and young people. These too were only gradually taken over by the churches as a part of their routine procedure. Today in our complex society new emphasis is being placed upon the laity as the People of God. The success of the church in our modern world is seen to depend upon its laymen, not because of their particular ability, but because of their involvement in the life of the world. The role of the pastor changes, becoming not less but more important as he seeks to aid the laity to function as the People of God in the totality of their lives.

What does this involve for the life of our local churches—for the local organizations of men, women, and young people? This too is a question that we need to face as we begin to look more closely at the life and work of our own denomination, of our own particular church.

THE UNITY OF THE CHURCH

Christ prayed that his disciples might be one, "even as thou, Father, art in me, and I in thee . . . that the world may believe that thou hast sent me" (John 17:20–24). Paul emphasized strongly the unity of believers (1 Cor. 1:10–13; Eph. 4:1–4), and to maintain that unity was himself prepared to die. Yet differences there were from the beginning. Paul and Barnabas went their separate ways. Judaizing Christians questioned Paul's apostolic authority. In Corinth there were factions, those who said, I belong to Paul, or Apollos, or Cephas, or Christ. But these various factions remained within the single fellowship. In the early church there were not only Catholic Christians, but Gnostics, Montanists, Marcionites, and Donatists; in the fourth and fifth and sixth centuries serious schisms occurred—Monophysite and Monothelite Churches arose which maintain their existence until the present day. The Roman Empire enforced unity within its bounds, but in 1054 there occurred the split between the older churches of the East and the newer churches of the West, a split which is perpetuated in the Orthodox and Roman Catholic Churches. Out of the Reformation grew the various Protestant bodies, most of which have reproduced themselves, and divided and re-divided on American soil. Most of these, however, as we have seen, are gathered into denominational families—Lutheran, Presbyterian (Reformed), Episcopal (Anglican), Methodist, Baptist, and Pentecostal—and in the last fifty years the ecumenical movement, tending toward both co-operation and union, has gained increasing momentum.

How is Christ's prayer to be answered in our own day? What relationship should there be between Presbyterian, Baptist, Methodist, Episcopal, and other churches? What relationship should we maintain with the various co-operative bodies—the National Council of Churches and the World Council of Churches? What part can the local church, of which we are members, play in the world mission of the church? How can we co-operate best with our fellow Christians in carrying out the Great Commission of our Lord, to make disciples of all nations, baptizing and teaching them to observe all that he commanded us? Such questions cannot be avoided, if we take seriously our Christian commitment.

Against this background, in the light of the church's nature and mission as set forth in the Scriptures, in the light of nearly two thousand years of church history, in the light of the present world situation, in the light of our membership in one particular church in one particular locality, we turn now, in the following chapters, to look more closely at the life and work of the denomination in which we are now called to serve and bear our own distinctive witness.

FOR CONSIDERATION

See the questions at end of each section, e.g., on pages 325, 327, 329, 330, 332, 333, 334.

*Presbyterian Church, U.S. Holding an Annual Meeting
of Its General Assembly*

26
PRESBYTERIAN
AND REFORMED

THE PRESBYTERIAN CHURCH IN THE UNITED STATES, of which
we are members, belongs to the Reformed and Presbyterian family of
churches, one of the four or five major branches of Protestantism.
Our fathers on the continent of Europe preferred the word "Reformed." They sought to organize no new church, rather to reform
the church which through the ages had departed in important respects
from the biblical norm. It is indeed one of the marks of the Reformed
and Presbyterian Churches that the church is always prepared to reform its life and work in the light of God's word as it becomes known
to them. In English-speaking lands the word "Presbyterian" came
into use because here the final struggle was with episcopacy—against
the autocratic power of rulers who sought to control the church
through the appointment of bishops. The word puts emphasis upon
the polity (organization) of the church: government through presbyters or elders, arranged in a series of ascending courts.

In the southern portion of the United States, where we are sub-
merged in a sea of Baptists, Presbyterians sometimes develop an infe-

riority complex. It helps our morale to observe that in broader areas this is not the case, that Presbyterian and Reformed are certainly the second, and perhaps the largest, Protestant body. Lutherans claim to be the largest Protestant family, and on paper this is indeed the case. But Lutherans count all baptized as members, and in Germany the majority of the inhabitants, and in Scandinavian countries 95 percent and more of the population, are baptized into the Lutheran Church in infancy, though the vast majority do not otherwise support the church. If bona fide members are counted there is reason to believe that Presbyterians would stand first, not second, in numbers. This is so, not because of great numbers in any one land, but because the Presbyterian and Reformed family of churches is so widely distributed throughout the earth. In the Alliance of Reformed Churches Throughout the World Holding the Presbyterian Order, for example, are ninety-six churches, from sixty-six countries, with a constituency of approximately fifty million.

Presbyterian churches are found today not only in England, Ireland, Scotland, and Wales, but also in most of the continental countries—including Austria, Belgium, Czechoslovakia, France, Germany, Greece, Hungary, Italy, Switzerland, and Yugoslavia—with a constituency totaling more than eighteen million.

There are Presbyterian and Reformed bodies in Africa with a constituency of approximately four million. They are found in Angola, Belgian Congo, British Cameroons, British Togoland, Cameroun, Egypt, Ethiopia, French Equatorial Africa, French Togoland, Ghana, Kenya, Liberia, Madagascar, Mozambique, Nigeria, Central Africa, South Africa, Basutoland, Southern Rhodesia, and Sudan.

In Latin America and the Caribbean there are sixteen Presbyterian and Reformed Churches, with a constituency of approximately one million members.

In Asia more than five million people are associated with the Reformed group of churches. They are located in British Borneo, Ceylon, China, India, Indonesia, Iran, Japan, Korea, Malaya, New Guinea (Dutch), Pakistan, Philippines, Syria, Lebanon, Taiwan, and Thailand.

Adherents of the Presbyterian and Reformed Churches of Australia, New Zealand, Tahiti, New Caledonia, and New Hebrides are estimated at more than a million and a half.

In North America there are sixteen and a half million people related to the Presbyterian family of churches—more than three million in Canada and over thirteen million in the United States. The largest Presbyterian church in this country is the United Presbyterian Church in the U.S.A., formed through the merger in 1958 of the Presbyterian Church in the U.S.A. and the United Presbyterian Church of North America. Our own Presbyterian Church in the United States, which established a separate existence in Civil War days, is second in size, with a membership now approaching the million mark. Among the smaller bodies are the original German Reformed Church (now a part of the United Church of Christ), the original Dutch Reformed Church (now known as the Reformed Church in America), the Cumberland Presbyterian Church, the Reformed Presbyterian Church (two bodies), the Associate Presbyterian Church, the Associate Reformed Presbyterian Church, the Orthodox Presbyterian Church, the Covenant Presbyterian Church, and the Bible Presbyterian Church.

There are some distinctive features which these Reformed and Presbyterian churches hold in common.

THE PRESBYTERIAN POLITY

First, a presbyterian polity (i.e., church government). Four major types of church government may be distinguished: (1) papal (monarchic), with government by a single ruler, the pope (Roman Catholic); (2) episcopal (oligarchic), with government by bishops (Orthodox, Anglican, American Methodist; though in most episcopal churches democratic elements have now been introduced); (3) congregational (pure democracy), in which all power is placed in the hands of the local congregation (Baptists, Disciples, and others); (4) presbyterian (representative democracy), in which representatives of the people (ruling and teaching elders) govern the church in a series of ascending courts.

Officers

The strength of the Presbyterian Church from the beginning has been found in this representative principle: laymen associated with the clergy in the government of the church, the unity of the church preserved through its series of courts. Such a church often moves slowly, but when it does move, it is likely to move massively. It is possible, of course, that ruling elders will not truly represent the people, that they will retard rather than stimulate the growth of the church; that is the danger that confronts all democratic governments. Our own church, along with other Presbyterian bodies, has sought to lessen this danger by permitting churches to choose their officers (elders and deacons) for limited periods of service. Ministers too sometimes overstay their time. But Presbyterian churches have always claimed the right to elect their own pastors and so long as this remains the case there will be periods when a church is without a pastor, and other times when the pastor remains longer than he or they would choose. To help in the movement of pastors, and to advise churches in the call of their ministers, commissions on the minister and his work are appointed in every presbytery.

Associated with ministers and elders in the government of the church are deacons. In apostolic days and in the early centuries, deacons were primarily concerned with the relief of human need (see Acts 6:1–7). In time this responsibility was taken out of their hands and the diaconate became merely a stepping-stone toward the priesthood (as it remains in Roman Catholic, Anglican, and Methodist Churches to the present day). Calvin attempted to restore the office of deacon to its original function. In Geneva they took over the care of the poor, the needy and distressed, including the sick (hospitals). The office of deacon declined in American Presbyterianism as elsewhere. When the office was revived, particularly in our own branch of the church, its responsibility in caring for the needy was again stressed; deacons were also given responsibility for the finances of the church and for the care of the church property. The first responsibility—in most churches—is now in name only; the two latter retain their importance.

Democracy in the Presbyterian Church has been fully applicable only to its male members. Women have always had the right to vote on the call of a pastor; they have had a voice in the election of their officers (elders and deacons); but they themselves have not been eligible to serve as ministers, elders, or deacons; for some time they were not permitted to speak in mixed audiences, much less to pray in the presence of men. Basis for this distinction was found in the missionary Letters of the Apostle Paul ("As in all the churches of the saints, the women should keep silence in the churches. For they are not permitted to speak, but should be subordinate . . . " [1 Cor. 14:33–34]; "I permit no woman to teach or to have authority over men . . ." [1 Tim. 2:12]). In recent times the idea has grown that Paul's words were applicable only to his own day, when woman's position in society was different from what it is today.

Our church took an important step forward in 1916, when the General Assembly ruled for the first time that women might pray and speak in public and carry on other activities in the local church if permitted by the session—with the one exception that they must not preach. In 1923 they were permitted for the first time to serve with men on the great boards of the church. Three years later a woman, the secretary of the Women's Auxiliary, was allowed for the first time to present her report in person to the General Assembly. In 1955 the General Assembly appointed an ad interim committee to make a thorough biblical study of the position of women in the church. This committee reported that in nearly all churches the world over women were taking a steadily increasing responsibility in the leadership of the affairs of the church, both on the local and higher levels, that many Reformed and Presbyterian churches (including the Presbyterian Church in the U.S.A.) permitted women to be elected and ordained to various offices in the church, and that this innovation had been informally approved by the Alliance of Reformed Churches Throughout the World Holding the Presbyterian System. The committee concluded that this movement seemed to be in response to the leadings of the Holy Spirit.

An amendment to our constitution that would permit women to be elected as elders and deacons was accepted by the assembly that heard this report and submitted to the presbyteries for their approval. The vote, however, was adverse: 39 in favor and 44 opposed. In 1963 the General Assembly once more approved an amendment to the constitution, this time permitting women to be ordained not only as elders and deacons, but also as ministers of the gospel. Presbyteries this time gave their overwhelming approval (53–27), and the amendment was finally approved and ratified by the General Assembly of 1964.

The movement to permit women to participate fully in the life of the church, which here reached its climax, has not been primarily a movement for "women's rights." It has been motivated throughout rather by a concern that women be permitted to serve their Lord in and through the church, which is his Body, with all their powers and to the full limit of their ability, not because they are women but because they are members of the household of God and each should serve with her own peculiar gifts. Supporters of the movement do not hold that men and women have "equal" (i.e., the same) gifts; rather, that they are complementary, the one to the other; that sharing more and more the same interests, they should increasingly co-operate in carrying on their Master's work; that the church should be able to draw upon the full resources at its disposal and encourage all its members to develop their fullest potentialities in the service of their Lord —in other words, to take seriously the priesthood of all believers.

Courts

The unity of the Presbyterian Church is preserved, as we have seen, by its series of ascending courts.

The *session,* including teaching and ruling elders, is the supreme judicatory (governing body) within the local church, all other organizations within the church being subject to its authority. The minister (teaching elder), however, is not a member of the local church, and he is responsible, so far as his message, his preaching and teaching of the word is concerned, not to the session, but to the presbytery, the second in the series of ascending courts which maintain the unity of the church.

The *presbytery* is composed of all ministers and one or more ruling elders from every church within a specified area, and has responsibility for the general welfare of the church within its own particular area.

Synods in our denomination are now—with one exception (Appalachia)—organized on state lines, though churches without the state are sometimes included (the Synod of Virginia, for example, includes isolated churches in West Virginia, Maryland, and Pennsylvania, in addition to the District of Columbia). The synod, not so important in actual practice as the presbytery, has general oversight of the work of the church within this larger area.

The highest court of our church, its bond of unity and peace, is the *General Assembly,* to which presbyteries elect commissioners (in proportion to their membership) including ruling and teaching elders in equal numbers.

The average church member knows only the work of his local church (and that in part). Through his gifts and through his representatives he is helping to carry on a far greater work which is essential for the effective functioning of his own local church, and which is helping to extend Christ's influence into the total life of our nation, and indeed to the uttermost parts of the earth.

Our fathers regarded this polity of the church as something that was God-given—that must operate in every aspect in strict accordance with the pattern set down in Scripture. We today do not find in Scripture so binding a scheme of organization; but we recognize that organization is essential if the work of the church is to proceed; and, in spite of defects (which are found in every type of organization, which are inherent indeed in human nature), we believe that our traditional polity, as it has developed through the years, is not only a sound one, but on the whole the best form of church government, and one which best accords with the general principles set forth in Scripture (see the Scripture listed on page 347).

THE PRESBYTERIAN CREED

Presbyterian churches are distinguished from others by their polity; historically also they have been creedal churches. There are churches today, like the Baptists, which profess to be noncreedal churches. It is true that they have no written creeds which have been formally adopted as a part of their constitution; but their traditional interpretation of Scripture becomes a creed no whit less binding, and in some ways even more so, than the written creeds of such churches as the Lutheran, Presbyterian, and Episcopal Churches. These latter churches, reaching back to the Reformation, adopted creeds at a time when it seemed imperative that those who repudiated the doctrines of Rome should declare their faith; they were confessions of faith on which men were prepared to take their stand at the cost sometimes of both life and goods.

Presbyterian Churches generally accept the Westminster Confession of Faith and the Larger and Shorter Catechisms, in which the doctrines of the confession are set forth more explicitly in the form of questions and answers, as a part of their constitution. However, this confession, drawn up in the language of the seventeenth century and setting forth answers to questions raised in that particular day, has never been imposed upon all members of the church. Those received into the church are required to answer only questions which the member of any evangelical body could answer—questions which have to do with their commitment to Jesus Christ as Savior and Lord and their readiness to serve Christ through the particular church in which they are seeking membership.

Ministers, elders, and deacons, on the other hand, are expected to accept the system of doctrine set forth in the confession—not every doctrine contained therein, but only those which are essential for the system as a whole. This was clearly said to be the case when the Presbyterian Church in America first adopted (1719) the confession as a part of its constitution, and has been explicitly reaffirmed from time to time in the course of our history. Who decides whether a particular doctrine is essential to the system as a whole? If there is any question about it in the mind of the officer to be ordained, he is expected to so inform the court (the session in the case of an elder or deacon, the presbytery in case of a minister) and leave the decision to them. In the course of time some doctrines (regarding predestination, for example) which seemed all-important to our fathers seem less important to their sons. So the presbyterian system provides for stability and change. The officers of the church accept a system of doctrine formulated in the seventeenth century as interpreted, however, by courts of the present day, in the light of their growing knowledge of Scripture. The Presbyterian Church, it may be added, has always been a theological church. It believes that what one thinks about God, about Christ, about life here and hereafter, and many other doctrines, is vitally important. Men preparing for the Presbyterian ministry give more attention to theology and to a study of the Scriptures in their original language than those of any other denominational family, excepting only the Lutheran and perhaps the Roman Catholic and Orthodox Churches.

Recognizing that the Westminster Confession of Faith is too long, and perhaps too stilted in its language, for popular usage in the present day, the General Assembly in 1962 approved a briefer statement of belief. This brief statement drawn up by an able committee of ministers and laymen does not become a part of our constitution but it does give a modern expression of the faith in simple terms that anyone can comprehend.

PRESBYTERIAN ECUMENICITY

The Presbyterian Church is distinguished from other Protestant bodies by its polity and creed; it has never assumed, however, as have some other bodies, that it is the only church of Christ. John Calvin labored more strenuously than any other churchman of his day to bind the scattered Protestant churches (including Lutheran, Reformed, and Episcopal) into a single body, allowing for differences in polity, worship, and creed. In general, though not always, Presbyterian and Reformed Churches have remained true to his ecumenical ideal. Our own church passed through an isolationist phase following the Civil War, as was natural perhaps under the circumstances; some isolationist trends have continued to the present day, and inevitably there are tensions as to the extent in which we should co-operate with other bodies, and under what circumstances we should unite with bodies which outwardly share our own faith and order.

The Presbyterian Church in the United States, however, recognizes all churches which preserve the word and the sacraments in their fundamental integrity as members of the one Body of Christ. This means in practice all churches which acknowledge the Deity of our Lord Jesus Christ. Some would except the Roman Catholic Church—but not as many as formerly. Our General Assembly no longer denies the validity of Roman Catholic baptism.

We dismiss our members freely to other evangelical bodies, and receive as readily members coming from such bodies. In most growing Presbyterian churches at the present time, 50 percent or more of the members have been reared in other denominations. We have no peculiar doctrines (concerning the mode of baptism, for example, or the validity of ministerial orders) which make such transfer of membership difficult. We open the Lord's table to all who profess his name. Presbyterians co-operate with other evangelical churches in their own community or state in every worthy enterprise, and often take the lead in such co-operative enterprises. We join with other major denominations in this and other lands in the work of the National and World Councils of Churches. True, opposition has come to our participation particularly in the National Council of Churches. Unless there is a decided change of sentiment, however, we shall retain our membership in both organizations, not because we agree with all that is said or done, but because of the contribution we can make through these organizations to the ongoing work of the Kingdom and because of the aid we receive in almost every phase of our own work. The desire to withdraw comes, it may be added, largely, indeed almost entirely, from those who are nonparticipants in their activities, not from those who represent our churches within these organizations, and not from those who have been given official responsibility for carrying on the benevolent work of our own denomination and who know therefore at firsthand the practical value of such aid.

One of the particular problems in this area which the Southern Presbyterian Church has had to face since 1865 is the problem of its relations with the Presbyterian Church U.S.A. (now the United Presbyterian Church in the U.S.A.). Three questions have been raised.

The first had to do with the establishment of full *fraternal relations*. In 1868 the Old School Northern Assembly acknowledged the legitimacy of the Southern Church, as it had refused to do in 1866. In 1869, the Old and New Schools now being reunited, the Northern Church declared that the offensive war declarations adopted by both bodies individually had no authority in the reunited body; and the following year, 1870, the U.S.A. Church appointed a committee to confer with one of our own regarding the opening of a friendly correspondence, looking forward to ultimate reunion. The Southern Church in reply drew up a severe indictment of the Northern Church in which, among other things, it charged that they had utterly betrayed the cause and Kingdom of our Lord Jesus Christ and had surrendered all the great testimonies of the church, of which we were now the sole remaining heirs. These were severe charges, fully as severe and just as unpardonable as the charges leveled against our own church by the Northern Assembly during the war years and after. Attention is called to them not to cast reflections on the fathers of our church but in order that we might realize that not all the wrong was on one side, that as a matter of fact both sections of the Presbyterian Church fell short of the spirit of Jesus in those difficult days. The first attempt to re-establish fraternal relations never got off the ground; this continued to be a pressing problem until 1882, seventeen years after the conclusion of the war, when the breach was finally healed. Both churches then withdrew the charges which they had leveled against the other[1] and a formal interchange of delegates was begun—marking the full resumption of fraternal relations.

Proposals for *union* began immediately and have continued to come up at intervals until the present time. Not until 1917, fifty years after the conclusion of the war, was the Southern Church willing even to consider such a possibility. From 1917 through 1922 negotiations continued, but the only type of union that our church was prepared to accept was not organic union, but a meaningless type of federal union, in which the Northern Church had no interest. In 1929 the Southern General Assembly, for the first time in its history, approved the idea of full organic union, and asked the U.S.A. Church to appoint a committee to work toward that end. This was regarded by many as a young man's Assembly, and the young men, it was said by the elders, had gotten a little bit out of hand. Subsequent assemblies quickly ended the negotiations.

In 1936 the Southern Church observed a Jubilee Year, the seventy-fifth anniversary of its founding as a denomination, and the following year the General Assembly once again approved organic union and asked the U.S.A. Church to appoint a committee on negotiations. These negotiations continued from 1937 to 1955, when the vote was taken and failed by one to carry even a majority of the presbyteries.[2]

The major grounds of opposition through the years to union with the "Northern" Church have been three: first, the doctrine of the "spirituality of the church," our differing views regarding the mission of the church; second, and more important in the later years, our supposed theological differences, many in our church feeling that the

U.S.A. Church is too liberal theologically; and in the third place, the racial issue, which, though it was not brought out in the open, was thought by many to be the dominant issue in the most recent discussion, as it was in fact in many of the earlier discussions.

While plans of union have so far failed, various plans for *co-operation* between the two Presbyterian Churches have been adopted. We do not compete on the foreign field; we seek not to compete on the home field. We work together on college and university campuses; we hold joint ownership of colleges and theological seminaries; synods and presbyteries, where there is serious overlapping, meet and plan their projects together.

In 1960 the Southern General Assembly adopted these resolutions.

> In this 100th year of the organization of our church and with the approaching centennial celebration of its founding, we are saddened that the division which came to our American Presbyterian family with a divided nation 100 years ago has not been healed even though the nation has long since been made one.
>
> We reaffirm the hope and prayer often expressed by previous Assemblies for the greatest possible unity in our Presbyterian family.
>
> We commend and encourage congregations, presbyteries, synods and agencies at all levels that are finding appropriate ways and means to increase Presbyterian cooperation and united efforts in their respective areas.
>
> At the Assembly level the Committee on Inter-Church Relations is instructed to confer with the corresponding body in the United Presbyterian Church in the U.S.A. and other Presbyterian bodies as to ways in which present tensions, where they exist, may be eased, where cooperation may be extended and made more fruitful, and to arrange, where advisable, for meetings of representatives of our boards and agencies for further exploration of ways and means of a greater united effort.[3]

The General Assembly of 1964 made a similar resolution. Here for the present the matter rests.

In the meantime, negotiations have been opened between the Presbyterian Church in the United States and the Reformed Church in America, looking toward further co-operation and possible merger between these two bodies. What the outcome of these negotiations will be cannot be foreseen at the time of writing.

Presbyterian in its order, Calvinist in its creed, ecumenical in its spirit, our denomination seeks today to carry out its mission in the world. What is involved in this mission? Important aspects will be considered in the chapters which follow.

FOR CONSIDERATION

1. What, as you see it, is the strength and the weakness of Presbyterian government?
*2. Consider Acts 6:1–4; 11:30; 14:23; 15:1–29; 20:17; 21:18; Philippians 1:1; 1 Timothy 3:1–8; 5:17; Titus 1:5–9; Ephesians 4:4. Do we have here a basis for presbyterian church government, assuming, as most scholars now agree, that "elder" and "bishop" were synonymous terms for the same office in New Testament times?
3. What, as you see it, are the values of a written confession of faith? Are there also handicaps?
4. Do Presbyterians place too much or too little emphasis on doctrine? Why do you think so?
5. Does the average Presbyterian understand the doctrine of his church? Of its polity (organization)? If not, why not, and how can it be remedied?
*6. Is it proper for the Presbyterian Church to co-operate with other Protestants in organizations which on occasion take stands to which some of its members take violent exception?
7. What co-operation is there between Christians in your own community? Are there other desirable types of co-operation that should be established?

A New Suburban Church Breaking Ground for Its First Building

27
THE BIBLICAL IMPERATIVE: TO MAKE DISCIPLES

THE BASIC RESPONSIBILITY of the church in every age has been to proclaim the gospel, to preach the Good News, to transmit the faith, to win disciples. Thus, in the beginning of his ministry Jesus "appointed twelve, to be with him, and to be sent out to preach . . ." (Mark 3:14). To Peter, who first acknowledged him as the Christ, Jesus said, "I will give you the keys of the kingdom of heaven . . ." (Matt. 16:19); to his disciples as a group, the risen Lord said, "Go . . . and make disciples of all nations . . ." (Matt. 28:19). Through the missionary laborers of many generations the faith finally came to our own forefathers; they in turn have sought to give it to others.

How has our own church discharged its responsibility?[1]

THE BACKGROUND

By the end of the Colonial period, Presbyterians, as we have seen (chapter 17), had become the second largest denomination in America. Their greatest strength was in the Middle Colonies and along the

348

frontier. In the South they were comparatively weak. They had been the first to bring the evangelical gospel into this region, where the masses of the people had not been reached by the established (Anglican) Church. But because of a lack of ministers (due in turn to the high educational qualifications required) they failed to retain a majority of their own people, the Scotch-Irish, much less win many of non-Presbyterian stock. The one exception was in eastern Virginia, where there was a revival that might have brought many into the Presbyterian Church had its leaders taken advantage of the situation. But after some feeble efforts on the Presbyterians' part, the Baptists came in and within a generation had laid the foundation for that numerical superiority in the South which they have retained to the present time.

After the Revolution, as we saw in chapter 19, came the great westward movement of population which resulted in the speedy settlement of the Mississippi Valley. The church's prime responsibility was to extend the gospel into the ever expanding frontier. Close on the heels of the pioneer trod the itinerant missionary or the more lowly colporteur, to be followed by the settled pastor. Because of their insistence on an educated ministry, Presbyterians fell far behind Methodists and Baptists, so far as number of members was concerned. This was particularly true in the South, where the existence of slavery served as an additional deterrent to missionaries from outside the region. Presbyterians accomplished far more, however, than other religious bodies. The educated Presbyterian ministers did not attract the uneducated masses, but they did gather to themselves a large proportion of the educated class in every community which they entered. By 1861 Presbyterians were the third largest denomination in the South, as in the nation as a whole.

In this year the Old School Presbyterian Church divided into Northern and Southern branches. The division was not due, ostensibly, to the outbreak of Civil War, but rather to the Gardiner Spring resolutions, adopted by the General Assembly which met in May, 1861, pledging allegiance to the federal government; Southern presbyteries thereupon withdrew, claiming that this resolution forced them out of the church. The General Assembly of the Presbyterian Church in the Confederate States of America (now the Presbyterian Church in the United States) was organized in Augusta, Georgia, on

December 4, 1861, with 47 presbyteries, 1275 churches, and a membership of 95,550.

In the next few years a number of smaller Presbyterian bodies were absorbed into the "Southern" Church. The most important of these were the United Synod (120 ministers, and 1200 members, representing New School Presbyterians in the South), some representatives of the A.R.P. Church in Kentucky and Alabama, the Presbytery of Patapsco (Maryland) in 1867, the majority of the Synod of Kentucky in 1868 (108 ministers and 9,800 members), and the majority of the Synod of Missouri in 1874, with 67 ministers and 8,000 members. These three latter bodies included southern sympathizers, practically forced out by the stubborn attitude of the northern assembly in the bitter aftermath of the war.

During the war years and for some time following (1865–1879) the Southern Church could do little in the way of church extension; impoverished by the war, they could barely maintain their existing churches. The General Assembly's Executive Committee on Home Missions became in fact, as also in name, a Committee on Sustentation (maintenance, support), i.e., holding their own rather than advancing.

With an improvement in its economic condition, the church resumed its missionary advance. Presbyteries and synods accepted responsibility for extension within their own bounds. Surplus funds in the hands of the assembly's committee were expended on the growing edges of the church, first Texas and later Florida. Oklahoma was open for settlement April 22, 1889, and cities sprouted like mushrooms, almost overnight. But our church's funds for church extension were required for Texas, and there was little left for Oklahoma. The comparative size of these two synods (Texas, one of the largest; Oklahoma, by far the smallest) illustrates the value, indeed the necessity, of home missions on an assembly-wide scale, if the church is to expand.

The Presbyterian Church in the United States, however, lacked resources in men and money to meet the spiritual needs of the hordes pouring even into Texas, and later into Florida. The Presbyterian Church in the U.S.A. (now the United Presbyterian Church in the U.S.A.) followed its own people with its own missionaries, and today these two major branches of the Presbyterian family divide the responsibility between them for building Presbyterianism in a number of our southern states. A succession of "comity agreements" (agreements allotting definite areas to each denomination involved) attempt with some success to lessen the waste of needless competition.

THE CHALLENGE: CHURCH EXTENSION

The Second World War wrought great changes in the South. The rapid growth of industry brought with it rising incomes, increases and also a shift in its population. In the decade of the fifties this population increase averaged a million a year. In the next fifteen years the U.S. Census Bureau estimated that the growth would be accelerated. Virginia and North Carolina were expected to grow approximately one million each, Texas three million, and Florida four million. In addition to the population increase, the shift of population was expected to continue from the rural areas to the cities, from the cities of the North and East to the cities of the South and the West, and from the centers of the city to their circumferences.

Each of these population movements has brought problems—the problem of the rural church, for example, where there is a declining population; the complex problem of the inner city, for which none of the older denominations so far has been able to find a solution; the problem of industrial communities and low wage areas, where Presbyterian churches are rarely successful; the problem of a declining neighborhood, where the church to survive needs to draw in members of a lower economic level.

In the Rural South

The great farm exodus, expected to continue for many years to come, means that the average rural church in the South faces a steadily declining population. However, some rural churches are being drawn into the orbits of the expanding cities.

Many rural churches, on the other hand, are located in sites which were appropriate for the horse-and-buggy days and for a rising rural population, but not for the present day in areas where population is declining. In addition, many rural areas are badly overchurched.

We should remember also that the church in the country is now faced with competition from many other agencies for the time and interests of the people. In any progressive community the church is now "but one of the groups or constellation of groups competing with each other for the time of the participating families of the community."

In the judgment of those who have studied the matter, the rural church, with notable exceptions, has not adapted its program to meet these rapidly changing environmental conditions.

"Rural life conditions have undergone tremendous changes in the United States in the last few decades," says S. H. Hobbs, Jr. "Perhaps no institution has changed as little as the country church. Everywhere in rural America horizons are enlarging. This applies to everything except the country church."

And yet, sociological studies reveal that in most rural communities in the South the church remains the most important social institution. A third of our members and two thirds of our churches are in the country.

The rural churches must remain vigorous, therefore, not only for their own sakes and not only for the sake of the urban churches which drain off their membership, but also for the sake of the nation, whose moral fiber is maintained by churches in city and country alike. To this end they require and deserve the help of urban churches and of the denomination as a whole.

Some of our rural churches, it may be, could be closed with no appreciable loss to the denomination. Others need to be relocated in areas where there is greater possibility for growth. Still others need to be grouped in some co-operative plan, denominational or interdenominational. The most practical and effective of these plans at present is the Larger Parish plan, by which two or more churches co-operate to provide for each individually and for two or more jointly a better total program than if each continues to work independently. The Larger Parish plan encourages joint projects, makes possible larger undertakings, and enables the co-operating churches to exert a larger influence in the community. When such a parish is organized, the people of the neighborhood respond and the churches grow. Through the multiplication of such parishes, the extension of co-operative activities, the training of lay leadership, the stimulation found in pastors' institutes and conferences, the research, guidance, and staff service of the Department of Rural Church in the Board of Church Extension, and above all through the prayers and activities of rural church members themselves, our country churches can and will be strengthened in the years to come.

In the Urban South

Available signs indicate that cities and metropolitan areas will continue to grow in the South as in the rest of the nation. They will grow because our southern farms have the highest birthrate in America and the greatest surplus population, because increasing mechanization means that fewer laborers will be required on the farms than are now required, and because new industrial opportunities are constantly arising. For many years this surplus population of the South moved largely to the cities of the North. In the future a larger proportion will remain in the South because industry itself is moving south.

People are moving not only to the city but within the city, and from the center out toward the circumference. This means that neighborhoods, all neighborhoods, are constantly changing; and that the church, if it is to continue to grow, or even to survive, must take these changes into account. As Dr. Leiffer puts it: "If the church is to serve the spiritual needs of men, it must in its planning be as skillful and as farsighted as the public-service company or the county highway commission, moving quickly into developing territories and reorienting its program in older areas as population changes take place." Actually the Church must be more farsighted. People moving into a new residence will on their own initiative make connections with the public service corporations, but they do not always on their own initiative make connection with the church. Men who have made a special study of church and urban life tell us that the church's best opportunity to win a newcomer into a community is within the first three months. Thereafter it becomes increasingly more difficult. "If people have been living in the area for ten years, without establishing a church connection," they tell us, "there is small chance that publicity or visitation will induce them to join the fellowship. Such people have made their contacts, habits are established, they have found satisfactions elsewhere. The inertia is too great for a call to produce much change in their attitudes. The church had its chance, but it was years ago."[2]

Urban communities, small or great, follow a regular pattern in their development and also in their decline. We cannot follow this developing pattern here, but we might recall that every city as it grows comes to have certain clearly defined areas—downtown, slum, declining areas, stable areas, growing residential section, and suburbs—and that in each of these areas the church has its own particular problems. Churches, and that means both pastors and people, must recognize these problems and take intelligent steps to meet them or they will inevitably decline. The task of the downtown church is conditioned by the fact that its members move increasingly to the outlying residential districts or suburbs. Many retain their membership in the central church, but eventually they or their children are likely to join the church in their own neighborhood.

It is hard for a church to remain in a downtown area, however, unless it somehow finds a way to minister to the people in its own neighborhood as well as to those who come in from the outside. The time may come when the downtown church ought to become an institutional church with a seven-day program intended for the people who live within its shadow, and when the presbytery or the denomination as a whole should give it the necessary funds to develop such a program.

The church in the city is also faced with the challenge of the slums, which, according to the estimate of Mark W. Dawber, hold approximately one third of our urban population. In the South this would include a large percentage of Negroes. This is the area with the highest percentage of disease, crime, and degeneracy, with the highest percentage of unchurched and, therefore, the highest percentage of need. It is difficult for the church to maintain any foothold here because it is hard to secure capable ministerial leadership, to recruit and hold an adequate membership, or to train capable leaders among the people themselves.

Beyond the deteriorated areas surrounding the main business zone we find the stable residential areas, most of whose land has been developed and whose general character has long since been determined. It sometimes seems that the church here needs to do nothing but continue its present successful program and all will be well. But that is a dangerous illusion. If the church is alert, it will no doubt discover that trends have developed which it needs to watch. Perhaps it is failing to reach certain elements of its natural constituency, its young people, for example, or its young adults, a failure which, if not remedied, will in time seriously affect the church's strength. The loss of some of its members by removal to more remote sections may indicate that the older population is beginning to migrate and a new and different population is moving in. And if the church does not succeed in reaching this newer population—the people moving into the new apartments or the new multiple dwellings, for example—it is in for trouble. Such a church may still render a helpful ministry to a people from a distance, but it makes little or no contribution to the people of its own neighborhood. It is not easy to adapt a church program to a changing neighborhood (particularly when the people come from different racial, cultural, social, or economic backgrounds), and it is not easy to win people in apartments who, for various reasons, are not so likely to seek out a church as those who own their own homes; but a church that does not adapt its program and seek new members fails to render its greatest ministry. And the time will come when it, too, must move, merge, live on at a dying rate, or finally close its doors. The tragedy is that so many do move away or close their doors while there are still hundreds of unchurched on every side.

The United Presbyterian Church in the U.S.A. is taking cognizance of this problem, and will greatly expand its assistance to churches in "inner city" areas. Funds will be used for new buildings, for pilot projects in inner city work, for training a staff to assist churches suffering from population changes in their areas, and for training programs for church leaders.

Our own church is beginning to move cautiously in the same direction. The need will become greater, not less, as time goes by.

American cities, as we have seen, tend to grow on their fringes. It is here that the fastest growth has occurred—almost half of the nation's increase in population during the last decade, two and a half times the rate of total population gain. And it is here that the U.S. Census Bureau sees the most rapid growth in the future—in the smaller urban and suburban communities adjoining our metropolitan centers.

Some of the new projected housing areas may prove to be a mistake, but unless the city itself ceases to grow—and often even so—many will become the important residential sections of the future. If a denomination, then, is not to fall hopelessly behind and to fail in its ministry to souls, it must watch for these new housing developments and at the right time and in the right way plant the nucleus of a new congregation.

"The wisdom displayed by ministers and laymen in adapting old churches or establishing new ones to serve the religious needs of this population," says Murray H. Leiffer, "will greatly influence the course of Protestantism for the next fifty years." Some would say for the next one hundred years.

Certainly it is in the growing residential areas of our southern cities that Presbyterianism today faces its greatest opportunities and its greatest challenge. Our church is weak, as we have seen, in the rural areas of the South; it is making little or no appeal to our rapidly growing industrial population; it does thrive in residential sections occupied by people with moderate or smaller income. Money wisely invested in a growing residential area of any one of our southern cities will return rich dividends in the years to come, dividends in souls and financial dividends as well, dividends which will in turn aid the benevolence program of our church in each and every phase.

As a result of our efforts, we organized for a number of years an average of one new church a week. Some of these new churches are now numbered among the largest churches in the General Assembly.

During the period 1926–1950 our denomination as a whole grew 50 percent. This was a growth greater that that of the Episcopal, the Methodist, the Disciples, the Presbyterian Church in the U.S.A., and many other groups. But it was not so rapid as that of the Roman Catholic Church which in the same period grew 53 percent, or that of the Southern Baptists who grew 100 percent, or that of the Mormons who grew 105 percent, or that of the Churches of Christ which grew 130 percent. And some of the newer sects—the Nazarenes, the Assemblies of God, and the Church of God in Christ—were growing ten times and in the case of the last church, twenty times as fast.

We do have much to show for our efforts, and yet compared with the total need we have done little more than scratch the surface. To give but one example, there were a few years ago over 273 incorporated places in Florida, most of which were and are growing by leaps and bounds, and in 164 of these there was no Presbyterian church, either U.S. or U.S.A.

To travel through the bounds of our church, to see in some areas, as in the Washington-Baltimore area, in Texas, or in Florida, miles on miles of new homes, giant apartment houses, various forms of multi-dwellings, and to realize that fifty or seventy-five or a hundred thousand dollars invested here and there would be repaid many times over within just a few years, to have it brought home that we do not have the funds either to give or to lend, leaves one sad, and even sick at heart.

The supreme opportunity which is now afforded us is not one which will continue forever, or which will be repeated in every generation. In the Colonial period the opportunity was given once and was then withdrawn; the pattern of religion in the South was fixed and has remained stable now for generations. In the post-Revolutionary period the opportunity was given once and was then withdrawn; the pattern of denominationalism in America was fixed and has remained stable until the present time, when once again the situation is fluid. Today the population of the South is once more on the move, and the best possible investment our church can make is to plant churches in the most strategic areas of our growing cities where they may become the great churches of tomorrow. We should not forget that every cause of the church stands to gain if we plant wisely and well; otherwise, every cause will ultimately lose. The decision which we are now making will determine our destiny for many generations to come. This is the third, it may be our last, opportunity to play a great role in American Protestantism.

Our Negro Churches

A particular problem which the Southern Church began to face immediately upon its organization, and which has continued to the present time, is our policy regarding our Negro constituency. In 1861 we had approximately fourteen thousand Negro members (the exact

number is uncertain)—not very many, but more than we have ever
had since. At the war's end the Negroes were not put out of the
southern churches, as many believe; they left by choice because they
wanted to organize churches which they could control under their
own leadership. The Baptist Church encouraged them in this effort,
and as a consequence became the dominant body among this race.
The Methodist Church hesitated and as a consequence lost two-thirds
of its Negro constituency.

Our own church expressed the desire that the Negroes remain in
the same position they had occupied before—in the white churches,
and, of course, segregated. When our fathers discovered that this
would not do, they offered to form separate Negro congregations under white sessions with white ministers, and then with their own officers, but still with white ministers. While we hesitated, all our Negro
members left us en masse, all except a few loyal family servants who
remained in the church of their old masters and friends.

Faced with this situation, we adopted in 1874 a new policy, based
on the Negroes' desire to have their own church. We sought to begin
again at the beginning: to organize Negro churches with Negro ministers to whom we had given a simple training, and when there were
enough of them, to set them aside into Negro presbyteries, later organizing an independent synod, with continuing financial aid. But it was
too late for such a policy. It proved an utter failure. We formed an
Afro-American Presbyterian Synod, but it could not stand. In 1916
we recognized our failure and organized what were left of our Negro
churches into Snedecor Memorial Synod. Theoretically, the goal of
our church was still the establishment of an independent Negro denomination. Practically, the Negro synod had become a constituent
and permanent part of our own church. Commissioners from the
Negro presbyteries came to our General Assembly, where they were
entertained as was then the custom, on a segregated basis.

In recent years two movements have developed among the Negroes which have special significance for the Church.

The first of these is the population movement—a movement of
the Negroes from the farms to the cities, and to the cities of the South
as well as to those of the North. Despite the exodus of the Negroes
from the South in recent years there were 3 percent more Negroes

in the region in 1950 than there were in 1940, though the ratio of Negroes in the South's population diminished from 23.8 percent to 21.6 percent. But Southern Negroes are now much more thickly congregated in the cities. Large-scale housing developments for Negroes have taken place in recent years in such cities as Memphis, Nashville, Atlanta, Orlando, Houston, and Louisville. In Richmond approximately 24,000 dwelling units formerly owned by whites were taken over by Negroes within five years. Numerous other cities have experienced similar changes, though perhaps not on so large a scale.

The second important movement among Negroes is what might be called a cultural movement. The status of the urban Negro is improving—economically, socially, politically (to some extent), and, above all, educationally. In almost every city a new class of Negro leader is emerging, including artists, businessmen, clergymen, dentists, editors, lawyers, physicians, social workers, and many others. But comparatively few educated Negroes are now entering the ministry. In the year 1955 only 96 Negro ministers graduated from all seminaries with a B.D. degree to serve the Baptist, Methodist, and Pentecostal Churches, which among them enroll most of the Negroes in America. The new generation of Negroes, particularly its leadership, is no longer willing to sit under the preaching of untrained ministers, and they are no longer attracted by the emotional type of religion that is found in the typical Negro church. Many are being lost, therefore, to the church.

In 1946 an ad interim committee reported on the status of our Negro work: 14,000 Negro members when our church was organized, 3,368 when the report was made; fifty-six Negro churches to show for all our efforts, only two of which were self-supporting; thirty-four active Negro ministers, the majority inadequately trained, all poorly paid, with the result that most of them were compelled to take on other work to support their families; Stillman Institute, our only school for Negroes, was a struggling junior college which fell far short of the requirements of a first-class educational institution. It was conditionally accredited by the Southern Association of Schools and Colleges, said the report, but this partial recognition was in danger of being withdrawn. The theological department had almost ceased to function, with one student that year and one course taught by a Methodist minister. The department of nurses' training no longer had any professional standing. There were evidences, continued the committee, of serious unrest among the student body, verging from time to time on open rebellion. The indication was that Stillman had lost the confidence of our Negro constituency.

It had lost the confidence of its Negro constituency, in large part, it may be added, although the committee did not say so publicly, because there were too many who retained the traditional attitude in the South for the Negro, a patronizing attitude which no longer permitted the "new" Negro to maintain his self-respect.

Following this report our General Assembly inaugurated a new policy: one which holds, for the first time, some promise of success. A new administration—with a changed attitude—took charge. A new Stillman, with a dedicated leadership and increased facilities, came into being. Its endowment was greatly increased, and it became a college of which we could be proud. Our Negro synod was dissolved and its presbyteries divided among the white synods. New churches were organized, and trained leadership provided. Most of the new churches became constituent members of the white presbyteries within whose borders they were located. Negro ministers began to be trained at our established seminaries. The result is that for the first time our work among the Negroes is really growing. It is appealing especially to the educated Negroes. The number of such Negroes has increased rapidly in recent years, but the number of educated Negro ministers has remained pitifully low. A recent count indicated that there were not a hundred Negro students with an A.B. degree preparing for the gospel ministry in all Protestant denominations combined. Our new approach, along with a trained Negro Presbyterian ministry, has enabled us to build a number of successful Negro churches in the South in recent years—churches with able ministers who draw about them some of the more influential members of their race.

Our church meanwhile is making some progress in integrating its Negro and white membership, a goal repeatedly approved by its highest court, the General Assembly. Negroes are received on an equal basis in our various church courts, in many, if not most of our church conferences and camps, in all of our theological seminaries, in most of our colleges. They are welcomed in the worship services of most of our churches. In some there is a mixed membership, and others are prepared to receive applicants for membership irrespective of color.

> If ... because of the redemptive love of Christ to whom each of us owes his own redemption, and for his sake, our whole church could show how the Cross makes all men brothers, what a convincing witness that would be [wrote Thomas W. Currie in a recent study book]! As Christ banishes paternalism, condescension, and cringing sloth, he forges us indeed more and more into the instruments by means of which he will batter down the gates of Hell.[3]

THE CHALLENGE: A NEW EVANGELISM

Basic for the growth of the church is some form of evangelism, for it is through evangelism that the church recruits the new members without whom it would soon wither and die. A larger proportion of the American population are members of the church today than ever before, and yet if a single generation falters in its task the labors of many previous generations may be dissipated.

Evangelism, by which the church lives and through which it witnesses to the world, has been defined as making the gospel of God's redeeming love in Christ known to those who do not know it, in hope that they may be turned to God in faith; and making it more effectively known to those who already live within the church, that their faith may grow in clarity and strength. Or, in the words of Dr. Nelson Bell: "Evangelism is presenting Jesus Christ in the power of the Holy Spirit so that men will put their trust in God through him, accept him as Saviour and Lord, serve him in the fellowship of his Church and follow him in daily living."

The types of evangelism are many. Some form of preaching evangelism is perhaps the most common. But there is also personal evangelism, in which children, young people, and adults are pointed to Christ by instruction offered in the Sunday school or elsewhere. Visitation evangelism, in which laymen, after a period of instruction, go two by two from house to house seeking commitments to Christ in the quiet of the home, has been one of the most popular and effective methods employed in recent years. Various forms of fellowship or cell evangelism have also been developed, in which people are brought into the friendship of a Christian group, with the purpose of bringing them to a decision for Christ. Mass evangelism, which played a great part in the earlier history of our nation, has been revived after a long period of decline, and has today both advocates and critics. Tract and book evangelism, in which literature is used as the principal means of witness, has vast possibilities which have hardly been tapped; radio and television evangelism are still in their infancy; and an evangelism which makes adequate use of the arts is yet to be born.

The evangelism of the future may be expected to learn from the mistakes of the past, and to venture out in new and as yet untried directions:

1. It will not be a mere duplication of the past, but will make use of methods both old and new.

2. It will deal with the total man, concerned not merely to save his soul but to make him a new man in Christ, as manifest in all the relations of life.

3. It will be interwoven into the program and life of the church, recognizing that the Christian life cannot develop in isolation, but that the newborn Christian must become an active unit in an established fellowship of worship and service.

4. It will appeal to every aspect of man's personality—thought, feeling, and will—and to no one of them in undue proportion.

5. It will be positive rather than negative in its emphasis, based not on prohibitions, especially of the narrow sort, but on the two great commandments, love to God and love to man.

6. It will grow out of a true conception of conversion, recognizing that a man can and must be radically changed as a result of the divine-human encounter, but that no two individuals come to God exactly alike.

7. It will be a call to total commitment.

8. It will be expressed in contemporary terms, and relevant to the needs and issues of its day.

9. It will make use of varied means of communication—radio, films, and television—which reach the ear and the eye of untold millions; tracts, which he who runs may read; articles and books for the more thoughtful; choral music, religious art, and drama with its pow-

erful appeal to the imagination. "Most direct and effective of all, when they are genuine expressions of faith and love, are concrete works of mercy that can make our faith live."

10. It will be directed to all groups, including those out of touch with the church, and not ordinarily reached by its message. "Many churches still do not realize that they have lost ground with particular social groups, because of a narrow or an irrelevant conception of the problems of modern man, or because they are too closely associated with certain social classes," declares a study document prepared for the Department of Evangelism of the World Council of Churches. "Too often, to the man in need, the Church appears as a body which speaks a language which few understand or is concerned with problems in which few are interested. Culturally and socially speaking it seems to many to be an anachronism, and this undermines its spiritual potency. The Church must learn to communicate its message for the new times."[4]

In Europe where the rift between church and the people is deeper than in America, a number of striking experiments have been undertaken, as we have seen, in an attempt to reach certain disaffected groups. Some of these experiments such as the Kirchentag in Germany, the Iona community in Scotland, and the Zoë movement in Greece have attracted international attention. But there are many other lesser known movements, in which points of contact are established in new and novel ways, especially with workers and intellectuals. And there is experimentation, though to a lesser degree, in our own land. Colleges and universities have their weeks of religious emphasis, which do not always fall into the same pattern. There are various attempts at industrial evangelism. Successful missions have been opened in the slums.

The lesson is clear. The evangelism of tomorrow must be conducted with flexibility. Varied forms of organization and strategy will be required. The needs of a changing world must be kept in mind. And no element or group in the population can be overlooked.

Evangelism is the task of the denomination as a whole, a responsibility which it seeks to fulfill in part through its Department of Evangelism in the Board of Church Extension, and the corresponding organizations within presbytery and synod. But it will never be fulfilled adequately except as it becomes the responsibility of the local congregation. We need an evangelizing congregation more than we need evangelists, for as Dr. George Sweazey points out in *Evangelism in the United States,* only a church can provide for that succession of steps by which an unbeliever can be brought to interest, to understanding, to decision, and to Christian living; can provide, in other words, a complete program of evangelism including contact, cultivation, commitment, and consecration. Too many local churches are content to serve their constituency without continuous systematic efforts to enlarge it. "It may be that we will be forced to learn a great deal from the Sects," suggests Richard Shaull, "for some of them, such as the Pentecostals, have discovered what it means for the local congregation to be a dynamic missionary community."[5]

This work of evangelism should be undertaken by all professing Christians. "The minister represents the paid salesman for Christianity," as Norman Victor Hope reminds us, "whereas the layman is the satisfied customer, who cannot help recommending something which he has found so richly satisfying."[6] Only the latter can carry the Christian witness into every aspect of our contemporary life. Laymen, like clergymen, differ greatly in the gifts that enable them to affirm and interpret for others the gospel they believe. "For very many Christians," says a report to the National Council of Churches, "the most fitting and effective medium of communication with their fellows is not talk, but thoughtful, perceptive, responsible action in the ever-pressing tangle of human need and personal involvement."[7] "For the individual Christian," declares the World Council's Study Document, "the normative service will most often be expressed through his secular calling: in daily work, in professional associations, and in community living.

"Through these day-to-day encounters the Gospel has its widest and closest contact with the world and they should be much more than occasions for pious declamations [which may] do more harm than good ... The Church must instruct and sustain its members in this encounter with the world and encourage new and pioneering experiments by the laity in witnessing to Christ through their secular calling."[8].

Dr. Roy G. Ross, General Secretary of the National Council of

Churches, recently observed that America was founded under the influences of a "vigorously proclaimed Gospel" and has developed her political and social institutions "under the constant scrutiny of the Church." But he warned that we are in danger if we assume that these Christian influences can be perpetuated without the constant "proclamation of the Gospel and the cultivation of the spiritual life." "America could be the nation which would tip the balance in determination of the faith which will eventually dominate the relation of nations," Dr. Ross declared. "However, she will never tip this balance in favor of a Christian ethos as over against complete secularism or nihilism until she first decides the faith by which she herself will live in today's world." He stressed that America can make the right decision only "if she is re-evangelized, re-educated and re-motivated by a Church with a clergy and laity on fire with deep conviction."[9]

To re-evangelize—that is the first task of the church; the second is to re-educate, and it is to this task that we must now turn.

FOR CONSIDERATION

1. "To make disciples" is the main task of the church: Do you agree with this statement? Why?
2. How does your own particular church attempt to fulfill this responsibility?
3. Is the growth of your church keeping pace with the growth of the community?
4. Is it reaching all types of people residing in the community? The newer types of people moving into the community?
5. Have new churches recently been built in your presbytery? Are new churches being projected?
6. Does your presbytery accept responsibility for carrying the gospel to the Negroes? Why or why not?
7. What forms of evangelism are employed in your church?
8. What would you add or subtract to what is said about the evangelism of the future on page 362?

A Small Adult Study Group Gathering for an Informal Discussion

28
"TEACHING THEM"

TEACHING THE CHRISTIAN FAITH is an essential function of the church. When a new church is built, if a choice is necessary, the religious education building is ordinarily constructed before the house of worship. No other activity of the church evokes the devoted service of so many of its members. For it is in and through the school of the church that our children are nurtured in the faith. Without its school, the church itself would wither and die. Or so it seems to us. It is hard to realize that the church has not always depended on the Sunday school, that the Sunday school is in fact comparatively recent in its origin and is still in the process of development.

CHRISTIAN EDUCATION IN HISTORY

Instruction of some sort there has always been. In the Great Commission, as recorded by Matthew, Jesus instructed his disciples to "make disciples of all nations, baptizing . . . [and] teaching them . . . " (Matt. 28:19–20). The earliest converts "continued stedfastly in the apostles' teaching" (Acts 2:42, A.S.V.). Teachers, as a distinct office, came to have recognized standing and are mentioned again and again as among the more important servants of the church (Acts 13:

1; 1 Cor. 12:28; Eph. 4:11). Timothy was instructed to entrust what he had received "to faithful men who will be able to teach others also" (2 Tim. 2:2). He was reminded that elders who ruled well were to be considered worthy of double honor, "especially those who labor in preaching and teaching" (1 Tim. 5:17).

The early church established catechumen classes in which candidates for admission to the church were instructed in the meaning of the faith. The rich ornamentation of churches in the later centuries—pictures, statues, frescoes, mosaics, for example—were justified on the ground that they constituted the Bible of the unlearned, visual education for the masses. The Protestant Reformers were compelled to find a way in which entire peoples could be instructed in evangelical truths which had been obscured for many generations. Schools were established, in whose curricula the Bible held a central position. Catechisms were prepared in which basic Christian truths were systematically set forth by means of questions and answers. Parents were expected to train their children, with the help of the catechism and through family devotions. Pastors catechized adults as well as children, to make sure that such instruction was not neglected, to make sure that adults themselves possessed the knowledge which it was their responsibility to transmit to the succeeding generation. This in general was the scheme of Christian education brought by our spiritual forebears to America.

In the early decades of the nineteenth century, it became apparent that the older method no longer sufficed. Public schools had not been established, and there was widespread illiteracy on the part of both young and old. Family instruction was neglected, and catechizing by the pastor could not supply the lack. Sunday schools for a time seemed to be the answer. Here children, and adults as well, were taught to read; Scripture was memorized and taught; the catechism continued to provide systematic instruction in the Christian faith; the labors of the pastor were aided by those of a host of voluntary workers, men and women. But the Sunday schools were not the sole reliance. Primary schools, secondary schools, colleges and universities, as they came to be established, first under religious auspices, and then increasingly under secular influence, offered additional instruction, religious as well as moral. Bible reading and prayer have lingered indeed in many grammar schools until the present day, when it appears they may be finally eradicated under the Supreme Court's new understanding of our constitutional provision for separation of church and state.

The growing secularization of the public schools, the widespread abdication of responsibility on the part of parents (particularly after the tender years) have placed increasing responsibility on the Sunday schools. Many advances have been made in this department of the church's work. Bible classes for adults became popular after the Civil War. Co-operation of the various denominations, which heretofore had prepared their own Bible studies in the preparation of the International Sunday School Lessons enabled lesson helps of higher order to be prepared. Teacher training courses sought to raise the level of instruction, to put at the disposal of teachers the latest educational knowledge and skills. Graded materials offered lessons more suitable to the various age levels.

Sunday schools have played indeed an indispensable role in the mission of the church. Devoted teachers have given far more than knowledge of Bible truths: They have cultivated love for Christ and his church—and it is through the Sunday school that most additions to the church have been won.

Yet it has become increasingly clear that much more needs to be done. The average child who has passed through the church school still does not possess a thorough knowledge of the Bible or of fundamental Christian doctrine. Too few are deeply committed to the cause of Christ, or to the task of living as a Christian in our modern world. And in accordance with the Great Commission, we are to teach men not only to know, but also to observe (i.e., to do) all that Christ has commanded us.

CURRENT EMPHASES IN CHRISTIAN EDUCATION

In recent years important developments have taken place in various areas related to the task of Christian education, which promise some improvement in this respect. Among them are the following:

A Clearer View of the Aim of Christian Education

There is coming to be a clearer understanding of the aim of Christian education—not primarily to transmit a body of knowledge (important as this may be), and certainly not to furnish rules of Christian conduct that apply to every situation, but rather to bring the child, the youth, the mature man and woman, to the place where they may hear and respond throughout life to the God who continues to address them personally in Christ.

Emphasis on the Home as the Primary Agent of Nurture

Some investigations have indicated that there is little correlation between church school attendance and ethical decisions, but a very high correlation, on the other hand, between parental guidance and Christian character. There can be little doubt that the basic stuff of religious belief and faith is established in early home experiences, before the child is of school age. The church has always recognized the importance of the Christian home. Today, as Christian education enters upon its new revolutionary phase, that importance is stressed even more, and more help is to be provided for the home.

Understanding of the Whole Church as Context of Education

There is growing recognition of the fact that it is not the minister, not the teachers in the church school alone, but the whole Christian community that nurtures its members, both young and old. This new trend in Christian education accords with contemporary trends in psychology which emphasize the importance of the group in all education processes. The church teaches through its corporate worship, through its observance of the church year, through the personal relations that exist between church members and between older and younger members, through pastoral services tendered to individuals, through the various expressions of Christian love to those who are in need, through the missionary activities of the church, through the formation of an inclusive fellowship that transcends the barriers found in other areas of life.

Emphasis on Education of Adults

An important development in the field of Christian education is the shift of emphasis from children to adults as the subject of education. It is not that children are less important but that adults are far more important than was formerly understood. Children learn largely by assimilation, by what is known as acculturation, in the home, in the community, and in the church. They learn from their parents, from their teachers, from association with their peers, from their impressions of the adult life about them, from the tone of the church and of the community as determined ultimately by adults. Adults maintain the church and carry on its mission in the world. To develop a mature faith and to witness effectively in their vocation they need to grow in their knowledge of the Bible, of the church, and the meaning of life as a member of the covenant community.

Improved Methodology

As a consequence of their new understanding of God's revelation and man's need, Christian education leaders have been led to re-examine and revise older methods of teaching the Bible and to make full use of the newer methods which have been tried and tested in harmony with modern understanding and with the nature of revelation itself.

Deepened and Enriched Content

A new emphasis is being placed on the Bible as the record of, or witness to, the revelation of God in Jesus Christ, through which he continues to speak to men, and on the principles of biblical interpretation.

There is also a new emphasis upon theology—the truth about God in relation to man. There was a time, it may be, when too much emphasis was placed upon intellectual assent to theological truth as an end in itself, to memorizing a catechism or creed which had little or no meaning for life. More emphasis is being placed now upon doctrine—the meaning of the Christian faith—and upon its relevance to life today.

An Improved Curriculum

Important curriculum revision has taken place in many leading denominations, including our own. The Covenant Life Curriculum on which we are now entering offers systematic instruction for every age

—such as we have never had before—in three important areas, Bible, Church, and Christian Life.

For Young People

Concern for the youth of the congregation has manifested itself in various ways throughout the years. There has always been concern to teach the Bible and doctrine; since the end of the nineteenth century, there has also been concern to meet the particular needs of youth. In the effort to meet particular needs, a youth organization (almost a "youth church") was emphasized for many years.

The first successful religious organization for youth was an interdenominational venture—Christian Endeavor—launched by Dr. Francis E. Clark in 1881. It spread rapidly among various Protestant bodies and remained the main reliance of our own denomination until the mid-thirties when, following in the footsteps of Baptists and Methodists, we began to build our own denominational program.

The "common commission plan" which called Senior High youth to consider and become involved in five comprehensive areas of the church's work (Christian faith, witness, outreach, citizenship, and fellowship) was soon developed by several denominations working together through the United Christian Youth Movement.

The Covenant Life Curriculum seeks to conserve values in former programs but to move on to more meaningful involvement of youth in the actual life and work of the church. Young people using CLC materials graded for particular age groups are studying each year in the same area as are adults (the Church this year, for example). Through youth planning committees or councils, they plan to follow up concerns and interests which spring from their study or from their everyday life. Planning, however, is always in the light of the program of work of the congregation, which claims prior attention; hopefully, some young people serve on committees and work groups of the congregation. Youth are responsible members of the church, not an auxiliary youth church.

What is the program for youth in your own church? What are its needs? Does it serve the young people as a means of participating in the life and work of the congregation, or does it set them apart from the congregation so that they must engage in trivial projects that have little relation to the mission of the church? What is the place in the church of nondenominational groups such as Girl Scouts and Boy Scouts? What is the responsibility of a congregation in sponsoring these?

A New Concern for the Community

For our purposes the community includes the various influences or areas of experience outside the home which influence the individual's development of values from childhood to the grave: institutions, public or private; organizations, social, cultural, athletic, or educational; peer groups, whether neighborhood gangs or executives of a corporation; mass communication media; papers and magazines; the political structure of city and nation.

The church is concerned about the community, so defined, because within the community are groups, influences, and situations which strengthen the church's work and also those which threaten it, forces which build up Christian character and forces which tend to tear it down, and also because it is in the community that the Christian must bear his witness and carry on his vocation as a follower of Christ.

It is for this reason in part that our Covenant Life Curriculum includes the three areas of concern just named: Bible, Church and Christian Life. It is in line with this understanding that our General Assembly has established a Division of Christian Action within the Board of Christian Education, whose responsibility it is to "aid and assist the various divisions of the Board in building the ideals of Christian living set forth in the Bible and included in the Standards of the Church as interpreted by the General Assembly, into an educational program of the Church ... "[1]

EDUCATIONAL AGENCIES

Education is provided not only in the church school, and from the pulpit, but also in programs offered by the Men of the Church, the Women of the Church, and the various organizations of the young people. Many churches now offer other periods and means of instruction—on the weekly church night, or in particular "schools" for limited periods.

The actual burden of instruction will always fall on the local churches—its individual members and its various organizations. The higher courts of the church offer guidance and support. The presbytery promotes rallies, retreats, camps, and conferences which serve to undergird the local church in its activities. It conducts training schools for teachers which only a few of the stronger churches could establish for themselves. The synod carries on similar work on a larger scale. In every synod is a director of Christian education, sometimes with a staff, who supplies technical assistance and aid where it may be needed, and who serves to co-ordinate and develop the program as a whole. Much attention has been given of late to the matter of vocational guidance. The General Assembly, through its Board of Christian Education, prepares the programs which are offered to the Men of the Church (programs for the Women of the Church are prepared by the Board of Women's Work) and to the various young people's organizations. It has prepared the Covenant Life Curriculum which is now in use throughout our church (a stupendous undertaking) and publishes the vast amount of literature which is necessary for the total program of Christian education.

Important supplements to the educational activities of the church are supplied by the church papers—the *Presbyterian Survey* (monthly), which is the official publication of the church, and which promotes the total program of the church; and the independent church papers (weeklies), *Christian Observer, The Presbyterian Outlook,* and *The Presbyterian Journal,* the first of which is primarily a family paper, and the last two of which serve both as news media and journals of opinion.

Last, but by no means least, are the various educational institutions of the church.

The Presbyterian Church has been interested in higher education throughout its history. John Craig, who was the first settled pastor among the Presbyterians in the back country, combined teaching with other ministerial duties, as did many, if not most, of the pastors who followed him. In Virginia, Augusta Academy, later known as Liberty Hall, and since the Civil War as Washington and Lee University, was established by Virginia Presbyterians west of the Blue Ridge as early as 1749. Hampden-Sydney College, the second oldest college in the

South, and the tenth oldest in the nation, opened its doors in the face of Anglican opposition, as a nonsectarian institution, on January 1, 1776. In North Carolina there were numerous classical schools opened after 1755 by ministers who had received their training in the College of New Jersey (now Princeton), a Presbyterian institution.

The importance of these various contributions to education in the Colonial period by the Presbyterians in the back country is more appreciated when it is realized that there was no system of public instruction south of the Mason-Dixon line in the Colonial period or long thereafter; that there were few schools of any sort in the older and wealthier Chesapeake and Carolina societies; that the prevailing theory of education brought to these regions from England was that education was for the upper class only, and of no concern to the people; that the Anglican Church, which prior to the Revolution was the established church in all the southern colonies, and which had sponsored William and Mary College, the one institution of higher learning in the South before 1776, was declining in strength; and that neither of the other evangelical denominations which had come into the South on the wings of the Great Awakening accepted as yet any educational responsibility.

After the Revolution, as we have seen, came the great westward movement of population which resulted in the speedy settlement of the Mississippi Valley. Because of their insistence on an educated ministry, Presbyterians fell far behind Methodists and Baptists so far as numbers were concerned, though they won more than other religious bodies on the frontier. The educated Presbyterian ministers did not attract the uneducated masses, but they did gather to themselves a large proportion of the educated class in every community which they entered. They also contributed far more to the educational development of the West and South—on every level—than those of any other church. Take higher education for example. In 1820 there were sixteen chartered colleges in the southern states which have survived to the present time. One of these had been established by the Roman Catholic Church and three by the Episcopal Church, all on the seaboard, and none of them flourishing; six had been established by Presbyterians, the only colleges in the interior; and there were five state universities. The two oldest of these, North Carolina and Georgia, were Presbyterian institutions in all but name, and in a third, the College of South Carolina, the Presbyterian influence was soon to become dominant.

This Presbyterian ascendancy in the field of education in the South continued until about 1840, after which it began to fade. Other denominations were now becoming educationally awakened, and the various states were assuming a larger proportion of the burden. After the Civil War, the impoverished church had more institutions than it could adequately support. It fell far behind in its educational efforts. Presbyterians continued to educate their sons and also their daughters, but did not adequately support their own denominational institutions. It is only comparatively recently that our church has begun to awaken to its responsibility to undergird and strengthen its centers of learning.

Today associated with our church are four theological seminaries (on which we depend for the education of our ministers), one school of Christian education (which trains lay workers in various areas of activity), fifteen Presbyterian colleges, two affiliated colleges, five junior colleges, four secondary schools, and two Presbyterian mission schools.

The General Assembly itself accepts responsibility for Stillman College[2] and for the Presbyterian School of Christian Education; other institutions are supported for the most part by synods, or, as in the case of the theological seminaries, by a group of synods.

In addition, synods support religious activities on the campus of all important colleges or universities within our bounds.

The support of this varied educational effort in our institutions of higher learning is vital, because from them come our educated leadership, including ministers, without whom the church could not long survive.

FOR CONSIDERATION

1. How adequately is the church fulfilling its educational task? Do young people and older folk know the essentials of the Christian faith? Are they finding relevant answers to the practical problems which they confront? Are they maturing in this realm as in others in which they take a vital interest?

2. Do you think that your own knowledge of the Bible, of Christian truth, has kept pace with your advancing knowledge in other fields?

3. Where does your own church school most need to be strengthened?

4. Should adults seeking admission into the church on confession or by certificate be required to receive instruction before their final acceptance?

5. Should the church make greater use of Christian art in some of its forms as an educational device?

6. What is the value of family devotions in Christian education? Are they practical in the modern family?

7. What are the most effective ways for a Christian family to transmit its faith? What are the greatest difficulties encountered in this endeavor?

8. Do you agree with the goal of Christian education as set forth on pages 368–369?

9. Does the church have any direct responsibility for shaping community patterns that affect Christian character?

10. Is it possible or desirable for men to become as well informed about the work of the church as are our women? How can this be done?

One Church Meeting Human Need Today—Through a Baby Clinic

29

"THE LEAST OF THESE"

Ministry to Those in Need

The church has always exercised a ministry of compassion and service. It can hardly do otherwise so long as it recognizes as its Lord One who will say, "As you did it to one of the least of these my brethren, you did it to me" (Matt. 25:40). The first officers were elected (Acts 6:1–6), as we have seen, to make certain that no one was overlooked in the daily distribution of supplies. For several centuries, relief of human need remained the prime function of the diaconate. After Constantine, in the Roman Empire, and throughout Europe in the Middle Ages, all charitable work was carried on under the auspices of the church. John Calvin sought to place this responsibility once again upon the deacons. They were made responsible not only for the finances of the church, but also for the management of the hospitals (the care of the sick) and for the distribution of relief. So in Scotland, the Rules of Discipline, drawn up by John Knox, recognized that physical relief should be provided under the auspices of the church for all unable to work. As life became more complex and as the citizens of the state were no longer automatically considered to be members of the church, responsibility for the relief of human need was necessarily assumed by the state. But the church has never held that it was relieved thereby of all responsibility.

In the Local Congregation

In our *Book of Church Order* (12–3) we read: "It is the duty of the Deacons, first of all, to minister to those who are in need, to the sick, to the friendless, and to any who may be in distress." Actually this is largely, if not altogether, overlooked in practice. Some boards of deacons grant a discretionary fund to the pastor, which he may use to aid those whom he deems worthy of relief; and at times, if there is a family of the church in dire distress (which does not often occur among our Presbyterian middle class constituency), the board of deacons takes more direct responsibility. But such limited action on the part of the deacons does not exhaust the congregation's present-day ministry of compassion and service. From our various religious bodies (and here surely the Presbyterian Church stands in the forefront) comes much, if not most, of the financial support of the various organizations included in the Community Chest, and many, if not most, of the professional and voluntary workers in these organizations. It is unfortunate that the church does not recognize more explicitly that this is a form of Christian service. The Women of the Church in their "circles" do provide systematically for volunteer services in many community enterprises.

In our modern rootless society, with so many families constantly on the move, the church also enables people to become acquainted; it promotes "togetherness," it offers friendship and hospitality to all who are willing to partake of it. It should not be overlooked either that church people do rally about those whom they know to be in any kind of distress. Such neighborly concern, such intimate personal services, in cases of prolonged illness, when death occurs, is not unimportant: It is in fact one of the important elements in the church's total pastoral services ("I was hungry and you gave me food . . . I was a stranger and you welcomed me . . . I was sick and you visited me" [Matt. 25:35–36]).

Here, as in other areas, the local congregation must always remain the basic unit. There are, however, some particular responsibilities which must be assumed by the larger units—presbyteries, synods, and General Assembly.

Through the Higher Courts

Shortly after the erection of the first synod (1719), there was established a "Pious Fund"—the beginning of our church's benevolent work. This Pious Fund was to be used for two purposes: to provide for itinerants among the new settlements (church extension), and to care for the widows and orphans of deceased ministers. Out of this Pious Fund came in time the "Presbyterian Ministers Fund," which continues its service today as the oldest life insurance company in America. When our denomination was organized in 1861 it erected an Executive Committee of Ministerial Relief in line with the practice of other major denominations in America. A minimum income (now eighteen hundred dollars, including other sources of income) is provided for the individual retired minister or his widow. Special contributions to this Relief Fund are made at the Christmas season through the annual Joy Gift. Following the example of other churches, however, our denomination now places its chief reliance upon the Ministers Annuity Fund, to which ministers and churches make annual payments—a scheme analogous to those developed by many business enterprises. In recent years coverage has been provided for all unordained personnel employed in the service of the church. Group insurance policies are also offered for medical attention. Administration of these services is in the hands of the Board of Annuities and Relief.

Our church established its first orphans' homes shortly after the close of the Civil War, particularly for the care of those whom the War had deprived of their natural support. As time went on, other homes for children were opened—one for every synod or group of synods. Today such institutions draw their children largely from broken homes. A host of young people have here received care and Christian nurture, manifest in their subsequent lives; many of them are now eminent ministers of the gospel. These homes have a deep hold on the affections of particular synods.

More recently homes for the aged have begun to be established, again on the synodical level. Need for such is generally recognized.

For increasing numbers of our more elderly citizens some institutional care must be provided. Government aid makes their construction comparatively easy, and the "guests" assume a considerable portion of the expense.

It is in foreign lands, where few public facilities exist, that the church has carried out most fully its ministry of compassion and relief. Here from the beginning medical missions have been a part of the evangelical enterprise. In some lands agricultural missions have been sustained. In Brazil, for example, a large proportion of the trained agronomists are graduates of the Gammon Institute, founded and supported until recently (with government aid) by our Southern Presbyterian mission. Other types of services have developed as there has been need—and opportunity.

For emergency relief on a large scale, Presbyterians join with other Protestant bodies in such ecumenical endeavors as Church World Service, sponsored by the National and World Councils of Churches.

CALL TO CHRISTIAN ACTION

At times through its history, the church has found it necessary to attack specific evils which take their toll in human happiness, and often in human life. Thus, as we have seen, the early church opposed abortion, the exposure of infants, and gladiatorial combats. It sought to lessen the evils of slavery; it struggled none too successfully against war. In the Middle Ages the church taught the mutual obligation of all orders in society and sought to establish the principles of a just wage. John Calvin held that church and state are jointly responsible for the establishment of a Christian society, and he and his successor, Beza, an outstanding scholar and Bible teacher of the Reformation, appeared in their pulpits as champions of the common man.

Toward the Building of a Nation

Puritans in New England sought to embody Christian ideals in their experiment "in the wilderness." Scotch-Irish Presbyterians came rather belatedly into the Southern Colonies along the Atlantic Seaboard, and were never as strong here as in the Middle Colonies. They made, however, significant contributions not only to the religious but also to the social and political life of the new nation that was coming into being. Four may be mentioned.

First, their contribution to an ordered society. Historians point out that organized Protestantism was the most influential institution of the back country. (The same could not be said of the older Chesapeake and Carolina societies.) The dominant church in the back country during the Colonial period was the Presbyterian. Its churches became nuclei, not only of the religious life, but of social, educational, civic, and military activities as well. It was a force making for stability —in some regions before the Colonial authorities were able to establish law and order.

Second, there was, as previously noted, the Presbyterian contribution to education.

Third, there was the contribution of the Southern Presbyterians to political freedom. Presbyterian dissenters, who occupied the frontiers beyond the mountains, were forced to bear the burden of the French and Indian War. Braddock's defeat at Pittsburgh in 1775 spread terror through Virginia. It was proposed to abandon all territory beyond the mountains to the enemy. In this panic of soul, it was the Reverend Samuel Davies, the most eloquent preacher in the colonies, who counseled calm and courage, and who cheered the volunteers who went to the front from eastern Virginia. Meanwhile, the inhabitants of the valley were exposed to the raid of ruthless savages, and the helpless inhabitants in utter consternation were counseling safety in flight. The Reverend John Craig wrote in his diary: "I opposed that scheme as a scandal to our nation, falling below our brave ancestors, making ourselves a reproach among Virginians, a dishonor to our friends at home, an evidence of cowardice, want of faith, and a noble Christian dependence on God, as able to save and deliver from the heathen; it would be," he added, "a lasting blot on our posterity." Craig advised the building of forts in convenient places for refuge. His appeal and example had its effect. "They required me," he continued in his diary, "to go before them in the work, which I did cheerfully, though it cost me one-third of my estates. The people very readily followed, and my congregation in less than two months was well fortified."

Not only did these Scotch-Irish Presbyterians bear the brunt of the French and Indian War in the South, they also made a mighty contribution to the winning of the Revolutionary War. At Abingdon in Virginia, and in Mecklenburg County in North Carolina, they were among the first to call for freedom from the British tyranny. Hanover Presbytery was the first ecclesiastical body to recognize and hail the Declaration of Independence. The Revolutionary War, so far as the Middle Colonies were concerned, was recognized as a Presbyterian war. The Scotch-Irish in Virginia and North Carolina, and most of those in South Carolina (as distinguished from the Scots), were solid in their support of the war. Their pastors appealed to the members of their church to participate in the struggle, and a number of them led their parishioners into battle. The battle of King's Mountain, which proved to be the turning point in the war, was won by Scotch-Irish pioneers from Virginia, the two Carolinas, and the Watauga settlements of what is now Tennessee, led by Presbyterian elders.

In the fourth place, we note the contribution of Southern Presbyterians to religious liberty. The Church of England, state-supported in the five Southern Colonies, was in Virginia, the strongest of the colonies, an exclusive church before 1688, and inhospitable, to say the least, after that date. It was Samuel Davies, the apostle of Presbyterianism in eastern Virginia, who broke down the resistance of the Colonial authorities and won a fuller right of religious toleration in Virginia, not only for Presbyterians, but for all dissenters from the established church.

After the battle for religious toleration came the long and decisive struggle for religious freedom, for complete separation of church and state, a struggle whose successful issue marks an epoch in the history of religious liberty. Virginia was the first modern state, indeed the first state in history, whose organic law provided for separation of church and state, which we have come to believe is for the best interests of both church and state. The principles wrought out here in Virginia later found expression in our Federal Constitution, and are treasured as one of the glories of America. Credit for this significant victory for religious freedom is generally given to the well-known Virginia statesmen, Thomas Jefferson and James Madison. But much of the credit, equal credit we might say, should go to the dissenters, Baptists and Presbyterians. The Baptists were the first and most consistent supporters of complete religious freedom, but the Presbyterians contributed statesmanlike papers which bore greater weight than the simple petitions of the Baptists. In addition, Hanover Presbytery sent lobbyists who met with committees and buttonholed legislators and spoke publicly as well as privately for their cause.

The "Spirituality of the Church"

Slavery became the all-absorbing issue in both church and state in the Antebellum period. There was much opposition to the institution of slavery in the South (in other denominations as well as in our own) before 1831. After 1831, the year of the Nat Turner insurrection (in which sixty or more whites were slain in southside Virginia), in a period when abolition venom was increasing, and when the South seemed to be increasingly dependent on the cotton raised by slave labor for its prosperity, the attitude changed: Southern apologists in both church and state began to defend the institution as beneficial to the Negroes as well as to the whites. On the defensive, morally, against the conscience generally of civilized man, theologians who were to mold the mind of Southern Presbyterianism developed a new doctrine of the "spirituality of the church." The church, they argued, cannot go beyond Scripture. Slavery is not condemned by the Bible: It was accepted by Jesus and the apostles; it cannot, therefore, be condemned by the church. The church, they further argued, is not concerned with social and political issues such as slavery.

Methodists and Baptists divided on this issue in 1845 and the New School Presbyterian Church followed suit in 1857. Old School Presbyterians, the main body so far as the South was concerned, remaining silent on the slavery issue, retained their unity until the outbreak of war. The southern presbyteries then withdrew, claiming that they had been forced out by a political decision of the Northern Assembly—the Gardiner Spring resolutions pledging loyalty of Presbyterians to the federal government.

The General Assembly of the Presbyterian Church in the Confederate States of America (now the Presbyterian Church in the United States) organized in Augusta, Georgia, on December 4, 1861, adopted an "Address to the Churches of Jesus Christ Throughout the World" in which it declared, in partial justification of its action, that "the provinces of church and state are perfectly distinct. They are as planets moving in different orbs."

This doctrine of the spirituality of the church came to be even more strongly held in the course of the war, as the Northern Church grew more bitter in its denunciation of both slavery and rebellion, and still more so in the dark days of Reconstruction. As the war drew toward its close, Abraham Lincoln, in his second inaugural address, pled for "malice toward none . . . charity for all." But the U.S.A. General Assembly, meeting in 1865, at the completion of the war, excoriated the Southern Church, founded, it was charged, to maintain the institution of slavery, and instructed their lower courts to receive no members from the Southern Church unless they confessed the sin of their former views regarding states' rights and slavery. When Southern sympathizers in Kentucky and Missouri protested these utterances, they were expelled from the Northern Assembly. These deliverances and these expulsions (the orphaned Kentucky and Missouri Presbyterians came into the Southern Church) not only strengthened the doctrine of the "spirituality of the church," but also greatly intensified the bitterness between the Northern and the Southern Churches.

From this time until approximately 1935, the generally accepted view of the Presbyterian Church in the United States was that its mission was limited to evangelism and to the fostering of an individual or family morality. Given by divine commission, its task was conceived to be in the strictest sense of the word "spiritual," that is, evangelistic and pietistic. During this period, the moral and ethical problems about which our church showed the most concern, almost the only problems on which the General Assembly offered any guidance for its members, were the problems of Sabbath observance, intemperance, and worldly amusements, including dancing, theater going, and card-playing. The church, meanwhile, had little or nothing to say about the social, racial, economic, national, and international problems that were peculiar to our region or that we in the South faced with the rest of the nation.

Acceptance of Wider Responsibility

Re-examination of this doctrine of the spirituality of the church began about the turn of the present century and was further stimulated by the Great Depression and its problems (beginning in 1929). In 1934 our General Assembly, moving cautiously, appointed a Committee of Social and Moral Welfare, whose sole duty was to define the scope and function of such a committee for the approval of the following assembly. In 1935 the General Assembly adopted the first report of this committee, one which defined or redefined the position of our church in this area, and which encouraged it to move forward in the years ahead. Said this report:

> We believe . . . that the Church in fulfillment of its spiritual function must interpret and present Christ's ideal for the individual and for society, must warn men of the presence of sin and of its effects in individual life and in the social life, must offer Christ to the individual and to society as the only Revealer of God and the only Redeemer of mankind, must seek with the spiritual weapons at its disposal to establish His Lordship in the hearts of all men, and over every area of human life . . . .
>
> . . . In accordance with Christ's command the Church must also teach men to love their neighbors as themselves and to do so . . . in the social sphere, as well as in the individual sphere, in the home, in the school, and in the Church, in industry and in politics, in racial contacts, and in international affairs . . . .
>
> It cannot discharge this part of its responsibility unless it deals with those actual evils in the individual life, and in the social order which threatens man's moral and spiritual development, which hinder the progress of God's Kingdom here on earth, and which produce needless suffering and distress among the children of men; unless in some definite and concrete fashion it encourages and stimulates its members to realize the ideals of Christ in their individual lives, in the life of each group of which they are participants and in the total life of the nation.[1]

Since that time the Committee on Social and Moral Welfare and its successors (now the Permanent Committee on Christian Relations) have brought in reports to the General Assembly on some specific problem or problems in this general area. Similar committees have been erected in many presbyteries and synods. Such reports do not become the law of the church. They do not bind the consciences of the members of the church. They are in effect pastoral letters addressed to the church, appealing to the consciences of those who will listen. And they provide documents which various organizations and groups within the church are invited to study. In recent years, a Division of Christian Action has been established within the Board of Christian Education. Its purpose is to incorporate Christian ideals into the total educational program of the church. It is significant that the third major theme included in the Covenant Life Curriculum—following the one story of the Bible, and the history of God's people, the church—is the Christian life.

"One of our greatest needs," ran a recent article in the *Presbyterian Survey,* "is a church technique that assembles people of opposing views for an honest confrontation of their differences."[2] Many will agree. Certainly no court, no minister, no piece of literature, can hand down the solution for the racial or other controversial problems that our churches face in this day and expect mature men and women to accept it from their lips as the final word in the matter. The solution may be found—or at least the steps must be taken to find a solution—many are convinced, as men and women meet in conference against the background of biblical study, and as they confront one another and think out the implications of the gospel for the problems that they meet in their actual experience. There are some promising beginnings in this direction but they need to be extended.

For a generation now the Presbyterian Church in the United States has officially accepted the idea that the gospel does have implications for the whole of life. The task of the present generation will be to find ways in which this concept can be accepted by the church membership as a whole, particularly our lay people, the People of God, who alone can translate the principle into practical reality. Only so can we be true to our Calvinistic, and also our Christian, heritage. And only so can we hope, in a measure, to fulfill our true spiritual mission.

FOR CONSIDERATION

*1. Read Psalm 72; Micah 6:1-8; Amos 5:10-24; Luke 4:14-21; Matthew 25:31-46. What light do these passages throw on the mission of the church?

2. How can the church best carry on its mission of compassion and sympathy at the present time?

3. What is being done in and through your own congregation toward this end? What more could be done?

4. What are the secular agencies which carry on such a ministry in your community?

5. How are these agencies related to the church? Could this relationship be improved?

6. What is the responsibility of the individual Christian in carrying out such a ministry?

*7. Does the church have a responsibility to speak on the larger moral and social issues before the American people—on such questions as segregation and integration? On the questions of war and peace?

8. Should such issues be discussed in the school of the church? In our men's and women's organizations? If so, under what circumstances and under what conditions or safeguards?

9. Would you favor the appointment of a committee on Christian action in your congregation?

10. Would you modify or amend in any way the statement on page 385?

Missionaries Bringing Medical Supplies and Bibles to Indians in Ecuador

30
"UNTO THE UTTERMOST PART OF THE EARTH"

A CHURCH HAS PRIMARY RESPONSIBILITY for meeting the spiritual needs of the people within its own community, neighborhood, or larger area. A local congregation, looking to its own opportunity and needs, recognizes, however, its responsibility to aid its denomination's wider efforts in the home field—presbytery, synod, and General Assembly; and this is done, as indicated, through its budgetary offerings.

But this is not enough. For a century and a half now, every Protestant denomination has recognized that it must do its part in spreading the gospel to other lands—not merely because this is a part of our Lord's command, not only because of our love for souls, but also because of our love for men, for humanity here and now. Christianity today has many foes; the battle line stretches around the world; responsibility for advance on important segments of that line has been accepted by us.[1]

GROWTH OF FOREIGN MISSIONS

The Home Base

Our first General Assembly (1861) adopted a remarkable declaration, remarkable because the new "nation" was at war, and its coasts were even then tightly blockaded. "The General Assembly," so ran the ringing statement, "desires distinctly and deliberately to inscribe on our Church's banner, as she now first unfolds in to the world ... His last command, 'Go ye into all the world and preach the gospel to every creature': regarding this as the great end of her organization, and obedience to it as the indispensable condition of her Lord's promised presence. ... "

It will have to be acknowledged that this challenging statement of purpose did not at the time express the mind or will of the church as a whole. It was some years before our churches were awakened in any true sense to their missionary responsibility, before a majority of our churches even contributed to the cause of world missions. In time, however, the Presbyterian Church in the United States became one of the leading missionary denominations in the country, judged by its per capita giving for this cause. Though such giving is low compared with that of a number of the younger sects, it is still high compared with that of most of the older denominations. Today world missions receives a larger amount, and a larger proportion of its askings, than any other assembly cause. It should be observed, however, that gifts for most other causes are divided among assembly, synod, presbytery, and local church. It might also be pointed out that the total number of missionaries (485) at the end of the year 1960 was thirty-two less than it had been in 1924, when the all-time maximum had been reached. Receipts for the Board of World Missions were more than double what they had been thirty years earlier, just about enough to offset the depreciation in the value of the dollar, though in the meantime the per capita wealth of the American people, in terms of actual purchasing value, had greatly increased. In other words, twice as many people (approximately) were giving the same amount of money (in actual purchasing power) as their fathers and mothers—half their number, and with less resources—had given a generation earlier.

Meanwhile, our opportunities and responsibilities have increased.

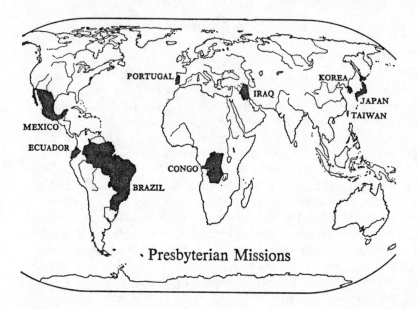

· Presbyterian Missions

Our Overseas Missions

In the Civil War period, with our borders blockaded, missionaries could not be sent to foreign lands; "foreign" mission work was confined to the Indians on our southwest border (subsequently transferred to home missions).

In 1867 we began our work beyond the waters—in China, and also in Italy. Two years later, work was begun in Colombia and Brazil; in Mexico and Greece in 1874; in Japan in 1885. Between 1890 and 1900 three new fields were entered: Africa (1890), Korea (1892), and Cuba (1899).

At the present time we have work in Europe, the Middle East, the Far East, Africa, and Latin America—a total of nine countries: Portugal, Iraq, Japan, Korea, Taiwan, the Congo, Brazil, Ecuador, and Mexico. In Portugal, Iraq, and Ecuador the work is carried on in cooperation with other bodies; in six we have independent missions.

The Rise of National Churches

In every land our purpose has been to aid in the development of a national church which in time could take over the responsibility for maintaining the gospel in its own land. Native churches have now arisen in nearly every country on the face of the globe, and the Christian community continues to grow in spite of all the difficulties encountered. Thus, in something less than a quarter of a century after 1925, at a time when the world was in the midst of disturbance and turmoil, the Protestant community increased 3 times in China and Korea, 5 times in Indonesia, from 6 to 8 times in the Philippines, Argentina, India, Mexico, Guatemala, and Cuba, 10 times in Puerto Rico, 11 times in the Belgian Congo, and 24 times in Brazil.[2] In 1916 there was an evangelistic community of 122,875 in all Latin America. In 1956 there were forty times as many, an estimated five million—more than two million in Brazil alone.

"The period under survey," says Dr. Lamott, "was very definitely one in which the Christian movement not only went forward from strength to strength but did so largely under its own power. Missionary forces in most of the countries suffered reduction and, in some cases and at certain times, almost depletion, but the church still went ahead. The figures presented above, therefore, represent the advance of the church rather than the advance of the foreign missionary movement in the areas studied. This is said not to disparage the work of the many efficient and devoted foreign missionaries working with and for the Younger Churches, the high quality of their contributions both in activity and in counsel, but to state a fact which many supporters of missions do not realize.

"This is seen further in a comparison of the number of ordained national workers as compared with the number of ordained foreign missionaries . . . in the Belgian Congo (for example) 354 to 147; Mexico 322 to 42; Cuba 237 to 22; Puerto Rico 159 to 25; Brazil 1,078 to 179; the Philippines 499 to 85; Indonesia 499 to 31."[3]

A recent Associated Press survey indicates that while Christianity's strength remains small in most Asiatic countries (the Philippines, where 83 percent of the population is Roman Catholic, is the one outstanding exception), it has nonetheless made creditable progress in an area where it has had to overcome cultural and language barriers nonexistent in the West. According to competent observers, Christianity in Asia continues to gain ground even while Western political influence declines.

"Christians in Japan 'weigh more than they count,' a feature article in Tokyo's [most influential paper] said recently. Pointing out that the total Christian population of 600,000 is but a tiny minority among the nation's 88 million people, the article listed outstanding statesmen, scholars, scientists, judges and businessmen who are Christians. The three elder statesmen of the Socialist party, which with 78 seats has the second-largest representation in the Diet, are Protestants, as are 15 others of the 250 members of that legislative body. Among outstanding Protestant citizens of Japan are the minister of finance, the director of the Atomic Power Research Institute, the presidents of several nationally known manufacturing companies and banks, and the former president of Keio University, who served as a private tutor to Crown Prince Akihito and was the official 'go-between' in arranging his recent [marriage]. The first two postwar presidents of Tokyo University, which ranks among the world's great educational institutions, were distinguished Protestants. Prominent Roman Catholics are less numerous, but among them are the chief justice of Japan's supreme court and a number of educators."[4]

Protestants in Syria and Lebanon are a small minority of the population, but in the National Evangelical Church (which has about 10,000 members) are 12 persons who work for embassies or legations, 101 professors and teachers, 47 medical doctors, 26 engineers, 15 nurses and social workers, and 14 bankers. Moreover, Protestant medical and educational institutions serve more than 30,000 people annually and have educated some of the most influential men of both countries.

The point to be held in mind is that in Asia, Africa, and Latin America indigenous churches have arisen, which are now independent of any foreign control and which possess their own institutions and trained leadership.

These churches have weaknesses enough (many of them reflections of similar weaknesses in the older churches); they face opposition greater in some respects than those faced by the older churches; yet it will be generally agreed that they are here to stay. And it is not to be forgotten that these younger churches are now producing some of our keenest and most penetrating evangelistic leaders and theological minds. As Bishop Manikam of India states, "Christianity is now in the process of becoming domesticated in the East." And the same could be said of Africa and Latin America.

THE NEW SITUATION

The fact that former mission churches have now come of age means that a new age in missionary activities has arrived.

Among the factors which must be taken into account are first the fact just emphasized, that in nearly every mission land there is now an indigenous or independent church or churches, indeed a world-wide network of so-called younger churches. Second is the fact that in nearly every land among these younger churches a new spirit of independence has arisen, seeking equality of status and protesting the western orientation of mission work. Recent independent nations in particular, in the pride of their new nationalism, resent any suggestion of dependence which could indicate a failure to have left behind the old colonial status. In this connection it needs to be noted that western civilization, once an asset to the missionary enterprise, is now, or at any time may become, a liability. This fact, along with the changing world situation, is one of the factors which require us to review all methods of missionary labor.

A third factor explaining the new day in missions is the growing realization, recognized by many, of course, from the beginning, that Christians of the West cannot evangelize the world through their own unaided efforts. We can assist and indeed must do so. But the major effort must finally come from the people themselves, and in fact this shift in emphasis is already beginning to take place. This in turn means that the older churches must seek in every way possible to strengthen the younger churches in order that they may more and more take over the work of evangelization in their own land. As Richard Shaull has written, "The church in each country is now the central reality. The important thing is to encourage its growth to the point where it can evangelize its people and do God's will in every area of national life. All mission strategy must center its attention on this task."[5] This means, in the judgment of many missionary statesmen, that the older churches of the West must increasingly put their resources at the disposal of the younger churches and serve and help them in every way possible as they struggle to meet the challenges and opportunities before them. According to Willis Church Lamott, "The young Churches stand today as the greatest forward step in fulfillment of the divine purpose that has taken place since Pentecost . . . The missionary movement is no longer an outreach of an established civilization into 'heathen' lands . . . It is a cooperative effort on the part of a world-wide fellowship to strengthen that fellowship until it shall express the will and purpose of its Lord and complete the work that he has set before it."[6]

The work of missions becomes, then, a co-operative task in which the older and younger churches work together to express the will and purpose of their Lord and to complete the work that he has set before them.

As our own church with others moves increasingly in this direction, we should have a greater sense of partnership with Christian bodies in other lands, and therefore of actual participation in the ongoing enterprise of world Christianity. What is our responsibility in this great enterprise?

OUR PRESENT RESPONSIBILITY

1. There is need for more missionaries. The thirteen years following World War II saw the largest offering of missionary life in any period of equal length in all our history—454 new missionaries. And yet, as we have seen, the total number of missionaries in 1960 was less than it had been in 1924, when we reached our all-time maximum. The need for missionaries, for more and more missionaries, for men and women, for ordained and unordained personnel, for well-trained specialists in a variety of fields, will remain urgent for many years to come.

2. There is, as indicated, need for increased financial support. In 1938, 10.5 percent of the church's total giving went to world missions; in 1957 only 4.4 percent. Men and money—these remain our most urgent needs.

3. There must be a new and more compelling motivation for world missions. The primary motivation of an earlier day was the salvation of souls—millions perishing eternally, the number augmented every passing second, for want of the Good News of Jesus and his love. This motive still moves many of those who go and a large number of those who give. But for many others it has lost its force. It is not, and has never been, the only motive. Men go because God's redemptive love has been revealed and that love cannot be concealed. They go be-

cause it is Christ's command, because they are convinced that he alone has the answer to the world's needs, because, as Bishop Neill says, Christ has a Kingdom and that Kingdom must be proclaimed; because a Christian world community has come into existence and that community, which is the only enduring community, must be extended. "The unsolved problem of human together-ness hangs over our generation with appalling menace," says Bishop Newbigin. "The Christian world mission holds the secret that can make mankind one family; this is the appeal to the youth of to-day."[7]

The Jerusalem Council stated the missionary imperative very simply: "We believe that men are made for Christ and cannot really live apart from him. Our fathers were impressed with the horror that men should die without Christ—we share that horror; we are also impressed with the horror that men should live without Christ.

"Herein lies the Christian motive; it is simple. We cannot live without Christ and we cannot bear to think of men living without him. We cannot be content to live in a world that is un-Christlike. We cannot be idle while the yearning of his heart for his brethren is unsatisfied ... Christ is our motive and Christ is our end. We must give nothing less, and we can give nothing more."[8]

There can be but little doubt that the missionary impulse in the older churches has dimmed in the last generation. If one has come to know God as he is revealed in Christ and to grasp his purpose as set forth in the New Testament, this cannot be. But so many have not yet grasped that purpose. We need a new vision and some slogan or call that will lead to a renewal of that missionary passion which possessed our fathers, and which will evoke from the ordinary Christian that response which God expects of our generation.

4. There must be a new conception of the church. Men must recognize that the church is "a world-wide, Spirit-filled fellowship existing for one purpose and one purpose only, to fulfill the world-wide purposes of God." "The Church," as Lamott points out, "is not an institution to be served or an organization to be perfected but a fellowship to be cultivated and extended ... ," a fellowship that levels all barriers and reconciles all men to one another because they have first been reconciled to God through Jesus Christ.

5. There must be a greater social concern. The Jerusalem Confer-

ence of 1929 recognized the relevance of the gospel for the whole man. The Madras Conference in 1938 raised the question of whether we should center upon individual conversion or upon social change, and answered emphatically, "We must do both." We in America need to recognize that any failure in brotherhood and every manifestation of national or racial prejudice is publicized abroad and does incalculable harm to the cause of Christ.

As Shaull reminds us: We Americans live in a glass house, visible to the whole world. [The Christian community] is called to confront all those who come in contact with it, from all corners of the world, on the university campus and in the local community, with an intensity of concern and a dynamic community life, the reality of which they cannot ignore and from the attraction of which they cannot easily escape.[9]

6. There must be a new sense of vocation on the part of laymen, especially on the part of the increasing number of laymen who travel and labor abroad. More citizens from nominal Christian countries are residing abroad for private, governmental, or commercial purposes at the present time than ever before. And the number is likely to increase. The Christians who are included in this group could become a striking force of incalculable significance. "The paid Christian worker is always to some extent the object of suspicion; the layman, who has no professional interest in the Church, can bear Christian witness in many places to which the professional Christian has no access, and all the more effectively because the genuineness of his testimony, spoken or unspoken, is more readily accepted."[10] Churches in Great Britain and Holland have begun to prepare some of their members for such service. Efforts so far have been on a small scale but may be expected to increase. In our country the United Presbyterian Church has begun to experiment in the same direction. The first "Institute on Overseas Churchmanship" held at Stony Point, New York, early in 1959 proved so successful that larger conferences are now in course of preparation.

7. There must be greater ecumenicity. Mission and ecumenicity in fact belong together; they are two aspects of the same thing. Jesus prayed that his disciples might be one in order that the world might know. Unity was to promote mission. So Paul, who labored so stren-

uously to propagate the faith, labored just as strenuously to preserve the unity of the church [1 Cor. 1:10; Eph. 4:1–3; Phil. 2:1–11]. And for the same reason. Unity for him, too, was in order for mission. Ecumenism which is concerned with the church in all the earth necessarily therefore involves both unity and mission. . . .

It was the felt needs of the mission field that gave rise to the modern ecumenical movement. The [native] indigenous Churches and the native leadership, which grew out of the mission activities, became impatient with the denominational divisions of the West which so greatly impeded their growth; missionaries could not help but see that denominational division and lack of world vision were interfering with the task to which they had devoted themselves. It was at the International Mission Conference held in Edinburgh in 1910 that steps were taken leading ultimately to the organization of the World Council of Churches.

It was the mission of the church also which gave rise to the National Council of Churches, in which the major Protestant bodies of the United States co-operate for their mutual advantage in those areas where they cannot work so well alone.

Through national councils of churches, through various regional and denominational groupings, and through the World Council of Churches, Christian bodies throughout the world, though aware of their differences, are co-ordinating their efforts in a wide variety of ways and are becoming more conscious of the God-given unities which bind them in common loyalty to the Lord and Savior Jesus Christ. Through such efforts a community of believers has come into existence which is now worldwide and which transcends barriers of nationality and race. Though still obscure in the eyes of the world, it may yet be regarded as the hope of the world. In it and in it alone are potentialities that enable it to function as the conscience, the heart, and the directive force of a distracted world that sadly needs to recover its spiritual bearings.

IN SUMMARY

As John Webster Grant reminds us: "The Church has become global to the point where the future of Christianity no longer depends upon the continuance of western supremacy. The newer Churches have not only become self-propagating in their own areas, the dream of a century ago. They have become capable of bearing the seeds of the Christian world mission . . . " And yet, as Grant exclaims: "How much more remains to be achieved! How pitiful our missionary enterprise appears—at least in numerical terms—when we compare the converts which have gathered in one hundred and fifty years with the Communists who have sprung up within forty! And this is only part, probably the least serious part of the story. Whereas Communists everywhere are thinking in terms of a world revolution, how slow is the average Christian to realize the universality of our faith! Would you suppose, from a casual visit to a local congregation, that the Christian Church was engaged in a worldwide struggle for the souls of men? Even among the congregations of one of our presbyteries or dioceses there is often less sense of a common enterprise than there is between Communist cells in Peiping and Guatemala. In a world where Christianity has a single task, there is often in our thinking a great gulf fixed between Church work and missionary work. We think of the local Church and the Church universal as two realities, when in fact they are two facets of one reality.

"It may even be in North America that except among those directly concerned, interest in the Church as a global fellowship is decreasing. A generation ago there was enthusiasm for the success of Christianity in Asia and Africa, although sometimes admittedly it was a patronizing enthusiasm. Today, when the Church has taken root throughout the world, we are ceasing to interest people in the world mission."[11]

Is Dr. Grant's indictment true? Of the church generally, of our own denomination in particular? There is some evidence, as we have seen, that missionary interest has decreased in recent years. If this be true, then the trend must be reversed.

We must give more and send more. The younger churches must be accepted as partners in a worldwide enterprise rather than as recipients of our foreign mission benevolence. To make this world fellowship real both in the West and abroad, there must be a greater exchange of leadership. Closer contacts must be established with churches in lands with other ideologies than our own. The missionary imperative must be recognized as basic—if not the primary concern of the church. It must be recognized also that the missionary task at home and abroad is one task, the task of each individual member and of each individual congregation.

The church, even in America, so far as active, working Christians are concerned, is a minority of the population. Even so, in Asia, not to speak of America, it is a far larger group than the one which Jesus described as "the salt of the earth" and "the light of the world." Members of this creative minority must function as salt and bear their witness to the light in their daily vocations, on weekdays as well as on the Sabbath. They must strive unceasingly that their local bodies become a witnessing group, a redemptive community, the people of God, exhibiting in their inner life and in the social relationships of church, family, and neighborhood a picture of Christianity in action. They must recognize and lead others to recognize that the local congregation is part of a world fellowship, in which God's purpose to make all men one in Christ is at long last become a reality; they must see and lead others to see that to strengthen this world fellowship in every way possible is the one great means of fulfilling God's will for our time.

FOR CONSIDERATION

1. Do you agree with the Foreign Mission Declaration of our first General Assembly (p. 389)? Why or why not?
2. In your estimation, does the rise of national churches in the various "mission" lands strengthen or diminish the foreign mission appeal? Why or why not?
3. Does the present world situation make missions more or less important? Why?
*4. Why, after all, should we give money and effort toward world missions? How would you answer this question if raised by a fellow church member? By an indifferent and skeptical outsider?
*5. How would you evaluate our present missionary responsibility as set forth on pages 394–397? What would you add to or subtract from the list?

The Church Dedicating Its Tithes, Offerings, and Services to the Lord

31
STEWARDS OF
GOD'S VARIED GRACE

THE CHURCH AT THE GRASS ROOTS—in Podunkville or Suburbia
or in the heart of Metropolis—is the church in microcosm: the
church of the Lord Jesus Christ in one particular area, at one particular point of time. The minister of this church is a minister of Jesus
Christ, who is the Head of the church universal (the "holy Catholic
Church" of the Apostles' Creed); members of this church are members of that church, which is the Body of Christ, "the fulness of him
who fills all in all." So the New Testament indicates. Paul, for example, wrote "to the church of God which is at Corinth, to those
sanctified in Christ Jesus, called to be saints together with all those
who in every place call on the name of our Lord Jesus Christ, both
their Lord and ours" (1 Cor. 1:2).

THE SERVICE OF WORSHIP

In this church, the church at the grass roots, the gospel is proclaimed, varying in language, yet essentially the same gospel that
Paul preached in Philippi, "Believe in the Lord Jesus Christ and you

will be saved"; the Scriptures are read, the same Scriptures which the church through the ages has held to be "inspired by God and profitable for teaching, for reproof, for correction, and for training in righteousness" (2 Tim. 3:16); hymns are sung as they were in ancient Colossae (Col. 3:16), but drawn now from a devotional treasury gathered through the ages; prayers are offered for all men, in accordance with apostolic instruction (1 Tim. 2:1–2); an offering is taken, as it was in ancient Corinth (1 Cor. 16:1); the sacraments (Baptism and the Lord's Supper) are observed, as they have been now for two thousand years.

Worship of course has varied—in content and in form—from age to age, from one land to another, from one denomination to another, from one congregation to another; yet the basic elements—Scripture, sermon, prayer, hymns, offering, sacrament—have remained.

Our Presbyterian tradition has placed emphasis upon word and sacraments. Wherever the word of God is truly preached and the sacraments properly administered, there, according to our understanding, is the church. That the word of God might be truly proclaimed and the sacraments properly administered Presbyterians have always insisted upon an educated ministry: For many years the requirements have been four years of college followed by three years in a theological seminary.

Zwingli, with whom our distinctive tradition begins, had retained some of the great days of the church year (Good Friday, Easter, Pentecost). Calvin's worship service included some liturgical elements: free prayer and fixed prayer, both had a part. But in the Puritan reaction against an imposed liturgy, all liturgical elements were dropped; worship came to be centered almost exclusively upon the sermon. In recent years Presbyterian churches are tending to recover some of the lost elements of their tradition. More place is given to congregational participation. Vestments have become common both in the choir and the pulpit. Old-fashioned hymns—actually hymns growing out of nineteenth-century revivalism (stressing the worshiper's response more than the divine initiative)—are sung less frequently. Christmas, Easter, Holy Week—the great days of the church year—are given a larger place. Sermons have been shortened. More attention is given to aesthetic elements.

In every denomination, including our own, worship is taken far more seriously than it was a generation back. In all, there has been something of a liturgical revival, growing out of a careful study of Scripture and a careful re-examination of elements within their own tradition.

We take it for granted that an offering shall be received as a part of the worship service on Sunday morning, that a portion of this offering shall be reserved for current expenses and a portion dispatched for the benevolent program of presbytery, synod, and General Assembly. Actually this procedure represents a comparatively recent development, the fruit of long experience, and a continuing attempt to apply biblical principles of stewardship to modern conditions.

TITHES AND OFFERINGS

The Old Testament religious establishment was supported by the tithes of the people imposed as a legal obligation. After the Resurrection, we read, "All who believed were together and had all things in common; and they sold their possessions and goods and distributed them to all, as any had need" (Acts 2:44–45). Not all disposed of their goods (Acts 5:1–4; 12:12), but enough was given to relieve cases of want, and such relief was then and for long afterwards the church's one benevolent enterprise. As the church grew, some fuller organization was required. Seven men (deacons?) were elected to take charge of the daily distribution (Acts 6:1–6). When famine arose, "the disciples [in Antioch] determined, every one according to his ability, to send relief to the brethren who lived in Judea; and they did so, sending it to the elders by the hand of Barnabas and Saul" (Acts 11:29–30). Paul later promoted a widespread effort to raise funds for "the poor saints" in Jerusalem from the church which he had founded on his various missionary journeys. In a letter to the Corinthians he laid down a procedure: "On the first day of every week, each of you is to put something aside and store it up, as he may prosper" (1 Cor. 16:2). In a later letter he held before them the example of the Macedonian churches: " . . . for in a severe test of affliction, their abundance of joy and their extreme poverty have overflowed in a wealth of liberality on their part. For they gave according to their means . . . and beyond their means, of their own free will

... but first they gave themselves to the Lord" (2 Cor. 8:2–5). Liberality in giving he recognized as one of the gifts of the Spirit on which the church depended for its progress. "Having gifts that differ according to the grace given to us, let us use them: if prophecy, in proportion to our faith; if service, in our serving; he who teaches, in his teaching; he who exhorts, in his exhortation; he who contributes, in liberality; he who gives aid, with zeal; he who does acts of mercy, with cheerfulness" (Rom. 12:6–8).

As the early church spread through the Roman Empire funds became necessary to support the clergy, who were now expected to give their full time to the service of the church; offerings for the poor were received on the Sabbath after the Eucharist (the Lord's Supper), in which the weekly worship service reached its climax, perhaps in recollection of Jesus' words, "As you did it to one of the least of these my brethren, you did it to me" (Matt. 25:40). Deacons reminded the well-to-do of their obligation to give in accordance with their means.

After Constantine, the church came to depend more on the support of the state. Wealthy benefactors bequeathed to it their lands and goods. In the Middle Ages, the church became the largest landowner throughout Europe, at a time when real estate was the most important source of wealth. All citizens, however, were required to tithe as a matter of religious obligation. After the Reformation, Protestant churches continued to draw much of their support from invested wealth, from government subsidy, or from public taxation. In many cases this still remains the case. Tithing meanwhile had fallen into disrepute. In the United States of America, the separation of church and state compelled all churches, for the first time since Constantine, to rely upon the voluntary support of their members. To train them to give this support was not an easy undertaking. Early Presbyterian churches depended upon subscription lists, circulated among the heads of families, for the salary of their minister. The majority of pastors were compelled to supplement the inadequate sums received by teaching school, by engaging in farming, or in some other remunerative occupation. There was no Sunday offering.

Voluntary societies were formed to support various benevolent projects (home missions, foreign missions, the education of ministerial students, the distribution of Bibles and tracts, and the like);

members of these societies made small contributions at regular intervals—sometimes as little as a penny a week. Women raised money
for special projects through bazaars, and this continued to be the case
until comparatively recently, when our General Assembly discouraged the practice as harmful to the best interests of Christian stewardship.

Pew rents, meanwhile, had supplanted the earlier subscription
list as the church's main financial effort. The choice seats in the sanc-
tuary were rented to the highest bidder.

The denomination gradually assumed responsibility for carrying
on benevolent projects which independent societies had originated.
Agents were appointed to visit the more important churches and to
take up collections for their particular interests. The number multiplied, until finally pastors in self-defense took over the responsibility
for promoting the various causes. A calendar was arranged. Each
cause was allotted its particular period. Annual collections were rec-
ommended, though for many years accepted only in part by a large
proportion of churches. In 1909 the General Assembly ordered that
collections for assembly's causes be reduced to eight: two for foreign
missions, two for home missions, two for ministerial education and
relief, one for Sabbath school missions and publication, one for Bible
cause. Under this system the collections for a specific cause suffered
greatly if, for example, during its particular month there was a series
of rainy Sundays.

Shortly before the Civil War a new interest in biblical principles
of giving had led the church to introduce (against the opposition of
those who held that the introduction of such mundane matters into
the worship service was dishonoring to God) the practice of a weekly
offering, as an important element in worship. In time duplex enve-
lopes became the vogue. Worshipers were invited to contribute each
week to current expenses and also to the benevolent causes designated for that particular month.

An advance step was taken in 1903 when individuals were asked
to pledge annual amounts for foreign missions. In 1910 this led to the
adoption of the every-member canvass as basic procedure—in which
every church member was invited annually to pledge definite amounts
for all the causes of the church. The following year this new plan was

rounded out by the adoption of an assembly budget, according to which the church would be asked to raise specified amounts for each assembly cause. A portion of this budget was assigned to the various synods. Each synod in turn drew up its own budget for the various causes of synod, and then transmitted the assembly's asking, along with its own, to the presbyteries—to each its own fair share of the total load. The presbytery in turn transmitted assembly's askings, synod's askings, and its asking to the local church—according to some agreed formula, taking into account the size and ability of each congregation. Worshipers now contributed each week to the total budget; that is, to the church's total benevolent enterprise. This in effect, with some refinements (such as the pre-budget canvass), remains the system now in use. Experimentation, however, continues. Various attempts have been made to equalize the budget, to make sure that each cause of the church receives its allotted proportion. The 1964 General Assembly adopted the idea of a central treasurer, which will contribute greatly to this end.

Along with budget and every-member canvass has gone an intensive stewardship campaign in the principles of biblical giving, each member of the church contributing every Sunday to the total work of the church: the Old Testament standard of the tithe as a minimum, being supplemented by the New Testament standard—as God has prospered us.

As a consequence of this effort the total and per capita giving of the church has greatly increased. That per capita giving is little enough compared, for example, with the Seventh-Day Adventist Church, whose average wealth is far below our own. Yet year after year we remain at the top or very near the top of all larger Protestant bodies in this country. It is to be feared, however, that the average attendant on the morning worship service gives to an enterprise—and a vast enterprise it has become—of which he has little or no understanding (our women are better informed than our men).

THE GIVER'S DOLLAR

When we make our offering on Sunday morning we should recognize that it is indeed an offering to our Lord, without which our worship would be hollow and insincere. We do not truly worship unless we give of ourselves (read Rom. 12:1–8), and it is through our means supplementing all other effort that we do give of ourselves—heart, mind, and will; bone, sinew, and muscle. Without the gifts of God's people, the work of the church, and therefore the mission of the church, would falter and fail. A portion of every dollar that we offer goes to support the work of our local congregation: to support the pastor, the director of Christian education, the janitor, to give some compensation to the choir director—and it may be, other professional aid—to maintain the church building, and all the varied activities of the church.

A portion of every dollar contributed through the local church goes to support the work of presbytery, most of it probably to the work of church extension: the planting of new churches, and partial aid until the church is able to become self-supporting. By such means the church grows. If the choice of a location has been wise, if an adequate plant has been provided for the initial stages, self-support will come without long delay, and the small investment will return large dividends in money, and—far more important—in lives.

A portion of every dollar placed in the collection plate goes to support the work of synod: its educational institutions (college or colleges and theological seminary), religious activities on the campuses of private and state institutions, weaker presbyteries with large opportunities for church extension, co-operative religious work, perhaps among migrants or in state penal institutions, synodical conferences for men, women, and youth.

A portion of every dollar contributed on Sunday morning goes to support the benevolent program of our General Assembly as a whole: the vast program carried on by the assembly's Boards of World Missions, Church Extension, Christian Education (this board is largely self-supporting), Annuities and Relief, and by more specialized agencies—the Historical Foundation, the Mountain Retreat Association, the *Presbyterian Survey,* the Presbyterian School of Christian Education, Stillman College, TRAV (Television, Radio and Audio-Visuals), the assembly's Committee on the Minister and His Work, for example.

Attendance on a meeting of the highest court of our church will open one's eyes. As the total effort of our church unfolds before him he cannot help but be impressed by the magnitude of the enterprise.

Every member of the church should read the official church magazine and one of the independent church papers in order that he may keep informed.

In many ways, in many lands, through the efforts of innumerable laborers, the work of the church, the work of our Lord, goes forward in our present day. Through our gifts each of us may have a part in the whole.

THE PEOPLE OF GOD

The church, as we have seen, is not a building, and it is much more than a worshiping congregation. It is the People of God—including the minister, but composed of all the members of the church. On occasion, the church in some specific area assembles for worship, for mutual edification and instruction. Where is the church on Monday morning, and during the days that follow? At the office, in the school, in the home, in innumerable gatherings of every variety: educational, cultural, political, economic, athletic, artistic, social. It is here, it may be, that our most vital Christian witness is borne, and it is here that Christian influence really begins to permeate the world.

There are some who serve the church at large—board secretaries, theological professors, evangelists-at-large. But the vast majority of church members find their niche in the local congregation—spread through the community for most of the week, at intervals gathered for renewed inspiration and strength, bearing now a common witness through their common worship. It is here in the local congregation that most of us make our contribution to the cause of Christ, and it is on the effectiveness of our witness here that the success of the church's mission throughout the world, in this and subsequent generations, ultimately depends.

But the local congregation can make its greatest contribution only as it looks beyond its own immediate interests and keeps ever in mind the fact that it is part of a larger whole, a part of the Body of Christ, which continues through the ages, which is spread throughout the earth—"the fulness of him who fills all in all." This is the fact which we confess when we repeat with Christians throughout the world the Apostles' Creed: "I believe in God the Father Almighty, Maker of heaven and earth; And in Jesus Christ His only Son our Lord . . . in the Holy Ghost; the holy Catholic Church . . ."

FOR CONSIDERATION

1. Some are distressed by the growing emphasis on liturgy as described on page 401. They fear that the prophetic element in worship is being minimized, that aesthetic elements (appealing to the senses rather than to intellect and will) are being over-emphasized. What is your judgment in the matter? Are the worship services of today more or less meaningful than those of yesterday? Wherein could the worship service of your own church be strengthened?

2. Is the money spent in the local congregation spent on ourselves, as sometimes charged, or is it money spent for the local mission of the church, a service to the community, an investment in the spiritual welfare of our children and our children's children for the glory of God? Is the money being well spent? Is the church promoting the right activities? Is any part of the church's mission in your particular community being neglected?

3. For what purposes are funds spent in your presbytery? How do you evaluate the work that is being done?

4. In what various ways can the average church member—you, for example—bear his witness for Christ?

5. How do we manifest our faith in the holy catholic church of the Apostles' Creed?

A BRIEF STATEMENT
OF BELIEF

GOD AND REVELATION

The living and true God has made himself known to all mankind through nature, mind, conscience, and history. He has especially revealed himself and his purpose for man in the variety of ways recorded in the Old and New Testaments. The Bible, as the written Word of God, sets forth what God has done and said in revealing his righteous judgment and love, culminating in Christ. The Spirit of God who inspired the writers of Scripture also illumines readers of Scripture as they seek his saving truth. The Bible calls men to an obedient response to the Gospel and is the supreme authority and indispensable guide for Christian faith and life.

God has revealed himself as the Creator, Sustainer, and Ruler of all that exists. In the exercise of his sovereign power in creation, history, and redemption, God is holy and perfect, abundant in goodness, and the source of all truth and freedom. He is just in his dealings with all the world; he requires that men live and act in justice; and he visits his wrath on all sin. He is gracious and merciful and does not desire that any should perish. Both his judgments and his mercies are expressions of his character as he pursues his redemptive purposes for man.

God is personal and he reveals himself as the Trinity of Father, Son, and Holy Spirit. It is the witness of the Scriptures, confirmed in Christian experience, that the God who creates and sustains us is the God who redeems us in Christ, and the God who works in our hearts as the Holy Spirit; and we believe that this threefold revelation manifests the true nature of God.

MAN AND SIN

God created man in his own image. As a created being, man is finite and dependent upon his Creator. Man can distinguish between right and wrong, and is morally responsible for his own actions. He reflects the image of God insofar as he lives in obedience to the will of God. A unique creature standing both within nature and above it, he is placed by God in authority over the world. It is, therefore, his responsibility to use all things for the glory of God. Although made in the image of God, man has fallen; and we, like all mankind before us, sin in our refusal to accept God as sovereign. We rebel against the will of God by arrogance and by despair. We thrust God from the center of life, rejecting divine control both of human life and the universe. From this perversity arises every specific sin, whether of negligence, perfunctory performance, or outright violation of the will of God.

Sin permeates and corrupts our entire being and burdens us more and more with fear, hostility, guilt and misery. Sin operates not only within individuals but also within society as a deceptive and oppressive power, so that even men of good will are unconsciously and unwillingly involved in the sins of society. Man cannot destroy the tyranny of sin in himself or in his world; his only hope is to be delivered from it by God.

CHRIST AND SALVATION

God, loving men and hating the sin which enslaves them, has acted for their salvation in history and especially through his covenant people. In the fullness of time, he sent his only, eternally begotten Son, born of the Virgin Mary. As truly God and truly man, Jesus Christ enables us to see God as he is and man as he ought to be. Through Christ's life, death, resurrection, and ascension, God won for man the decisive victory over sin and death and established his Kingdom among men. Through Christ, bearing on the cross the consequences of our sin, God exposed the true nature of sin as our repudiation of God. Through Christ, bearing on the cross the guilt of our sin, God forgives us and reconciles us to himself. By raising his Son from the dead, God conquers sin and death for us.

God has an eternal, inclusive purpose for his world, which embraces the free and responsible choices of man and everything which occurs in all creation. This purpose of God will surely be accomplished. In executing his purpose, God chooses men in Christ and calls forth the faith which unites them with Christ, releasing them from bondage to sin and death into freedom, obedience, and life. Likewise God in his sovereign purpose executes judgment upon sinful man.

Man cannot earn or deserve God's salvation but receives it through faith by the enabling power of the Holy Spirit. In faith, man believes and receives God's promise of grace and mercy in Christ, is assured of his acceptance for Christ's sake in spite of his sinfulness, and responds to God in grateful love and loyalty.

In repentance, man, through the work of the Holy Spirit, recognizes himself as he is, turns from his sin, and redirects his life increasingly in accordance with God's will. The Christian life is a continuing process of growth which reaches its final fullfillment only in the life to come.

THE CHURCH AND THE MEANS OF GRACE

The true Church is the whole community, on earth and in heaven, of those called by God into fellowship with him and with one another to know and do his will. As the body of Christ, the Church on earth is the instrument through which God continues to proclaim and apply the benefits of his redemptive work and to establish his Kingdom.

The Church in the world has many branches, all of which are subject to sin and to error. Depending on how closely they conform to the will of Christ as head of the Church, denominations and congregations are more or less pure in worship, doctrine, and practice. The Presbyterian Church follows scriptural precedent in its representative government by elders (presbyters). These elders govern only in courts of regular gradation. The form of government of a church, however, is not essential to its validity. The visible church is composed of those who profess their faith in Jesus Christ, together with their children.

Through the Church, God provides certain means for developing the Christian mind and conscience and for maturing faith, hope, and love. Primary among these means are the preaching, teaching, and study of the Word; public and private prayer; and the sacraments.

The Bible becomes a means of grace through preaching, teaching, and private study, as the Holy Spirit speaks to human needs and reveals the living Word of God who is Jesus Christ. It illuminates man's thought and experience as it provides an occasion for the Holy Spirit's work of redemption and as it testifies to the working of God, but it is not intended to be a substitute for science and inquiry. In preaching and teaching, the Church proclaims and interprets the mighty acts of God in history and seeks to relate them to every phase of human life. The prayerful and diligent study of the Scriptures guides the Christian in his relationships with God and his fellow man, and in his personal life.

Christian prayer is communion with God in the name of Jesus Christ through the inspiration and guidance of the Holy Spirit. In prayers, alone or with others, we acknowledge God's greatness and goodness, confess our sins, express our love to him, rejoice in his blessings, present our needs and those of others, receive from him guidance and strength, and joyfully dedicate ourselves to his will. To pray in the name of Christ, our Mediator, is not to repeat a formula, but to trust his redemptive work, to ask for his intercession, to depend upon his presence with us and to desire what he has taught us to value and believe.

Christ gave to the Church through his apostles the sacraments of Baptism and the Lord's Supper as visible signs and assurances of the Gospel. Baptism sets forth, by the symbolic use of water, the cleansing and regenerating love of God through the work of the Holy Spirit; in this sacrament we and our children are assured that we are members of the covenant family of God, and are publicly accepted into fellowship with Christ and his Church. The Lord's Supper sets forth, by the symbolic use of bread and wine, the death of Christ for our salvation; in this sacrament we have communion with the risen Christ, who gives himself to us as we receive in faith the bread and wine for the nourishment of our Christian life. Being assured of his forgiving and sustaining love, we renew our dedication and enjoy fellowship with the whole people of God. The Lord's table is open to members of all churches who have publicly professed Jesus Christ as Saviour and Lord and who come in penitence and faith.

CHRISTIAN LIFE AND WORK

Each Christian is called to be a servant of God in all of life, so that we must seek God's will for the work we do and for the manner in which we do it. Christian vocation may be found in any work where our own abilities and interests best meet the legitimate needs of God's world. The Church is charged under God with the obligation to seek out the most responsible and effective Christian leadership. It is the special role of the ordained ministry, including elders and deacons, to perform particular services in the life of the Church and to strengthen every Christian in the discharge of the responsibilities of the priesthood of all believers in the Church and the world. For the Christian, all life becomes significant as he does his daily work with dedication and diligence out of love for God and for his neighbor.

The range of Christian responsibility is as wide as human life. The Christian must recognize, but not accept as inevitable, the world as it is, distorted and torn by sin. Christians as individuals and as groups have the right and the duty to examine in the light of the Word of God the effects on human personality of social institutions and practices. As servants of the sovereign will of God, Christians are under obligation to their fellow men and to unborn generations to shape and influence these institutions and practices so that the world may be brought more nearly into conformity with the purpose of God for his creation. The Church's concern for the reign of God in the world is essential to its basic responsibility both for evangelism and for Christian nurture.

We believe that our destiny and that of the world are not subject to chance or fate, but to the just and loving sovereignty of God. In this assurance we face the problems of suffering and evil. Faith in the purpose and providence of God assures us of his presence in suffering and of his power to give it meaning. We are confident that no form of evil can separate us from the love of God, that God works in all things for good, and that evil will ultimately be overcome. Therefore, while we cannot fully understand the pain and evil of the present world, we can offer ourselves as active instruments of God's will in their conquest.

JUDGMENT AND THE LIFE TO COME

Eternal life is the gift of God. We are assured by the promises of the Gospel, by our relation to Christ, and by his resurrection that death does not put an end to personal existence, but that we too shall be raised from the dead. Those who have accepted the forgiving love of God in Christ enter into eternal life in fellowship with God and his people. This new life begins in the present world and is fulfilled in the resurrection of the body and the world to come. Those who have rejected the love of God bring upon themselves his judgment and shut themselves outside the fellowship of God and his people.

As Christ came once in humility, he will return in glory for the final judgment and for the consummation of his universal Kingdom. The work and promises of Jesus Christ give assurance that the age-long struggle between sin and grace will in God's good time have an end; all the power of evil will be destroyed, and God's holy, wise, and loving purposes will be accomplished.

The Brief Statement

This statement of belief has been prepared to present in the language of our time the historic Christian doctrine set forth in Scripture and affirmed by the Presbyterian Church. In a brief statement it has not been possible to treat all doctrines, or to cover fully the doctrines which have been treated. The conditions of history and the limitations of human mind and language are such that no statement of Christian doctrine can be either final or complete. Nevertheless, this affirmation is submitted in the hope that it will be used for the glory of God and the edification of the church.

Charles L. King, *Chairman*	Kenneth J. Foreman	Laurence F. Kinney
Felix B. Gear, *Vice Chairman*	Roland M. Frye	James G. Leyburn
John H. Leith, *Secretary*	Warner L. Hall	J. R. McCain
Wade H. Boggs, Jr.	T. B. Jackson	Harry M. Moffett, Jr.
Mary L. Boney	Ashby Johnson	David L. Stitt

NOTES

CHAPTER 1 THE CHURCH: ITS NATURE AND MISSION
1. Donald G. Miller, *The Nature and Mission of the Church* (Richmond: John Knox Press, 1962), pp. 16–20.

CHAPTER 2 THE CHURCH WINS THE EMPIRE
1. As quoted by Joseph Cullent Ayer, *A Source Book for Ancient History* (New York: Charles Scribner's Sons, 1913), p. 21.
2. *Ibid.,* p. 19.
3. *Ibid.,* p. 53.
4. Kenneth Scott Latourette, *A History of the Expansion of Christianity,* Vol. I, *The First Five Centuries* (New York and London: Harper & Row, Publishers, Incorporated, 1937), p. 112.
5. As quoted by Ayer, *op. cit.,* pp. 6–7.
6. *Ibid.,* p. 71.
7. As quoted by J. Stevenson (ed.), *A New Eusebius—Documents Illustrative of the History of the Church to A.D. 337* (New York: The Macmillan Company, 1957), pp. 13–14.
8. *Ibid.,* p. 16.
9. *Ibid.,* p. 39.
10. This monogram consists of the two letters Chi (X) and Rho (P) which are in Greek the first two letters of the name "Christ."
11. See Gordon J. Laing, *Survivals of Roman Religion* (New York: Longmans, Green and Company, 1931). Courtesy of David McKay Company, Inc.
12. G. H. C. MacGregor and A. C. Purdy, *Jew and Greek: Tutors Unto Christ* (London: I. Nicholson and Watson, Ltd., 1936), p. 288.
13. As paraphrased by John Foster, *After the Apostles* (London: Student Christian Movement Press Limited, 1961), p. 12.
14. Latourette, *A History of the Expansion of Christianity,* Vol. I, *The First Five Centuries,* pp. 364–365.
15. As quoted by Hans Lietzmann, *From Constantine to Julian* ("A History of the Early Church" [London: Lutterworth Press, 1950]), III, 278.
16. Henry Melville Gwatkin, *Early Church History to A.D. 313* (New York: Macmillan & Co. Ltd., 1912), I, 234–235. Used by permission.
17. T. R. Glover, *The Jesus of History* (New York: Association Press, 1917), pp. 200–201.
18. Robert M. Grant, *The Sword and the Cross* (New York: The Macmillan Company, 1955), p. 59. Used by permission.

CHAPTER 3 CHURCH AND STATE ARE UNITED
1. As quoted by Ayer, *op. cit.,* pp. 371–372.
2. *Ibid.,* p. 367.
3. *Ibid.,* pp. 559–560.

415

4. J. R. Palanque, Pierre de Labriolle *et al.*, *The Church in the Christian Roman Empire*, trans. E. C. Messenger *et al.* (London: Burns, Oates & Washbourne, Ltd., 1952), II, 569–570. Used by permission of Burns & Oates, Ltd., and The Macmillan Company.
5. As quoted in Palanque, De Labriolle *et al.*, p. 716.
6. Palanque, De Labriolle *et al., op. cit.*, p. 569.
7. Ayer, *op. cit.*, pp. 390–391.
8. See Palanque, De Labriolle *et al., op. cit.*, p. 700.
9. Winthrop S. Hudson, *The Story of the Christian Church* (New York: Harper & Row, Publishers, Incorporated, 1958), p. 25.

CHAPTER 4 THE CHURCH TIGHTENS ITS ORGANIZATION

1. In Acts 15 we read that "the apostles and the elders [of the church in Jerusalem] were gathered together to consider" a very important issue which had been raised in the church, and that the final decision in the matter was one approved by "the apostles and the elders, with the whole church" (15:6, 22). It would appear from this passage that the apostles did not exercise arbitrary or absolute power within the church.
2. Stevenson, *op. cit.*, p. 48.

CHAPTER 5 THE CHURCH ELABORATES ITS WORSHIP

1. "The Letter of Ignatius, Bishop of Antioch, To the Magnesians," *Early Christian Fathers*, ed. Cyril C. Richardson ("Library of Christian Classics" [Philadelphia: The Westminster Press, 1953]), I, 96.
2. As quoted by Philip Schaff, *History of the Christian Church* (New York: Charles Scribner's Sons, 1923), II, 204.
3. As quoted by Henry Bettenson, *Documents of the Christian Church* (New York: Oxford University Press, 1947), pp. 94–95.
4. Ilion T. Jones, *A Historical Approach to Evangelical Worship* (Nashville: Abingdon Press, 1954), p. 94.
5. *Ibid.*
6. *Ibid.*, p. 96.
7. As quoted by Palanque, De Labriolle *et al., op. cit.*, p. 525.

CHAPTER 6 THE CHURCH DEFINES ITS BELIEF

1. George Hodges, *The Early Church from Ignatius to Augustine* (New York: Houghton Mifflin Company, 1915), pp. 128–129.
2. As quoted by Bettenson, *op. cit.*, p. 36.
3. *Ibid.*, p. 73.
4. Donald Baillie, *God Was in Christ* (New York: Charles Scribner's Sons, 1948), p. 83.
5. As quoted by Bettenson, *op. cit.*, p. 130.
6. This tale of the heresies and of the birth of orthodoxy may have seemed long and confused to the new reader, but we have touched only the high spots of a fascinating story. Those who want more details and discussion should read a short history of doctrine, or any textbook in theology (see Bibliography).
7. Williston Walker, *A History of the Christian Church* (Rev. ed.; New York: Charles Scribner's Sons, 1959), p. 160.
8. See Philip Schaff, *op. cit.*, III, 993–994.

9. As quoted by Ayer, *op. cit.*, p. 475.

10. Reinhold Seeburg, *Text-Book of the History of Doctrines* (Grand Rapids: Baker Book House, 1958), II, 26.

CHAPTER 7 THE CHURCH SERVES AND SURVIVES THE EMPIRE

1. Edmund H. Oliver, *The Social Achievements of the Christian Church* (Toronto: Board of Evangelism and Social Service of The United Church of Canada, 1930), pp. 35–36.

2. From Richardson, *op. cit.*, pp. 216–218.

3. Gwatkin, *op. cit.*, p. 73.

4. Will Durant, *The Story of Civilization*, Vol. IV, *The Age of Faith* (New York: Simon and Schuster, Inc., 1950), p. 76.

5. Ayer, *op. cit.*, pp. 60–61.

6. Oliver, *op. cit.*, p. 76.

7. Charles M. Jacobs, *The Story of the Church* (Philadelphia: The Muhlenberg Press, 1925), pp. 73–74. Used by permission of Fortress Press.

8. Philip Schaff, *op. cit.*, IV, 82–83.

9. Ayer, *op. cit.*, p. 531.

10. Henry Kendall Booth, *The Great Galilean Returns* (New York and London: Charles Scribner's Sons, 1936), pp. 103–104.

CHAPTER 8 THE CHURCH GAINS AND LOSES

1. James Hastings Nichols, *History of Christianity, 1650–1950* (New York: Copyright © 1956 The Ronald Press Company), pp. 3–4.

2. From Ireland also came the first extensive penitential books, in which appropriate satisfactions were assessed for specific sins.

3. The Venerable Bede, *The Ecclesiastical History of the English Nation,* 731 A.D. (London: Henry G. Bond, York Street, Covent Garden, 1849), Book I, chap. 13, p. 95.

4. The account of Boniface's labors is adapted from *Apostles of Medieval Europe* by G. F. Maclear (New York: The Macmillan Company, 1869), pp. 110–128.

5. John H. Leith (ed.), *Creeds of the Churches: A Reader in Christian Doctrine from the Bible to the Present* (Garden City, N.Y.: Doubleday & Company, Inc., 1963), pp. 55–56.

6. George Sale (trans.), *The Koran* (Philadelphia: J. W. Moore, 1850), Chap. IV, p. 69.

7. David Schaff, *History of the Christian Church* (New York: Charles Scribner's Sons, 1923), V, 229.

8. As quoted by Will Durant, *op. cit.*, pp. 591–592.

9. *Ibid.*

CHAPTER 9 THE POPES EXTEND THEIR POWERS

1. James H. Robinson, *An Introduction to the History of Western Europe*, ed. James H. Shotwell (Short ed.; New York and Boston: Ginn and Company, 1946), p. 73.

2. As quoted by William Shaw Kerr, *A Handbook on the Papacy* (London: Marshall & Scott, Ltd., 1950), p. 209.

3. *Ibid.*

4. James Bryce, *The Holy Roman Empire* (London: Macmillan & Co., Ltd., 1906), p. 99.

5. As quoted by Bettenson, *op. cit.*, p. 141, from R. D. G. Laffan, *Select Documents of European History, 800–1492* (New York: Henry Holt & Co., 1930–1931).

6. It was during Charlemagne's reign, it may be noted, that the new calendar numbering the years from the Incarnation of the Lord (B.C. and A.D.) came into general use.

7. Walker, *A History of the Christian Church*, p. 188.

8. Philip Schaff, *op. cit.*, IV, 283–284.

9. See David Schaff, *op. cit.*, V, 44–45.

10. John T. McNeill, *Makers of Christianity* (New York: Holt, Rinehart and Winston, Inc., 1935), II, 68–69.

11. Leighton Pullan, *From Justinian to Luther* (Oxford: The Clarendon Press, 1930), p. 147.

12. As quoted by Bettenson, *op. cit.*, pp. 161–163.

13. Gilbert Bagnani, *Rome and the Papacy* (New York: Thomas H. Crowell, 1929), p. 168.

14. Walker, *A History of the Christian Church*, p. 267.

15. Bettenson, *op. cit.*, p. 192.

16. Jacobs, *op. cit.*, pp. 170–171.

17. As quoted by A. W. Ward *et al.* (eds.), *The Cambridge Modern History* (New York: The Macmillan Company, 1904), II, 10–11.

18. Hudson, *op. cit.*, p. 36.

19. *Ibid.*, pp. 48–49.

CHAPTER 10 ROMAN CATHOLIC THEOLOGY TAKES FORM
1. Indulgences, it may be pointed out, are no longer sold, but are granted for a number of designated acts or practices.

CHAPTER 11 NEW MOVEMENTS STIR WITHIN THE CHURCH
1. Gilbert K. Chesterton, *St. Francis of Assisi* (New York: George H. Doran Co., 1941), pp. 141–142.

2. Rufus M. Jones, *The Luminous Trail* (New York: The Macmillan Company, 1947), pp. 77–78. Used by permission.

3. David Schaff, *op. cit.*, V, 388–389.

4. Thomas a Kempis, *The Imitation of Christ*, trans. William Benham ("The Harvard Classics" [New York: P. F. Collier & Son, 1909]), VII, Book III, 21:1, p. 294.

5. *Ibid.*, Book I, 1:3, pp. 213–214.

6. *Ibid.*, 14:1, p. 226.

7. *Ibid.*, Book III, 21:1, p. 294.

8. David Schaff, *op. cit.*, V, p. 514.

9. In Paris, for example, LeFebvre was teaching the Pauline doctrine of justification by faith long before Luther came upon the scene.

CHAPTER 12 LUTHERAN CHURCHES ARE ESTABLISHED
1. As quoted by Roland H. Bainton, *Here I Stand: A Life of Martin Luther* (New York and Nashville: Abingdon Press, 1950), p. 45.

2. Martin Luther, *A Commentary on St. Paul's Epistle to the Galatians* (London: James Clarke & Co. Ltd., 1953), pp. 157–158.

3. Bainton, *op. cit.*, p. 78.

4. Walker, *A History of the Christian Church*, p. 308.

5. Bettenson, *op. cit.*, p. 284.

6. *Ibid.*, p. 285.

7. Hudson, *op. cit.*, p. 60.

CHAPTER 13 REFORMED AND PRESBYTERIAN CHURCHES SPREAD

1. Lutheran churches in Europe count as members all of the baptized.

2. A. C. McGiffert, *Protestant Thought Before Kant* (New York: Charles Scribner's Sons, 1924), p. 70.

3. E. Troeltsch, *The Social Teaching of the Christian Churches*, trans. Olive Wyon (New York: The Macmillan Company, 1931), II, 622. Used by permission.

4. Preserved Smith, *The Age of the Reformation* (New York: Holt, Rinehart and Winston, Inc., 1920), p. 204.

5. *Ibid.*, pp. 208–210.

6. T. M. Lindsay, *A History of the Reformation* (New York: Charles Scribner's Sons, 1922), II, 257.

7. Smith, *op. cit.*, p. 254.

8. Williston Walker, *The Reformation*, ed. John Fulton ("Ten Epochs of Church History" [New York: Charles Scribner's Sons, 1900]), pp. 317–318.

9. Lindsay, *op. cit.*, p. 309.

10. Walker, *The Reformation*, p. 330.

CHAPTER 14 "RADICAL" MOVEMENTS APPEAR

1. Franklin Littell, *The Anabaptist View of the Church*, ed. Jas. H. Nichols & William Panck ("Studies in Church History" [Boston: Beacon Press, 1958]), VIII, 29.

CHAPTER 15 REFORMATION COMES TO ENGLAND

1. Norman Towar Boggs, *The Christian Saga* (New York: The Macmillan Company, 1931), II, 721, 733.

2. J. R. Green, *Short History of the English People* (New York: Harper and Brothers, Publishers, 1876), p. 455.

3. *Ibid.*, p. 461.

4. Later, in agreement with the Scotch forces whose aid had been sought in the war with Charles, the purpose of Parliament, through the Westminster Assembly, was "to reform the church after the Presbyterian model."

5. Gaius Jackson Slosser, *The Westminster Assembly and Standards* (Privately printed, n.d.), p. 26.

6. The early Quakers were active, however, in many humanitarian efforts. As a writer in the *Schaff-Herzog Encyclopedia* has written: "In the recognition of the equal rights of women, in the abolition of slavery and the slave trade, in the protection and instruction of the Indians and the weaker races of mankind, in the amelioration of penal laws and prison discipline, in the adoption of enlightened methods for the care and relief of the insane, in testimony against war, intemperance, oaths, corrupting books and amusements, extravagance, insincerity, and vain display, it has been in the forefront of Christian reformers

... "; *The New Schaff-Herzog Encyclopedia of Religious Knowledge* (New York: Funk and Wagnalls Company, 1909), IV, 394.
7. Green, *op. cit.,* Chap. VIII, sect. 10.
8. *Ibid.,* Chap. IX, sect. 2.

CHAPTER 16 COUNTER-REFORMATION DEVELOPS
1. Smith, *op. cit.,* p. 388.
2. L. Fuerbringer, Th. Engelder, P. E. Kretzmann, *The Concordia Encyclopedia* (St. Louis: Concordia Publishing House, 1927), pp. 375–376.
3. Walker, *The Reformation,* p. 402.

CHAPTER 17 THE CHURCH COMES TO THE AMERICAS
1. Leonard W. Bacon, *A History of American Christianity* ("The American Church History Series" [New York: The Christian Literature Company, 1897]), XIII, 8.
2. As quoted by William Warren Sweet, *The Story of Religion in America* (New York: Harper & Row, Publishers, Incorporated, 1950), p. 91.

CHAPTER 18 THE CHURCH ABSORBS NEW KNOWLEDGE
1. A. C. McGiffert, *op. cit.,* p. 147.
2. *Ibid.*
3. See John Dillenberger and Claude Welch, *Protestant Christianity Interpreted Through Its Development* (New York: Charles Scribner's Sons, 1954), pp. 189–198.
4. *Ibid.,* p. 268.
5. *Ibid.,* pp. 269–282.

CHAPTER 19 THE CHURCH EXTENDS ITS BORDERS
1. Henry K. Rowe, *The History of Religion in the United States* (New York: The Macmillan Company, 1924), p. 79. Used by permission.
2. Peter J. Mode, *The Frontier Spirit in American Christianity* (New York: The Macmillan Company, 1923), p. 41.
3. From *Great Christian Books* by Hugh Martin. Copyright 1946 by W. L. Jenkins. The Westminster Press, pp. 101–102. Used by permission.

CHAPTER 20 THE CHURCH IN AMERICA GROWS AND PROLIFERATES
1. Taxation for the support of the Congregational Churches continued for some time longer, ending in New Hampshire in 1817, in Connecticut in 1818, and in Massachusetts not until 1833.
2. The International Convention of Disciples of Christ has recently voted to change their name to International Convention of Christian Churches (Disciples of Christ).
3. John B. Holt, "Holiness Religion," *American Sociological Review* (October, 1940), pp. 740–747.
4. As quoted by Charles S. Braden, *These Also Believe* (New York: The Macmillan Company, 1949), p. 170.

CHAPTER 21 THE CHURCH BECOMES CONCERNED ABOUT SOCIETY
1. Francis H. Stead, *The Story of Social Christianity* (London: James Clarke & Co. Ltd., 1924), II, 184–185.

2. R. H. Tawney, *Religion and the Rise of Capitalism* (London: John Murray, 1926), pp. 188–189.

3. *Ibid.,* pp. 192–193.

4. Karl Marx and Friedrich Engels, *Manifesto of the Communist Party,* ed. Friedrich Engels (Chicago: Charles H. Kerr and Co., 1888), p. 58.

5. *Christianity in the Light of Modern Knowledge—A Collective Work* (New York: Harcourt, Brace and Co., 1929), pp. 753–754. Used by permission of Blackie & Son Limited, Glasgow, Scotland.

CHAPTER 22 THE CHURCH SEEKS TO RECOVER ITS LOST UNITY

1. Henry Pitt Van Dusen, *What Is the Church Doing?* (London: Student Christian Movement Press Limited, 1943), p. 40.

2. In late 1963 the General Assembly of the National Council approved realignment of these varied activities under five main divisions and three administrative or supporting offices.

3. W. A. Visser 't Hooft (ed.), *The New Delhi Report* (New York: Association Press, 1961), p. 152.

4. W. A. Visser 't Hooft (ed.), *The Evanston Report* (London: Student Christian Movement Press Limited, 1955), p. 306.

CHAPTER 23 ROMAN CATHOLICISM MEETS NEW CONDITIONS

1. The Jesuit Order was restored after the fall of Napoleon and quickly recovered its former ascendancy.

2. Walker, *The Reformation,* p. 525.

3. Winfred Ernest Garrison, *Catholicism and the American Mind* (Chicago: Willet, Clark & Colby, 1928), pp. 94–95.

4. Though the pope is declared to be infallible only under circumstances just mentioned, a recent pope (Pius XII) reminded theologians of the Church (in 1950) that pronouncements of the Supreme Pontiff in his encyclicals must also be accorded their "full assent" and that a question which he has decided can no longer be the object of free discussion among theologians.

CHAPTER 24 THE CHURCH FACES A CHANGING WORLD

1. Adapted from Ernest T. Thompson, *Tomorrow's Church, Tomorrow's World* (Richmond: John Knox Press, 1960), pp. 7–26.

2. David L. Cohn, "The Great Turning Point," *The Saturday Review* (May 16, 1953), p. 11; quoted by Ernest T. Thompson, *op. cit.,* p. 8.

3. Denis de Rougemont, "The Conquest of Anarchy," *The Saturday Review* (January 13, 1951), p. 17; quoted by Thompson, *op. cit.,* p. 13.

4. Paul Hutchinson, *The New Ordeal of Christianity* (New York: Association Press, 1957), pp. 86–87; quoted by Thompson, *op. cit.,* p. 14.

5. Kenneth Scott Latourette, *Christianity in a Revolutionary Age,* Vol. IV, *The Twentieth Century in Europe* (New York: Harper & Row, Publishers, Incorporated, 1961), pp 540–541.

6. Sydney E. Ahlstrom, "Theology and the Present-Day Revival," in *Religion in American Society. The Annals of the American Academy of Political and Social Science* (November, 1960), p. 30.

CHAPTER 25 YESTERDAY AND TODAY: A REVIEW AND A LOOK AHEAD
(none)

CHAPTER 26 PRESBYTERIAN AND REFORMED
1. The Northern Church excepted the charge of rebellion.
2. A three-fourths vote is required by the church's constitution in cases of church union.
3. *Minutes of the General Assembly of the Presbyterian Church in the United States (1960)*, p. 77.

CHAPTER 27 THE BIBLICAL IMPERATIVE: TO MAKE DISCIPLES
1. The material in this chapter is largely adapted from Ernest T. Thompson, *op. cit.*, pp. 49–72.
2. Murray H. Leiffer, *City and Church in Transition* (Chicago: Willett, Clark & Co., 1938), p. 277.
3. Thomas W. Currie, *Our Cities for Christ* (Atlanta: Board of Church Extension of the Presbyterian Church, 1954), p. 9; quoted by Thompson, *op. cit.*, pp. 67–68.
4. From *Theology for Evangelism,* a study document prepared for the Division of Studies, Department of Evangelism of the World Council of Churches, p. 2; quoted by Thompson, *op. cit.*, p. 70.
5. M. Richard Shaull, "The Service of the Church," *The Reformed and Presbyterian World* (December, 1958), XXV, No. 4, 158–165; quoted by Thompson, *op. cit.*, p. 71.
6. Norman Victor Hope, "The Evangelistic Challenge Today," *Religion in Life* (Winter, 1950–1951), XX, No. 1, 78; quoted by Thompson, *op. cit.*, p. 71.
7. From *The Good News of God: The Nature and Task of Evangelism,* report of a Special Commission appointed by the General Board of the National Council of the Churches of Christ in the U.S.A., p. 18; quoted by Thompson, *op. cit.*, p. 71.
8. From *Theology for Evangelism, op. cit.*, p. 12; quoted by Thompson, *op. cit.*, pp. 71–72.
9. From *Religious News Service* (December 1, 1958); quoted by Thompson, *op. cit.*, p. 72.

CHAPTER 28 "TEACHING THEM"
1. *Minutes of the General Assembly of the Presbyterian Church in the United States (1958)*, pp. 88–89.
2. Stillman College was organized originally under General Assembly auspices, particularly for the training of a Negro ministry.

CHAPTER 29 "THE LEAST OF THESE"
1. *Minutes of the General Assembly of the Presbyterian Church in the United States (1935)*, pp. 93–94.
2. Brooks Hays, "Set in the South," *Presbyterian Survey,* (January, 1961), p. 13.

CHAPTER 30 "UNTO THE UTTERMOST PART OF THE EARTH"
1. The material in this chapter is largely adapted from Ernest Trice Thompson, *op. cit.*, pp. 98–124.
2. The figures are given in Willis Church Lamott, *Revolution in Missions* (New York: The Macmillan Company, 1954), p. 87; quoted by Thompson, *op. cit.*, p. 101.

3. *Ibid.*, p. 88; quoted by Thompson, *loc. cit.*

4. From "Minority Influences Japanese Nation," *The Christian Century* (April 22, 1959), LXXVI, No. 16, 469–470; quoted by Thompson, *op. cit.*, pp. 101–102.

5. Richard Shaull, *Encounter with Revolution* (New York: Association Press, 1955), pp. 135–136; quoted by Thompson, *op. cit.*, p. 104.

6. Lamott, *op. cit.*, pp. 21–22; quoted by Thompson, *loc. cit.*

7. Lesslie Newbigen, *One Body, One Gospel, One World* (Published for the International Missionary Council by Wm. Carling and Company, Ltd., London, 1958), p. 13; quoted by Thompson, *op. cit.*, pp. 115–117.

8. Lamott, *op. cit.*, p. 157; quoted by Thompson, *op. cit.*, p. 117.

9. Shaull, *Encounter with Revolution*, pp. 116, 119; quoted by Thompson, *op. cit.*, pp. 117–118.

10. Stephen Neill, *The Unfinished Task* (London: Lutterworth Press, 1957), p. 217; quoted by Thompson, *op. cit.*, p. 118.

11. John Webster Grant, *World Church: Achievement or Hope?* (Toronto, Canada: The United Church Publishing House, 1956), pp. 38–39; quoted by Thompson, *op. cit.*, pp. 122–123.

CHAPTER 31 STEWARDS OF GOD'S VARIED GRACE

(none)

CHRONOLOGICAL TABLE

Important dates in church and secular history; time spans are indicated by the initial date, e.g., 1653 Cromwell: The Commonwealth.

29 Crucifixion of Jesus	410 Alaric sacks Rome
43 Execution of James	426 Augustine writes *City of God*
50 Missionary journeys of Paul	432 Patrick comes to Ireland
64 Neronian persecution	440 Leo I: Petrine theory of papacy
70 Destruction of Jerusalem	449 Anglo-Saxons invade England
112 Correspondence: Pliny and Trajan	451 Council of Chalcedon
132 Jewish revolt under Bar Cochba	476 Last "Roman" emperor deposed
150 Justin's *Apology*	481 Clovis, king of the Franks
155 Martyrdom of Polycarp	526 Benedict: The Benedictine Rule
161 Reign of Marcus Aurelius	563 Columba comes to Iona
250 Decius: First persecution	570 Mohammed born
303 Diocletian: Second persecution	590 Gregory I becomes bishop of Rome
312 Battle of Mulvian Bridge: Conversion of Constantine	664 England: Synod of Whitby accepts Roman tradition
325 Council of Nicaea	732 Charles Martel halts Mohammedans
367 Athanasius: First New Testament canon in its present form	800 Charlemagne: Roman emperor
392 Theodosius: Ban on pagan worship	988 Russia: Conversion of Vladimir I

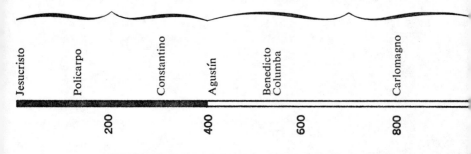

Jesucristo	Policarpo	Constantino	Agustín	Benedicto / Columba	Carlomagno

200   400   600   800

1603 James VI of Scotland becomes James I of England and Scotland	1706 First presbytery in Colonies
1607 Settlement of Jamestown	1717 First synod in American Colonies
1611 King James Bible	1722 Moravians begin missionary activity
1616 Death of Shakespeare	1726 Great Scotch-Irish migration begins
1619 Synod of Dort	1739 John Wesley: Aldersgate experience
1620 The Pilgrim Fathers	1740 Great Awakening in America
1633 Recantation of Galileo	1741 Handel's *Messiah*
1640 America: First Presbyterian Church	1776 Declaration of Independence
1647 Westminster Assembly draws up Presbyterian Standards	1792 William Carey: Beginning of modern missions
1648 Peace of Westphalia	1799 Schleiermacher's *Addresses on Religion*
1653 Cromwell: The Commonwealth	
1660 Charles II restored to throne	
1682 Makemie: Missionary to America	
1685 Revocation of Edict of Nantes	
1685 James II: "Killing time"	
1689 William and Mary: Toleration Act	

1054 Schism of East and West	1509 Birth of John Calvin
1073 Pope Hildebrand (Gregory VII)	1516 Erasmus' Greek New Testament
1096 The Crusades begin	1517 Luther's *Ninety-Five Theses*
1176 Peter Waldo begins preaching	1520 Luther is excommunicated
1198 Innocent III ascends papal throne	Magellan sails around the world
1210 Francis of Assisi gathers disciples	1521 Luther before the Diet of Worms
1215 England: The Magna Charta	1522 Zwingli begins Zürich Reformation
1216 Beginning of Dominican Order	1525 Tyndale: New Testament into English
1232 Inquisition established	1534 Henry VIII breaks with Rome
1265 Thomas Aquinas begins *Summa*	1536 *The Institutes of the Christian*
1272 Last Crusade ends in failure	*Religion*: Calvin comes to Geneva
1302 Boniface VIII: Bull *Unam Sanctam*	1540 Loyola founds the Jesuit Order
1309 Beginning of Avignon "captivity"	1545 Council of Trent opens
1378 Beginning of Great Schism	1546 Death of Luther
1382 Wycliffe: Bible into English	1555 Peace of Augsburg
1414 Council of Constance opens	1558 The Elizabethan Settlement
1415 Thomas à Kempis' *Imitation of Christ*	1560 Knox leads Scotch Reformation
1417 John Hus burned	1562 First Huguenot War
1429 Joan of Arc	1564 Death of Calvin
1434 Printing press invented	1572 Massacre of St. Bartholomew's Day
1453 Fall of Constantinople	1581 Independence of Holland
1483 Birth of Luther	1588 Defeat of Spanish Armada
1492 Columbus discovers America	1598 Edict of Nantes

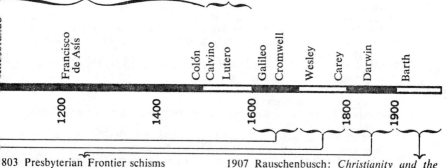

1803 Presbyterian Frontier schisms	1907 Rauschenbusch: *Christianity and the*
1816 American Bible Society formed	*Social Crisis*
1837 Old-New School Division	1908 Federal Council of Churches
1848 Marx: *Communist Manifesto*	1910 Edinburgh Missionary Conference
1854 Dogma of Immaculate Conception	1914 First World War begins
1859 Darwin: *Origin of Species*	1917 Communist Revolution in Russia
1861 Civil War begins in U.S.A.	1919 Barth's *Commentary on Romans*
Organization of Presbyterian	opens new theological era
Church in Confederate States	1929 Mussolini: Vatican State created
1864 Plus IX: *Syllabus of Errors*	1939 Second World War begins
1870 Dogma of Papal Inerrancy	1948 Amsterdam: World Council of
Popes deprived of temporal power	Churches
1875 Mary Baker Eddy: Christian Science	1950 National Council of Churches
1876 Graf-Welhausen theory opens new	1962 Vatican Council II begins
era in biblical criticism	
1886 Student Volunteer Movement	

A SELECTED
BIBLIOGRAPHY

BAINTON, ROLAND H. *Here I Stand: A Life of Martin Luther.* New York and Nashville: Abingdon Press, 1950. 422 pp. Paperback.
———. *Early Christianity.* Princeton, N.J.: D. Van Nostrand Company, Inc., 1960. Paperback.
———. *The Medieval Church.* Princeton, N.J.: D. Van Nostrand Company, Inc., 1962. 192 pp. Paperback.
———. *The Age of the Reformation.* Princeton, N.J.: D. Van Nostrand Company, Inc., 1956. 192 pp. Paperback.
BRAUER, JERALD C. *Protestantism in America: A Narrative History.* Philadelphia: The Westminster Press, 1953. 307 pp.
CRAGG, GERALD R. *The Church and the Age of Reason: 1648–1789.* Bristol, England: Hodder & Stoughton, 1962. 299 pp. Available in paperback also.
DENDY, MARSHALL C. *The Understanding and Use of the Catechism.* Richmond: The CLC Press. In preparation as of this writing.
DILLENBERGER, JOHN, and WELCH, CLAUDE. *Protestant Christianity Interpreted Through Its Development.* New York: Charles Scribner's Sons, 1954. 340 pp. A popular and readable account of Protestant thought from the Reformation to the present day.
JANSEN, JOHN F. *The Nature of Christian Worship.* Richmond: The CLC Press. In preparation as of this writing.
LINGLE, WALTER L. *Presbyterians: Their History and Beliefs.* Rev. ed. Richmond: John Knox Press, 1960. Paperback.
STEVENSON, WILLIAM. *The Story of the Reformation.* Richmond: John Knox Press, 1963. 206 pp. Paperback.
STICKELBERGER, EMANUEL. *Calvin: A Life.* Translated by David Georg Gelzer. Richmond: John Knox Press, 1954. 174 pp.
STREET, T. WATSON. *The Story of Southern Presbyterians.* Richmond: John Knox Press, 1961. 134 pp. A brief account in paperback.
THOMPSON, ERNEST TRICE. *Presbyterians in the South: Volume One, 1607–1861.* Richmond: John Knox Press, 1963. 629 pp. A much fuller account. Volume Two in preparation.
VIDLER, ALEC R. *The Church in an Age of Revolution: 1789 to the Present Day.* Baltimore: Penguin Books, 1961. 287 pp. Paperback.
WALKER, WILLISTON. *A History of the Christian Church.* New York: Charles Scribner's Sons, 1947. 624 pp. Revised in 1959. The best one-volume history.

Some of the books referred to in this text may not be available for purchase in bookstores. Perhaps one of your local libraries can provide them.

GLOSSARY

ARIANISM—A heresy affirming that Jesus Christ is made, not begotten, by the Father. Thus Jesus is a part of creation, more than man but less than God.

ASCETIC—As noun, means a person who shuns comforts and luxuries and lives on the barest necessities. As adjective, it refers to that kind of life.

ASCETICISM—The theory that God rewards us (with "merit") for going without comforts and living in deliberate hardship. The theory is that an ascetic life is holier than any other kind. Ascetics abounded in the early Christian church; unmarried, many even refused to look at a woman from a distance.

BYZANTINE—Refers to the Byzantine Empire, the eastern half of the Roman Empire, with capital at Byzantium. Name changed to Constantinople after Constantine the Great. Present name Istanbul, in Turkey.

CANON—A list; especially of books officially recognized by a church as divinely inspired and therefore authoritative for religious faith and moral practice.

CHARISMATIC—Refers to extraordinary powers or gifts bestowed by the Holy Spirit. A charismatic is a person with such outstanding gifts.

COMITY—An arrangement among churches or denominations according to which each church is assigned a definite territory within which the other churches agree not to interfere or to start work of their own.

DIALOGUE—Contemporary jargon for "discussion."

DIOCESE—The area of a bishop's jurisdiction.

DISPENSATIONALISM—The theory of religious history as presented in the notes to the Scofield Bible, for example. The essence of it is twofold: that all promises of the Old Testament to Israel must be literally fulfilled; and that there are seven successive dispensations or methods by which God deals with his people. This theory has been officially rejected as heretical by the Southern Presbyterian Church.

DISSIDENT—Dissenting or seceding.

DOCETISM—The theory that Jesus Christ's human body was not real but a kind of illusion. The word comes from the Greek word meaning "to seem"; Docetists say that Christ is divine but only *seems* to be human.

DOGMA—A religious formula or statement which is definite and officially adopted by the church. In the Roman Catholic Church a dogma is beyond criticism, cannot be changed or given up. Protestants regard all dogmas as subject to review and revision for good cause.

ECUMENICAL (kindred nouns: ecumenism, ecumenicity)—Church-wide (when referring to the church) or worldwide. An ecumenical council is one attended by representative leaders from all parts of the Christian world. Owing to the East-West and Catholic-Protestant split, no council today is actually ecumenical, though some are called so.

ESOTERIC—Known only by, or to, a closed circle of people "in the know." Doctrines taught secretly to a chosen few. Private-stock ideas.

EXPONENT—As used in a study of ideas, the word means one who stands up

427

for and takes seriously and defends some idea, plan, or policy. Any "Mr. Republican" would be an exponent of Republican ideas.

HERETIC—A Christian who rejects some basic Christian doctrine. A heretical idea is one which the church rejects. The act or habit of supporting a heretical idea is called heresy.

ICONOCLASM—Comes from Greek words meaning "to break images"; means the attitude or actions of one who goes about breaking images. The iconoclastic controversy in the church was the argument (often violent) over whether it is right to venerate images (pictures or statues). In general the eastern churches favored the veneration of pictures, not statues, while the western churches continued (to this day) to venerate both. Both East and West agreed that the image was not the direct object of worship but was a symbol of a spiritual reality. Protestants point out the real danger of image-veneration turning, in practice, into outright idolatry.

INDIGENOUS—Native.

LEGATE—Official representative; envoy.

METROPOLITAN—The top bishop of an ecclesiastical (church) district.

MONASTICISM—Withdrawing from the world to an abbey or cloister and living there an ascetic life in company with others of the same sex. This is supposed, by those who practice or admire it, to be specially holy. A monastic is one who lives in one of these "orders."

POLITY (no connection with politics)—Any form of church government is called that church's polity. Reformed Churches have a presbyterian polity.

PREMILLENNARIANISM (one who believes in it being a premillennarian)—The doctrine that the second coming of Christ is very near, and that after his coming, Christ will personally rule the world for one thousand years.

SALIC FRANKS—A Frankish (Germanic) people, or collection of tribes, living in Germany in the Dark Ages between the Meuse and Scheldt Rivers.

SCHISMATIC (in America pronounced "Sizmatic," or "Skizmatic")—From the Greek word *schizo*, "to split." A schismatic church is a split-off church. Catholics accuse Protestants of schism because Protestants have left the mother-church. Protestants accuse Catholics of schism because they have left the simplicities of the church of the New Testament.

SEE—Charge or territory of a bishop.

SYLLABUS—An annotated list of things or events or declarations. The Syllabus of Errors was a document issued by the Pope in the nineteenth century giving an extended list of modern practices (public schools and democracy being two of them) which Catholics were solemnly warned against.

THEOSOPHY—A somewhat vague combination of "metaphysics" and mysticism, neither theology nor philosophy. Prevalent in India and California.

TONSURE—A shaving of a portion of the head, as a symbol of religious devotion. Different monastic orders adopted different styles of cutting or shaving the hair of their scalps. Argument over the right shape of the tonsure was one of the factors leading to the great schism between eastern and western Christian churches.

VISIGOTHS—Goths who lived in western Gaul (France).

INDEX OF
SCRIPTURE PASSAGES

429

INDEX

431

438 INDEX

Lutheran Church—*continued*
　in ecumenical movement, 298
　government of, 326
　membership, 176, 336
　in Reformation, 170, 176, 187
　view of church and state, 313
　worship in, 329–330

Macarius, 94
Madison, James, 258, 382
Madras Conference 1938, 396
Malaya, 336
Man, doctrine of, 243–244, 249
Manichaeism, 81
Manz, Felix, 198
Marco Polo, 76
Marcion, 68
Marcionites, 334
Maronite Church, 113
Marriage; *see* Sacraments
Marsilius, 159
Martin V, 133
Marx, Karl; *see* Communism
Mary, worship of, 62–64, 140, 144,
　306–307, 327, 329
Mary, Queen of Scots; *see*
　Reformation in Scotland
Mass; 144–145. *see also* Roman
　Catholic Church, sacraments of
Mattys, Jan, 200
Maurus, 145
Melanchthon, 173
Melville, Andrew, 194–195
Mendicants; *see* Monasticism
Mennonites, 200–201, 212, 239
Methodist Church
　in America, 256, 259, 260, 265,
　　266, 274, 334, 349, 371, 374
　beginnings of, 245, 256, 333
　divisions in, 267, 271, 276, 383
　in ecumenical movement, 298
　Negro constituency, 271, 358, 359
Methodist Episcopal Church in
　America, 266
Methodist Protestant Church, 276
Mexico, 303, 390, 391
Millennialism, 251
Mills, B. Fay, 260

Ministers
　education of, or educational
　　requirements for, 401
　support of, 403
Missionary Education Movement,
　293
Missions; *see also* Carey, William
　early missionaries, 324–325
　international conferences, 287,
　　295–297
　modern movement, 261–263,
　　390–399
　results of, 44, 319, 397
　support of, 404–405
　types of, 380
Modernists, 251
Mohammed, 112
Mohammedans, 79, 111, 112–113
Monarchianism; *see* Heresies;
　concerning Trinity
Monasticism
　development of, 93–96, 106, 138,
　　148–154
　orders of, 148–154, 159, 167, 233,
　　301
Monophysite Church, 334
Monophysitism; *see* Heresies
Monothelite Church, 334
Monothelitism; *see* Heresies
Montanists, 334
Moody, Dwight L., 260
Moravian Church, 239, 254, 261
Mormon Church (Church of Latter-
　Day Saints), 269–271, 356
Münzer, Thomas, 201
Mystery religions, 29–30, 59, 61, 62
Mysticism, 154–157

National Association of Evangelicals,
　294
National churches, 390–391
National Council of Churches of
　Christ, 286, 293, 294, 334, 344,
　364, 380, 397
Near East, 79
Negroes; *see also* Presbyterian
　Church in the United States
　churches of, 357–358